west twine 537

THE DRAMA OF TRANSITION

THE DRAMA
OF TRANSITION

Native and Exotic Playcraft

By

ISAAC GOLDBERG 1887-

PUBLISHERS
STEWART KIDD COMPANY
CINCINNATI

23-2060

PN
1861
G6

Printed in the United States of America
THE CAXTON PRESS
"Everybody for Books."   This is one of the Interlaken Library

TO MY WIFE
ELSIE FRIEDA

THE ACTOR'S PROLOGUE

Once more the mimicry begins
With its compounded heritage—
Of hopes, of fears, of sorrows and of sins.
Once more a little stage
Pretends to hold symmetrical a play,
Pointed by art, or rounded, or made square,
While all the time not here on the stage but
    there
Within you proceeds the authentic play.
And each of you, a player,
Day after day,
Performs behind a curtaining breast
Some part which we make partly manifest.

We, too, are living stranger plays than these
And wearing, or off-stripping in some inner
    room,
Life's mask of mimicries;
But in this rôle of scapegoat we assume,
Besides our own, your solaces, your sins,
Your worst, your best.

And, therefore, whether we appear to jest
Or to be solemn, we request
That you let first your eyes and ears and then
    your hands attest
Our humanness—if we speak true
Some accent of that deeper play containing you.

WITTER BYNNER.

FOREWORD

In a sense, despite the title of this book, there is
no such thing as a transition drama. Playwrights
follow their calling for money or for fame, or for
whatever else you will, but not for the purpose of
establishing compact compartments in a historical
survey. A world always in flux is a world ever in
transition; change is the law of life. Indeed, Mr.
Dukes, in an excellent book upon the drama, has
made use of the term transition in a sense quite the
opposite to that which it bears in our present title.
Employing as his example the German designation
Uebergangsmensch (i. e., one belonging to the transition), he selected it for its connotation of advance-
ment to an ever beckoning goal. His conception
of transition-men was thus the heroic one of leaders
at first reviled, then but half understood even by
their admirers, and only at last triumphant among
the few who really count. That is a valid interpretation and one of which Mr. Dukes made such
good use that some ten years later a countrywoman
of his, Storm Jameson, elaborated it into a valiant
book which, together with that of Mr. Dukes and
other contemporary critics of the drama, will receive due consideration in the pages that follow.[1]
The more current acceptation of transition, how-

---

[1] Mr. Havelock Ellis, in the Postscript to the sixth and final volume of his remarkable *Studies in the Psychology of Sex*, has expressed the dynamic conception of
transition so well that I cannot forbear quoting him (pages 641-642): "But the
wise man, standing midway between both parties and sympathizing with each,
knows that we are ever in the stage of transition. The present is in every age
merely the shifting point at which past and future meet, and we can have no
quarrel with either. There can be no world without traditions; neither can there

ever, is that of a comparative lull in creative activity and of a period marked rather by the decline from high achievements, by restlessness, experiment, and eager groping.

It would be easy, of course, to begin a survey of immediate causes with the late madness in Europe, just as the older historians began their tomes with the Creation. But just as the Creation, to modern history, is a rather recent date in the career of this globe, so were disintegrating forces at work before 1914, and it may well be that the war, far from being a cause of artistic disintegration, was a vast economic effect of influences that had long been at work in every sphere of human activity.

In any event, between the peaks lie valleys. If some, like Miss Jameson, prefer to leap from peak to peak, that is their enviable privilege; the exercise is strenuous, but exhilarating, and is taken less often only because few critics possess the seven-league boots that hold the secret of these gigantic strides. Yet there must be occasional repose even from peak-climbing; it is good to rest the eye upon undulating prairies and even modest meadows. They are part of the same mother earth, though not so near the moon, and they have their own amenities. Rome was not built in a day, nor did Ibsen or Strindberg or Hauptmann rise up over night, blown out of an intangible fancy. Let there be no misunderstanding on this score, and let no terrestrial analogies mislead us; disparagement of

be any life without movement. As Heracleitus knew at the outset of modern philosophy, we cannot bathe twice in the same stream, though, as we know today, the stream still flows in an unending circle. There is never a moment when the new dawn is not breaking over the earth, and never a moment when the sunset ceases to die. It is well to greet serenely even the first glimmer of dawn when we see it, not hastening toward it with undue speed, nor leaving the sunset without gratitude for the undying light that once was dawn."

the lofty is the farthest from my intention. If such a modest book as this did not, on the whole, contribute to a better appreciation of the outstanding few, I should consider it a waste of time and paper. Not that the lofty few should be left on the lonely heights of their eminence; storms must brew around these peaks and the winds of criticism hurl back and forth. The past has played altogether too much havoc with eminence for us to feel too sure of our opinions. Out of the humbler ranks, however, some day the rare genius arises; it is good to know his ancestry, to learn what men, what works, what spiritual attitudes, preceded him and helped to shape him even as he was casting off their spell. For such is the paradox of the artist; he rebels against the very material he employs.

The matter of this book is largely so new to the English-speaking world that I have found it necessary to include a far greater proportion of expositive detail than I should have wished. Since there is little use in discussing values in the absence of anything like concrete examples, I have been fairly generous with outlines of plot and with biographical information. In the case of no country, however, was it my intention to speak of every author or to consider, chronologically or critically, every play of the authors chosen. Where are these plays being written, and under what circumstances? Who are the writers? What are they trying to do? How are they succeeding? These are the questions I first asked myself and which I am now trying to answer. They determine quite clearly the method of treatment: a minimum of biography, attention wherever called for to the content of the play, and, most important, the adumbration of a critical opinion. Included in the critical remarks are the opinions of foreign critics upon the work under discussion. My own opinions, which pretend to no finality, are those of an inquisitive, cosmopolitan nature that deals in labels with repugnance, as the necessary evils they are, and that abhors more than anything else such pedantries as cosmic cataloguing. It might be said, indeed, that dramatic criticism itself, like the drama which it deals with, is in a state of transition. Certainly, as far as the English-speaking peoples are concerned, the tendency is away from dogmatism, irrelevant preaching, moralizing, propaganda of social, economic, and political ideals and what not else that obscures the essentially lyrical nature of art. For this reason I have placed, before the chapters upon drama in various parts of the world, a survey of recent works upon dramatic criticism; I have selected chiefly the books of writers whose attitude enriches my own. Their common attribute is a desire to escape the limitations of academic, traditional thought, to have done with the artificial restrictions that hedge in discussion, which should be as free as the art that it treats. Yet it is instructive to note how each, in his own particular freedom, may reach conclusions not only independent but divergent. For criticism is an art, the critic an artist, and as such, an autonomous being justified by his product alone.

If, then, this book does not treat of peaks, there may be a few hills in it worth the climb. The Spanish dramatists, for example, may not remould the society in which they flourish, but, on the other hand, they illustrate it and thus make amends for

artistic shortcomings by serving as quasi-social documents. And, at that, it is a question whether in
an occasional play Echegaray, Galdós, or Benavente, for all that may be urged against them, have
not risen to creative vision. Of the novelty-seekers,
the Italians and Germans seem most active. They
may be rash, impetuous, at times ludicrous, yet there
is something tonic in their eager restlessness. After
all, it is easy to sit by the ancient fires and sing
hymns to the past; but that past is always there
for us to return to; it has been appraised and re-
appraised, and will be yet again. Even where the
deed proves abortive, the spirit of the "new" is the
essence of all living. Pope's merely shrewd couplet,

> Be not the first by whom the new are tried,
> Nor yet the last to lay the old aside,

may serve as the miniature *vade mecum* for intellectual cowards; to the adventurous spirit it is but
a snivelling rhyme. The Yiddish drama, exotic as
it may appear, exhibits all the stages—in highly
concentrated form—that have characterized nations
with a far older theatrical tradition; it has produced
men capable of artistic abnegation and creative
vision, and although its claims may easily be exaggerated by devotees, it yields its own peculiar
contribution to the general story of modern drama.
The same may be said of the drama in South America, where the stage, for all practical purposes, was
born but yesterday.

In dealing with these milieus, these men and their
work, I have made use of every available source to
throw light upon the fuller significance of their
strivings. The sterner limits of æsthetic criticism—

I refer to the method followed by Benedetto Croce and his disciples—might reject certain details as superfluous or irrelevant, and I am not sure that such an attitude would be unjustifiable. This is not, however, a book of pure criticism; neither is it addressed primarily to specialists; the nature of the material calls for treatment that shall be at once biographical, historical, geographical, as well as critical. I am addressing chiefly those seeking more intimate contact with the ebb and flow of dramatic activity, and have thus been discursive, discussive, informative, according to the relative ignorance prevailing upon the subjects under consideration.

Some of the text has appeared previously in books (as introductory matter), magazines, and newspapers. Though such text has in many cases been thoroughly revised, I wish to thank the editors of the various publications for permission to make additional use of the material. Among these are: the Boston Evening Transcript, the Christian Science Monitor, the New York Tribune, the Literary Review (New York Evening Post), the Freeman, the Bookman, the Stratford Journal, and the Menorah Journal. Among the publishers of books to whom I am similarly indebted are: Mr. Harrison Hale Schaff, of Luce and Company, Boston; Brentano's; Mr. B. W. Huebsch; the Stratford Co., Publishers, of Boston.

I wish, at the same time, to point out that much of the matter has been radically altered; one is not so infallible that the years bring no change in outlook or opinion. Wherefore I would ask that, in any case where I have in this book expressed an opinion upon a writer or subject previously dis-

cussed by me in any article or other book, the
previous expression be cancelled and the present
one be taken as the more mature. Perhaps not so
near the truth—wherever that elusive chit may
dwell—but let us cherish a while the illusion that
our latest opinions are the best![1]

In order to preserve a certain unity in each division, occasional repetition has been rendered necessary.   For suggestions as to possible changes in
later editions, the author may be addressed in care
of the publishers.

ISAAC GOLDBERG.

Roxbury, Massachusetts, 1922.

[1] The plans for this book originally included chapters upon England and Ireland,
but the material fast outgrew the limits set. Happily more than one book deals
with contemporary English dramatists. For Ireland I would recommend Mr.
Ernest A. Boyd's *The Contemporary Drama of Ireland.*

CONTENTS

2

17

18 CONTENTS

BACKGROUNDS OF CONTEMPORARY DRAMATIC CRITICISM

BACKGROUNDS OF CONTEMPORARY DRAMATIC CRITICISM

Human reason? One might as well ask the reason of life itself. We call evil whatever opposes our good. We call madness whatever opposes our reason. But it's all one. . . . It's all—life, the fecund mother of joys and inexplicable sorrows.
  —The Doctor, in Benavente's *Alma Triunfante*,
    Act III.

I

"Nobody's right—but they all think they are right. . . . A lot they know," murmurs Liliom, in Molnar's play of that name, dying, in his ignorance, with more wisdom upon his lips than understanding in his heart. He was speaking of a larger world than criticism, but his words are equally applicable to a realm he would never have comprehended. There was once, in greater numbers than exist to-day, a type of mind that looked to criticism for certainty, for an escape from feeling and thought rather than an induction into them, for a regiment of names drawn duly up in companies and marshaled according to rank. That type is precisely the kind that asks of criticism the one thing neither it nor life can give and that fails to bring to it or to life the one thing upon which they both are nourished—an open, restless, inquiring spirit.

21

Life itself, except to those who harbor implicit faith, yields no discoverable meaning. The whence, the wherefore, the whither are the sides of a triangle far more eternal than the passional imbroglios that weave their net of sex upon the stage. Only in art does the mystery receive a momentary, illusory solution—a different one in each author and in each work. For a brief while the impressions prisoned in book or play create an illusion of order amid chaos, of significance amid multiform meaninglessness. "The world asks an ancient query," runs the Jewish folk song. And, as when in our childhood games the Priest of Paris lost his hat, some say this and some say that. Yet, to revert to the fathomless philosophy of the folk song, as ingenuous in its depth as was Liliom in his nonchalant farewell, "the ancient question still remains."

If, then, we shall not look to art for certainties, neither shall we seek them in criticism. The pompous will continue to emit their Rhadamanthine judgments. Let them. The gulls will go on drinking the easy draught; they will have pocketfuls of labels for every product, and if the work do not fit the label, why, give short shrift to the work! Let them, too. The wiser of us will plod along on our quest for beauty, content with the pleasures of the road and not brooding overmuch upon the destination. Let us, therefore, dismiss at the outset both certainty and the literary hierarchies that it connotes. By no means are we to relinquish the right to entertain opinions; but let us be modest even in our occasional cocksureness. Opinions are only human; they change with us. And what is criticism but the listing of disciplined opinions?

Life being in our sense of the word meaningless, art often becomes the faith of the faithless. Art imposes a meaning upon things, and one of the measures of the artist is the success with which his inner passion fuses the elements of his make-believe world into a higher reality. If, as Croce maintains, art is essentially successful expression, by that same token there are as many worlds as there are original individuals to express and to appreciate. And since criticism is itself an art, it creates, out of the materials with which it deals, a world of its own,—again different in each critic and in each of the critic's works. The world of criticism, as the world of art, is the world of the individual, the personality.

II

Few examples could better illustrate the inevitable divergence of the most enlightened opinion than the attitude of three of our leading contemporary critics toward one of the most popular of latter-day playwrights. Storm Jameson, as her *Modern Drama in Europe* reveals, is one of the sternest appraisers of the drama—a veritable Nietzsche in knickers, smashing her way through the idols of the day with almost forbidding asperity. Ludwig Lewisohn, as sensitive as she to the philosophy inherent in drama and even more sensitive to beauty than she or Nathan, is every whit as exigent. Now, what becomes of Sir James Barrie in their hands?

This is Jameson's estimate:[1]

"Mr. Barrie is not a Romantic, though he is here in their company. His work eludes classification,

---

[1] *Modern Drama in Europe.* By Storm Jameson, New York, 1920, pp. 211, 212.

as does the work of all men who are masters of their art. There is nothing like it in the whole of modern drama, and though to be unique is not to be great therefore, few will be found to withhold from Mr. Barrie any honouring word. Yet is 'great' an epithet of too little humanity for his whimsical and tender art. There should be words to do it honour, but they do not come readily, as does the praise we find for plays that leave us heart-whole. They should be gracious words, and kindly, like the work that waits their tribute, needing it so little.

"But the drama of J. M. Barrie has other qualities than those of grace and loving kindness, and other arts than the wizardry that sets men's thoughts wandering in forgotten places and their eyes searching for forgotten dreams. There is pity, infinite pity, and—lest that become intolerable—infinite courage, defying suffering and age and death itself. Pity and courage alike have a fine, keen edge. There is nothing sentimental in the mind that called them out, giving them life and form—the form, maybe, of an awkward boy, or a 'queer old divert' of a charwoman: it is a shrewd mind, quick to see the absurdity of our unconscious posturings even when it smiles at them.

"And if the true artist is he who makes life finer and nobler than it is, then is the author of *Quality Street* and *The Old Lady Shows Her Medals* indubitably an artist, touching life with gentle fingers, making it braver, and sweeter to our lips. So that somewhere among the hierarchy of those great dramatists who took gods and heroes and made them types of humanity, must be found a place—lowly, if it is to please him—for the dramatist who took a charwoman and made her a symbol of man's immortal divinity."

The passage amounts almost to a lapse from the lofty standards set for herself in this most trenchant of contemporary books upon the drama. For a moment she seems to become sentimental with that very sentimentality which she fails to note in Barrie —and how could one help note it in his later plays any more than one could overlook the descent of Maeterlinck in his more recent productions? Almost she exemplifies that unconditional surrender which Professor Phelps prescribes as the sole possible confrontation of Barrie.

Nathan occupies here a middle position. To him, Barrie is "the triumph of sugar over diabetes."

And now Lewisohn:[1]

"His plays are commended for their purity. He surrounds with the gentlest pathos and all the beauty he can comprehend a triviality of soul that is as shameful as one hopes it rare. Spiritual triviality— we come very close to Barrie with that phrase. He makes harsh things sweetish and grave things frivolous and noble things to seem of small account. No wonder he is popular among all the shedders of easy, comfortable tears. He dramatizes the cloud in order to display its silver lining. . . . Barrie's imagination is as uncontrolled as his ideas are feeble and conventional. Yet this is the dramatist whose position is seriously undebated. This purveyor of sentimental comedy to the unthinking crowd deceives the semi-judicious by moments of literary charm and deftness and mellow grace that recall the years when he wrote *Sentimental Tommie*

---

[1] *The Drama and the Stage.* New York, 1922, pages 177, 178.

and *Margaret Ogilvie*. But those years are gone. His noisy stage successes have left him increasingly bare of scruple, of seriousness, of artistic and intellectual coherence. They have left him 'whimsical' and false and defeated in the midst of wealth and fame."

The humor of the situation lies in this: that the casual reader of Jameson and Lewisohn would almost with a certainty, coming across these passages, have ascribed the first to Lewisohn and the second to Jameson. It is as if Jameson, in her Nietzschean demands upon the drama, had decided for a moment to relent, lest her requirements, growing over taut, strain the bonds of reason. And as if Lewisohn, sensitive to beauty as a matrix to the vibrations of the recording needle, felt a need to harden in the face of a dangerous substitute. Pilate asked two questions too few. He should have added, What is Goodness? What is Beauty? Then the problem of art would have been posed in full. Another eternal triangle!

III

We are prepared, now, for the widest differences of opinion as to what constitutes the proper attitude toward the drama and as to what the drama itself may be. And though the most divergent sources yield similar definitions, even here the differences begin with the very rise of the curtain.

What is a play?

No, we shall not go back to Aristotle, the eternal precursor; he has a finger in every critical pie, whether or not he is mentioned. To stress our point we need go no farther than our own day.

"The only really valid definition of the dramatic is: Any representation of imaginary personages which is capable of interesting an average audience assembled in a theatre." Thus William Archer, in his *Playmaking: A Manual of Craftsmanship*, page 48. That word "average" sticks in one's throat; it explains Lewisohn's half-surprise that a man "can translate Ibsen and write *The Green Goddess* with equal cheerfulness."

"Good drama is anything that interests an intelligently emotional group of persons assembled together in an illuminated hall. Molière, wise among dramatists, said as much, though in somewhat more, and doubtless too, sweeping words. Throughout the ages of drama there will be always Romanticists of one sort or another, brave and splendid spirits, who will have to free themselves from the definition and limitations imposed upon them by the neo-Bossus and Boileaus, and the small-portion Voltaires, Laharpes, and Marmontels." Thus Nathan,[1] whose "intelligently emotional" is so vast an improvement over Archer's "average" that it excludes it implicitly and connotes an entire attitude toward all of life.

With a similar impatience, Lewisohn writes:[2]

"Let us have done, first of all, then, with this verbiage.

"A play is a dialogue which, when spoken by actors from a platform, holds the minds of men through its culmination toward some physical or spiritual end.

"The power and depth of that sense of culmination is the measure of the play's dramatic life.

[1] *The Critic and the Drama*, by George Jean Nathan, New York, 1922.
[2] *The Drama and the Stage.* Pages 4, 5.

"Any dialogue that has dramatic life can be acted on any stage.

"A born dramatist can write drama without ever having seen a theatre. If an audience refuses to hear him, it is because the soul of his work is alien from that audience's collective soul.

"The popular playwright is not he who understands either the theatre or the drama best, but he who flatters men most and disturbs them least."

How far we have gone from Mr. Archer's "average" now! Yet all three definitions carry a sense of liberation from the old, cramping rules. Nor is that freedom a mere relaxation of discipline, any more than is the newer criticism, with its refusal to erect fixed standards, a renunciation of control. It is, on the contrary, a sterner attitude than ever, a more exacting demand upon self in the advance toward complete selfhood—a renunciation, indeed, of external rules that enable one to dispense with the ardors of thought, since all things have their measure foreordained. This shifting of criticism from quasi-objective to avowedly subjective ground, besides clarifying the inevitably personal character of all criticism, imposes new obligations upon the critic. Mere theoretical structures no longer suffice; taste, in Spingarn's[1] words synonymous at its highest with artistic creation, must go deeper than ever before; far from applying a set of rules from without, it must probe within and re-create the work of art. Far from settling anything, then, such an attitude unsettles everything. It is part of a centrifugal world-spirit that finds expression in such unrelated personalities as a Baroja in Spain, penning novels of

---

[1] *Creative Criticism.* Essays on the Unity of Genius and Taste. By J. E. Spingarn. New York, 1917. This book is indispensable.

disintegration; a Shestov in Russia, proclaiming the disunity of philosophy and declaring all things possible; a Rodó in Spanish America, emphasizing the love of truth as distinct from truth itself. (Did not Nietzsche write: "We should not let ourselves be burnt for our opinions themselves, of which we can never be quite sure, but we may perhaps do so for the right to hold and change them?" And has not this, sifted through Mencken, become: "If I knew what was true, I'd probably be willing to sweat and strive for it, and maybe even to die for it, to the tune of bugle blasts. But so far I have not found it"?[1]) The person of true culture thus grows more and more into the individual, the personality that every true artist contains. Long since released from his tribal loyalties in matters of politics (let us hope so, at least), he is thrown upon his own inner resources, and the wealth of those resources determines the richness and the fruitfulness of his perceptions as well as of his response. Criticism is worth precisely as much as the critic.

IV

That even the spirit of liberation may tend to crystallize into dogma is shown by the first of the contemporary attitudes toward the drama with which we deal. I call this the Dukes-Jameson theory, because although Storm Jameson, in her recent *Modern Drama in Europe*, elaborates the aristocratic, philosophic attitude, it was stated succinctly some ten years before by Ashley Dukes, in his *Modern Dramatists*. "Tolerance smoothes the way of life," he wrote, "but it is the most insidious

---

[1] *In Defense of Women*, 2nd ed. New York, 1922. Page xviii.

enemy of art. It spells compromise, and compromise and criticism cannot be on speaking terms. . . ." The work of art is "individual and indefinable. It will be simply the expression of a personality through the medium of a craft. If the craft fails, the personality may be distorted, but if the personality fails, the craft is useless. The great need of the theatre, then, is not conformity to this school or that, but the service of writers who are at once free spirits and good workmen. Freedom is their own possession, but good workmanship can be learned in some measure from the masters."[1]

And who are Dukes' masters?

They are implicit in his critical creed: "It is dogmatic, because it is written from a definite standpoint, and its judgments depend upon an absolute standard of value. To write of any group of authors, dramatic or otherwise, without such a standard, is to debase the coinage of criticism and to insult the artist."[1] The Dukes standard is what he calls modernity. His modernists are "in touch with, or in advance of, the thought of their own time; . . . their work breaks new paths, offers new forms and modes of expression; . . . the men and women they create do not merely reflect the conditions under which they live and the spirit of their age, but are dynamic, developing continually, offering a criticism of those conditions, and so projecting themselves into the future and making history." Mere imitation gives way to selection; description yields to interpretation. Nor does modernity depend upon modern subject-matter. "Hugo von Hofmannsthal, who has hitherto based most of his plays

---

[1] *Modern Dramatists.* By Ashley Dukes. Chicago (n. d.).

either upon the tragic legends of Greece or the Italian Renaissance period, is clearly more of a 'modern' than Sudermann, who writes of present-day Germany." And, more to our present purpose, in his consideration of John Galsworthy: "It should be the tritest commonplace to say that no playwright can make great drama out of little people."[1]

Jameson, in the main, takes the Dukes standard and covers much the same ground in greater detail. Like him, she pivots modern drama upon Strindberg and Ibsen; with him, she repudiates the whole realistic production. "Expressed in another form, this distinction between good and bad artists becomes a question whether the artist has given of a superabundant vitality to re-create life, or whether he has merely taken the facts of life to manufacture his work. The first is a sign of strength, the latter a sign of weakness. The first gave us the finest drama of Ibsen; the latter is giving us the plays of Mr. Arnold Bennet." . . . "The drama of to-day is a drama of anarchy; dramatists have forgotten how to imagine finely. They offer us studies of little lives, with nothing of inspiration in them, and they demand praise for fidelity or sincerity; meaning thereby failure to interpret the life they draw, or to create other than a bad copy of what all can see and need no imagination to comprehend. . . . It is Nietzsche's great æsthetic service that he hated this anarchy of the non-artistic, teaching that artists should not see things as they are—they should see them fuller, simpler, stronger.' "[2] . . . "Dramatically speaking, souls are not equal. Great plays cannot be written of little souls."[3]

---

[1] *Modern Dramatists.* Page 149.
[2] *Modern Drama in Europe.* XIII—XXVI..
[3] *Modern Drama in Europe.* Page 12.

To all intents and purposes, then, Jameson and
Dukes see the passing drama from the same seats.
Neither book is as well known in the United States
as it should be, and it is safe to predict for each a
growing importance in the library of the theatre.
Each is as stern with art as it asks the artist to be
with life. Each, in its dogmatism, possesses almost
the rigidity of an ethical code, with Jameson insisting upon the joy born of power and all but reject-
ing any sympathy born of understanding, which is
itself a power. Yet toward the end she can write,
"To-morrow sleeps in each man's brain," and
throughout her valiant volume she dances in the
sun of this life's perpetual discontent, aglow with
the zest of high adventure.

Less dogmatic, as exclusive of mediocrity but
closer to the core of artistic impulse, is the so-called
Carlyle-Goethe-Croce-Spingarn theory to which Mr.
Joel Elias Spingarn, in a volume important inversely
to its modest proportions, first called serious attention. The battle between the objective, dogmatic
critic and the impressionist is as "old as the earliest
reflection on the subject of poetry. Modern literature begins with the same doubts, the same quarrel.
In the sixteenth century the Italians were formulat-
ing that classical code which imposed itself on Europe
for two centuries, and which, even in our generation,
Brunetière has merely disguised under the trappings
of natural science. They evolved the dramatic
unities,[1] and all those rules which Pope imagined to
be 'Nature still but Nature methodized.' But at

---

[1] Inasmuch as this is not a book for specialists, I may be pardoned the remark that Aristotle did not erect the so-called three unities, which, as Spingarn
states, were later evolved. The simple fact needs frequent restatement, for one
is constantly meeting, in the most up-to-date works, references to Aristotle as the
originator of the famous trio of unities. "It is difficult to believe," writes Gilbert

the very moment when their spokesman Scaliger was saying that 'Aristotle is our perpetual emperor, the perpetual dictator of the fine arts,' another Italian, Pietro Aretino, was insisting that there is no rule except the whim of genius and no standard of judgment beyond individual taste."[1]

To the Germans of the epoch stretching from Herder to Hegel we owe the enunciation of the doctrine of art as expression. Carlyle interpreted it to the English. " 'There is a destructive and a creative or constructive criticism,' said Goethe; the first measures and tests literature according to mechanical standards, the second answers the fundamental questions: 'What has the writer proposed to himself to do? and How far has he succeeded in carrying out his own plan?'" Carlyle, in his essay on Goethe, almost uses Goethe's own words when he says that the critic's first and foremost duty is to make plain to himself "what the poet's aim really and truly was, how the task he has to do stood before his eye, and how far, with such materials as were afforded him, he has fulfilled it."

Such a conception of criticism involves a radical revision of views. Rules, as rules, disappear. Since each work of art is a law unto itself, *genres*, representing an artificial system of cataloguing, follow the rules into oblivion. Style, in the sense of rhetorical embellishment, goes with them, for the work of art is an indivisible entity. Moral judgment of literature becomes an anachronism. "To say that poetry is

Norwood in his *Greek Tragedy* (London, 1920, note 1, page 42), "that Aristotle never mentions the 'Three Unities.' On the Unity of Action he has, of course, much to say; the Unity of Time is dismissed in one casual sentence. As to the Unity of Place there is not a word. It is signally violated in the *Eumenides* and the *Ajax*."

[1] *Creative Criticism.* See the entire first lecture, pages 3-44.

3

moral or immoral is as meaningless as to say that
an equilateral triangle is moral and an isosceles
triangle immoral, or to speak of the immorality of a
musical chord or a Gothic arch." . . . "No
critic of authority now tests literature by the standards of ethics."

It follows, from the Crocean conception of art as
successful expression, that technique cannot be separate from art any more than can style—that the
epoch and the environment of an artist's labors are
of interest as history or sociology, but not as art.
These are assumed; the central interest is transferred to what the poet has done with his material.
If *genres* disappear, so must the conception of the
evolution of literature and of the origins of art,
"for art has no origin separate from man's life."

I am not asking the reader to accept Croce's
philosophy; I am trying to prepare him for an appreciation of the Croce-Spingarn attitude toward the
drama. "We have done," says Spingarn, "with the
confusion between the drama and the theatre which
has permeated criticism for over half a century.
The theory that the drama is not a creative art,
but a mere product of the physical exigencies of the
theatre, is as old as the sixteenth century. An
Italian scholar of that age was the first to maintain
that plays are intended to be acted on a stage, under
certain restricted physical conditions, and before a
large and heterogeneous crowd. Dramatic performance has developed out of these conditions, and the
test of its excellence is therefore the pleasure it
gives to the mixed audience that supports it. This
idea was taken hold of by some of the German
romanticists for the purpose of justifying the Shake-

spearean drama in its apparent divergence from the classical 'rules.' Shakespeare cannot be judged by the rules of the Greek theatre (so ran their argument), for the drama is an inevitable product of theatrical conditions. These conditions in Elizabethan England were not the same as those of Pereclean Athens; and it is therefore absurd to judge Shakespeare's practice by that of Sophocles. Here, at least, the idea helped to bring Shakespeare home to many new hearts by ridding the age of mistaken prejudices, and served a useful purpose, as a specious argument may persuade men to contribute to a noble work, or a mad fanatic may rid the world of a tyrant. But with this achievement its usefulness but not its life was ended. It has been developed into a system and become a dogma of dramatic critics; it is our contemporary equivalent for the 'rules' of seventeenth-century pedantry. As a matter of fact, the dramatic artist is to be judged by no other standard than that applied to any other creative artist: What has he tried to express, and how has he expressed it? It is true that the theatre is not only an art but a business, and the so-called 'success' of a play is of vital interest to the theatre in so far as it is a commercial undertaking. 'The success may justify the playwright,' said an old French critic, 'but it may not be so easy to justify the success.' The test of 'success' is an economic test, and concerns not art or the criticism of art, but political economy. Valuable contributions to economic and social history have been made by students who have investigated the changing conditions of the theatre and the vicissitudes of taste on the part of theatrical audiences; but these have the same relation to criticism and to the drama as art that a history of the publisher's trade and its influence on the personal fortunes of poets would bear to the history of poetry."

This severe scrutiny of all extraneous elements is the more important since here, in the United States, technique has long been a word to conjure with, and of late there has been a tendency to stress the appurtenances of drama—the scenery, the lighting, the stage mechanism—to the hurt of the creative spectator. Bound up with this, too, is another problem of criticism: the relation of the printed to the acted play.

"The first to challenge this theory of the drama" (i. e., the so-called "closet drama") "was a scholar and critic of the Renaissance, Lodovico Castelvetro, who published an Italian version of Aristotle's *Poetics* in 1570. . . . Castelvetro certainly takes issue with Aristotle on the question whether the drama exhibits its real power in the study or in the theatre. 'Non è vero quello che Aristotele dice,' he says: it simply is not true, what Aristotle says, that the value of a play can be discovered by reading in the same way as by theatrical representation, for the reason that a few highly gifted and imaginative men might be able to judge a play in this way, whereas everyone, the gifted and ignorant alike, can follow and appreciate a play when it is acted. . . . In order to understand what the drama is, and what is the peculiar pleasure that it affords to men, we must examine the conditions of the physical theatre and realize what is to be found there. The fact that the drama is intended for the stage, that it is to be acted, must form the basis of every true theory of tragedy or comedy."[1]

This prepares us for Diderot's exaltation of the actor as the real creator of the play, and to his theory of what we now call the psychology of the crowd, which, as Spingarn points out, had been foreshadowed in Bacon's *De Augmentis*, as well as by Castelvetro himself. Lessing, in his *Hamburgische Dramaturgie*, returns to the Aristotelian conception. "Indeed, he forestalls Lamb's theory that a great play cannot be properly acted at all: 'A masterpiece is rarely as well represented as it is written; mediocrity always fares better with the actors.' "

The circle of contradictions is complete. Here we have Lewisohn saying that a naturally gifted dramatist need never see the inside of a theatre; and here is Lamb, supported by Spingarn, averring that the audience may remain away as well. The exploitation of crowd-psychology I am ready to dismiss without recall. It is for the most part a concession to the lower tastes of the mob, which can wear frock coats as well as smocks. No one hears anything about crowd psychology when a poet reads his verses in a public hall; everyone condemns the orator who makes his cheap appeal to this very characteristic of crowds. That appeal is

---

[1] Spingarn, *Creative Criticism.* Pages 47-96, lecture on Dramatic Criticism and The Theatre.

The best-known contemporary defender of the Castelvetro attitude in this country is Brander Matthews. In his essay on Francisque Sarcey (*Studies on the Stage*) he says: "A play is written not to be read, primarily, but to be acted. M. Coquelin has recently pointed out that if Shakespeare and Molière . . . were both careless as to the printing of their plays, it was because they both knew that these plays were written for the theatre, and that only in the theatre could they be judged properly. Seen by the light of the lamps, a play has quite another complexion from what it bears in the library. Passages pale and dull . . . when read coldly by the eyes, are lighted up by the inner fire of passion when presented in the theatre; and the solid structure of the action, without which a drama is naught, may stand forth in bolder relief on the stage."

just as cheap when made in an auditorium that houses a drama. Back of every work of art, more important than the nation or the people that gave it birth, stands the individual, the personality. Though as a human being he may form part of the crowd, as an artist he is its enemy, or at least independent of its dictates. The crowd, indeed, is the very symbol of that imperfect reality which the artist would not so much escape as make over. Though the product be read or heard or witnessed by the thousands, it is primarily a bridge of expression leading from one to one. Art being, then, the communication of significant personality, the material and the milieu and the manner are secondary; better still, they are incidental attributes. They are not the essence of art, which lies in a personal permutation of those elements into an organic whole. When the artist's work finds an understanding goal, the circuit of personality is complete. Art begins and ends in the individual. For it, the "crowd" simply does not exist.

And, from the standpoint of Croce and Spingarn, representing æsthetic criticism, "the theatre simply does not exist." To such criticism, "a theatre means only the appearance at any one time or in any one country, as Croce puts it, of a 'series of artistic souls.' When these artistic souls appear theatres will spring up like mushrooms to house them, and the humblest garret will serve as an eyrie for their art. But all these external conditions are merely dead material which has no æsthetic significance outside the poet's soul; and only in the poet's art should we seek to find them." . . . "To say, therefore, that playwrights write for the stage, that poets write for money, that painters paint to be 'hung,' is to confuse mere stimulus with creative impulse." . . . "For the true dramatic critic will transfer his interest from the drama itself to the 'laws of the theatre' or the 'conditions of the theatre' only when the lover studies the 'laws of love' and the 'conditions of love' instead of the lady's beauty and his own soul."

The Croce-Spingarn criterion of pure æsthetics is a severe discipline. Although, as a strong personality and a merry impressionist, George Jean Nathan accepts many of its implications, he rebels against the acceptance of any one theory. "There are as many sound and apt species of criticism as there are works to be criticized. To say that art must be criticized only after this formula or after that is to say that art must be contrived only out of this formula or out of that. As every work of art is an entity, a thing in itself, so is every piece of criticism an entity, a thing in itself. That *Thus Spake Zarathustra* must inevitably be criticized by the canons of the identical 'theory' with which one criticizes *Tristan and Isolde* is surely difficult reasoning.

"To the Goethe-Carlyle doctrine that the critic's duty lies alone in discerning the artist's aim, his point of view, and, finally, his execution of the task before him, it is easy enough to subscribe, but certainly this is not a 'theory' of criticism so much as it is the foundation for a theory. To advance it as a theory, full-grown, full-fledged and flapping, as it has been advanced by the Italian Croce and his admirers, is to publish the preface to a book without the book itself. Accepted as a theory complete in itself, it fails by virtue of its several undeveloped intrinsic problems, chief among which is its neglect to consider the undeniable fact that, though each work of art is indubitably an entity and so to be considered, there is yet in creative art what may be termed an æsthetic genealogy that bears heavily upon comprehensive criticism and that renders the artist's aim, his point of view, and his execution of the task before him susceptible to a criticism predicated in a measure upon the work of the sound artist who has just preceded him.

"The Goethe-Carlyle hypothesis is a little too liberal. It calls for qualifications. It gives the artist too much ground, and the critic too little. To discern the artist's aim, to discern the artist's point of view, are phrases that require an amount of plumbing and not a few footnotes. It is entirely possible, for example, that the immediate point of view of an artist may be faulty, yet the execution of his immediate task exceedingly fine. If carefully planned triumph in art is an entity, so also may be undesigned triumph. . . . All things considered, it were perhaps better that the critical theory under discussion, if it be accepted at all, be turned end foremost: that the artist's execution of the task before him be considered either apart from his aim and point of view, or that it be considered first, and then—with not too much insistence upon them— his point of view and his aim. . . . In its very effort to avoid pigeon-holing, the Goethe-Carlyle theory pigeon-holes itself. . . . That there may not be contradictions in the contentions here set forth I am not sure. But I advance no fixed, definite theory of my own; I advance merely contradictions of certain of the phases of theories held by others, and contradictions are ever in the habit of begetting contradictions. . . . The Goethe-Carlyle theory, properly rigid and unyielding so far as emotional groundlings are concerned, may, I believe, at times safely be chucked under the chin and offered a communication of gipsy ardour by the critic whose emotions are the residuum of trial, test, and experience."[1]

Nathan, whose views upon the crowd in the theatre coincide quite with those of Spingarn and the Croceans, takes an opposite stand upon the relation between the printed play and the acted. For once, at least, he is in definite agreement with Brander Matthews, thus proving that criticism, like politics, betimes makes strange bedfellows. "To hold that the drama as an art may achieve its highest end read by the individual and not acted in the theatre, is to hold that music as an art may achieve its highest end played by but one instrument and not by an orchestra. The theatre is the drama's orchestra. Upon the wood of its boards and the wind of its puppets is the melody of drama in all its full richness sounded."[2]

Something valid there seems in Nathan's attitude toward the Goethe-Carlyle theory that has been elaborated into a rather formidable apparatus by Croce. More valid than ever, indeed, when we confront some of the Italian's followers, who become more Crocean than Croce. Here is Mr. Ainslie, for example, in the preface to his translation of *Ariosto*, *Shakespeare, and Corneille*, asserting that "Croce's theory of the independence and autonomy of the

---

[1] George Jean Nathan. *The Critic and the Drama*, chapter on Æsthetic Jurisprudence, pages 3-26.
[2] *The Critic and The Drama*. Chapter on The Place of the Theater, pages 65-66.

æsthetic fact, which is intuition-expression, and of the essentially lyrical character of all art, is the only one that completely and satisfactorily explains the problem of poetry and the fine arts." But Croce himself, in his most recent work, gives the best answer to such self-destructive superlativity and to Nathan's impatience with too tightly ringed theory. Commenting upon the word "illogica," he writes that it means "not entirely harmonized," and applies to the system of every man and every philosopher, who always possesses some aspect not harmonized and not logical. This aspect, he goes on, is precisely the source whence springs the new thought or the so-called new progress.[1] It is indicative that Croce, in this very passage that treats of the illogicality of Dante's system, parenthetically applies the observation to the systems of all men. Artistic personality thus is a triumph over logic, and Nathan's numerous contradictions, to add yet another to his list, may not artistically be contradicted.

We are not yet done, however, with the varied attitudes of our divergent free spirits. For, just as Lewisohn and Spingarn seem to flout the theatre and the audience, so now comes a young Scotchman and suggests that perhaps criticism itself is false at the very core.

"What," asks Edwin Muir, "if all the assumptions on which we have thus far judged art should be—erroneous? What if every system of æsthetics and every criticism should be, not merely wrong here and there, but, by their very existence, the standing, immemorial misunderstanding of art? In

[1] *La Poesia di Dante.* Benedetto Croce. Bari, 1921, page 55.

short, what if questions regarding the function and the 'meaning' of art simply should not be asked at all, and, in any case, should never be answered? These inquiries have drawn forth and written this edifying essay.[1]

"My thesis is that art can be comprehended on one hypothesis only, that this hypothesis concerns the universe, and that, in the history of the universe, it has very seldom been consciously held. The hundred and one philosophers who have constructed theories of art have certainly not held it: their systems of æsthetics are to be found, each killed with an appropriate comment, in the terrifying appendix to Signor Croce's book. Signor Croce made only one error in that almost infallible work: he should finally, as an exercise in impartiality, have sent his own theory to the guillotine and have become his own executioner. But unfortunately he could not refute himself."[2]

That hypothesis Muir states in the following terms: "Art delights us precisely because it takes us out of the realm of duty, of reason, and of necessity. It does not moralize or humanize us nor remind us of eternal justice. It carries us into a world which is neither necessary nor necessitated, but perfectly arbitrary and free, and gives us freely something inconceivably rich and magical, not because we deserve it nor even because we 'need' it, but simply as a final golden superfluous drop to our filled cup. Delight is the feeling which we ex-

---

[1] See the two articles on The Truth About Art in *The Freeman* for February 15 and March 15, 1922.

[2] Croce could not very well commit philosophic suicide, of course; but the reference to his casual passage in the book on Dante, which I give several paragraphs back, reveals him in a fairly human, even humble, attitude. That one reference indeed might be made the basis for a negation of all philosophy.

perience when we receive something great or beautiful without needing it. And art gives us this feeling. . . . The plainest truth about art is that it is superfluous, and springs out of superfluity; to give it a use one has to strain and falsify not only art, but the terms one uses. . . . In the end, the presence in the universe of superfluity is only made possible by setting at the ultimate bounds of existence chance, irrationality, folly. Then all things become, as they are, possible.[1] Then freedom is gained perhaps for the first time. This choice, once it is made, commits us to several assumptions. For instance, that there is no connexion whatever between a thing's necessity—to the 'world' or to anything else—and its right to exist. Everything exists as a perfectly unnecessary thing: we ourselves, philosophies, literatures, and States, as well as butterflies and planets. It is only after they have come into existence that we make them into necessaries. We are not entitled to condemn anything because it has no function; on the contrary, to be without a function is to be free, to be rich. The greatest things have been done by men who have had no function; for to do a thing freely is to be great."

From which premises Mr. Muir deduces the superfluity of that other art, criticism. But not on that account should it be abolished, any more than art itself.

"From all this it follows—that criticism should be abolished? On the contrary. It has the same right to exist as every other superfluous thing. Its justification is that it fulfills no use; that it is, like art,

[1] So, too, the Russian epigrammatic philosopher Leo Shestov, one of whose books is actually named in its English Version, *All Things Are Possible.*

expression. But if a thing is not useful it cannot be important? This is the great orthodox heresy about the universe which makes it such a dull place to live in. The superfluous things are the important things, the justification of life, the saving grace whereby the useful and the necessary are redeemed. For life also is finally expression, and not task nor instrument."

Mr. Muir, then, has been playing with paradox. In the very act of denying art and criticism he creates them. He is like the vaudevillian who exclaims, "Women! women! We can't get along with them and we can't get along without them!" Now, that vaudevillian has merely been expressing a fundamentally useless and only half-serious rebellion against an indispensable half of life. So, too, Muir, who cannot get along with criticism and cannot get along without it.

V

We agreed, at the outset, not to look to criticism for certainty; surely we have not at any moment here been in danger of encountering it. But, on the other hand, we have encountered something far more precious: a high sense of adventure, of personal freedom, intellectual courage. One thing should, moreover, be definitely impressed before abandoning this survey: that this progression away from fixed standards not only does not shirk the burdens of intellectual effort, but adds to them. It is not that bugaboo of irresponsibility and license as opposed to responsible liberty. There is nothing more intellectually degrading than a supine adherence to literary authority; it numbs and even destroys the personality. There is nothing more exhilarating, on the other hand, than the freedom that comes with true selfhood; far from shirking, even in the moral sense, it seeks new responsibilities for the sheer joy of vanquishing them. It is the eternal spirit of nonconformity, conforming only to its own true self.

From these general considerations we come now to concerns more immediate, if less related, to pure criticism. In a book aiming to throw light upon the current drama in a number of countries the question of nationalism naturally arises. In an era of psychoanalysis, during which the shadow (and sunshine) of Freud is cast upon the novel, the influence of that noted investigator upon the drama is of historical and social interest. In an epoch that has, in our own country, witnessed the resurgence of Puritanism, the ancient killjoy of censorship enters a second childhood and compels the artist to take up the cudgels anew. I will deal with these matters summarily, even at the risk of appearing dogmatic. And if a flash of temper gleam forth it is not the lesser part of social criticism—as of any other variety—to be human as well as superior.

Nationalism in Art. In the sense of propaganda, nationalism has no more place in art than morality or any other set of rules. Neither, for that matter, has internationality. It is an illusion, for example, that advanced drama must follow economics in theme and make the proletariat its hero. In the artistic sense, the Greek dramas are more contemporaneous with us than many a self-conscious proletarian drama that collapses from sheer hollowness. All these attitudes, however, may serve as the passional centre from which radiates a full circle of human significance. Hauptmann's *Weavers*, incidentally, makes good propaganda for the downtrodden; but that is not the core of the play, which is revelatory and not hortatory. So, too, if Galsworthy's *Strife* attracts the radical element, it had its origin in something deeper than a desire to support the working class. Indeed, it is common experience, at every performance of the play, to hear the members of the *audience* take sides, particularly during the meeting of the strikers' representatives with the company's board of directors. A *play* that takes sides, however, may be excellent thought, admirable humanity, and what not else, but as a work of art (and that is what we are now interested in) it is as dishonest as a game with marked cards or with loaded dice. So, too, the "national" play. It may be fine patriotism or whatever you like, but it is not art, unless that nationalism or internationalism is at the center, not at the periphery, of the action,—unless these elements are ingredients of the inspiration (if we may talk of art in terms of the cook book), and not the preordained end toward which all events are willy-nilly to be directed. If art is not a pulpit, neither is it a recruiting station.

The dramatist, moreover, who writes a play as a conscious citizen of a nation to which he ascribes certain "national" characteristics runs the risk of vitiating his work through false assumptions, even as the critic who interprets that play in the light of those same assumptions. We take it so easily for granted that every German must write ponderously, forgetting the winged words of Nietzsche; that every Spaniard must wallow in blood spilt at the behest of the point of honor, forgetting a Benavente who flounts all the canons of home-made and imported dramaturgy; that Russians must be morbid, what though Gogol's *Revizor* punctures the theory. This is not to say that national characteristics do not exist, or that they lack importance in art. But just in proportion as the artist accepts them unquestioningly, and the critic, too, he surrenders part of that free personality which is the sign and seal of the creative genius.

In literature, nationalism is a term that requires extensive modification even in the minds of scholars, who forget the immense importance of that cross-fertilization which is always going on in the realm of ideas. And ideas have no country.

National personality is, of course, a different matter. It has been often explained, but in few places, recently, so well as in Señor Madariaga's book of essays, *Shelley and Calderón*. "It is, indeed, in relation to national character that the study of foreign literature is most illuminating, and, if there are such things as foreign literatures, it is less to the multiplicity of languages than to the multiplicity of national characters that we owe them—witness the differences between American and English, Swiss and German, Spanish and Spanish-American literatures. A national character may be defined as a set of tendencies determined by the relative strength of the tendencies which compose it. All tendencies are in all men, and that is the basis of human unity and solidarity. It cannot be said that one people is intelligent and another one is not; that one lacks imagination and another one moral sense. All peoples possess all the elementary essences of human nature; but all peoples do not possess them in equal proportions. Hence national character. For a difference in quality is but a synthesis of quantitative differences."[1]

We may sum up the attitude toward nationalism in drama by saying that when it appears as something consciously imposed by the artist upon his material, it is extraneous,—an excrescence, a parasite, and vitiating; when it is exhaled from his work as one of its integral characteristics, it is part and parcel of the creative personality and, as such, a component of art.

Freud and the Contemporary Drama. With the psychoanalysts, the various transformations of the theory of sexual repression and their importance to neuropathy we have here no concern. It was certain from the start, however, that Freud was to have an extensive influence upon the literature of the day, particularly as literature itself, from the Freudian standpoint, is a species of dreaming, of wish-fulfillment, amenable to the dream interpretation that has brought fame to this Viennese Jew. Freud himself applied his methods to literary products. In our own country Jones, Coriat, Prescott, and others have done the same. The very name of the most widely known "complex" is taken from a Greek tragedy, as is its sister situation. Mr. Albert Mordell, in two books,[2] has sought to apply the Freudian method to criticism itself. But psychoanalytic criticism of literature, at best, uses the literary product as a starting-point for biological analysis; it does not properly enter the æsthetic field. Its true function is elucidation, not appreciation,—

---

[1] *Shelley and Calderón.* By Salvador de Madariaga. New York (n. d.).
[2] *The Erotic Motive in Literature.* New York, 1919. *The Literature of Ecstasy.* New York, 1921.

4

understanding and not beauty, science and not art. It may explain the genesis of a work of art, but aids æsthetic enjoyment only through whatever light it may cast upon the foundations of personality. This, it may be added, is all that the chief Freudians attempt, and they have without a doubt brought to literary investigation some of the most important processes that students have learned.[1]

The assertion that we all live a common life in the unconscious gave to universality in art a new meaning; we no longer scratch Russians to find Tartars, we scratch civilization and come upon savagery. More important still, the Freudians centered interest upon the necessity of the liberated personality; the literary process thus becomes synonymous with released repressions. Writers, always in search of new themes, were bound to seize upon the unknown continent discovered by the new Columbus; they were bound, too, to render themselves and the discoverer ridiculous by over-emphasis, misapplication, inartistic use of material, and all the other exaggerations into which novelty beguiles the unwary. Sophocles, writing as an artist probing the human soul, knew nothing about psychoanalysis, nor about the Œdipus situation, yet Freud went to him for a symbol; the difference between the ancient Greek and Mr. D. H. Lawrence is that the one knew nothing about these "complexes" and the other—despite his natural gifts as a novelist and a

---

[1] I would refer the interested reader to a recent volume issued at Washington: *Psychoanalysis and the Drama*, by Smith Ely Jeliffe and Louise Brink, 1922. The plays considered as texts for psychoanalytic doctrine are Chesterton's *Magic*, Gliddens and Marcin's *Eyes of Youth*, Raphael's *Peter Ibbetson*, Tolstoi's *Redemption*, Kennedy's *The Army With Banners*, Benrimo-Hazelton's *The Willow Tree*, Hazelton-Cochrane-Benrimo's *The Yellow Jacket*, Barrie's *Dear Brutus* and Benelli's *The Jest*. The danger of such studies as these is that value as a text may be confused with æsthetic value, and I am not sure that the authors have not fallen more than once into this very error.

dissector of souls—seems to know nothing else. Sophocles, to continue the strange comparison for the sake of our point, anticipated Freud by being true to human nature; Lawrence, particularly of late, is true rather to Freud. I do not disparage his novels, of which I admire the earliest most. I do, however, believe that the author's self-conscious Freudianism has spoiled page after page of his work; much in this should have been saved for his little treatise, which, thank Heaven, he did not decide to turn into a novel as well, with all its misty mysticism and involved psycho-poetry.

We shall note, then, in one country after the other, how the newer dramatists, like their fellow novelists, were quick to seize upon the psychoanalytic suggestions: Glaspell and O'Neill in the United States, not to mention the lesser fry, who were sure to misunderstand and garble; Evreinov in Russia, whose monodrama, as I try to show, fairly follows the Freudian dream-structure and attempts to apply the single-person point of view; some of the "grotesque" school of Italy, who, not content, like Wedekind, to write plays that suggest a nightmare, actually direct that the actors shall employ the nightmare technique; the German Expressionists. Not that the dream mechanism is new upon the stage; but the contemporary dramatist, as often as not, makes a conscious use of it as the result of the Freudianism in the air; and by Freudianism I mean not merely the particular theory of Freud, but the psychoanalytic atmosphere in general. To the critic the question is, not how successfully the artist has proved Freud, but how successfully he has used this suggestion, as any other, to create a vital play. Sophocles, Shakespeare, Goethe, all did it before Freud himself was dreamed of; others will do it in spite of the contagion of Freudianism. Each generation must have its intellectual slang of thought, if so we may call it. The day before yesterday we spoke in terms of Spencer and Darwin; yesterday it was Nietzsche; this morning it was Freud, this afternoon Einstein. To-morrow —? These are but incidentals to the artist, who must speak a language of all time; if Freud can provide the inner stimulus, let it be he; or any other, provided the work of art appear.

Censorship of the Stage. Mention of Freud and censorship in the same breath tempts one to amusing animadversions upon the psychology of the reformer. Somewhere the irreverent Mencken has expressed a fear that few of them would be equal to the most ordinary temptations; as Freud might put it, their very super-activity as reformers is itself a form of combating the impulses within them which they would throttle in others. But I leave this to the psychopaths, who, I hope, will make a good job of it. My own concern here is with the censors and the stage; the stage daily seems to be getting the worst of it.

To state my personal attitude in the shortest possible form: I am unequivocally opposed to any form of censorship whatsoever. Rather than yield to the reformers on the most minor point, as a playwright I would withdraw from the field and write plays to be printed for private distribution. Let us distinguish between art and business, however. There is a fortune invested in the theatre as a commercial institution; managers must live; so

must playwrights; if that living collides with powerful reformers, the managers—none too eager as a
body for the interests of art—are as business men
justified in seeking to placate the powers.   But let
not these powers deceive themselves; they are not
advancing public morality one step by such a
"conversion" of the managers, who, were it possible,
would send them all a-packing at the first opportunity.   Having said which, let us leave the managers to their business, and may it prosper.

The censor has no more right to dictate to the
artist than has the manager himself.   And to dictate in matters of sex is to choke the stream at its
very source.   Jameson has sneered at the importance
given to sex in the contemporary play, relegating it
as a factor in life to a position far below that of the
Nietzschean will to power.   No doubt the future
will witness a diminished position occupied by sex
in daily thought and in art, for with a change in
attitude toward our moral problems—and there are
few things in history that change so often and that
agree in different countries so little during the same
eras—will come a lessening of the morbid preoccupation with a beautiful well-spring that the eternal
censors have defiled.   Yet, Jameson notwithstanding, there will be such a preoccupation as long as
men are men and women, women; it is an eternal
theme; it is at the centre of life, and for the censor
to govern its expression is ridiculously like letting
the prison be run by the jail-birds.   If a play is
frankly and commercially indecent, that is a problem for the police; we are not interested in it.   The
artist, however, to the censor, is as east to west,
and never the twain shall meet.   His business is

self-expression and self-communication; just in so far as he yields an inch of his ground to the enemy, he surrenders so much of his birthright. Rather sex rampant than any form of censorship, for at least we should be sincere savages. There is no compromise here; even thought of compromise is, on the artist's part, surrender. For an author's society, then, to treat with the reformers, may be good business; it is high treason to art. To agree upon the selection of a catholic body of censors may placate the multitude and may educate the censorious; but in principle it is just such high treason. For, at bottom, the censorship represents the intrusion of theology. It is founded upon the very uncertain proposition that the flesh is evil,—a transvaluation of all art values. It knows nothing of the spirit, much as it may prate about it. It is the negation of art.

It presents, moreover, another danger,—that of the censorship of ideas. Indeed, the censorship we have just been discussing is nothing but control of a central idea. From the attempt to control the expression of sex to that of controlling expression of unpopular ideas upon economics, politics, and other matters that involve the stability of institutions favoring the dominance of class or caste, is but a short step. Religious repression and politico-economic oppression are ugly twin sisters.

"You're not a respectable man," says the cajoling Mrs. Muskat, trying to flatter Liliom into returning to his position at the merry-go-round. "You're an artist." Well, let no such distinction frighten us. Nor the curse of conformity that hangs like a pall over the entire country, until a thinker

like Santayana may write: "Though it calls itself
the land of freedom, it is really the land of compulsions, and one of the greatest compulsions is that we
must think and feel alike. . . ." Censorship tends
to just such conformity; it is the denial of artistic
personality; as a member of the body politic, the
writer, if he be worthy of his salt, must fight it as
best he can; as an artist, he will ignore it.

And so we return to poor Liliom: "Nobody's
right—but they all think they are right. . . . A
lot they know." One thing, however, we may
know: that amid the eternal uncertainty, we have
the right to select, for ourselves, our particular
views, amenable to such change as experience and
a deeper life may bring; that choosing is either our
own work or we are slaves.

"Every dramatist," Mr. Lewisohn has written,
"accepts or rejects the ideas upon which characters
act. He shapes the consequences of their actions
according to his sense of the quality of the ideas
that urge them on. Upon his view of the world,
upon his reaction to moral ideas, will depend his
choice and conduct of his fable and the end to which
he brings the lives of which he treats. It is a better
preparation for the career of a dramatist to have
watched the actions of a few villagers and to have
brooded over those actions at that spiritual core
where criticism and creation are one than to have
read all the manuals of play-writing and stagecraft
in the world and be an expert on lighting and decoration. Shun the theatre. It is a place of confusion for the dramatist. Beethoven wrote his symphonies in a little room. They can be played by

twenty men or by a hundred, in a barn or a temple. The mechanism of production is not your business; it is your servant. Your business is with man and his world and the ideas that reconcile him to it or drive him to despair.

"It is, then, his vision of the world and of the will that dictates the dramatist's choice and treatment of a fable. Accident has nothing to do with it; ingenuity has nothing to do with it. You hear stories of plays 'tinkered with on the road.' Mr. Belasco takes a manuscript and rewrites it. A dramatist whose play can be 'tinkered with' or rewritten or revised by an alien hand has not begun to comprehend the elementary conditions of any art. His play may not be inevitable under the aspect of eternity. He is but a man. He is, perhaps, but a manikin. But it must seem inevitable to him. It must be so interwoven with his profoundest perceptions, instincts, convictions, that he is willing to labor for it, starve for it, die for it. Unless it is an inseparable part of his own soul's integrity—it is nothing. Why have the managers the habit of demanding changes, revisions, adaptations for the needs of this season, that theatre, a certain star? Because they are not dealing with dramatists at all, but with mechanics, journeymen, hacks. There can be no compromise on this question. This is the final test. Do you think that your play can be changed by another or for another's convenience or use? Destroy it and work with your hands. This does not mean that your play is perfect. Having destroyed it, you yourself may relive its sources in experience, dig deeper into your own soul, and create it afresh. But if Mr. Belasco thinks he can use it after laying upon it a judicious hand, be sure that only the fire will cleanse it and your shame."[1]

An age of transition is not one in which the highest attainments of the drama may be studied. Yet it may exhibit the sincere strivings of the artist and reveal the lowly origins of future greatness. In any case, as a human spectacle, it is absorbing. We turn to it now, to view it in the light of such liberal principles as may have been gathered from the preceding pages. We demand intellectual freedom of the playwrights; we must begin by ourselves possessing it.

---

[1] *World, Will, and Word*, in The Literary Review, January 21, 1922.

SPAIN

SPAIN

JOSÉ ECHEGARAY

To all but his countrymen, José Echegaray was the author of *The Great Galeoto* and little else; to the history of his nation's drama he will perhaps remain little more. Yet, when he passed away upon September 15, 1916, Spain lost one of the most remarkable figures that it has reared in recent years. For fatal fertility, for sheer versatility of talents, he was notable even in a land that had produced a Lope de Vega with his fifteen hundred dramas. For four decades he fairly dominated the Spanish stage, at the same time making for himself a reputation as scientist, mathematician, publicist, orator, educator, moralist, and, I believe, authority upon bridge construction. Perhaps it was this dazzling career, rather than his few worthy plays, that influenced the Nobel commission, in 1904, to award the prize for literature to him, in company of the Provençal poet, Mistral. Surely the dramatic output of the protean publicist had earned the distinction more through quantity than quality. Long before 1904 his most significant work for the stage had been completed. In English he had been known through *The Great Galeoto*, which has been translated a number of times and given upon the stage in at least two acting versions: that by Maude Banks and a freer (and not altogether adequate) version by Charles Nirdligner, known as *The World*

61

and His Wife, and acted by Faversham. One other of his plays, *Mariana,* was also once familiar to English audiences in occasional performances by Mrs. Patrick Campbell.

It is now more than forty-five years since Echegaray made his unpretentious and somewhat mature début upon the Spanish stage, with a clever one-act play entitled *El Libro Talonario* (*The Check Book*). Before that date he had been known to the intellectual public in some of the numerous capacities I have just mentioned. His speeches in favor of free trade, especially, had won the approbation of the nation's leading minds. But upon the event of *The Check Book* the public was asked to accept the versatile figure in a new rôle, and it was not long before the resourceful Spaniard had added another province to his conquests.

His attraction to the stage was largely the result of the success there won by his younger brother Miguel, whose comedies are still popular in Spain. Echegaray, the older, produced his first play at the age of forty-two—a fact which explains much in the subsequent career of the dramatist. He brought to the stage a vast political acumen, a mature life of constant study and activity, a mind naturally given over to moral, mathematical, and social considerations. His was not the steady growth of the artist groping in the recesses of creative fancy; he came to the theatre with a view of life that was well defined. In the drama he saw, not so much a vehicle for art, not a form in which to encase beauty, but rather a means for exploiting his own particular moral principles. He is thus frankly a writer of problem plays, and it must be confessed at the out-

set that for the most part he has allowed his thesis
to predominate, much to the cost of any higher
dramatic art.

Echegaray, moreover, is in many respects quite
as significant to the history of the Spanish stage as
he is to the stage itself. Not since the days of the
classical epoch has a dramatic author been received
so widely in his own land; he is the first of the
modern Spanish playwrights to have procured ample
recognition outside the limits of his nation's borders.
To him came the vogue that was denied Tamayo y
Baus (author of *A New Drama*), who was an in-
finitely more artistic spirit; to him came the popularity that Lopez de Ayala could not attain, despite his superior poetic gifts. While much of this
popularity may be ascribed to reasons none too
flattering to the methods of *The Great Galeoto's*
creator, some of it was due, no doubt, to the more
cosmopolitan outlook of this thinker—to his tendency to break the bonds of a narrowing nationalism.
Where so many of the Spanish dramatists were
content to be Spanish, Echegaray, in his best plays,
becomes European.

It is important to notice in connection with his
dramas that Echegaray has helped to alter the very
pivot upon which the Spanish stage revolves—the
so-called *punto de honor*, the point of honor.[1] This
peculiar moral code has for its central idea the
absolute chastity of the female. Woman becomes a
sublimated concept that is not even to be gazed
upon covetously with impunity. The insistence

[1] The point of honor has been referred to Moorish influence (Cf. Viel Castel, *Revue des Deux Mondes*, pages 397, 442, 1841), and to the Italians (Donald Clive Stuart, *Romanic Review*, Vol. I, Nos. 3, 4). It is, in essence, as drama, a special-ized form of the "eternal triangle."

upon her lily-white purity becomes a fierce, almost voluptuously virtuous passion on the part of her natural protector, man.   For more than two centuries the stage in Spain had been trammeled by the point of honor, which is less intelligible to the Anglo-Saxon than to a Latin audience.   Not even the great Lope de Vega had entirely overcome the narrowing influence of such an ethical punctilio which, in one of the greatest of the classical dramas, *Del Rey Abajo Ninguno* (*None Beneath the King*), by Rojas y Zorrilla, reaches a climax of artistic beauty and irrational injustice to blameless womanhood.   From the standpoint of the *punto de honor* Echegaray's plays may be said to mark a transitional stage.   The frankly masculine view inherent in the point of honor gives way in his best work to an attitude more just to woman.   In none of his pieces, however, does he reach the independence of that more radical spirit, Pérez Galdós, as exhibited in the justly noted *Electra*.

Echegaray's general conception of the dramatist's sphere may be best studied in the preface to his first social drama, *Como Empieza Y Como Acaba* (*The Beginning and the End*), produced on November 9, 1876.   This is also the first of a triolgy which possesses as its motif the persistence of an evil deed through several generations.   The author's dramatic mainspring is here presented as "the logic of fatality," which, he says, "dominates when moral liberty cedes to passion its place in the human soul."   The dramatist, then, would have us consider him a fatalist, and he has elsewhere said that "Fate writes greater tragedies than playwrights," but a close study of his several score of plays shows clearly that his Fate is purely a social phenomenon—the familiar and inevitable opposition of society as a whole to the desires of the individual.

Of Greek fate there is little or nothing in the Spanish playwright, although he has succeeded as no other in his own land in giving to the world about us all the characteristics of a cold, impersonal, implacable fate. In his better plays he has risen above his theories. We cannot take seriously to-day a dramatist who justifies the incongruities of his work by referring back to newspaper originals, or to such a metaphysical formula as the "logic of fatality." Logic and fate are really two antithetical concepts, and to link them creates a paradox whose ill effect is easily discernible in the many melodramas of Echegaray, where improbability clashes against absurdity and the curtain descends on a crescendo of empty effect.

The motif par excellence of Echegaray's dramas is the conflict between two inherently opposing duties or forces. Now it is a daughter who sacrifices her own happiness in order to shield her father from the consequences of an indiscretion; now it is a son who, in order to save his father from disgrace, gives up a happy marriage. Again, we find a scientist pitted against the cohorts of superstition, or a father who assumes responsibility for the crime of his illegitimate son, thus expiating his own crime against society. The characters of these plays all seem to exist for the satisfaction of their morbid desires for self-sacrifice and expiation. From this standpoint the theatre of Echegaray presents a long procession of illegitimate children, of heroines in ill-merited dishonor, heroes of the exaggerated Hugoesque type,

5

villains too often reminiscent of the nickel novel "hair-raiser." So that he has created many situations, innumerable problems, but little character.

Of humor there is little enough in this serious Spaniard. His moral aim accords ill with undue levity. The most irreconcilable opponent of the playwright must admit, however, that he excels in harrowing efforts, in a certain gloomy power, in a sheer vehemence and momentum of language that carry along the worst of his plays. Quite negligible on the whole as a poet, he is scarcely more eminent as a writer of dramatic prose, yet there is a power in his phraseology, an attraction in his figurative speech, in the Oriental profusion of his bizarre conceptions, that does much to redeem his other deficiencies. There is little continental artistry in the average Echegaray production. He lacked the power of self-criticism, of technical finesse; he was a moral force rather than an artistic spirit. His fancy would penetrate a situation, his mind would supply a contention, his powerful language could easily fuse the whole, and his electric energy thus galvanized a play into existence.

It may be questioned whether the Spaniard wrote any really notable work after the memorable date of *El Gran Galeoto*, 1881. Since then he added much to the bulk of his labors, but not usually of a quality to enhance his reputation. Beginning in 1874, and writing incessantly, he registered a surprisingly small number of failures for a dramatist of such prolific talent. In such plays as *La Esposa del Vengador* (*The Avenger's Bride*) and *En el Puño de la Espada* (*On the Sword's Point*), he actually revived the waning melodrama in Spain and lent it

new life, infusing a vigor and a cult of the grandiose
that he had imbibed from Victor Hugo and the elder
Dumas. It was through the younger Dumas and
through Henrik Ibsen, together with a host of minor
influences, that he was soon led to the social drama,
a form to which his very temperament, as well as
the traditions of his national stage, was bound
sooner or later to carry him. This, nevertheless,
did not prevent Blanco García from writing that the
social drama was "more averse than favorable" to
his spirit—a criticism, perhaps, that shows a personal aversion to the type of drama rather than a
critical distinction. Echegaray was eclectic by
nature and environment, and his work reflects the
dominant tendencies of his time, yet there is also
the imprint of his own rigid personality.

Three years after his début he startled his audiences with *O Locura O Santidad?* (*Madman or Saint?*)
in which the influence of Ibsen first appears to any
appreciable extent. The play, one of the three or
four worthy companions to *The Great Galeoto*, presents many analogies to *Brand*, which may have
inspired the Spaniard in his first signal effort. Just
as the Norwegian priest sacrifices the spirit to the
letter, creating a hell of ruin in his search for heaven,
so, too, Lorenzo, discovering that his name and his
fortune are in reality not his own, is brought to the
verge of insanity by the clash of the two opposing
forces—his daughter's happiness in marriage to a
noble, which cannot take place under the true state
of circumstances (at least Lorenzo's honesty protests against it, despite the plebeian willingness of
the parties concerned), and Lorenzo's "duty" to relinquish his name and fortune. This would destroy,

too, the happiness of his mother (through whose ruse his plans of sacrifice are frustrated) and of his wife.

The struggle leads Lorenzo to the asylum, while we are left to hope that all will right itself in time. Was Lorenzo a madman or a saint, so to insist upon his duty?

Between this play and *El Gran Galeoto* intervened eleven dramas of varying merit, among these the play which, I believe, can well claim the odious distinction of being the worst ever penned by its author—*Mar Sin Orillas* (*The Shoreless Sea*). It is one of the puzzles of the human intellect that the mind capable of *The Great Galeoto* should be able to descend to the puerile ineptitude and absurdity of *The Shoreless Sea*. The point of honor is here urged to farcical extremes—piracy, rape, intrigue, all crowd the stage amidst a veritable tissue of confusions. When a single word might save the insipid heroine, she prefers to maintain an ambiguous silence before her equally silly husband. Repudiated by him, she plunges into the sea. Presently a message arrives, proving the wife innocent of the charge which her husband has preferred against her. Seized with grief at his harshness, the husband follows his wife into the ocean. All of which was so destined by the author from the very start.

Most of the plays that followed *The Great Galeoto* tend but to repeat the ever-recurrent motifs of the playwright—illegitimate offspring, outraged honor, malicious slander, social error, fanaticism, materialism, snobbery, and so on, through the gamut of all possible social complications. Nor is Echegaray free from such trite devices as "the papers," and those recitations of antecedent events that usually, on our own stage, take the form of "twenty years ago," etc., to the accompaniment of tremolo music. "The papers," indeed, come near to spoiling such a play as *Madman or Saint?*

In *The Great Galeoto* we find Echegaray at his best. It is with justice recognized not only as the Spaniard's masterpiece, but as an addition to world-literature. For once in his career the author almost frees himself from the devices of cheap melodrama. Here is no villain of the regular type, no hero, no heroine—all are victims of a society which in itself means no harm. Therein lies the essence of the tragedy. The casual remark, the fitting smile, these are the elements that start Madrid talking of Julian and his wife, Theodora, and of Ernesto, their ward, whom the world says is usurping the position of Julian. With unswerving impetus, with the very impersonality of fate, the play develops to its conclusion. At the end Julian is killed by the apparent revelation of his wife's love for Ernesto, yet neither the wife nor the ward has been really guilty. Madrid's tongues have forced them together—slander has forged its unthinking lies to the heat of apparent truth.[1]

Few plays present such a powerful, logical, convincing study of gossip and its evil consequences. The art of the play is in its simple power.

---

[1] The name of "The Great Galeoto" is derived from the story of Paolo and Francesca in Dante's Divine Comedy. "Galeotto fu il libro e chi lo scrisse" says Francesca as she tells the story of the memorable day when she and Paul forgot themselves. Galeotto (Galehault) was the intermediary between Lancelot and Guinevere, and thus did the book they were reading serve as intermediary between Paul and Francesca. Even so does the gossip of the world serve as the intermediary that forces Ernesto and Theodora together. It is interesting to note, in this regard, that the germ of *The Great Galeoto* already appeared in *Como Empieza Y Como Acaba*. In the latter play the heroine, Magdalena, in reading Dante (together with Shakespeare, a great favorite of the author), comes across the identical passage which suggested the dramatist's greatest work.

But four personages occupy the central position, yet in them we feel palpitate the heart of the town— they present, indeed, the world in miniature, so keenly do we feel their presence, the effect of each word and of each action.

This salient drama has been compared to various plays. Sheridan's *School for Scandal* has been mentioned as a frivolous antecedent. *Othello*, too, has been adduced as an example of the malignant effect of gossip. But in *Othello* it is the personal villany of an Iago, not the impersonal, unintentional force of society, that leads to the tragedy. For *El Gran Galeoto* is the drama of "They say." To my mind, a better comparison than either is none other than *Much Ado About Nothing*. For here we have the comedy of "They say." The play is all the more comic in that it represents a knowing piece of amiable malice; the Spanish drama is all the more dramatic in that it is the story of an unintentional, impersonal infamy.

The Great Galeoto reveals the influence of Ibsen in a marked degree. Even more so, speaking directly, does *El Hijo de Don Juan* (*The Son of Don Juan*), which has erroneously been termed the Spanish *Ghosts*. Frankly deriving its inspiration from the Norwegian tragedy, Echegaray's play shows a difference in treatment and in point of view which really entitle the play to be called original. Whereas Ibsen's *Ghosts* shifts the blame of Oswald's plight back to the society which forced Mrs. Alving to dwell with her debauched husband, Echegaray would seem to indicate that the fault of Lázaro's insanity lay only in his father's failure to live a moral life.

Although the Spaniard goes into such horrible details as would have quite unnerved Ibsen himself, he yet fails to penetrate into the social basis of his protagonist's insanity. Or, if he does penetrate, he rests his hope for betterment upon the individual.

Echegaray's play is further complicated by the fact that his doomed hero is engaged to be married, thereby providing a typical Echegarayan struggle—shall he marry, knowing his moral duty not to? Must he then give up his only hope for happiness? Truly terrible in conception and in treatment is the scene where Lázaro's father detects his son, wild in debauch, tippling with the very mistress he himself has known too well. When at last the curtain descends on the cry of Lázaro for the sun (borrowed from Ibsen because of its beauty, says Echegaray), the father, in anguish, cries out, "I, too, have asked for it!"

The coupling of the names of Echegaray and Ibsen, largely due to this play, has been much overdone by critics who have not taken the trouble to examine the works of Echegaray extensively. There are really more differences between the two than similarities. In the first place, Ibsen is by far the greater artist. He chooses between prose and verse with discrimination, while the Spaniard seems to waver between the two with uncertainty. Ibsen is the master dramaturge, where Echegaray is too often a bungler with peculiar talents that save his work from failure. Ibsen is an artist in search of ideas; he grows from play to play in both art and thought. Echegaray's art is, excepting three or four plays, a negligible quantity; his ideas are certain from the start—he came with them to the stage; it is his art that he gropes about for, never to discover it for good, heedless of the critics, intent on moral purpose alone. *Mariana* and *El Loco Dios* (*The Divine Madman*), 1900, also reveal the influence of Ibsen. The second of these plays has been termed by Fitzmaurice-Kelly, I believe, an unintentional parody of the Norwegian's symbolism.

Although both Ibsen and Echegaray recognize the rôle of society in life, yet the Spaniard would seek self-realization in self-repression, while the Norwegian hopes for the realization of self through the expansion of self. Ibsen is an out-and-out radical; Echegaray is that peculiar, but familiar, type who to the radical seems conservative and to the conservative seems radical.

Gloomy as Ibsen himself is Echegaray in his more powerful moments; as insistent as, and less swerving than, Tolstoi in his moral purpose. Unsusceptible to the attacks of critics, he has rarely ventured to defend his works except upon the basis of morals. His ideal is at once of the past and of the future. With a vigor that takes him back, on the one hand, to Calderón he unites a modernity that brings him forward, on the other, to Ibsen and the social philosophers. His work, I believe, represents a transitional period in the history of the Spanish stage. As early as 1903 Bernard Shaw had said of him that he was made of the stuff that crosses borders—a prophecy which bore fulfillment on the English stage some three years later.[1]

---

[1] The Shavian endorsement of such playwrights as Echegaray and Brieux is one of the paradoxes of the Irishman's career. In both, Shaw saw more than was there.

Most of the preceding section on Echegaray consists of a ruthless condensation of a book I wrote upon him as part of the requirements for the Ph.D. degree in Romance Languages (Harvard, 1912). I thought little of Echegaray then; I think less now—as of so many other things. The doctorial thesis reposes in the university archives. There let it rest *in pace*.

To say that Echegaray, on the whole, is a bad playwright because he is a belated romantic is as futile a toying with terms as to pronounce any other writer great because he happens to be an opportune realist. Echegaray, in general, is an inferior dramatist because the plays themselves are vitiated at their source. They do not develop from a core of passion, produced inevitably by the clash of character and circumstance. They are the artificial result of a passion that they do not contain.

"Spanish dramatists," writes Storm Jameson, "are making their way towards a national drama almost untouched by the restless spirit that stirred Italy. Their conception of life is singularly simple. In Italy a revolt against the forms of modern life; in France, with the exception of Brieux, cynical and witty ridicule of folly; in England, save from the Celtic Shaw, no very savage indignation; in the north, generally, a dramatic view of life limited to social institutions and conditions. But Spanish dramatists, with the rare exception of Dicenta, are not in revolt against anything, least of all against life."[1] With the rare exception of Dicenta?[2] Then where was Benito Pérez Galdós, whose labors Jameson overlooks in their entirety, what though, as a woman in revolt, she should have been one of the first to proclaim the ideological virtues of *Electra?* Galdós may not be the dramatist of genius

[1] *Modern Drama in Europe.* Pages 230-231.

[2] Joaquin Dicenta, 1860-1916. Yet *Juan José*, Dicenta's central drama, is not a proletarian play; primarily it turns upon a pivot of frustrated passion. The workingman, robbed of his mistress-sweetheart by his employer, who later discharges him for venturing to assert his prior rights, finally slays both the unfaithful woman and her tempter. Of course it is easy to detect a symbol here, if one is so minded, revealing the maddened proletarian slaying both his own interests as well as his employer's in anarchic revolt. The play itself is a strange commingling of realism and romanticism; its sweep is as surely romantic as its detail is true to life. It stirs even the reader, despite its shortcomings.

that Ramón Pérez de Ayala[1] has sought to make him out, but surely he should have merited a few words in a resumé of modern Spanish drama that devotes half of its space to Echegaray. Of capital importance to the course of modern thought in Spain, eminent as a novelist, beloved as a personality, Galdós bridges the gap between the Spain of yesterday that was Echegaray and the Spain of to-day that is, upon the stage, Benavente.

BENITO PÉREZ GALDÓS

The life of the noted writer stretches across a span of seventy-five years—years rich in history, not only for his beloved Spain, but for the entire world. Born at Las Palmas, in the Canary Islands, on May 10, 1845, he was sent to Madrid in 1863 to study law. An unwilling student he was, like so many others of the literary tribe, and, again like them, he drifted into journalism and thence to literature, readily making a name for himself among the Liberal element. As early as this he had already tried his hand at art, for in 1862, at the Exposition in Santa Cruz de Tenerife, he was awarded honorable mention for sketches entitled *La Magdalena* and *Un Boceto Historico*, as well as for an oil-painting called "Una Alquería." Nor did his love of the pencil and brush abandon him entirely, for later he illustrated his own books in a manner that called forth the praise of professional artists, and designed the last resting place of his famous friend Pereda. That friendship, by the way, which was begun early in the career of the author who yesterday was mourned wherever the Spanish tongue is spoken,

---

[1] See his *Las Máscaras*, 2 vols, 1919, Madrid.

was one of the strangest as well as one of the most
beautiful in literary history, and deserves pages and
pages by itself; about it, a paragraph presently.

The man was strangely reticent; it has been suggested by a noted Spanish critic that perhaps he
put so much of himself into his voluminous productions that he really cared little to discuss whatever
he may have omitted; in any case, when asked by
even so great a figure as Clarín (Leopoldo Alas) for
details as to his early life, Galdós replied in more
condensed fashion than a scant encyclopædic reference. He would offer little beyond the fact that
he arrived in Madrid in 1863, and that during the
three or four years that preceded the revolution of
1868 he made several attempts at writing pieces for
the theatre, only one of which he was at all content
with, though he was glad that it had never reached
the "boards." The passage is important because,
years later, when Galdós again approached the stage,
this time with a great reputation as a novelist behind him, his aims were obscured by critics who
were somewhat too ready to discover that the
novelist was trying to corrupt drama by grafting
upon it procedures that belonged only in long nar-
ratives. Galdós, it appears, was in reality returning to an early love, and not all Spanish theatrical
critics are inclined to agree with Fitzmaurice-
Kelly's recent judgment that "his diffuse, exuberant
genius was scarcely accommodated to the conventions of theatrical form." (Enc. Britannica, 11th
edition.)

In 1867 the idea came to him for his first book,
La Fontana de Oro, which he himself describes as a
work with a certain revolutionary tendency. He

began it in Madrid, completed it in Spain, and no sooner did he return to Spain than the revolution broke out. He received the new state of affairs most enthusiastically. It was at this stage (from 1868 to 1872) that he made the acquaintance of the famous regional novelist, Pereda. At their first meeting it seemed that each had read everything the other had written, and the friendship was dissolved only by the death of the older man. Here was Galdós, the standard-bearer of liberalism, of anti-clericalism, of modernism in the broader sense of the word, a bosom friend of the man who stood squarely against everything that fired him who was later to write *Doña Perfecta* and *Electra*. Intellectually speaking, black could be no greater contrast to white than were the ideas and the ideals that animated Pereda and Galdós; yet despite the mutterings of friends and foes, despite the passing of years that brought them often into conflict, they lived in growing intimacy, traveled much together over the picturesque provinces of Spain, and seemed to symbolize, by their unbroken fellowship, the fact that, underlying all the antagonism which divides men into warring camps, into clashing sects, is a fundamental humanity that bridges all gaps. Is there not something ironical in the picture of Galdós and Pereda shaking hands above the battle, as it were, while down below their adherents fought out the bitter conflict of orthodoxy versus liberalism, of faith against science? Better still, is there not something that laughs gently at sects and sectarians in the familiar story of the determined battle of books that was waged between the Liberal and the Tory?—a battle in which even opponents of Galdós are forced to admit that Pereda came out second best? The two men met, above even their own personal battles, as man and man. There is, to me at least, something in that friendship which refutes the narrower applications of the theories each held.

Clarín has described Galdós as he looked in his prime, after he had published several of his Episodios Nacionales (those National Episodes which constitute a veritable epic of Spanish history, as well as one of Galdós' chief claims to enduring fame)—the forehead that bespoke genius and passions; the penetrating eyes that conveyed the impression of tenderness not unmingled with guile—a certain innocent, artist's guile. The author dressed neither well nor badly. He was as little inclined to talk as to write of himself, but on the other hand, made a willing as well as skillful listener, aptly steering the conversation by means of well-directed questions. He had no use for the more rhetorical aspects of the writer's craft; indeed, he has been accused by grammarians as sinning against the language's purity. With all respect to grammar, it was never meant to worry great writers; if a man has not conquered the prudish chit in his schoolhood days, he must do without her later. For one person who writes well, how many thousands write correctly! Galdós was, moreover, fond of retiring early; he was not what one could call a society man; even the theatre, into which he aspired to attract his own audiences, was a wearying spectacle to him and left him with a headache. A man, then, who believed in hard work and the simple life; who carried on the great tradition of Spanish fecundity; who fought for advanced thought, now leading the crowd, now led by it; who virtually made his country's history live anew in a series of romances that have more than once, and by critics of accepted authority, been compared to Balzac for the wonderful array of living characters and to Dickens for the humanity and the humor that inform them.

Mention of Dickens reminds us, too, that Galdós was much influenced by English literature, with which he was very familiar. His foreign excursions took him most frequently to London and Leopoldo Alas has said that, in his opinion, Galdós would go to Great Britain "for customs, politics, and men, . . . but not for women." The references to Balzac and Dickens are not new; years ago Rafael Altamira pointed out that the resemblance to Dickens was more in the faculty for creating types than in the vein of humor.

It is said that Galdós' first suggestion for his famous series of National Episodes came from the noted French literary twins, Erckmann and Chatrian, who are still considered by many to be a single person, largely owing, perhaps, to the usual coupling of the names by a hyphen. For this purpose he resorted to a most rigorous plan of documentation; "old charters, old letters, old newspapers were collected by him with the minuteness of a German archivist," writes Fitzmaurice-Kelly; "no novelist was ever more thoroughly equipped as regards the details of his period. *Trafalgar*, the first volume of the Episodios Nacionales, appeared in 1879. . . . The author's aim was to write the national epic of the nineteenth century in prose, and he so completely succeeded that, long before the first series ended in 1881, he took rank among the foremost novelists of his time. A second series of Episodios Nacionales . . . was brought to a close in 1883, and was, like its predecessor, a monument of industry and exact knowledge of realism and romantic conception; and he carried on the Episodios Nacionales into a fourth series, raising the total of the volumes to forty. In fecundity and power of creating character, Pérez Galdós vies with Balzac."

The National Episodes, however, represent but a part of Pérez Galdós' prose labors; indeed, there are not lacking Spanish critics who, though they acknowledge the supreme virtues of the Episodes, find the most interesting of the man's novels in his contemporary series—the books dealing with the social and religious problems of modern life. Here, too, his astonishing faculty of observation, his skill in construction, his bold assault upon current evils, his unflagging inventiveness, attest the genius of Galdós. One wonders whether Fitzmaurice-Kelly, the noted English Hispanophile, still considers the prose labors of Galdós broad, but lacking solidity. At any rate, this characterization, which appeared in his history of Spanish literature, is not repeated in the article upon Pérez Galdós to be found in the latest edition of the Britannica.

Among the best of the contemporary novels are *Doña Perfecta* (1876), which has been used as a text book in our schools, and has been translated into English; *Gloria* (1877); *La Familia de León Roch* (1878), *Angel Guerra* (1891). To these many would wish to add the exquisite *Marianela* (known here in at least two editions for school use, as well as a translation into English), and *Fortunata y Jacinta*.[1]

Galdós' theatrical career really begins with the production of *Realidad*, which was adapted for the stage from two of his prose works, *Realidad* and *La Incognita*. The next year (1893) witnessed the production of *La Loca de La Casa*, which was followed by *La de San Quintin*, *Los Condenados*, and *Voluntad*. In 1896 *Doña Perfecta* was translated to the scene. Five years later occurred one of the most important theatrical representations in the history of the Spanish stage: the production of the much-discussed, much-maligned, much-fought, and vituperated *Electra*, of which more in a moment. In 1902 came *Alma y Vida*; next year, *Mariucha*; 1904 saw the dramatization of the excellent novel, *El Abuelo*, which has been likened to *King Lear* for its theme. In 1915 came the socialistic *Celia en los infernos* and *San Simón*, and in 1916, when the author was already past seventy, *El Tacaño Salomón*.

Manuel Bueno, the well-known Madrid theatrical

---

[1] Professor J. D. M. Ford, of Harvard, in his recent *Main Currents of Spanish Literature*, challenges Galdós' enthusiasts in characteristically fair, outspoken words. After admitting that Galdós attacks real evils, and that he does not lack courage, the noted scholar adds that "his courage is not one worthy of unqualified praise, for it is on occasion dangerously like the courage of the fanatic. He assails fanaticism in the religious constitution of his fellow Spaniards, and he exposes himself to the charge that he is himself a fanatic in his methods of doing so.

"The *Doña Perfecta*, which, out of all his novels, has made most noise abroad, illustrates what happens when his antipathies take one of their most determined forms, anti-clericalism. In this book he gives but a perverted idea of religion, of Catholicism as practiced in Spain. No one can prove a rule of life by basing his arguments upon the abnormal, the monstrous, the exceptional in human nature; and again, the intrinsic goodness of a religious system is not vitiated by the excesses of a few fanatic and unintelligent believers." Ford advances similar objections to other of the Galdós romances. Here, of course, the reader is more or less unconsciously swayed by his stand upon the matters under discussion. Thousands of readers cannot view the books in this light; perhaps the critic does not exist who can read controversial works with utter impartiality and impersonality. Until criticism shall have been made a science (which means never) such impersonality will be a word for critics to toy with. Yet in works of a controversial nature it is doubly obligatory upon the author to play his game fairly. There is food for thought, too, in Ford's statement that Pereda, in those novels in which he tried to refute Galdós' theses, "was too hide-bound in his own conservatism to meet the other novelist effectively on his own ground."

critic, who is by no means always inclined to optimistic views upon the national drama, softens perceptibly in the presence of Galdós' plays. For the sake of the grandiose themes and their treatment he is ready to forgive him things that could not be pardoned in a writer of less merit. He agrees at once that Galdós has brought novelistic methods to the theatre, but what, he asks, of that? Who has decreed, outside of critics who look upon books and the stage as material for text-book utterances, that all analysis must be confined to the novel and all synthesis to the stage, and that never the twain must meet? Galdós' plays belie that assertion, and that is why his work for the stage is, "like *La Celestina*, an intermediate form between theatre and novel, possessing the fascinating fibre of the first and the noble eloquence of the second." One must admire, above all, the boldness of the man, he tells us, in thus flouting the conventional canons of stage-technique. Galdós refused, moreover, to pander to the taste for blatant rhetoric that Echegaray knew so well how to satisfy. With all his faults, Bueno receives Galdós into the theatrical fold—he did from the first, when others were finding fault and when the public was turning a cold shoulder—with these affectionate words: "We are with Galdós body and soul, because his work has opened to us a road which, were it not for this great writer, would be irreparably closed to us."

It is the brilliant stylist and exquisite conteur Ramón Pérez de Ayala who has erected Galdós into a quasi-Shakesperean figure, at the same time tearing Benavente rudely from the pedestal upon which contemporary criticism has placed him. With reference to both men, the author of that quaint and fascinating book *Belarmino y Apolonio* is well worth knowing; he is, to say the least, original, and his commentary is such a welcome relief from the pompous maunderings of so many of his inferiors, that it is a tonic, even when one is compelled to disagree with him. It is true that his clever remarks are often founded upon the process of giving new meanings to old words and thus polishing up old thoughts,—that, despite his airy manner, he has little new to say. It is true that he has a habit of treating his subjects in tripartite divisions that recall both Cæsar's Gallia and the Ciceronian phraseology. It is true, too, that by reading out of Galdós' plays a mass of theory, he reads into them an artistic value that is absent. He talks much of impersonality, yet tells us little of Galdós and much of himself. He does not criticize or reveal the play under consideration so much as use it, and avowedly, as the basis of commentary. Now, no one has a quarrel with this sort of thing. Its sole justification is the quality of the man who does it, and in Pérez de Ayala, whether as critic, poet, or novelist, there is a distinctly personal savor that creates art even when it leaves one's opinions unaltered.

To this critic Galdós' work is all nineteenth century Spain. "In Don Benito Pérez Galdós, as in Shakespeare, it is clearly to be seen that the author has conceived the dramatic work as a whole in which at every moment the action is co-ordinated with the place where it occurs, the character with the physical appearance of the personage, the dialogue with the attitude and the composition, the phrase with the manner, the voice with the gesture,—in short,

the spiritual with the plastic element. Without
this condition there is no great dramatic art."
Again: "This fusion of the figure with the milieu
and the infiltration of the ambient with the personage, in the manner of osmosis and endosmosis
between the spirit and the environment, is a salient
characteristic of the most original and intense of
modern literary art, the Russian. It is likewise the
dominant trait of the Galdosian production of the
entire second epoch or manner, whether through influence of Russian literature, or through deter-
minism of the contemporary sensibility, I do not
know." Galdós, according to this view, crowns the
Spanish novel as Cervantes starts it; he reforms
Spanish drama as Cervantes tried to, in the direction of simplicity and realism, although "Cervantes
did not succeed in becoming the chief dramatist of
his day, and Galdós is, without dispute, the greatest
of ours and one of the first in any age or place."

In what appears, to most, the exaggeration of this
last citation there is, none the less, a kernel of
measurable truth. Galdos' plays, unlike Echegaray's, do develop from a core of passion that is
the play itself. They reveal a healthy disregard for
the conventions of stage technique. They do not
yield readily to the arrogant confines of the proscenium, and tend to overflow the banks of the accepted form. But in so doing they exercise a liber-
ating influence; they rebel, rather than, like Echegaray's numerous monstrosities, conform. They are
the plastic revelation of the thought that they contain. Often the personages are so humanly conceived and presented that, like all significant human
beings, they become symbols—symbols not in the

sterile sense of allegory, but in the sense of meaningful life. It is thus possible for Pérez de Ayala, in considering Galdós' *La Loca de la Casa* (1893) to indicate Pepete as the incarnation of egoism and capitalism overshooting the mark, and Victoria as his socialistic, counterbalancing wife. Incidentally, the critic points out that Pepete's "Nietzscheism" precedes by several years Clarín's introduction of the German's name to Spain. It is because of Galdós' power to create the illusion of humanity that Ayala may declare, "Perhaps you sympathize more with some than with others of the figures or personages in Cervantes; but it is certain that their father, in the moment of engendering them, sympathized with all alike. We will say the same of Galdós' figures."

So, in his various plays—there are about a score —Galdós is viewed as defending the conservation of the species and the reason, the instinct (conservation) favoring the individual versus the species and the reason favoring the species versus the individual. "Such is the tragedy of human history and the life of man: the perpetual struggle between these two just causes." And what is to reconcile these irreconcilables? The will, by which we are to understand the love of love.

Manuel Bueno, though not the stylist that Ayala is, can speak of Galdós in the same reverential terms. "Galdós' art fascinates me," he has written in his criticism of *Mariucha*, "fascinates me because it answers to deep aspirations of youth, because it translates the restless spirit of our times, because it is boldly destructive and frank without hypocrisy." In Mariucha we have a spiritual sister to Ibsen's Nora and Hedda; as she is a rebel, so is the play regarded as an essay in Nietzschean transmutation of values.

Of *El Abuelo* (1904), Bueno speaks in terms of extravagance unmatched by Pérez de Ayala. "Hamlet, spying upon the words and the gestures of his mother and his uncle to track the origin of the crime, is less tragic than the Count of Albrit seeking, through the smiling adolescence of Nell and Dolly, the tell-tale indication of the maternal guilt." Dolly becomes an "Antigone more beautiful within the ideal than the Greek virgin herself." And the play as a whole is "the greatest work produced by the contemporary national theatre. If it were permissible to assign rank to works of art, I should place it between *King Lear* and *Brand;* that is, the most intense of Shakespeare and the deepest of Ibsen. The thinker and the artist have reached, in *El Abuelo*, the loftiest height accessible to genius."

Such admiration, such panegyric, may be understood without being shared. There is no question as to the hold which Galdós exerts upon the liberal minds of his nation. In much of what his commentators write, the artist is confused with the social personality. Perhaps one must be such a Spaniard as Ayala or Bueno to behold in *El Abuelo* the tragic eminence assigned to it in the radiant words just quoted. Surely one may range himself among Galdós' admirers without assenting to what seems rhetorical expansion rather than critical comprehension.

Let us pause for a few moments upon *El Abuelo* (*The Grandfather*), which dates from 1904, three years after *Electra*. It is, in essence, almost a dramatization of the Tennysonian lines,

Kind hearts are more than coronets,
And simple faith than Norman blood.

The Count of Albrit, a proud nobleman fallen
upon evil days, is tortured by a maddening doubt
as to which of his granddaughters, Dolly or Nelly,
is the real daughter of his deceased son and which
the spurious. He returns to his former manor at
La Pardina to meet his daughter-in-law Lucretia,
who at first cannot bring herself to tell him the
truth. He decides to watch the children closely for
a sign of the noble blood to reveal itself by word or
deed. At first perplexed, he decides finally upon
Dolly. Yet it is the selfish Nelly who is the real
one, as the disgruntled Senén discloses in a moment
of anger against Lucretia, and as Lucretia herself
tells her confessor. The Count, fairly crazed, for
he has come to love Dolly, decides: "Now I see that
human thought, human calculations, and human
plans are as nothing! All these are nothing but
rust that corrodes and decays; what endures is that
which dwells within! The soul can never die!"

What does one see in the play, approaching it
without a knowledge of its importance to the modern
Spanish drama and equally ignorant of the exalted
opinion in which Galdós is held by Ayala and
Bueno? To speak the humble truth,—a fairly well
constructed piece, containing two or three genuinely moving scenes, and somewhat marred by the
use of such conventional makeshifts as "papers,"
"proofs," and revelations made by crossed under-
lings. There are unnecessary "asides"; unnecessary,
not because the "aside" should be ruthlessly rooted
out of contemporary drama (I do not believe it
need be), but because in this case nothing that they

convey could not with equal ease and greater effectiveness have been conveyed by facial expression and gesture. These defects are compensated for, and richly, by the very intensity of Galdós' conception; he saw, what Echegaray may never have imagined, that there is a place upon the stage for calmness, for passion that does not tear itself to tatters. But Shakespeare, *Hamlet?* Let us be moderate, gentlemen! Echegaray, upon the production of *El Gran Galeoto*, was hailed as a second Shakespeare. Maeterlinck, too, after the presentation of *La Princesse Maleine*, was brought by Octave Mirbeau to the attention of a skeptical world with the same crushing praise. And, as we shall presently note, Benavente's camp-followers have not lagged behind the procession of puffery. No. It is not here that Galdós' importance lies. Both Echegaray before him and Benavente after have helped to obscure his service to a stage cluttered with "efectismo"—the easily attained sensationalism of external effects and coups de théâtre. Galdós had a glimpse of what the contemporary dramatist, at his best, is rapidly attaining. In a day when "technique" was everything, he despised it. Nor was it because he could not have written in the Scribe-Sarcey tradition; the genius capable of creating his novelistic world was easily equal to a task that is assimilated without too much trouble by any competent college student to-day. It was because he felt its restraining influence, because drama to him meant something more than an exercise in form and genre. So that, if the semi-confined outlook of Echegaray may be traced back to Calderón, the plays of Galdós belong rather, like those of Benavente, in the tradition of Lope de Vega. That way lies a formal freedom which is the mirror of an inner liberation.

La de San Quintin (englished as *The Duchess of San Quentin*) belongs to the earlier Galdosian plays, 1894. The work deals chiefly with the love of young Victor for the Duchess Rosario, a year younger than he. She is an aristocrat fallen into financial difficulties; he is the supposed son of Don César de Buendia, a tight-fisted, lecherous, semi-invalid of fifty-five. Through the Marquis de Falfan de los Godos, who has been wronged by Don César, Rosario comes into letters proving that Victor is not the natural son of Don César. This she makes known, choosing Victor, the socialist idealist, in preference to Don César, the crafty widower who has made love to her. The happy couple, representing the union of enlightened aristocracy and the rising proletariat, look to the future with confidence. Where old Don José, almost a nonagenarian, sees the death of a world, Victor and Rosario behold the dawn of a new era.

The vision of the play is that which inspires most of the author's labors; the whole is vivified by Galdós' passion for truth to self, for truth at all costs, for social progress. There are suggestions of Ibsen's *Pillars of Society*, as well as *The Wild Duck*.

But one cannot help wishing that these unnecessary asides, these epistolary imbroglios, these mysteries of parentage and melodramatic revelations, together with the other trappings of a style that is outmoded because it never sank its roots into passional genuineness, were absent. Galdós did not look upon life as does Mr. Galsworthy, for example.

The Englishman sees it deeply, sees it steadily and
perhaps whole, yet is prone to treat it as if it laid
itself out in patterns of easily grasped symmet-
ricality; there seems, at times, and especially in
such a later work as *The Skin Game*, a readiness to
employ stenciled detail in the elaboration of a pattern that is meant to be anything but stenciled.[1]
Something of this same incongruity informs the
major portion of Galdós' plays. It is particularly
disconcerting in such a piece as *Electra*, 1901, which
created a veritable furore in the intellectual life of
the nation. It was a personal as much as an artistic triumph. As was to be expected, the con-
servatives launched their propaganda against the
subversive drama. It is recorded that "in one city
the actors were obliged to leave the theatre before
the performance in order to escape violence at the
hands of the clericals. In another, the members of
the company were refused lodging and were obliged
to spend the night in the streets. Even from the
pulpit and the confessional, says Galdós himself,
war was waged against the work."[2]

[1] This same effect is produced upon me by Galsworthy's *The Mob*, a play
which seems to prove that not even the most noble attitude can make a good
piece of art unless the life of art itself be respected. There is more than one appeal
in the play to that very mob whose political and emotional unreason is pointed
out by the author; as a playwright he appeals to that very mob spirit in his
audience, with the effects of passing parades, with the coincidence of Hubert's
death in battle at the moment of the first national victory, with the foreshadowing
of that death in the dream recited by Hubert's wife. Galsworthy begs part of the
question by making the nation at war with a *little* opponent. Would More's position have been less logical if the fight were an equal one? And is it the mob that
starts wars or ends them? His shorter pieces reveal, in more marked degree,
something of the same incongruity that I am trying to explain in Galdós. (See,
for example, *The First and Last*, with its sudden entrances, burned "papers"
(Echegaray!), union of aristocracy and slums, double suicide, all inside of a one-
act play that requires three scenes with thirty hours between I and II and two
months between II and III, and the curtain lowered in the third scene to denote
the passing of three hours. Yet Phelps can say that "he has never produced anything negligible." (*Essays on Modern Dramatists*. New York, 1921.)

[2] *Contemporary Spanish Dramatists:* Plays by Pérez Galdós, Linares Rivas,
Marquina, Zamacois, Dicenta, and the Quintero brothers, translated with an
introduction by Charles Alfred Turrell. Boston, 1919, page 11.
  For Galdos' *The Duchess of San Quentin* as well as for Echegaray's *The Great
Galeoto*, and Guimera's *Daniela* see *Masterpieces of Modern Spanish Drama*, edited
by Barrett H. Clark, Cincinnati, 1922.

Here again we encounter the anomaly of a fresh outlook upon life with an outmoded technique,—an anomaly that seems to mirror the transitional position of Galdós in both Spanish drama and Spanish thought. The play is an attack upon the imposition of the religious life upon healthy young womanhood and the means used to bring this about. (In this play, for example, Electra is told that she is Maximo's sister.) Yet, despite all the opposition brought to bear, Maximo, a widower with two children, marries Electra. His successful suit may be taken to symbolize the triumph of science over clericalism in Spain. The third act, representing Maximo's laboratory, is an excellent piece of stage symbolism done in the best manner; the action and the symbol here are part and parcel of each other; just as the metals are fused in the laboratory, so are Maximo and Electra fused in their affection, and so has Galdós fused the component elements into an organic unity. It is easy to dismiss the last scene but one, in which Electra beholds her mother, as a visible representation of the maiden's conscience or inner debate, but there are other qualms that seize the critic. Here is the brief scene:

THE SHADE: I am your mother, and I come to calm the anxieties of your loving heart. My voice will restore peace to your conscience. No bond of nature unites you to the man you have chosen for a husband. That which you heard was an invention dictated by affection to bring you into our company and to the peace of this holy house.

ELECTRA: Oh, Mother, what consolation you bring me!

THE SHADE: I am telling you the truth, and I give it strength and hope. Accept, my daughter, as a test of

the temple of your heart, this transitory seclusion, and
bear no ill will to those who brought you here. . . .
If marital love and the pleasures of the family call your
soul, allow yourself to abandon this sweet attraction and
do not pretend to a holiness that you cannot attain.
God is everywhere. . . . I do not know how to find
Him outside of here. . . . Seek Him in the world
along paths better than mine, and . . . (*The Shade
is silent and disappears as the voice of Maximo is heard.*)

MAXIMO (*in the door*): Electra!

ELECTRA (*running toward him*): Ah!

PANTOJA (*at the right*): My daughter, where are you?

MARQUIS: Here, with us.

MAXIMO: She is ours.

PANTOJA: Are you running away from me?

MAXIMO: No, she is not running away. . . . She
has come to life.

We have seen that Galdós' critics fall naturally
into the habit of symbolistic interpretation, and that
Galdós himself so creates his characters that they
live as symbols of flesh and blood, not literary al-
gebra. So here Pantoja may be regarded as representing the clerical party; Cuesta, modern business; the Marquis, the ancient aristocracy, "joining
hands with Science (Maximo) to save Spain (Electra)
and bring her to a new life." It should be emphasized, however, that the play is a human progress
absolutely independent of any such interpretation. And it is a sad commentary upon Spanish
life that when Spaniards do revolt, they must revolt, in their art, against conditions and views that
elsewhere belong rather to the history of mental
liberation than to the catalogue of man's contemporaneous obstruction. . . . I write this, and
then think of recent happenings in the United

States. Wherefore let silence be the better part of condescension.

The remaining plays of Galdós are in similar revolt against bigotry, against social convention, benumbing tradition; *Celia en los infiernos*, 1915, is an addition to the proletarian drama imperfectly projected by Dicenta; *Sor Simona*, 1915, is a proclamation of love as the begetter of peace, of humanity as the only real country of the world. And yet Storm Jameson could write that "Spanish dramatists, with the rare exception of Dicenta, are not in revolt against anything, least of all against life." Rather than Dicenta, a distinctly minor figure, that rare exception should have been Benito Pérez Galdós. Surely he was not in revolt against life, but just as surely was he a rebel against the conventions and traditions that impede its freer play. He did not create for the stage a form fully adequate to the artistic illumination of that spiritual rebellion, perhaps because he did not see fully into its deeper implications. At any rate, his form impresses one as intermediate; he fought evils rather than illuminated a new day. He was held back by the very past that he opposed. He was himself too deeply rooted in the soil out of which he sought to rise. This, rather than any addiction to special methods, explains his shortcomings as a dramatist. When Ayala and Bueno exalt him to the skies, it is the person and the idealist who is worthy of the praise, not the dramatic artist. Art is a province in which most of us are far nobler than our works. If we would be nobler still, as all lovers of beauty are noble, we should be ready to read the distinction.

"THE GENERATION OF '98"

It is significant that when the so-called "generation of '98" rose in determined rebellion against the trammelling past of Spain, venting its venom upon Echegaray and all that he stood for, they not only excepted Galdós from that past, but in a large sense built upon him. In a similar situation, the youthful Italians dealt similarly with Giovanni Verga, who was excepted from the condemnation heaped chiefly upon the druggingly sweet D'Annunzio as the continuator and chief abettor of the national vices: cult of woman and worship of the past. It is a wise generation of youths that looks beyond dates and remembers that Youth is an attribute of the spirit rather than a mark upon a calendar.

Perhaps the most laconic form in which the revolt of these young men has found expression is the characteristically succinct, tart quintet of paragraphs that Baroja gives to it in his *Youth and Egolatry:*

". . . During the years 1898 to 1900," he writes, "a number of young men suddenly found themselves thrown together in Madrid, whose only rule was the principle that the immediate past did not exist for them.

"This aggregation of authors and artists might have seemed to have been brought together under some leadership, and to have been directed to some purpose; yet one who entertained such an assumption would have been mistaken.

"Chance brought us together for a moment, a very brief moment, to be followed by a general dispersal. There were days when thirty or forty young

men, apprentices in the art of writing, sat around
the tables in the old Café de Madrid.

"Doubtless such gatherings of new men, eager to
interfere in and influence the operations of the
social system, yet without either the warrant of
tradition or any proved ability to do so, are common upon a larger scale in all revolutions.

"As we neither had, nor could have had, in the
nature of the case, a task to perform, we soon
found that we were divided into small groups, and
finally broke up altogether."[1]

This is far from telling the whole story, of course,
but Baroja, in pointing out the lack of cohesion and
the subsequent dispersal of the youthful icono-
clasts, touches upon two vital considerations.

The defeat of Spain by the United States in 1898
was rather a goad to the rebellion of the intel-
lectuals than the cause of the overturn.   Dissatisfaction had for a long time disturbed the hegemony
of the bourgeois.   Had not Costa proclaimed that
the sepulchre of the Cid must be locked under
double key?   And was not the sense of realism—the
true heritage of the literary Spaniard—already keen
in the liberal Galdós as well as the orthodox Pereda?
But the intense pessimism of the innovators, besides returning to this healthy sense of reality, accomplished far more.   They threw out of the window
the cluttering, vacuous rhetoric of the Castilian
orator; they sought and found a less turbid, clearer,
more plastic poetry; they opened wide the nation's

---

[1] See the English version by Jacob S. Fassett, Jr., and Frances L. Phillips,
New York, 1920, with a pertinent introduction by Henry L. Mencken.
    For the case against the "generation of '98," see the prodigious *Historia de la
Lengua y Literatura Castellana, comprendidos los autores hispano-americanos*, by
D. Julio Cejador y Frauca, Vol. X.   Madrid, 1919.   The author slashes his way
through a thicket of quotations, repetitions, and objurgations until, perhaps wearied
by his own protests, he almost sells his case through a frank admission of the
benefits conferred upon Spanish literature by the generation he is combating.

doors and let the winds of Europe blow lustily through the house; they scandalized the neighbors with all manner of new-fangled notions. Desultory as their labors were, unconsolidated by community of purpose or awareness of direction, they reshaped the national literature. "In the literature of Spain," wrote Azorín (José Martínez Ruiz), one of the most noted of the rebels, "the generation of '98 represents a renaissance; more or less ample, or narrow, if you will, but when all is said and done, a renaissance. . . . A renaissance is simply the fecundation of the national thought by foreign thought." And so, upon the minds of Darío, Valle-Inclán, Baroja, Unamuno, Maeztu, Ortega y Gasset, Bueno, and Benavente played the minds of the greater Europeans. Through these representatives of the new Spain entered D'Annunzio, Ibsen, Tolstoi, Amiel, Spencer, Verlaine, Nietzsche, and the honorable rest. Nietzsche, Verlaine, and Gautier were general rather than specific influences; each man, for himself, responded to specific stimuli. For Baroja there were Dickens, Poe, Balzac; for Benavente, there were Shakespeare, Musset, and the modern French dramatists. The *Institución Libre de Enseñanza* became a veritable symbol of "national masochism," whose aim was, in Cejador's words, to "de-hispanize and de-Christianize Spain."

The revolt against the theatre was crystallized in the manifesto issued against Echegaray at the time when the rest of the nation was celebrating his reception of the Nobel Prize.

Benavente, as one of the eager '98-ers, became a participant in the intellectual life of Europe; his prose—even apart from his dramas—shows a sensitiveness to shades of thought and an exquisite æsthetic adjustment that are the chief contribution of the restless youths among which he grew to artistic maturity. Everything that the theatre of Echegaray is, the theatre of Benavente is not. His work, which is not to be fully understood without a knowledge of the insurgents whose ranks he once fought in, forms one of their chief claims upon historic glory. Just as Baroja, in the novel, is seemingly the apostle of a philosophic centrifugalism, so in the drama is Benavente the shifting, disintegrating Protean, as instable as the life he pictures, constant only in his inconstancy. And to cap the brief but lively history of the drama's rebels among the '98-ers, Benavente himself only yesterday received the very Nobel Prize that was the signal for Echegaray's condemnation, and received it—so impatient are the young and so intent upon their own accession to fame—at the very moment that he was the target of powerful thrusts and attacks from which he does not emerge unscathed.

JACINTO BENAVENTE

The most outspoken as well as the best-informed of the anti-Benaventians is that same Pérez de Ayala in whom Galdós finds his panegyrist. He does not deny the dramatist "uncommon talent, inexhaustible acuteness, fluency, and elegance of language, copious repertory of rhetorical and scenic artifices. But all these gifts together entail particularly vituperable and harmful consequences, for they are pressed into the service of a mistaken conception of dramatic art." Their fruit in Benavente, according to this analysis, is "pharasaism, sophism, conceptism, which are to ideas what the press is to words." And Benavente's versatility? "Examining, as a whole, in panoramic fashion, the complete theatrical production of Don Jacinto Benavente, we become at once aware that the landscape before us is a strange region whose flora and fauna correspond neither to the torrid nor the frigid zone, but to some epicene, transitional zone in which the climate changes arbitrarily from hot to cold and from cold to hot without ever reaching great extremes." . . . "Benavente's theatre is . . . precisely anti-theatrical, the opposite to dramatic art. It is a theatre of middle terms, without action or passion, and therefore without motivation or characters, and, what is worse, without genuine reality. It is a merely oral theatre, which, for its perfect scenic realization, does not require actors in the true sense. . . ."

In the later plays of the Spaniard, Pérez de Ayala discovers a growing apostolic fervor, as, for example, in *La Ciudad alegre y confiada,* which is dubbed "not drama but staged politics." *La Princesa Bebé,* to him, is "neither passion nor fantasy." *La Malquerida* (played here by Nance O'Neil as *The Passion Flower*) becomes a mere "detective play" (*drama policiaco*). *The Governor's Wife* is dismissed as a piece that bored the public, who laughed only at the suggestive quips. Not even the quality of Benavente's salaciousness is to Ayala's taste, for, "granted the public's acceptance of a gross reference to sex, a cultured, well-balanced spectator will be less disgusted by the merry, frank, natural, sound allusions, as in the Greek and Latin

7

classics, in our classics, in the writers of the Italian renaissance, in Shakespeare, than by the moody, veiled, morbid allusions, which suggest morose, sinful pleasures." Again, apropos of *Los Cachorros*, "his drama, in my sincere but perhaps mistaken opinion, does not proceed immediately from life; it is intellectual, literary, theatre of the theatre. But within this category of merely literary drama, I believe that Benavente, in view of his talent, acuteness, and culture, is many cubits higher than similar authors (for example, Linares Rivas), and that his works admit no comparison with the others of the same species."

From such opinions as these to the appreciations of Benavente by John Garrett Underhill, who discovered him to English readers and playgoers, and whose translations and their accompanying introductions are so easily accessible[1] as to render any account of the playwright's life unnecessary in these pages, is, in more ways than one, a leap of three thousand miles across the sea. Mr. Underhill is fully aware and duly appreciative of the change wrought by Benavente upon the Spanish stage. "Only a master of the theatre could be so independent of its parade; rather he has espoused every reform by which the stage might be broadened or made more sincere. The theatre has been his workshop, and after each period of productivity he has withdrawn from public view . . . returning again with a fresh orientation and a keener sense of living values. 'Ah!' he exclaims, in the second volume of his Table Talk, 'let us have done with all counterfeits, of which the most common in the

---

[1] *Plays by Jacinto Benavente*. Two series. New York, 1917, 1919.

theatre are these: the confusion of the vapid with the literary, of the dull with the profound, of the extravagant with the new, the banal with the poetic, the gross with the courageous and bold. All these equivocations invariably end in one other—an empty house, which is explained by saying that the play failed because it was art, and the public was unable to appreciate art. But the true art of the theatre is to do good business, and to do good business you must do good art. Shakespeare and Molière were both managers, and as managers both made a great deal of money.'[1]

"No dramatist is less theatrical, yet none has written more theatrical plays. . . . The real dramas of Benavente, in which he has expressed his impressions of life without hesitation or reserve, and made a distinctive contribution to the theatre, are far more numerous" (i. e., than his secondary one-act pieces, musical plays, translations from the English, Catalan, and French and occasional pieces.) . . . "Benavente has . . . tried his hand at almost every genre, and he has been successful in them all—peasant dramas and the tragedy of blood, so long associated with Spain in the minds of foreigners, satires of provincial and metropolitan society, of the aristocracy, dramas of the middle class, court comedy in the most subtle and refined of forms, in which by birth and breeding the personages are all royal. He has written romantic comedies and dramas, rococo spectacles, imaginative fairy plays of genuine poetic worth. Only the play in verse has remained unattempted, implying, as it

[1] A brief but effective refutation of such an oft-repeated fallacy as occurs in Benavente's talk of Shakespeare and Molière is made by Ludwig Lewisohn in his *The Drama and the Stage*, pages 16, 17.

no doubt does, through its diction a certain artificiality in the very process of thought.[1]   In all these different genres he has moved with consummate ease, without the suggestion of effort, until the drama of character has seemed the most facile and casual of arts."

In Benavente's style Mr. Underhill discovers one of the most complex and highly personal in literature.   The Spaniard is concerned not so much with ideas as with thought in process of formulation. Plot, as such, is of secondary moment, while the tendency of the man's art is altogether "away from the plastic toward the insubstantial, the transparent. What he had accomplished with satire he next essays with plot, turning his attention to its secondary and suggestive values, to the inferences which wait upon them, and the atmosphere which they create."   All this is interesting not only for its illumination of Benavente's method, but for its analogy with procedure that is loosely labeled Expressionist and associated with the young German experimenters rather than with Benavente in Spain or O'Neill in the United States.   The futuristic currents, it may be added in passing, flow weak upon the Spanish stage; they are almost confined to the prose and poetry of such groups as the Ultra, with an affinity to the Dadas and the host of pullulating "isms" that run the continuous literary vaudeville show of Europe.

Truth—let us be careful with that chameleon-word—does not always lie in the middle.   But in the case of Benavente, if Underhill does him some-

---

[1] Recent Italian dramatists have in practice disproved this theory.   There is no valid argument against the poetic play.   All it needs is—poets.

thing more than justice, surely Ayala does him
something less. Men do not write fourscore plays
of unvarying merit. If they are Latins they suffer,
even more than Anglo-Saxons, who are fond of
considering themselves a colder race, from the undue praise and the undue depreciation of friends
and enemies; they acquire a quantitative outlook
upon output; they mistake theory for execution,
theme for projection. So that we may agree at
once that not every play by Benavente is worth
reading or producing; that critics like Ayala have
been unjustly harsh, as critics like Bueno and
Andrés González Blanco have been unjustly eulo-
gistic. "Shakespeare returned to life," exclaims
González Blanco,[1] writing of the play *Señora Ama*,
"would sign this drama with pride!" (Shades of
the immortal Will, what comparisons are committed
in thy name!) Donina, declares Manuel Bueno,
referring to one of the protagonists of *La Noche del
Sábado* (*Witches' Sabbath*) "is a creature that recalls
the women of Shakespeare," whereupon, in his enthusiasm, he makes of Portia the daughter of Shy-
lock![2] Now *Witches' Sabbath* is a highly original
and interesting production,—one of the cycloramic
spectacles that form, for some, the chief contribution of Benavente to the technical renovation of
modern Spanish drama. But why burden it under
such a mountain of praise? Nor, on the other hand,
should the excess of his critics be allowed to obscure
the genuine values of the dramatist.

Benavente, as is now well known, was, in his
earlier days, a traveler with a circus, perhaps a

[1] *Los Dramaturgos Españoles Contemporáneos*, p. 131 et seq. Valencia.
[2] *Teatro Español Contemporáneo*, pp. 144-151. Madrid.

performer in the ring. His entire output for the
theatre may be viewed as a vast circus ring with
Benavente as sprightly, antic master, cracking his
whip and summoning in dazzling succession a motley
of clowns, now cynical with the sneer of satire, now
sad with the traditional heritage of the mummer's
melancholy, now provocatively admonitory, now
nonchalantly anarchical, but ever the conscious
clown of the ring. There is, in the man's most
characteristic labors, a sophistication that almost
militates against depth of passion; whether he weeps
or he cries, he is never so absorbed that he cannot
pause for introspection, for self-analysis. It is no
accident that his beginnings, toward the end of the
nineteenth century, are made in satire, and that his
most famous work, *Los Intereses Creados* (played in
the United States as *The Bonds of Interest* and in
England as *The Bias of the World*) is satire so sublimated that, from viewing mankind as a tangled
string of puppets, it takes the logical step of con-
verting them frankly into puppet figures upon the
stage. Remember that Benavente's plays, like
Baroja's novels, for all the *madrilenismo* of both
writers, are centrifugal; they proceed from a common center, but do not return; they elude ready
classification because they were born of a spirit
hostile to the artificial ease of order. There is
neither morality nor immorality in Benavente, who
is amoral, and Martínez Sierra is right in changing
his figure when he says that Benavente's work resembles him as if it were himself "reflected in a
mirror . . . or rather, in the flowing crystal of
a brook."[1]   To characterize the man's work—as

---

[1] See his *Introduccion* to the Nelson edition of three Benavente plays (*Los Intereses Creados, Al Natural, Rosas de Otoño*).

apart from whatever artistic values we may assign
to it—one needs words that do not stand still, that
mock, that snicker, that brood, that shift forever
restlessly like the colored glass of the kaleidoscope,
into patterns new and alluring. The stupid iteration of Echegaray, who could not even in *El Gran
Galeoto* abandon his shabby artifices, gives way to
colorful variety; even when we know that the new
patterns are but bits of tinted glass thrown together
at a venture by a turn of the kaleidoscope, we are
grateful for the change.

It is not necessary, even were it here feasible, to
go over every play that Benavente has written.
Some of them are avowed trifles that fulfill their
purpose of enlivening the passing hour; nor should
one overlook, even among these, such a deep little
episode as *La Verdad* (*The Truth*), in which a young
lady, placed in a position where she may, if she
desires, overhear in hiding what her sweetheart has
to say about her to his boon companions, finally
refuses the opportunity. For, if there is a hypocrisy
of virtue, may there not be, too, a hypocrisy which
assumes vices? And whatever her sweetheart says,
whether complimentary or derogatory,—how is
she to know which words carry the real truth? Then
there is the bonbon called *El Principe Que Todo Lo
Aprendió En Los Libros* (*The Prince Who Learned
Everything Out of Books*), written for the Children's
Theatre he founded, together with the actor Porro-
dón, in 1911. This is a charming little juvenile
satire, not without application to adults, containing
mild gibes at the court, at book-learning, and the
"practical" life, and constituting, in certain minor
respects, a young folks' Don Quixote. For the prince

believes all he has read in the fairy books,—only in this case the strength of his belief carries him through. Tonino, the buffoon, with his stomachic greed, is the Sancho of the play as La Vieja, the prince's good fairy, is the Dulcinea who "comes true."

The characteristic Benavente is to be found rather in such arresting performances as *La Gobernadora* (1901), *La Noche del Sábado* (1903), *La Princesa Bebé* (published in 1905, but withheld from the stage until 1909), *Los Intereses Creados* (1907), and *La Malquerida* (1913). In these his satire, his irony, are at their most pungent; his wit is at its sharpest, his skill at suggesting psychology through a minimum of words and actions most fine. Around these, and the few others that might be grouped with them, are clustered a score of minor works, illuminative of his best rather than illustrative of it. As, for example, *El Automóvil* (1902), which followed fast upon *Alma Triunfante* of the same December. If I mention *The Automobile* at all, it is because in this fairly clever farce I seem to find a sort of "rehearsal" for the writing of the widely acclaimed *Bonds of Interest* of five years later. Its essential theme is the same as that of *Los Intereses Creados;* Margarita, former sweetheart of Federico, steals him away in an automobile just bought from the Marquis by Hilario, father of Federico's affianced, María Luisa. A scandal results, and the engaged couple break off, though at bottom still in love. Margarita is a romantic, stage-struck madcap; she half convinces herself that she will ennoble her character by "renouncing" Federico (à la Dame aux Camelias!), and before she is through, she has so entangled the virtuous men and ladies that they are forced to accept in silence her fanciful and theatrical explanation of Federico's "escapade." Here, as in the later play, cleverness devises its own extrication; there are a number of funny scenes, but the distance between this and *The Bonds of Interest* is continental; in *The Automobile* the persons are largely puppets; in *Los Intereses Creados*, the puppets are more than persons, living a life that is their own and a symbolic life dependent not upon arbitrary, parallel meanings, but upon the significance that radiates from all genuine personalities. Bueno, a fellow '98-er of Benavente's, has been extravagant in praise of the other piece, *Alma Triunfante*. "It is the elegy of life's nothingness," he writes,[1] "of the tragic void of our souls." Perhaps. But Bueno is too prone to discuss ethical implications rather than the æsthetic index of the play, which is not very high. A woman, crazed by the loss of her child, has been in the asylum for five years, during which time her husband has a child by another. This she discovers when she returns to her house. Rather than admit her knowledge, however, she would feign a return of insanity, so as to remove herself from his path. He, sincerely penitent, is led to confess all to her, whereupon she accepts the daughter as partly hers and pardons all concerned. Her doctor has been deceived, while the priest has known the truth all along, through the wife's confessor, and it is through him that she is led to the more human conclusion. The doctor-priest balance swings evenly between science and religion, which are reconciled in an all-embracing human love. As here, so in *Rosas de Otoño* (1905), pardon and hope seem the

---

[1] *Teatro Español Contemporáneo*, pages 137-144.

woman's lot. There is sympathy for woman, yet she is depicted as being too weak in will to accomplish what her intellect approves. She may rebel, but gives in at last, while man purchases forgiveness at the price of a little hollow flattery. Here, as in *La Fuerza Bruta* (1908), Martínez Sierra beholds support of bourgeois morality; there is a closer analogy, however, between *Brute Force* and *Alma Triunfante*, wherein the emphasis is placed rather upon sacrifice than upon pardon. And those who assert that Benavente is never "preachy" would do well to consult the close of *La Fuerza Bruta*. To this group we may assign *Los Malhechores del Bien* (*The Evil-Doers of Good*, 1905), which is not, as some have maintained, an anti-clerical diatribe. It is a satire against the essential immorality of a certain type of charity-giving as prevalent in England as in France, in Germany as in the United States,—a condescending patronage that robs its beneficiaries of will, manhood, personality.

Benavente, in an interview, is reported to have expressed a choice of *Señora Ama* (1908) as his best play. For that reason, as well as because of the commendations that González Blanco and his ilk have laid upon it with a trowel, it is worth while dwelling upon for a paragraph. It is in three acts. The protagonist is much in love with her erring husband; she overlooks his numerous transgressions and even prides herself upon his conquests, for if he is so popular with the ladies, then all the more credit to her for having won him. . . . But when a child begins to grow in her bosom she becomes strict, for no bad example must be set before the boy (so she wills the sex) after he is born. . . .

Once again she forgives her husband, assuring him
that heaven has done the same. There is little
effectiveness to the play whether as psychology,
action, character portrayal, or narrative. "This is
worse than among the Moors!" exclaims Rosa in
the first act. "Then there's no religion here, no
morality, no shame?" . . . "Quit your fussing!"
is Julita's reply. "There are simply men and
women. . . ." Yes, but for an advanced playwright like Benavente, too many of the men reap
the pleasures of vice, while the women are left with
the solace of virtue, a sweet word that one finds
in the dictionaries. Yet who shall blame overmuch
if he depicts his people as they are? These are not,
after all, his best plays. They are not the ones he
wrote in the mood of *Princess Bebé*, of which he
declared: "Sometimes I say what I think, sometimes I have regard for the opinions of others."
No; in these, he has a certain "regard for the opinions
of others," which is good business and ratifies what
the author has written in connection with art and
money-making.

Rather let us return to the salient series that
starts with *La Gobernadora*. In these one imagines
one discovers Benavente in the core, not upon the
rim, of his work. The satire and the irony in them
are not the detached commentary that may be found
in his lesser social pieces; they are the overtones of
the action and the personages, vibrating with the
fundamental tone and coloring its timbre. The
very frames merge with the pictures they contain
until they dissolve in the variegated detail. It was
Benavente, not Echegaray, that Shaw should have
"discovered" circa 1903. Far more versatile than

Pirandello, the Spaniard more resembles his English contemporary in his radiant technical insouciance, his ventilation of current notions, his ready wit, his intellectual curiosity. One looks in vain through Benavente, however, for Barbaras, Candidas, predacious Anns and their life-force brood. One looks in vain for meticulous stage-directions, which Benavente avoids, and logorrheic prefaces. The Spaniard lacks almost entirely the Irishman's ethical preoccupations, though, curiously enough, no one has come away from Shaw with a hampered sense of personal liberty. Benavente's is not a discursive world; it is rather a compact, pyrotechnic institution where the rockets glare, the wheels spin a while, and then the display is over. He dazzles the mind and leaves the heart curiously indifferent,—perhaps because he is himself an indifferent spectator. Once again, like Baroja, he produces the impression of a man who has sat down upon the banks of life to watch the stream flow by. He does not, like Shaw, plunge into the waters and get himself gloriously wet; he is like those shapely maidens who expend their effort upon a beautiful bathing suit that is never meant to be kissed by the waves. But—and this is the important consideration—he has projected into his best works just this instable, aloof, yet inquisitive attitude toward life, and drama can do little more than vivify an attitude.

The governor's wife of the play thus named is one of Benavente's wise brood who works her will upon the surrounding society through a subtle knowledge of human nature. "She has made her husband, and she knows how to recall every detail of the making that she may gain some new end.

She can switch back and forth between two decisions as one who flies gracefully from the trapeze of opportunism to the trapeze of self-interest. Next to nothing in the life of the town escapes her interference. She plays off the townsfolk to her ceaseless advantage. She can keep the proper secretary, guide, counsellor, and friend to her husband—and agreeable lover to herself. And all this she does with a marvelous *savoir-faire*, a bird-like vivacity, an inimitable grace, the lightest of innuendo. Like a knowing lark, she scales singing the heavens of self-interest and self-will. If for a moment she flutters downward, this Doña Josefina still charms piquantly. With reason she tempts comédiennes. Mrs. Fiske should play her in America.

"This precious pair are well companioned—in the gubernatorial 'palace'—by a bent-shouldered, soft-spoken old henchman, who knows every byway of duplicity, hypocrisy, and self-interest in Moraleda; in the town itself, by a whole troop of fitting denizens. Across the scene comes and goes 'the richest man in Moraleda,' who would order its morals and manners, its downsittings and uprisings according to his own notions and for his own profit, and who is by no means choice or considerate in his methods. The spectator salutes him as one well known in the Moraledas even of pure and young America. Behind him trail a gabbing wife, a shallow, pettish daughter. Near her are two, three, and four gallants, pretending to the ways of the frivolous, knowing world as it appears, say the 300 miles from the nearest capital. Again the spectator salutes them gladly; ten chances to one he has encountered them no farther away than our own Middle West. In

the middle distance or farther into the offing a
tradesman, an actor, a manager, the rector of the
university, women 'snippy' and women vacuous;
while here and there passes and repasses a distinc-
tively Spanish character—for the most part folk of
the bull ring. All these dwell together busily, even
happily, in Moraleda, because they are all tarred
with the same stick—the stick with which Benavente first prods and smears the governor, the governor's lady, and the rich, the mean, the arrogant
Don Baldomero. The end of the stick is sharp, the
acid on it bites through the tar. Details aside, the
comedy of *The Governor's Wife* is as true as truth,
and as savory, in Moraledas the world over. Out
of the tares of human nature Benavente has brought
to bloom a flower of the theatre. Into fifty novels
Balzac had need to pack his 'human comedy.'
The Spaniard has compressed his into one brief
play."[1]

Even more kaleidoscopic than *La Gobernadora* is
the *Witches' Sabbath* (*La Noche del Sábado*), subtitled by the author "a novel for the stage in five
tableaux." But this scenic novel does not employ
the technique of the Galdosian play, in which the
author of the National Episodes deliberately flouted
theatrical convention and mingled genres in a manner
to astound the academic. Neither does it revert to
the habit of some of Benavente's lesser plays, in
which the plot is narrated rather than presented in
action and word. It is dramaturgically akin to the
Expressionistic methods that it preceded; to such
slices of life as Molnar's *Liliom;* to the irregular

[1] H. T. Parker, in the *Boston Evening Transcript*, May 19, 1920, on a day following the performance of the play, in Underhill's translation, by the Harvard Dramatic Club, Cambridge, Mass.

stage patterns that Wedekind employed before
Kaiser, Hasenclever, and the other new Germans,
that Hauptmann has used in such recent plays as
Der Weisse Heiland, and that one, William Shakespeare by name, used in blissful ignorance of our
contemporary "isms." It is a free form that is the
result, or rather the other aspect, of a free conception. Shall it irk us that the work is not Spanish
in atmosphere or psychology? The action, supposed
to take place in a winter resort upon the Riviera,
"situated near the boundary between Italy and
France," has, in reality, a less local setting, and the
boundaries are more exactly those between no two
countries, but between you and me. With his early
fondness for the lector whom Drinkwater but yesterday brought to our stage in his *Abraham Lincoln*,
Benavente prologues his play—as he is later to do
with *The Bonds of Interest*—with a brief, poetic
prelude.

It is Saturday night. Earth, sea, and sky blend in
refulgent harmony—light, waves, mountain tops, and
groves smile with the freshness of a world new-born,
ignorant of sorrow and of death. Gods and heroes,
nymphs and fawns should inhabit this enchanted shore;
love and wisdom alone are worthy to contemplate its
beauty. The idylls of Theocritus and the eclogues of
Virgil breathe the spirit of its poesy, or if perchance a
poet of our unquiet time may turn to it to glorify his
melancholy, let it be the divine Shelley, worshiper of
the eternal harmony of Beauty, Truth, and Good, who
refused to set bounds and limits to the infinite, adoring
God in all his works. The ritual of his worship shall be
the passionate litany of the holy poet of Assisi, the
universal lover, who greeted all things with his song of

ardent flame: Brother Sun, Brother Sea, Brother Birds, Brother Wolf—all brothers!

Into this enchanted scene, by Nature so lavishly endowed, comes man. It is the fashionable winter season —*à la mode*—man has chosen his earthly paradise well; for paradise indeed it is. He flees from the cold and the chill of the North, but he brings the chill of his life with him; he flees from his life, but his life follows and overtakes him. Every pathway beneath his feet opens into an inferno like Dante's, above whose portals is inscribed the legend:

> Through me the way is to the city dolent,
> Through me the way is to eternal dole,
> Through me the way among the people lost.

Whereupon the motley tale begins. A sordid story of a mother, Imperia, mistress of Prince Florencio, and Donina, daughter of Imperia, who loves Nunu but cannot win him. Nunu, knowing his power over Donina, tries to trade her to her mother's paramour. Donina, trapped in a low resort and defending herself against the Prince's attack, slays him. For a while she is kept alive by the attentions of Nunu,—attentions purchased by her mother, unknown to the languishing daughter,—until, the secret of his assiduity out, she dies, while her mother leaves with the other Prince, Michael Alexander.

Plot in Benavente is of itself next to nothing. In his dramatic pointillage the detail is almost all. Now it is a snatch of dialogue: "We become impossible socially," says Leonardo, "not because of what people know about us, but because of what they imagine we may know about them." "Precisely," replies Etelvina. "We ought always to say what we know of everybody, not out of malice, but in the

interest of truth and good feeling. All of us are
made of the same clay. Virtue is merely relative—
it consists of those vices one does not possess. If it
had been virtuous not to eat apples, and I had been
Eve, man would never have fallen. I cannot abide
the sight of apples; although I do not complain of
those that eat them. No doubt they have good
reasons." Or, as the Signore says, somewhat later:
"For the most part, people know about as much
about life as they do about the theatre—they see
the play, that is all; the real show goes on behind
the scenes." (Here, it seems to me, Benavente has
uttered an unconscious critique of his own drama;
one does get the impression, often, that his personages are keeping something from the spectator.)
Again, it is an entire section of the play that stands
out as a miniature piece within a piece, as in the
original third scene of this scenic novel:

We are like witches, says Imperia, meeting on
Saturday night. I was a little girl when I first heard
the legend, and you remind me of it now. There was a
poor woman who lived near our house. She was very old,
and apparently very respectable. She lived alone, and
you would have said that she was a good woman. Her
house was clean; she worked in the garden by day, busy
with her flowers, or fed the pigeons; at night she sewed a
little on her quaint old clothes. She was never idle—
it was a calm and peaceful life, lived openly in the sun.
But people said that she was a witch, and every Saturday
at midnight, as the clock struck twelve, she mounted a
broomstick and flew away to the witches' lair, and there
with the other witches she did homage to Satan; and if
you could surprise them then, you would see them as
they really were. One day, some time later, at dawn on a
Sunday morning, the old woman was found dead, out of

her bed, at some distance from her house, in an open field, and there was a dagger in her heart. But nobody could ever find the assassin nor discover any motive for the murder, nor could anyone ever explain the reason that woman should have been found in that place on that morning, when she had been seen closing the door of her house as usual the night before, and in the morning when they carried the body there, the door was still closed.

RINALDI: But you don't really mean? . . . Nonsense! Then you would have to believe in witches.

IMPERIA: No, not in such witches. But there comes a Saturday Night in all our lives, even the most peaceful of them, when our souls, like the witches, fly to their lairs. We exist for days to reach one hour which is vital and real. Then our witches' souls take flight, some toward their hopes and ambitions, some toward their vices, their follies, others toward their loves—toward something which is far from and alien to our lives, but which has always smouldered in us, and at heart is what we are.

Such is the quasi-Freudian witches' sabbath of the play, which, if any palpable deduction may be made from its rapidly reeling visions, suggests a defense of the soul's repressions. "To achieve anything in life we must destroy reality," concludes Imperia, "and thrust aside the phantoms of fact, which confuse and hem us round, to follow the only reality, the flight of our witches' spirits on Saturday Night, as they turn to their ideal—some toward evil, to be lost in the shadows forever like spectres of the night, others toward good, to dwell eternally in it, the children of love and light."[1] It is the Ibsen

---

[1] The excerpts are from Mr. Underhill's translation of the play as it appeared in *Poet Lore*, spring number, 1918. The same issue contains a suggestive article by Mr. Underhill on "Benavente As a Modern."

call to selfhood that echoes in the words of this
puppet-woman. Perhaps the characters talk now
and then as if they were preaching at the audience?
It is not enough to reply that Shaw's personages are
merely the playwright's mouthpieces, something in
the manner of yesterday's trick motion picture in
which every performer in the play had the same
face. Modern conversation is a reflection of modern
problems. Intelligent folk are forever discussing
life. There is more drama in a searching analysis
of vital contemporary issues than in all the action
that ever packed a melodrama circus.

Storm Jameson, who beholds in Benavente the
hope of the Spanish drama, is wiser than those
Spaniards who have called the versatile Jacinto
foreign in artistic spirit. Behind his affinities with
the modern Frenchmen and contemporary culture,
she beholds the spirit of Lope de Vega, with that
classic spirit's tradition of suppleness, his skill in
construction, his "splendour of movement and
music; living, distinctive characters. Only a new
creative activity could give fresh life to his pageant
of emotion and colour, filling it with the more complex life of modernity, taking the highest from past
and present, and making it afresh for the new age.
. . . His (i. e., Benavente's) comedies have exquisite fantasy, poetic grace, technical perfection,
and intellectual distinction. Where they fail is in
an occasional careless handling of their finest qualities. . . . Fantasy overshadows reality, to the
marring of dramatic proportion."

It is in *The Bonds of Interest* that she finds the
quintessence of these qualities,—a piece none the
less original, provocative, illuminating, salient in

modern drama, for its failure when offered to New York by the Theatre Guild in 1919. Small need to go out of Spain for its forerunners,—realistic, individualistic Spain with its roster of ribald rogues that begins with the sixteenth-century *Lazarillo de Tormes* and comes right down into our own day. Nor, as we glance toward the past for the inevitable rivals who said our good things before us, should we forget, in considering the contemporary breaking away from stage forms, that already at the close of the fifteenth century Spain had its *Tragicomedia di Calisto y Melibea* (the famous *Celestina*). This play, a novel in dialogue, has in its various editions sixteen, twenty-one, and twenty-two acts. Realism, pessimism, passion, imagination,—all these are in the medieval work of the Jewish laywer, Fernando de Rojas. It is good that we should recall betimes our eternal contemporaries.

The play by which Benavente is best known out of his native land is a symbolic, marionette drama in which are restored to a new and glorious life the puppets of the Commedia dell' Arte. And the play, not the plot, is the thing. Crispin, the shameless cynic, archetype of wordly rascality, paving the way for Leandro's marriage, so that the debts they have both incurred may be paid, is a veritable human summary of the will to achieve. He is the minor Mephisto to Leandro's minor Faust. He is, rather than a separate individual, another of Leandro's selves,—the grosser metal that holds together the golden nobility of his master's soul, or, to invert our philosophy, the adventurous spirit that transcends Leandro's bourgeois ethics. It is Leandro who, redeemed by true love, is ready to

confess his life-lie; it is Crispin who prevails upon
him with more worldly counsel, and who, by his
uncanny cleverness, so embroils the other puppets
in a network of inter-related interests that they
cannot expose his own misdoings without doing hurt
to themselves.   Such plays illuminate life by epito-
mizing it.

Yet note how Benavente is himself the cynic
even in the prologue that he puts into the mouth
of Crispin; how, after presenting the play as a child
of the antique farce, lifted by Lope de Rueda,
Shakespeare, and Molière to high estate, he offers
it as "a little play of puppets, impossible in theme,
without any reality at all.   You will soon see how
everything happens in it that could never happen,
how its personages are not real men and women,
nor the shadows of them, but dolls or marionettes
of paste and cardboard, moving upon wires which
are visible even in a little light and to the dimmest
eye.   They are the grotesque masks of the Italian
Commedia dell' Arte, not as boisterous as they once
were, because they have aged with the years and
have been able to think much in so long a time.
The author is aware that so primitive a spectacle is
unworthy of the culture of these days; he throws
himself upon your courtesy and upon your goodness
of heart.   He only asks that you should make yourselves as young as possible.   The world has grown
old, but art never can reconcile itself to growing
old, and so, to seem young again, it descends to
these fripperies.   And that is the reason that these
outworn puppets have presumed to come to amuse
you to-night with their child's play."

Here we have a sort of anti-technique; an art that

seeks not so much to conceal itself as to invite attention to its operation. It is one of the many signs of the reaction against realism that stirs upon the stage of every nation and invades not only the precincts of scenery and playcraft, but even of acting.[1] The prologue is spoken in the mood of the man who declaims it; the epilogue, from Silvia, is a mirror of her own gentle soul:

You have seen how these puppets have been moved by plain and obvious strings, like men and women in the farces of our lives—strings which were their interests, their passions, and all the illusions and petty miseries of their state. Some are pulled by the feet to lives of restless and weary wandering; some by the hands to toil with pain, to struggle with bitterness, to strike with cunning, to slay with violence and rage. But into the hearts of all there descends sometimes from heaven an invisible thread, as if it were woven out of the sunlight and the moonbeams, the invisible thread of love, which makes these men and women, as it does these puppets which seem like men, almost divine, and brings to our foreheads the smile and splendors of the dawn, lends wings to our drooping spirits, and whispers to us still that this farce is not all a farce, that there is something noble, something divine in our lives which is true and which is eternal, and which shall not close when the farce of life shall close.

And just as Crispin and Leandro are but varying aspects of the same individual, so are the Crispin of the prologue and the Silvia of the epilogue but varying aspects of the author himself.

It is this dualism in Benavente that explains, if it does not wholly justify, Ayala's accusation of

---

[1] See Macgowan's *The Theatre of To-morrow*, pages 148-159.

preachiness.   One might, as a critical *tour de force*,
go through the Spaniard's dramas and play the
game of citing Scripture against the Scriptures.
Benavente could thus, on isolated evidence, be made
out an anti-upper-class satirist (*Gente Conocida*), a
sentimental bourgeois (*Rosas de Otoño*), a psychological investigator (*La Malquerida*), and what not
else.   So that, if Jameson attributes too much to
Benavente's feelings when she says of him that he
"cannot always hold his naked hate and anger from
tearing in pieces the dramatic fitness of speech and
character," she hits the nail on the head in the
crisp statement that follows fast upon the other:
"The short measure of the dramatist is filled up by
the preacher.   So that not all the radiant beauty of
style, nor the clear, deep passion, nor the tenderness, can carry his tragedies to the peaks that first
catch the sun.   Yet he does fly, and the wings are
the wings of a god."   Nor are those who know her
theory of the modern drama surprised to find her
interpreting Crispin as the man who "will live
dangerously or not at all.   This is more than exquisite dialogue, more than fantasy in perfect form:
it is an artistic criticism of life, the highest form of
comedy; a criticism of the world in which the noble
must needs save himself by the baser, where love
and morality are pawns in the game of the masters
of life.   And through it all, beneath the grace in
which it clothes itself, is the pulse of creative life."
And, were she seeking support for such an interpretation, she would find plenty in Benavente's *Princess
Bebé*, wherein Princess Helena bluntly asks, "How
would any human life be possible if we were not
able to outwit the social laws?"   Yet it is this same

Helena who can inquire: "Why this insane desire to shut ourselves off from each other, to ticket and classify ourselves, to create distinctions between us, and fancy that we are superior to our fellows, when we are all equal and all belong to the same race, the poor, despised, human race, which spends all its time dividing itself and hating itself and marking itself off into classes and castes and individuals, when all the sympathy and all the love in our hearts which might bind us together would be too little even then among so many to alleviate the sorrows of life?" It is quite as difficult to pin his creatures down as to glue the label to his elusive self.

Benavente's significance to the drama of to-day— and it would receive a prompter recognition did he write in French in a capital so proclamative as Paris of its minor and major glories—lies in a versatility that is more than mere dramaturgic virtuosity. His restlessness, his cynicism, his emotional dualism, are part and parcel not only of our peculiar modernity, but of every richer nature that has brooded upon the tragi-comedy of life. Hence his shifting of attitudes, his disregard of conventional form, his creative instability. Hence, too, the fusion, not always complete, between reality and fantasy. Echegaray was merely prolific; Benavente's fecundity is qualitative as well as quantitative. Echegaray stamped ready-made ideas into the prevailing dramatic forms; Benavente's intellectual resiliency created its own amorphous ambient. Yet something in the man's intellect seems to suppress the emotional fervor that alone could nourish living creatures rather than sublimated symbols. His plays, with their thin fables and their rich dialogues, suggest those pages of the Talmud in which islets of text are submerged in an ocean of commentary. Not so much excess of emotion, as Jameson would have it, but excess of intellectuality, interferes with the dramatic fitness of speech and character. Can this be a prevision of our future society, wherein, as in Shaw's latest legend of longevity, the flesh and its passions shall have evaporated into atmospheric thought? And shall the fruit of the Shavian rebellion be nothing but this fleshless abstraction from the carnal roots of life? No, youth will have none of it, not even a youth that is born wise out of Shavian eggs hatched in Methuselania.[1]

---

[1] I must postpone to some other occasion a consideration of the two Quintero brothers, Serafín and Joaquín, who are so intimately connected with the history of the *género chico* in Spain. Inasmuch as they would prove of particular interest to those interested in the one-act play and the little theatre, I may mention that the best treatment of them in English may be found in the Introduction to the text edition of *Doña Clarines* and *Mañana de Sol*, by S. Griswold Morley. The Quinteros' *Malvaloca* is published in New York; their *A Sunny Morning* is most easily available in *Fifty Contemporary One-Act Plays*, edited by Frank Shay and Pierre Loving (Cincinnati); *The Fountain of Youth* (*La Flor de la Vida*) is also issued at Cincinnati.

ITALY

ITALY

Italian critics of the drama, who are not any more cheerful than the rest of the tribe, have as much reason as any to bewail the low state into which the drama has fallen. There have not been lacking scholars who even deny that a genuinely national stage exists; since Tullio Fornioni, in 1885, started the ball a-rolling it has been given powerful shoves by such men as Mario Pilo, Salvatore Barzilai and V. Morello. Only yesterday Signor Guido Ruberti, in his closely packed two-volume book upon *Il teatro contemporaneo in Europa*, renews the discussion, and in his section upon the realistic Italian drama (I, 211) declares bluntly, "The truth is that Italy has never had a truly national theatre." In the ensuing commentary he indicates that there is, in the very nature of the Italian people, a certain quality that is anti-dramatic in effect; the spiritual and material difficulties experienced by the nation while other countries were conquering a greater or less degree of liberty caused it to turn in upon itself, accustoming it, perforce, to a "singular mental habit of adaptation and conciliation; a remarkable equilibrium that succeeds in fusing within itself the most diverse tendencies, harmonizing them in a supreme ideal that is neither skepticism nor austere faith, neither absolute indifferentism nor unreflecting passion, yet feeds upon and communicates all these." The Italian conscience, moreover, unlike the Slavic, finds its great problems settled in ad-

125

vance by its creed, thus removing, or at least greatly
modifying, one of the mainsprings of dramatic action. In the powerful scenes of passionate crime
the critic sees but added proof of the primitiveness
of his people; upon them, he tells us, the currents
of modern thought make little impression.

For much of the delay in the achieving of a
national theatre the influence of France is blamed,
—the same France[1] in whom Spanish-American
critics fear a denationalizing allurement, in whom
Portuguese students behold a decentralizing siren,
in whom Brazilian youth of autonomous aspirations
point out a Gallicizing evil. Again, the presence of
so many well-defined regions, each with its own
psychology, its own pride, its own determination to
preserve its spiritual independence, acts as a hindrance to the formation of a distinctly recognizable
national drama. The Italian dialect stage is an important institution; Rome, Sicily, Milan, Bologna,
Venice, Naples,—these are, from the standpoint of
the drama, fairly nations within a nation, and even
the better-known Italian playwrights are proud to
write for them. Verga and Pirandello are intimately
associated with their native Sicily, Bracco with his
beloved Naples, Sabatino Lopez with his Tuscan
birthplace.

If, then, it is yet a problem whether Italy's drama
be truly national as an institution, there can be no
question as to the activity of its stage. The war,
as everywhere else, precipitated an intellectual turmoil; forces that had been slowly gathering burst
forth as if caused rather than merely hastened by
the conflict; there were sudden conversions, as wit-

---

[1] "Questa Italia teatrale che ha per capo Parigi," says Benelli in the foreword
to his newest play, Alì.

ness the philosophical volte-face of Giovanni Papini
in his often beautiful yet often tediously maundering *Storia di Cristo* and the just as maundering but
far less beautiful play by Sem Benelli, called *Ali*.
In such novels as Mario Puccini's *Viva l'anarchia!*
and Borgese's *Rubè*, one could see the wavering of
the Italian intellectual. The light cast by such books
as these illuminated the turbid maelstrom of swirling ideas; to be sure, the light fell upon confusion,
yet out of that confusion something like comprehensible units of activity emerge, not without significance for the immediate future of the country.
Marinetti's Futurism, only part of a larger lunacy,
may not be dismissed in toto any more than may the
German Expressionists or the once rampant Dada-
ists, whose wild exploits, often meaningless, are yet
not without meaning. The so-called "grotesque"
theatre, similarly symptomatic of a social state, is
clearer in performance and claims at least one significant figure in Pirandello. Such poetic attempts
as Morselli's *Glauco* and Forzano's *Sly* show that
even in the midst of disorder may come plays of
sweetness in which something of classic permanence
inheres. If these days, then, show for Italy little
in the nature of definite, indisputable accomplishment, the era is one of experiment in many directions.

There is Francesco Scardaoni's proposal for a new
theatre that shall become nothing less than a temple;
it must not be defiled by problems nor be clouded by
too much poetic incense; it must house pure beauty.
In the ecstatic words that conclude his essay upon
a new "Theory of the Tragedy," which forms one
of the two prefaces—not to speak of an autobio-

graphic postlude—to his recent play *Nel Grande Silenzio* he proclaims:

"The stage is an altar upon which Beauty consecrates its rites, and Beauty is the religion of life.

"All the rites of all religions were originally tragic pantomime; metaphysical deviations and false divinities prevented development and dispersed values.

"Without tragic celebration no rites exist, and without rites there is no religion.

"Whence it appears that the religion of Beauty is supreme.

"The temples became theatres; it is now time for the theatres to become temples."[1]

This doctrine the writer develops in a rather long essay, in which he advances the "unity of beauty" as the sole worthy unity. Truth to tell, he has but changed names. His new unity is hardly novel. He does perform a valuable service, however, in pointing out that the interpretation of life upon the stage may be infinite, and should not be restricted to a single point of view, and that because of this variety of existence, the opportunity for beauty by combining experiences into new harmonies is rich. And since we must have "isms", he presents us with a new one: "Dramatic Polyphonism." Here, however, he has touched upon a genuinely important consideration. He would, for example, deny supremacy even to dialogue upon the stage.[2] Conventional text-books upon the drama usually assert that dialogue is the distinguishing attribute of the

---

[1] It is interesting to note that the Russian Sologub has, in his *Theatre of the Single Will*, developed a similar theory of the theatre as becoming once again a temple. ". . . The hour will come," he says, "when, in the transcendence of body and spirit, we shall come together in liturgical ceremony, in sacramental rites."

[2] Compare Evreinov's subordination of the spoken word in his "monodrama."

drama—that no sooner do two people get to conversing than the elements of drama are already
present. Not so for Signor Scardaoni. Just as we
have become accustomed to doing away with lay
figures like the regular hero, heroine, villain, comic
man, and so on, and witness with pleasure plays in
which the personages fuse into the natural group of
human beings that they form off stage, so does
Scardaoni look forward to a drama in which even
dialogue has been robbed of its supremacy and been
made to fuse with the other elements of the play—
the pauses of silence, for instance, the words, gestures, lights, colors, which combine to establish a
"cosmic zone."

Scardaoni's essays repay the reading. Like all
enthusiasts, he has simply forgotten to extend his
theories to the tolerant point of allowing other views
of the stage. Even as he refuses to allow dialogue
to dominate the theatre, forcing it to fuse with
other elements into a perfect whole, so he should be
willing to recognize that not even his cult of beauty
should occupy the stage-temple to the exclusion of
all other forms. Just because life is so manifold in
its phases we are ready, nay eager, for new aspects
of the drama. But just as surely is it impossible
for any one aspect to sweep aside all the others
with an essay.

There is Achille Ricciardi, with his interesting
Theatre of Color. His book, *Il Teatro del Colore*, is
dedicated to Gabriel d'Annunzio, who first invited
him to write it, and he promises to follow it with
another that shall occupy itself with an "artistic
offensive." Despite the fact that the book saw the
light only in recent years, the theories contained in

it were developed as far back as 1906, and it is not
without ill-repressed dissatisfaction that the author
saw his ideas appropriated by Sem Benelli and mentioned in the Italian press as emanating from that
source.

Ricciardi is not so dogmatic in his assertions as
Scardaoni. He does not insist that the theatre of
color is the only possible theatre, and that in it lies
the sole hope of the drama's future. He recognizes
that there are types of play to which his ideas do
not apply. On the other hand, he is well satisfied,
and quite readily convinces the reader, that the possibilities of color as employed in dramatic representations have been only scratched upon the surface. We have too long been content to use color
merely as a decorative element, overlooking the
fact that, so to speak, it has a life of its own, a rich
treasury of emotive connotations, and may be employed as a distinctly psychological factor, with
gradations, combinations and climaxes all its own.
In a fairly long preliminary discussion he enters
into an abridged history of color-values, carefully
distinguishing previous attempts from his own. He
insists that his innovation possesses primary æsthetic
significance. "Even the color of the clothes determines the psychology of the dramatic person.
. . . In the development of the drama the color
of the costumes follows the ascent of the emotions.
Every event takes place in a special atmosphere,
with its individual color. . . ."

Ricciardi believes that the proper sphere for the
application of this theory is in plays of a fantastic
character. There is no doubt that it may be applied, in modified form, to any play of worth. Only

one serious objection (and not at all an insurmount-
able one, as far as practical production is concerned)
may be suggested. Do colors affect all persons the
same way? And granted this, do colors affect all
persons in the same way at the same time? If not,
how can full use of the colors as a psychological
factor be made? It should be remembered that
Ricciardi is not concerned primarily with color as
decoration or as symbol, but as a vital factor such
as sound is in music. The innovator seems to feel
the validity of this objection, for toward the close
of his exposition he asserts that certain values of
color—he calls them moral—are widespread, such
as red and blue for happy moods, and white for
purity. Moreover, colors in motion, production of
contrasts, and so on, possess psychological effects of
their own, and doubtless the words of the piece
could suggest subtly the influences intended. Color,
then, is here not the equivalent of other sensations,
"but it modifies their tone and thus creates something sui generis."

Ricciardi seems to establish very firmly his position as the genuine innovator in this regard. It is
of interest to note how constant is the deference of
both Scardaoni and Ricciardi (as well as more than
one other of the innovators in the United States,
Germany, and elsewhere) to Greek models and ancient procedure. Behind all the agitation lies clearly
a yearning for spiritual freedom. To Ricciardi as
to Scardaoni, there is something of the rite in the
drama; the former would even seek his ideal stage
upon the Mediterranean, thus returning to the
open air of the ancients.

In Benelli's most recent play we shall witness the

effect of the war upon one of the chief ante-bellum
playwrights of Italy. This done, for a few pages
we shall revert to the recently deceased dean of
Italian letters, Giovanni Verga, whose modest plays
yet constitute for some the hope of a national
renaissance in the drama. We shall then be ready
to appreciate the actual direction—or rather directions—taken by that drama since Verga's *Cavalleria
Rusticana,* now in the poetic play (whether in prose
or verse) of a Morselli or a Forzano, now in the
futuristic orgasms of Marinetti, and particularly in
the "grotesque" school which received its name from
a queer production by Chiarelli, and counts among
its followers a motley band over which the gifted
Pirandello easily assumes supremacy.

BENELLI'S NEW APOSTOLATE

Ali (*Wings*) was first produced at the Teatro
Manzoni, in Milan, on March 14 of this year, with
Alda Borelli in the chief feminine part of Marta and
Tullio Carminati in the mystical part of Luca.
As one of the consequences of the critical discussion
aroused by the production we have a long foreword
by the author, entitled "Words to be Read Before
the Drama and After," nor is he hesitant, in the
course of this polemical prologue, about asking his
reader to go over the play more than once, lest important detail escape him. If the evidence of the
play itself were not sufficient, surely the tone and
temper of these preliminary pages would show that
Benelli was in an apostolic mood. One may even
see in his abandonment of verse an added pledge of
his seriousness. Yet more than a little of the old
Benelli is there—the Benelli whose fondness for the

past prisons him even when he would be most
modern; whose psychology is fairly one-sided, and
never more so than in his newest production; who
is so centered upon the harsher aspects of the human
soul that he must be harsh even in his portrayal of
a Christ-like figure such as Luca in *Wings*. It is
easy to believe that the Italian, goaded by many
suggestions that he was falling into a rut in his
"theatre," determined to refute the innuendoes with
a play that should present a new phase of his art.
What is more likely is that *Wings*, his first play in
six years, represents the response of a sensitive soul
to the brutalities of a conflict in which he shared,
not unmindful of the brutality nor of the necessity.
For the rest, it is useful to recall that the remarkable conversion of the heritic Papini is but a symptom of what is occurring in contemporary Italy.
Wings may not be Benelli's return to "the" faith,
but it surely signals a powerful affirmation of faith
and even suggests—nothing less—the influence of
an Ibsen who, thirty-five years ago, wrote *Brand*.

The play, for all this eloquent defense, is not one
of Benelli's best. In fact, with the exception of a few
high moments in the fourth and last acts, it is rather
dull and static, and one may gather as fruitful a
notion of what it is all about from the somewhat
hectic foreword as from the sultry symbolistic drama
that follows. That the action is autobiographical
Benelli denies, although he is ready enough to admit that it mirrors his "unspeakable torment"
amidst the vertiginous life through which we are
passing. The point of view coincides with that of
his poem, *L'Altare;* he is confident that life has a
mission, and seeks a goal which he calls "the har-

mony of individual, free forces," in which shall be found paradise. Such a quest involves martyrdom, and *Wings* is the drama of that self-immolation. To the short-sighted folk who denied to *Wings* any essential dramatic character because its protagonist does not emerge victorious, he replies that Luca's defeat is the very element that renders *Ali* a tragedy. "Human impotence is the greatest truth that the tragic poets of all times and all places have expressed. The greatest tragedy of all lies in the Unattainable!" He composed this drama, then, "in my own way, and not according to the conventions of the theatre. I have never done otherwise." (What! Never, signore?) "The word 'theatrical' I consider silly. Give me the proper bridge, and I'll lead on to the stage for you any charm, any creature, any event."

From this to righteous wrath against the commercial stage is but another little bridge, and Sem Benelli crosses it, crying somewhat vainly and with unconscious humor, "The theatre is but a market-place to-day!" (With his *Jest* in its seventeenth edition and sixtieth thousand to date!) The truth is that Benelli has discovered the difficulties that beset *Wings*, and this his foreword shows clearly. In his indignation against the French importations to the Italian theatre he is more than a little justified; but why in all conscience should he, who has helped so greatly to enamour the Italians of their past, ridicule them for their fondness for Harlequin and Puncinello? And why, after satirizing those who wished to learn the meaning of his drama, does he proceed forthwith to offer an elucidation? And why, too, his acrimonious assault upon the reviewers, against whom he seems to feel so well fortified?

Is it not a trifle possible that Benelli himself has a feeling of failure? If he has not such a feeling, then he has confused his prophetic fervor with dramatic values, and in so doing has but followed the example of more than one of the reviewers to whom he is so ineffectively saucy. He has set himself an ascetic ideal, broader than that embraced by any one religion. Benelli, born of Jews, himself tells us that his Luca, "who might also be a Catholic," is tormented by a vaster mystery—to love without sin, even at the cost of not loving at all. "Rather be sterile than sinful." And to the objection that sin is unconquerable and perhaps even necessary, since everybody sins, he replies, "It is not necessary. Sin is the infamy of man, not the infamy of God." Toward the end of the foreword, speaking half for his protagonist and half for himself, Benelli concludes:

I cannot help being a martyr, for the good that I glimpse is too great and will destroy my real good. . . . Martyrdom is the flower of a fruit that has no season. Martyrdom is the only consolation of my littleness. The sole weapon that I have with which to demonstrate my truth, for I have not offered only arguments—I have offered my life. The greatest martyrdom is that which the asserter of an idea imposes upon himself when he proclaims, "I no longer belong to anybody."

Thus speaks not a dramatist but a preacher. He may be noble, he may win our sympathies, even our devotion, but if he has not written a good drama he is not a good dramatist. And judged by the standards of drama rather than of religious vision, Benelli, in this play, suffers a fall from grace. *Wings* is dull; it is repetitious; it does not begin to move until the play is nearly over; it is preachy, all-too-preachy, unredeemed by humor, by human pliability, by psychological insight, by any sort of action. At times it is wooden; at best it bursts into occasional flights of fanatic eloquence, and for a moment here and there a human trait emanates from personages. Then woman may rail at man's spiritual infidelity; then man may become a thrall to visions that tear him from earthly bonds, only to meet, between him and his longings, the eternal wall of flesh. But what are such moments against long stretches of ranting, of mystical maundering, of arid conversation, or worse, debate? Benelli denies that he is Luca, yet after one has read the play—and, in due courtesy to the author's wishes, read again the foreword—one feels that Luca, not Benelli, must have written that preamble.

The play opens just after Luca has lost his wife Anna, in whose death he finds it is impossible to believe. To his skeptical physician-friend, Giovanni, he confides the strange thoughts that have come to overwhelm him, and unbosoms himself about his domestic relations and his own sad life. His wife's people—foreigners—do not think well of him because he is "an Italian first, and only then an artist." His mother's career has been overcast by illicit love. And in him burns the nostalgia of martyrdom. "Evil is conquered only by good. . . . Renunciation, Giovanni! I have thought to die thus. I no longer desire to live, to be. This suspense, this everlasting farewell, this conquest of horror, recollection, affection, everything, fill me with such power that nothing remains but to conquer death." Luca masters his grief and is soon known as the chief of a small cult; he refuses to write for a newspaper that asks his beliefs; he refuses to debate with his opponents, although within a few minutes of his refusal he is hotly engaged in an exposition of his faith; he has entered into relations with Marta, a woman whose flesh has led her to the spirit, and to whose body Luca's soul has descended. She feels her ascent as plainly as she feels his sense of retrogression, and it torments her even as later Luca's unbending self-righteousness is to torment his mother. Yet there are times when she floods him with a passion that overwhelms and convinces even herself. At the end of the second act, he cries to her: "Ah, Marta, Marta! If you were not the truth, I should be betrayed by the very smile of the universe, for I see only you upon earth!" And she, in response: "I believe you! I believe you!"

Yet neither here speaks sober belief, for to Luca, the apostle, this woman is sin and hindrance; and to Marta a self-sacrificing, redeemed soul, Luca is the prey to a fleshless delusion. Soon another trial assails Luca. His delicate little son, who has been cared for at a religious institution, dies on the same day that the father has been attacked in his schoolroom by a mob that did not understand. The little one's death seems to be the decisive element in completing Luca's separation from Marta; until now it has been a spiritual division; henceforth it will be corporeal as well. He leaves her, as he believes, forever.

Marta follows him, however, to the house of his mother, where for a month he has been acting strangely. The two women meet, each in sorrow, anguished that they have no hold upon the man of their thoughts. Returning, as is his wont, at sunset from a day of contemplation on the heights, Luca encounters them. In the one he beholds the woman who for the while enslaved his senses; in the other, the one who early became a slave to her own, thus blighting his memory of her. The sight of both hardens his soul; he curses the blind passion that enmeshed him and them and the world. But neither are they silent—they to whose love he has been blind. "Silence, mother!" he cries. "I can no longer listen to you. You're no longer mother to me. You're a woman!" And she, in an outburst:

Yes, I am a woman. And what have you given to me as your mother? You followed that father of yours who sent me away! Now I can see you as you really are, after almost thirty years! What have you given me as your mother? As a woman I won love! Have I anything to boast of as a mother? I became a mother by accident, without desiring it; and my son flees me! But love did not betray me! He who made me over is dead, but I love him still! As between my love and you, it's you who are the stranger! And if there is anyone here who does not know what pardon means, it is you! And if there is one here who does not know what love means, it is you! . . . Leave my house. The nearer we are to each other, the more strangers we. Let me alone!

For the first time a latent doubt finds voice in Luca, and he says in characteristic fashion: "I doubt! I doubt! . . . Martyrdom! In his hour of despair, he who cannot sufficiently affirm his

truth can always through his self-sacrifice disturb
that humanity which does not understand him.
And now I desire martyrdom." Is it any wonder
that his mother calls him out of his mind and reminds him that his dream has led him to insult his
mother and despise the woman who brought him
her love? Now it is Marta's turn to appear. Bru-
tally Luca tells her that he no longer loves her.

MARTA: Then tell me; tell me the truth. While I,
with my vast, all-embracing love, fashioned of light and
faith, of joy and veneration, was giving all of me to you,
serving you, rendering myself truly worthy of you as I
imagined you to be, were you then truly worthy of me,
as I was thus transformed?

LUCA: Don't ask me!

MARTA (*with an outcry*): Tell me!

LUCA: No, no, no. I was merely smitten with your
beauty, your flesh, your softness, by voluptuousness.
. . . Every time that I had you, the more you bent
yourself to my desires, the more I felt degraded. I felt
forever upon the verge of sin, ignominy, stultification;
and I fell thousands of times. . . . I fled you! If I
were to have continued living with you I'd have had either
to die infamously or curse you without cease. That is the
truth.

In her horror at this revelation Marta draws a
revolver from her bag and shoots him. At once she
is seized with remorse and his mother rushes to his
side. "You have done well," he gasps to Marta,
and to his mother, "I . . . I . . . the truth.
. . . I . . . the light!" The gardener, hearing the shot, runs upon the scene. Luca, fearing lest
Marta's crime become known, manages to declare
that he has shot himself, and his parting injunction
to the women is to love each other. "Dying, I

learn for the first time the sweetness of that pardon
which at last opens for me the gates of my earth
. . . Paradise."

The play contains hints of poetry, but little of
the vital spark. In characterization it is especially
weak; Luca is hardly more than a mouthpiece,
while Marta and Luca's mother are convenient
foils and interlocutors. Giovanni and Professor
Torre are stiff variants of the "raisonneur," who
was once so familiar a figure in the French drama
that Benelli scorns. Quaranta is the most rigid of
stage types, serving but to draw out Luca by his
opposition and to perform a lightning-like conversion from which he recoils with equal rapidity.
One may question the necessity of having Anna's
parents appear in the first act, after which they are
almost forgotten. Anna herself is not seen, though
her presence fills the opening scene. In all seriousness, I believe that the one plausible character in
the play is the gardener, Pietro, who appears for a
few minutes in the closing act, but who, during those
fleeting moments, behaves himself like a human
being. For the few changes of mind that Luca experiences we are hardly prepared; between act one
and act two he has already formed a cult and taken
a mistress, despite the ascetic exaltation and longing for paradise in the beginning. All this is possible and natural, but must we take it on Benelli's
word in the case of a play centered about Luca's
Messianic figure? Let others judge the ideas and
idealism of the play. As drama it is quite unin-
spiring and without effect. To use Benelli's own
words, he has not discovered the right "bridge"
that leads to the opening of such material.

GIOVANNI VERGA

With the recent passing of Verga (1840-1922) Italy lost the dean of her letters—a powerful solitary figure whose stylistic austerity and personal aloofness foredoomed him to the lonely eminence that was his. He is intimately associated, in the history of his country's letters, with the movement known in the peninsula as "verism," and out of it as realism and naturalism. Verism, of course, has its distinguishing characteristics, but it is part of the great anti-romantic reaction and in Verga found such vigorous, artistic expression—and withal so arrestingly personal—that even to-day more than one of the "young" writers is not ashamed to acknowledge the influence of the deceased master. Labels mattered little to him. "Words, words, words," he once declared. "Naturalism, psychologism! There's room for everything, and the work of art may be born of any 'ism.' Let it be born—that is the main thing!" He had as little liking for the term "verist" as Ibsen for the appellation Ibsenite, and was so aloof that when, in 1920, his countrymen honored him on his eightieth birthday, many had to be informed all over again that his *I Malavoglia* (1881) was one of the best novels of its age, and that its author was one of the most solid glories of latter-day Italian literature. That he was the author of the intense *Cavalleria Rusticana*, out of which was made the libretto of Mascagni's mellifluous opera, was matter of more common knowledge.

He was born in Catania, and began his career as a writer of conventional novels redolent of the

French feuilletons; his very first (unprinted) work was an extensive novel inspired by George Washington and American Independence. Yet in a deeper sense the work of Verga is a psychological unity, and close study of the early books shows the young Verga to be father to the older. The novel that caps his creations, *I Malavoglia*, was intended to be the first of a trilogy devoted to a study of what he named "the vanquished" (i vinti), but after the second of the series, *Mastro-don Gesualdo* (1888), he appears to have abandoned the project.

In Verga's novels there seems to exist a certain parallel to the labors of Thomas Hardy, whose life, too, ran parallel to the great Italian's. In both the same underlying pessimism, in both the same masked pity. Signor Linati has also suggested Verga's affinity to Synge, for his deep insight into the lives of the humble fisherfolk. By these tokens we are in the presence of a figure whose influence among the newer novelists will prove strong and salutary.

Verga's atmosphere is naturally in good measure that of his native scene, where life is lived amidst a ferocious intensity of passions and a crushing belief in fate. His so-called impersonality should not mislead his readers, however. "It is not to comply with a Flaubertian æsthetics," writes Luigi Russo in his recent book upon Verga, "that the author of *Cavalleria Rusticana* tries not to intervene in his tale; it is because his model, the Sicilian peasant, is convinced that he himself does not intervene in the conduct of his own life."

Verga's position as a dramatist is secondary, yet Ruberti accords to the stage version of *Cavalleria*

Rusticana an importance to Italian dramaturgy
comparable to the significance of *I Malavoglia* to
the Italian novel. "The entire theatrical production of Giovanni Verga," he writes, "is contained
in a little volume of pocket size, about four hundred
pages long; yet there will come a day when we'll
go back to it to discover inside the sincerest and
most artistic representation of life that our theatre
produced toward the close of the nineteenth century."

Perhaps that praise is a tribute rather than a
criticism, yet the one-act *Cavalleria Rusticana* is a
gem of its kind. This should not be confused with
the libretto of the opera, which, though true to the
tale of the play, necessarily leaves out those very
qualities that make of the original a miniature
masterpiece. The drama, first produced in Rome
in 1884, with Duse in the role of Santuzza, immediately created a deep impression because of its
spontaneous presentation of life in the raw. Here,
in the words of Renato Simoni, we have a "hundred
dramas in a single act." Nor is the statement
merely another sample of Latin rhetorical exaggeration. In all of Verga's work for the stage the elemental theme is love; he is most successful when
nearest to the primal substratum of passion. The
one excursion into what an anemic social class calls
love was made, I believe, in his *Caccia alla Volpe*
(*The Fox-Hunt*), which is itself a puny, anemic
performance. French subtleties of irridescent amour-
ettes were not for Verga's vigorous middle years.
For the rest, he seemed to prefer the succinct form,
so that later plays, such as *In Portirneria*, *Caccia
al Lupo*, *La Lupa*, are not full length.

It is in the presence of a simple play like *Caval-*

leria Rusticana that one person, at least, feels the inadequacy of the Dukes-Jameson aristocratic theory of the drama.   These are simple folk, humble, "vanquished" souls that struck their creator from the first with a sense of their stark significance.   In Verga, like the eternal modern that he is, nothing is settled; he is enigmatic, sphinx-like.   And so, too, his characters, out of whose very dumbness rises the eloquence of human symbols.   *Rustic Chivalry* leaves one with a haunting sense of a fate that overhangs us all; not a Greek fate, but a fate that courses in our veins and laughs at our puny institutions and our solemn ring of defenses against the incursions of the originary beast.   For a simple, powerful miniature such as this, one could easily spare the numerous "triumphs" of a later Niccodemi, the lucubrations of grotesque mummers whose present virtue lies, not in accomplishment, but in a search for new paths.

In Portineria (*At the Porter's Lodge*) is a pathetic little play in which all the trouble is caused by love misplaced.   Now it is the sickly sister Malia who is fond of Chiarini; but Chiarini loves the other sister, who, in turn, places her affections elsewhere.   And thus the chain of unhappiness is forged link by link, fettering them all to misery.   *La Lupa* (*The She-Wolf*) is an unrelenting portrayal of a mother who pursues the husband of her daughter.   Of the two dramatic sketches *The Wolf-Hunt* and *The Fox-Hunt*, *The Wolf-Hunt* is easily the better; just as in *In Portineria* the various links of true and virtuous love combine to make a chain of unhappiness, so here the links of illicit passion unite in a chain of evil.   It would seem that to Verga there is something in the very nature of passion which foredooms its victims to misfortune, whether that passion burgeon in the heart of the pure or burn in the bosom of the transgressor. The wolf of *The Wolf-Hunt* is a man who has deserted one woman to pay attentions to the wife of another man; when trapped, however, his first concern is not to shield or to save the wife, but to rescue his own hide. The fox-hunt of the second sketch shows the comic aspect of the same situation, but Verga is here on unfamiliar or unattractive ground.

Verga found no followers; it is as a personality rather than as a model that he is to-day a power among the small band of artists. There is, in his labors, a tonic elementalism that makes for the illusive permanence of literary glory; his *Cavalleria Rusticana*, at least, will long be a focal point in the story of the Italian drama.

ENRICO LUIGI MORSELLI

The short life of Morselli (1882-1921) was as checkered as it could be made by a youthful thirst for adventure, a goading poverty, and an underlying spiritual restlessness. Born at Pesaro, he was early taken by his parents to Modena and soon thence to Florence. Here he finished the courses given at the elementary schools and advanced to the university, where for two years he devoted himself to the study of medicine and letters, which, judging solely from contemporary literature, seem to have a powerful affinity for one another. He took no degree, but his intercourse with such minds as Papini and Prezzolini helped to sharpen his wits, and later, when he needed a little friendly notice,

Papini beat the drum for him with those sharp, staccato thumps for which he is noted—or was noted, before the astounding conversion that is signalized in his recent *Storia di Cristo*. To Papini, indeed, Morselli owes not a little for his crossing of the Italian border and for exaltation as a writer of modern tragedy that lifts him clearly above both D'Annunzio and Sem Benelli.

"Morselli," wrote Papini of the tragedy *Glauco* in one of the numbers of the short-lived *La Vraie Italie,*—a monthly published by him in French for the dissemination of a broader knowledge of Italian cultural life—"does not follow pedantically the elaborated myths and the learned reconstructions of the Hellenists. He is not a patient and boresome archæologist like D'Annunzio; he cares very little for erudite bric-a-brac, for local color, for the scenery and supernumeraries that serve to conceal the impotency of the impotent. He penetrates to the very core of the psychological action and into the very soul of his personages. . . . He transports us into a magic world that is almost outside of time, but in that mythical and prehistoric world we behold men who suffer, love, who betray, who take pleasure with the puissant frankness of elemental humanity. He uses the myth so as to obtain a superior lyric freedom that shall permit him to depict life in its very essence. He thus stands apart from all the makers of classic pastiches with which our literature has been infested from the sixteenth century down to D'Annunzio and Benelli."

It is easy to see that Papini was here quite as much interested in damning his pet aversions as in praising the most noted of his friend's productions.

The trumpet-blast, however, did reveal Morselli to the outside world.

According to the evidence available, Morselli's life at Florence was a strange admixture of ardent study and wild debauch. In his twentieth year, in company of his friend Valerio Ratti, he suddenly launched upon a sea voyage, and before he returned to Florence he had wandered from Capetown to Buenos Aires, to Cornwall, to London, to Paris, earning his living now by his pen, now by the most cheeky imposture. Once back in Italy—"the most penitent and happy of prodigal sons"—Morselli founded a large commercial and industrial review called *Mercurio*, which ran for no less than five years and died of—honesty. In order to marry he was compelled to borrow 150 lire to proceed with the ceremony; this was but the beginning of straits that brought him often the pangs of hunger. His mind reverted to writing, and the result was that peculiar little book called *Favole per i re d'oggi* (*Fables for the Kings of Today*). Here we encounter just that combination of the ancient and the contemporary that strikes the reader of his tragedies; there is, moreover, a certain cynical outlook upon life, a philosophic scorn of man the individual that so often companions a love of him in the abstract. (Was it not Mephisto who, in W. S. Gilbert's little-known adaptation of *Faust* called *Gretchen* inveighed against the holy tribe,

> Who pray for mankind in the aggregate
> And damn them all in detail!)

The encouraging reception of the book resulted in the composition of the one-act *Acqua sul Fuoco*

(*Water Upon Fire*), a charming little piece, comparable for its sentiment, its irony, and its tenderness to Pirandello's *Sicilian Limes*. The play made very little impression, and Morselli returned to Pesaro convinced that he had not been cut out for a dramatist. His next refuge was poetry, and he set about the writing of *Orione*, his first tragedy, which is poetic not in the narrow sense of rhymes and meters, but in the ampler one of outlook, atmosphere, implication. Originally produced in 1910, it made the tour of Milan, Trieste, Modena, and Florence. The author, who was encountering plenty of opposition among his fellow-craftsmen, was accused of classicism, and perhaps to refute the charge wrote the modern play *La Prigione* (*The Prison*), which Tina di Lorenzo acted in Milan, Turin, Florence, and South America. Close upon this followed *Il Domatore Gastone*, an amusing one-act skit, in which an animal-tamer finds his hazardous occupation quite pacific in comparison with the taming of two determined young skirted animals of a more closely related species.

Soon we discover Morselli in the "movies" as an actor, and he readily advances to the position of director. The war, however, cuts short his cinematographic ventures. His noted tragedy *Glauco* is now beginning to take shape; he reads the first draught to the composer Franchetti, who is so struck with it that he immediately acquires the rights to set it to music. A period of illness intervenes, and it is not until he is out of the sanatorium that Morselli writes the final draught in twenty days at Blevio. He leaves the sole copy in the compartment of a railroad car, and it is recovered only

after a campaign of telephone calls and telegrams.
From one manager to another it travels until at
last it is produced through the enterprise of Virgilio Talli and acted in triumph by Annibale Be-
trone, proving to be the greatest success since
Benelli's *La Cena delle Beffe* (*The Supper of Jests*).
The furore created by *Glauco* led, of course, to the
republication of Morselli's other labors; he had already been working upon two tragedies, *Dafne e
Cloe* and *Belfagor;* now he considered a new modern
play as well, to be called *L'Incontro*. In 1919 he
was awarded the government prize of 6,000 lire for
Glauco, and his future seemed assured. Declining
health, however, led to his early death from tuberculosis of the lungs.

Morselli's fiction comprises the *Favole per i re
d'oggi, Storie da ridere . . . e da piangere* (*Tales
for Laughter . . . and Tears*), and *Il trio Stefania.*
The fables, as we have seen, are filled with cynicism, irony, bantering mockery. Beneath the sneers
is a spirit of tolerance and a withdrawal that enables
the author to consider his fellow-men as if he were
a god endowed with a sense of laughter and of
human frailties. The tales for laughter and for
tears are not divided into those meant for pleasure
and those written to agitate the emotions. The
title, I imagine, signifies that each tale contains
both elements in a very human blend. As the
writer declares in that strange tale *Italien, Liebe,
Blut!—a German novel left half completed through my
own good offices*—"I was made that way: I would
laugh and laugh, yet at bottom I took everything
seriously, even as now, when I no longer laugh."
The man is, then, fundamentally ironic and

symbolic in his outlook upon life. This does not
have to be read into his lines; it is there, in body
and in spirit, often in the very title. Even his
modern play, *La Prigione*, is thus symbolic, standing for the mental torture and confinement of sus-
taining a family-lie, of "putting on a front." It is
written in the vein of Giacosa, but tinted throughout with the dramatist's personal methods. As to
Orione and *Glauco*, the first, written about ten years
earlier than the second, is not so good, because of
its diffuseness and because it carries less poetic
conviction. The symbolism is less effective, and
while the action is excellent in scenes, it is neither
so cumulative nor so climactic as in the later play.
Orione, the god, is less impressive than Glauco, the
seeker, and Merope is less colorful than Glauco's
sweetheart, Scylla.

Morselli's tragedies are both singularly free of
scenic trappings and rhetorical inflation. There is
a beautiful simplicity in his language which one
need not be an Italian to appreciate. He writes a
prose that is akin to poetry without being of that
vapory, deliquescent variety considered by some
"poetic". He knows the secret of a broad, rhythmic
action in which the pictorial, the dramatic, and the
vocal blend into a meaningful harmony. Out of
two classic myths he creates two modern symbols.
Glaucus is a Sicilian, in love with Scylla, and hears
the sirens and tritons summon him to that wealth
and glory of which he dreams; to him glory is even
more than Scylla, and so great is her love that she
helps him rob her father, that the foundations of
his venture may be assured. Off fares Glaucus on
his eager quest, resisting temptation on the way,

returning successful only to find Scylla dead. Just
as *Glaucus* symbolizes, in its beautiful simplicity,
the great cost at which fame is purchased, so *Orion*
reveals in similar, though less effective fashion, the
littleness of man before the powers of nature and
of death. Orion, earth-born, and defying all earth's
creatures, after slaying the monster of the forest,
dies from the sting of a scorpion that he deems beneath his notice. Morselli, in these plays, has renewed eternal truths for us. That is perhaps the
essence of enduring art.

Some Italian critics have objected to the symbolic interpretation of these two plays in particular.
Yet surely, even considering the tragedies in the
strictest manner that so exacting a philosopher as
Benedetto Croce would require, one is justified in
noting the symbols that the author has unmis-
takably put into them as part of his personality
rather than as a predetermined intention. And so
considered, *Orione* breathes a sense of man's help-
less position in the face of nature's immutable laws,
even as *Glauco* suggests man's tardy recognition
that glory is less than love. "Qualunque vita è
abietta si è fatta al solo scopo di vivere! . . . e qualunque vita è santa se un fine l'illumina! . . ."
exclaims Jacopo in *La Prigione*. "Any life is base
if it be concerned only with living, and any life is
holy if a purpose illumine it." We have Morselli's
own word for it that he aimed to create a little
beauty through his writings, and his interpretation
of the word "purpose" by no means signifies an art
marred by the obtrusion of moral preachment.

Morselli's position in the contemporary letters of
his country is not an inconsiderable one, and already

secure.   The triumphant reception of *Glauco* by a national audience trained in the best traditions of the poetic drama led more than one critic to behold in the young playwright the precursor of a new, peculiarly modern, poetic tragedy.   Amid the ruck of fantastic productions that infested the "grotesque" theatre, with its pieces labeled "visions," "confessions", "parables" — anything, indeed, but drama or comedy—Morselli developed an idiom and an atmosphere all his own.   His early death was a genuine loss to the Italian stage, for with D'Annunzio's heroics and Benelli's reversion to prose and apostolic mysticism, Italy needs more than ever the unpretentious beauty, the pure line, and the harmonious colors that Morselli would have added to its store.   When a *Glauco* or a *Sly* can appear so close to one another, why, after all, should artistic souls lie awake nights worrying about the "nationalism" of the Italian theatre?

GIOVACCHINO FORZANO

Something of this unpretentious beauty, this color, this pure line, is in the play in verse that recently raised Giovacchino Forzano from the ranks of the opera librettists to the rarer precincts of the poetic drama.

It was inevitable that *Sly*, suggested by the Induction to Shakespeare's *Taming of the Shrew*, should, after the triumph it won in its native Italy, claim the attention of the London in which the action of the piece is laid.   This London, it is true, is the capital of the seventeenth century's early days, yet so successfully has the erstwhile Italian librettist assimilated the mood and manner of his

subject that only yesterday London rose to the
first English performances of the play. It was as
much of a novelty there as in the Italy whence it
came, and it should prove no less appealing and
successful when Mr. Belasco produces it here. It
has the charm and poetry of a play by Barrie—
some of Christopher Sly's own old wine poured into
a new bottle. With this single play Forzano emerges
from the ranks of the mediocrities and justly lays
claim to such consideration as is granted to artists
of creative imagination. We have the word of so
practiced a playgoer as the dramatist Marco Praga
that *Sly* in performance was an unmixed delight.
Upon the printed page *Sly* is no less a delight unmixed. It has verve, body, glamor, a gift for robust
humor as for tender fancy; it can be stoutly coarse
without descending to ribaldry, softly amorous
without a too noticeable lapse into sentimentality.
To Italians it must have come as a doubly welcome
relief from heavy D'Annunzian vapors and Benellian
harshness that had not yet become apostolic, as
well as from the grotesqueries above which only
a Pirandello and a few others can raise their heads.
Forzano is no Rostand, and *Sly* is no *Cyrano*, but
there are analogous external as well as internal
reasons for the success that greeted both.

In adding as subtitle of the play, "the Legend of
the Awakened Sleeper," Forzano consciously relates
his plot to the Oriental theme that made its way in
one form or another from the *Arabian Nights* into
Europe, early appearing in Italy and in such
Spanish pieces as Calderón's *Life Is a Dream*.
For the purposes of his drama he adds to the characters presented in the Shakesperian Induction and

changes certain relationships. Sly is not here a
tinker, but a vagabond tavern troubadour; the
Elizabethan jesting Lord becomes the Count of
Westmoreland, to whom Forzano gives a willful,
wayward mistress, Dolly. The cruel deceit is carried out, as in the second scene of the Induction,
but with the added complications that a Dolly
(instead of Shakespeare's page disguised as a woman)
may develop. And Sly's fate, as we shall see, is
followed to the end.

The Italian play is in three acts and four scenes.
The first act takes us to "The Hawk's Tavern,"
where a drinking bout is in progress, set off by a
rout of chess-players, bag-pipers, wags, and a scold-
ing hostess. There is John Plake, drunk to the gills,
boasting of the new part that he is to take in the
"tragedy written by my friend William Shakespeare"; he is to be the first gravedigger, and knows
his part so well that he has even been able to dig
up some of the best bottles in the tavern cellar
without digging down into his pocket to pay the
score. The drunker he gets, the more he longs for
the rhyming tippler, Sly, his bosom pal and chorister
of the roisterers. A battle over his refusal to pay
is suddenly interrupted by the entrance of Dolly,
who, having grasped the situation, throws a purse
to the hostess and restores quiet. Dolly, bored by
the creaking courtliness of her routine life has
escaped in quest of adventure; the Count, however,
knows her haunts and is quick to trail her to The
Hawk. At first he would have her off at once, but
the entreaties of the guests and his own need for
diversion prevail upon him and he and his retinue

remain. Plake, moodier than ever, yearns for his
boon companion. Of a sudden Sly's voice is heard
from the outside; he is fleeing from Snare, who
would lock him up for unpaid debts.

> Where is that drunkard
> Of a Sly whom I must lock up in jail?

Prosaic, but fateful words these that Sly yet will
hear on a rueful day. Now, however, with nobility
for an audience, friends for a chorus, and comfort
flowing cheerily from generous bottles, he is moved
to song, and sings his lilting tale of the lovelorn
bear. With new gulps come new moods, until his
self-pitying philosophy rises from his cups:

> But drink! drink!
> When you're not drinking,
> Sly, who are you?
> Tell them, poor Sly—these folks that call you
> Tippler, drunken sot! . . .
> A tavern minstrel . . . juggler . . .
> Itinerant hawker . . . you scribble verses
> For births, deaths, and marriages . . .
> You're a jack of all trades . . .
> Yet remain a sad wretch!
> A tatterdemalion!
> Try to raise your eyes to a beautiful woman! . . .
>   She laughs with compassion! . . .
> Your home, your kingdom,
> Your paradise: the tavern!
> I would give . . . my life (now I make you laugh)
> Just to hear
> The voice of a woman . . . or of a child
> Say to me (*he sobs*),
> "Good day to you, Sly." (*He drinks and kisses the
>   beaker. He can hardly stand.*)

You! You save me! Yes! When I have drunk
I am transformed!
And I'm a king!
Nay! More than king!
More than a living creature!
This body of mine
Melts at the will of fancy!
And I become . . . a silver cloud!
I ride astride the horned moon
And scour the heavens in quest of verses!

This Cyranesque outpouring touches Dolly's heart
and suggests to the Count a pleasant manner of
winding up the evening. His plan quickly matures,
and even Sly's companions are drunk enough to see
the cream of the jest. All but Plake, who cannot
drink in mock salutation to His Highness-to-be,
Chris Sly.

The second act transports us to the Count's
gilded palace; his attendants and Dolly have been
well instructed in the parts they are to play when
Sly awakens from his drunken stupor. Sly, according to their plot, has been in delirious sleep for ten
years, during which he has imagined himself to be
the vagabond versifier of his only too real career.
Dolly is his sad, but prayerful wife, who daily during these years has besought heaven for his return
to reason. And this is the eventful day of that
return. Slowly the awakened toper is convinced—
or perhaps he is yet drunk enough to see truth in
the hoax—and the climax comes when he is told
that even now his wife is at the little church of the
castle, still praying and as yet not apprised of his
miraculous cure. From afar comes the echo-like
sound of her orisons, chorused by a murmur of

feminine voices that support her entreaties. Trumpets and bells announce the restoration of the supposed nobleman's reason, and Sly heads the grand procession into the great hall. This leads us to the second scene—that of the hall, into which Sly is received by a veritable chorus of the nobility and its entourage. One thing is on Sly's mind: his wife; here is the height of the farce, and here the height of Sly's incredulity. No, this must be a dream— as soon as he shall stretch forth his arms to embrace her she will vanish as so often in the past. When his fears find poetic voice—for is not Sly a tippling troubadour?—Dolly is so affected by the genuineness of his aspirations that she forgets the part she has been taught and begins to feel a real response to the feigned potentate who can make love so much better than the Count. To Sly, who is afraid that his "madness" will return if he dares to touch her, she whispers encouragement:

Sly . . . Sly . . . fear not . . . Your madness will not return. . . . I am indeed your wife. . . . (*to calm him*) and I love you, . . . I love you. . . .

Again and again she must say the words, inciting him to poetic delirium. Still he hesitates to touch her, while she bids him, now feigning nothing, not to fear. "Dare. . . . Sly . . . dare. . . ."

And Sly dares. He kisses her, when out of the air comes the voice of the Count, simulating that of Snare in the first act:

Where is that drunkard
Of a Sly whom I must lock up in jail?

The kiss is a signal for the sudden appearance of the courtly train; the laughing outburst of the concealed nobles wakes Sly rudely from a dream indeed, but a dream that has had one incontestable reality. He refuses to be separated from Dolly, whom he holds in close embrace.

> You have laughed me to scorn! You! You have
>   laughed me to scorn!
> And you should be condemned
> To remain lifelong
> Thus . . . tight in my arms . . .
> And under my kisses! . . .

Sly is thrust into the cellar, there to ruminate upon his fall. The Count bids him adieu with a derisive couplet, while Dolly, leaning against the marble balustrade, watches the attendants through tear-filled eyes as they drag the disillusioned poet off into the gloom.

The closing act takes place in the cellar, where Sly indulges in a long soliloquy. Murder wells up in his heart, and then love. Dolly's kiss was true, it was sincere.

> In that moment . . . I vow . . . that woman
> That woman . . . (*finally daring to speak the words*)
>   loved me!
> She loved me! Yes, she loved me. . . .
> I felt it! She loved me! And now . . . now . . .
>   (*as if mad with joy, weeping and laughing*)
> Think, Sly, just think,
> If this be true,
> Something of the jest remains with you. . . .
> The most precious part is yours! You're no longer
>   alone!
> The gloom of your hell has been cleft!
> There is a hope of sunlight even for you!

This is your victory!
Life is beautiful, Sly!   Life is beautiful
Even for you!
Even for you!

But how shall he taste the fruits of this vengeance,
this victory? He beholds visions of seeing Dolly
again, of freeing her. Then follows the realization
of the truth. At this very moment his Dolly may
be in the arms of another. The thought maddens
him. Go back to the tavern? No. The jest has
tricked him doubly; it has held out love and snatched
it away, it has raised him above his surroundings.

Now I have had a glimpse of paradise, and I, too,
Demand my share! Yes, I demand it!

By the bottle he has lived; by the bottle he shall
die. With a grim sense of humor he breaks a bottle
against the stone table and severs the veins of his
wrist, gasping that "upon the dead are placed the
emblems of their nobility." Now he will no longer
wake to new delusions; now he may wish all. As
he lies there dying Dolly comes stealing in to beg
his forgiveness for the part she played in the cruel
jest. At first she does not notice his condition. Did
he not feel that she would come to see him, she asks.
And soon she is holding a dead man in her arms.

It seems entirely probable that Forzano began
this piece as a libretto and soon saw that it was
too good to be drowned out by tones. In describ-
ing it one falls naturally into the jargon of Italian
opera. As one reads, one can easily pick out the
entrances, soli, duets, choruses, and all the other
earmarks of conventional opera. Dolly's prayer be-

hind the scenes, accompanied by the feminine voices, is as reminiscent of *Il Trovatore* as is Sly's pitying soliloquy of *I Pagliacci;* Sly's song of the lovesick bear has numerous relatives in the operatic repertory, although Forzano here has rendered it an integral part of the action, and even a mirror of Sly's own fate, as it is significantly parodied in the second act. In the reading, at least, the last act comes as a sort of anti-climax; the act consists almost entirely of Sly's farewell to the world, with the final appearance of Dolly in time to provide his last vision of Paradise. Yet it links itself naturally to all that has gone before, and is in sombre contrast to the vinous gayety of the opening scene and the cruel bantering of the second. The verse is of free, flowing, spontaneous character, never rigid or academic. Poetry suffuses the whole from beginning to end in company of romance that runs the gamut of the moods. Shakespeare's tinker here becomes the symbol of man's fearless but futile rebellion against disillusionment.

FRANCESCO T. MARINETTI

Marinetti's futuristic extravagances, which possess the grand consistency of a philosophic system invading every department of human activity, are not a phenomenon apart in the intellectual hurly-burly of contemporary existence. With varying degree of intensity this impatient desire to dump overboard the impedimenta of the past and start anew, untrammeled by circumspection or tradition, rises in Spain, in Germany, in France, under names that resemble each other only in the "ism" that wags like a frisky tail at the end. No amount of

insurgent impatience and extravagance should obscure, however, the symptomatic significance of the
strivings; there is a soul of goodness in all things
evil, even in the laughing madness of the Dada-
ists.   Besides, who shall pretend, from a glimpse
at the source, to predict the size of the rivers that
may flow from it miles down the mountain sides?
The Futurists reared a numerous and a noisy brood;
in art, in poetry, in the drama, their impulse has
been felt, not permanently perhaps, but perceptibly;
their theories are as false as any that seek to en-
compass all creation in a dogma, their performances
add strangeness to that inherent falsity.   It is not
the "nouveau frisson" that they seek; a thrill is
doubtless too long and must be heightened to a
culminating orgasm.   And if it is difficult to speak
of these newer "isms" without lapsing into the
phraseology of the consultation room and of the
psychoanalyst, it is doubtless because some of the
proponents of the cults invite the attention of the
neurologist rather than the scrutiny of the critic.
All this has been said before of the advocates of
novelty; something in the most curious and restless
of us resists the suggestion of change.   Let us note
down our thoughts, then, with becoming humility,
and extract, from the welter of newer activities
what seems most likely to prove of productive,
creative value.   If the new turns out to be old, and
has been advanced only on the score of newness,
obviously this relegates it to the background; if it
lays undue emphasis upon the part of a whole, again
obviously that excess should be indicated as an excess rather than as a contribution.   If, again, there
is something valid in the spirit of the performance,

11

despite its artistic shortcomings, the knowledge is important; it may lack significance to art, but possesses value for an understanding of the artist's impulse. Back of all this seeming fatuity lies a desire to escape from the mere repetition of reality in art; it is, in its own way, part of the protest against narrow realism that is evidenced as much in the work of the German Expressionists, let us say, as in the stylists of the new scenery and what Mr. Macgowan has called "the theatre of to-morrow."

Marinetti, like his spectacular countryman D'Annunzio, has a gift for self-advertisement, and came to the notice of the rest of the world through the suppression of his novel *Mafarka the Futurist* by the Italian Comstocks. That was about fourteen years ago, and his acquittal was speedily followed (February 20, 1909) by a manifesto of Futurism in the Paris *Figaro*. Since then, it would seem, the Futurists have been as busy with the writing of manifestoes as with the exemplification of their theories; it is doubtful whether anything that has come from them contains the germs of permanency —to which, of course, they might reply that permanency is anti-futuristic—but there is no doubt that the various manifestoes make interesting reading. They are a running commentary upon the futility of contemporary existence, expressive of a violent reaction against every stabilizing force in civilization. Everyone is familiar with the Futurist proposal to abolish Italy's past by selling her museums and art collections and purchasing with the proceeds the newest engines of warfare. Speed, violence, mob action, are the new gods.

With special reference to the stage, the earliest Futurist pronunciamento called for the Variety Theatre, a mad hodge-podge of acrobatics, practical jokes, blending of the performers with the spectators, caricature, pantomime, and what not under the sun else. Here, for example, are some of the innovations called for by the manifesto:

"The Variety Theatre is to have no traditions, dogmas, nor masters, and is to be nurtured upon 'speedy actuality.'

"It is to be absolutely practical, seeking to divert the public with comical effects, erotic excitation, and imaginative surprises, which must be incessantly renewed by the combined efforts of authors, actors, and stage hands.

"It must run the entire gamut of stupidity, imbecility, absurdity, thrusting the intelligence insensibly to the very brink of madness.

"The Variety Theatre is the only one to employ the collaboration of the public, which does not remain static, like a stupid spectator, but takes boisterous part in the action, singing with the performers, accompanying the orchestra, conversing in improvised talk and bizarre dialogues with the actors. The latter are to pick clownish quarrels with the musicians.

"The Variety Theatre uses the smoke of cigars and cigarettes to fuse the atmosphere of the auditorium with that of the stage. And since the public thus collaborates with the ingenuity of the actor, the action takes place simultaneously upon the stage, in the boxes, and in the pit.

"Such a theatre is a school of sincerity, particularly instructive to the male, since it exalts his rapacious instincts and strips from woman all the veils of romantic illusion that so long have swathed her. At the same time it brings out woman's 'admirable animal traits,' thus re-establishing sex upon a primitive basis. It provides, moreover, a school of heroism, seeking to incite men to break all existing records for athletic pursuits. It is a school of subtlety, of complications and cerebral synthesis, for its clowns, sleight-of-hand men, lightning cal culators, and the rest of that tribe; here a single dance, representing the discussion of diplomatists over the Morocco and the Congo questions, may be the equivalent of at least three years of study in foreign politics.

"Love is here to be shown up for the natural thing it is, stripped of the romantic languors, the carnal obsessions, the mysteries, and anti-hygienic idealisms that have led a parasitic existence upon it.

"Perspective, proportion, time, and space are annihilated, together with the Solemn, the Sacred, the Sublime of Art with a capital A." Psychology is to be relegated to the academic past whence it sprung, and in its stead is to be enthroned what Marinetti christens *fisicofollia*, a word constructed in antithesis to psychology and signifying, as the opposite to mental order, physical abandon.

If these extracts from the manifesto seem extravagant, what shall we say to the detailed advice given by its framer to the operators of this Variety Theatre? The singers are to be compelled to paint their bare necks, their arms, and particularly to dye their hair every seductive color; the performer is to be interrupted and made to deliver a revolutionary harangue; the seats are to be covered with glue in

certain parts of the auditorium, thus adding to the
amusement of the spectators by the discomfiture
of the unfortunate parties; the same seat is to be
sold to some ten persons, thus making sure of confusion and argument; free tickets are to be given
to semi-lunatics, who will cause more trouble with
their obscene gestures, their pinching of women,
and other eccentricities; powders provocative of
itching and sneezing are to be scattered about.

"Prostitute systematically upon the stage all
classical art, representing, for example, during a
single evening, all the Greek, French, and Italian
tragedies condensed into a ludicrous potpourri.
Enliven the works of Beethoven, Wagner, Bach,
Bellini, and Chopin with the interpolation of Neapol-
itan songs. Represent side by side on the stage
Zacconi, Duse, Mayol, Sarah Bernhardt, and Fre-
goli. Perform a Beethoven symphony backwards,
beginning on the last note. Reduce all Shakespeare
to a single act. . . . Have *Ernani* given by actors
enclosed up to the neck in sacks. Grease the boards
of the stage so as to ensure diverting tumbles at
the most tragic moment of the action.

"Encourage in every way the genre of the American eccentrics, their effects of exalting grotesquerie,
of horrifying dynamism, their coarse sallies, their
enormous brutality, their trick vests, and their
pantaloons, deep as the holds of ships, from which
there will issue forth, with thousands of other things,
the great futuristic hilarity that will rejuvenate the
face of the world."

There is another, and perhaps more important
document of the Futurists concerning the modern
theatre, signed by Marinetti, Emilio Settimelli, and

Bruno Corra at Milan, January 11, 1915, and February 18 of the same year. They call it, in direct contradiction of facts easily verifiable, "our first words upon the theatre."

This time the Variety Theatre is considered only of precursory importance; the label has become Synthetic Futurist Theatre, "atechnical, dynamic, simultaneous, autonomous, alogical, and unreal." The war, which to them was a species of intensified Futurism, had strengthened their belief in the theatre as a national influence. Ninety per cent of the Italian people goes to the theatre, it proclaimed, while only ten per cent reads books and reviews. Wherefore—as if nothing else had ever been said previously upon the matter—the necessity of a Futuristic theatre.

That theatre must be synthetic, must pack into a few minutes and into a few words and gestures countless situations, feelings, ideas, sensations, facts, and symbols. Such innovators as Ibsen, Maeterlinck, Andreiev, Claudel, and Shaw never aimed at a true synthesis; at best they are but semi-futuristic, and essentially static. "We are convinced that, mechanically, through brevity, we can create an absolutely new theatre, in perfect harmony with our vertiginously speedy and laconic (sic) futurist sensibility. Our acts must also be instants. . . . With such an essential and synthetic brevity our theatre can sustain and even overcome the competition of the Cinematograph."

That theatre must be anti-technical, opposing every precept of the dramaturgic text-book with its imposing array of playcraft. "We wish to destroy Technique, which from the Greeks down to the

present day, instead of becoming more simple, has
waxed ever more dogmatic, more stupidly logical,
meticulous, pedantic, stifling." Away, then, with
a hundred pages where one will suffice, simply because the public wishes to be convinced of the
reality of a person; away with any distinction between theatricality and untheatricality; away with
villains and heroes, imitation of reality, with the
desire to explain the action through minute logic,
"when even in real life we can never grasp an event
in its entirety, with all its causes and consequences,
since reality vibrates about us" in a chaotic confusion of inter-related fragments. "For example,
it is stupid to represent upon the stage a contest
between two persons, always in a clear, logical order,
while in our actual experience with life we find
almost exclusively fragments of dispute which our
activity as modern persons has brought to our
attention for a moment in the car, in a café, in a
station, and which have remained filmed (*cinemat-
ografati*) upon our souls as dynamic, fragmentary
symphonies of gestures, words, sounds, and lights."

That theatre must be dynamic and simultaneous.
"We believe that a thing is of value according as it
has been improvised (hours, minutes, seconds), and
not prepared for a long time (months, years, centuries)." And the signers point out in italics that
the greater part of their plays have been written
in the theatre, virtually improvised; they pooh-pooh
Shakespeare, fall asleep over Ibsen's lines. Absolute dynamism is their program, through the compenetration of different times and places. Hence
their *simultaneità*, in which time and space are
abolished.

That theatre must be autonomous, alogical, unreal. It is born of (1) "our frantic passion for actual life, velocitous, fragmentary, elegant, complicated, cynical, muscular, fleeting, futuristic; and (2) our ultra-modern cerebral conception of art, according to which no logic, no tradition, no technique, no opportunism may be imposed upon the genius of the artist, who must be concerned solely with the creation of synthetic expressions of cerebral energy possessing the absolute value of novelty."

Together with this novelty of outlook and execution comes a novelty of nomenclature. Contemporary Italy, I believe, has more different designations for its dramatic products than any other nation of the Western world. Among these Marinettian novelties are the *battute in libertà* (free lines; i. e., improvisations by the actors); the *simultaneità* (simultaneity, in which the action takes place in a fourth-dimensional world wherein time and space no longer exist); the *compenetrazione*, wherein the emphasis is placed upon the interpenetration of temporal and spatial elements; the *poemetto animato* (animated short poem); the *sensazione sceneggiata* (the scenified sensation); the *ilarità dialogata* (hilarious dialogue), and a similar array of "extralogical discussions," "deformations," ad libitum.

The plays produced upon this plan have actually been given by various dramatic companies and have been received enthusiastically (if we may credit the manifesto) by the publics of many cities.

As to Marinetti's own plays, we are not here so much concerned with his *La Momie Sanglante* (*The Bleeding Mummy*) or his *Il Re Baldoria* (*King Hubbub*, 1909), which is to me as fat and fatuous

as the fleshly potentate whose gory exploits it
chronicles. Nothing of dynamic synthesis about
this satire upon parliamentarism that takes place
in the realm of Block-heads at some undetermined
epoch in the Middle Ages. Nor, for that matter,
is there anything novel or arresting in the longest
of the synthetic plays that Marinetti issued in book
form in 1920 under the title of *Elettricità Sessuale.*
(The titular play was produced in 1909 in a French
version.) *Sexual Electricity* is a play of facile symbolism, the interpretation of which is reinforced by
the protagonist, who is named Marinetti, thus
further indicating his spokesmanship for the author.
Few dramas could be more conventional in technique; it even opens with an expository conversation between two servants! Its purpose is to glorify
the Futurist views as to marriage and sex in general,
and its satire is so obvious, so transparent, that it
amounts almost to direct harangue. Far more interesting as experiemnts in the new forms are the
short pieces that make up the remainder of the
collection. Some of these are little more than
animated cartoons of moral or political import; they
employ the "flash-back" methods of the moving-
picture, the "insert" methods of both film and car-
toon. One of them uses the tripartite stage of the
medieval theatre in which heaven, earth, and hell
are simultaneously visible. Another, called a "drama
of objects," gives voices to inanimate articles of
furniture, while a companion drama, not even en-
dowing the chairs of the action with voices, actually
manages to create an atmosphere of anticipation by
the shifting shadows of the chairs waiting for the
guests to arrive. There are "plays" calling only for

the appearance of hands in various positions above a stretched curtain and consisting of twenty directions for the various positions; there is neither continuity nor climax, the hands of each "scene" telling their story by their attitude alone. For example, direction number 3: "Two masculine hands (of different persons) clasp one another firmly;" number 14, "a feminine hand waves a handkerchief with yearnful languor, crushed and grieving;" number 19, "a masculine hand with the forefinger rigidly pointing in a position of energetic command." The feet likewise have a play to themselves. One of the most interesting of the pieces, which is two pages long, consists solely of stage directions and the revelation of an officer's room on a summer's night. Here, literally, the picture tells the story.

As an illustration of the plays, I translate one of the least esoteric, called *On a Moonlit Night*, "alogical compenetration." As the author explains in his note, "The heavy-paunched man is not a symbol, but an *anti-logical synthesis* of many sensations: fear of future reality, cold and solitude of the night, vision of life twenty years after, and so on."

SCENE: *A Garden; a Bench.*

HE: What a beautiful night! Let's sit down here. . . .
SHE: How fragrant the air is!
HE: We are all alone, we two, in this vast garden. . . . Aren't you afraid?
SHE: No . . . no . . . I am so happy to be here alone with you.
A STOUT, HEAVY-PAUNCHED GENTLEMAN (*enters from a side path, approaches the couple, sits down upon the bench beside them. They do not see him, however, as if he were*

invisible): Hum! Hum! (*He stares at the maiden while she speaks.*)

SHE: Did you feel that breeze?

THE STOUT, HEAVY-PAUNCHED GENTLEMAN: Hum! Hum! (*He stares at the young man while the latter speaks.*)

HE: It isn't the breeze.

SHE: But isn't there really anybody in this garden?

HE: Only the watchman yonder in his cottage. He's asleep. Come here, closer. . . . Give me your lips. . . . So.

THE STOUT, HEAVY-PAUNCHED GENTLEMAN: Hum! Hum! (*Looks at his watch by the light of the moon, rises, walks about pensively in front of the two as they kiss, and then sits down again.*)

SHE: What a beautiful night it is!

HE: How fragrant the air is!

THE STOUT, HEAVY-PAUNCHED GENTLEMAN: Hum! Hum!

HE: Why do you tremble? Did something frighten you?

SHE: No. Kiss me again.

THE STOUT, HEAVY-PAUNCHED GENTLEMAN (*looks again at his watch by the light of the moon, rises, walks behind the bench, unseen, and lightly touches first her shoulder, then his, and disappears slowly into the background.*)

SHE: What a shudder!

HE: It's getting somewhat cold. . . .

SHE: Late, too.

HE: Let's go in. What do you say?

Has Marinetti added anything to the dramatic art with these curious experiments? Hardly a tittle. After all the Futuristic verbiage about conventional technique, he returns to it in the titular piece, as we have seen; there is nothing in the other plays

that has not for decades formed the stock-in-trade
of stage mechanics. Visions of heavenly beatitudes,
of Gretchens meant to allure Fausts, of fantastic
dreams, are a commonplace of melodrama, which
often has annihilated time and space in precisely
Marinettian manner, though with different intentions. And what is more common, more of the
past, than his arid allegory and symbolism? In
these miniature plays, if we may call them such,
Marinetti has achieved novelty of emphasis rather
than of matter or conception; he has taken the part
for the whole.

The chief importance, then, of the Futurist attack
upon the contemporary drama is that it has thrown
a lurid light upon the weaknesses of conventional
technique. Beneath all the nonsense and futility
of the Variety Theatre, beneath all the blatant
nomenclature of the Synthetic Play, lies a valid
striving away from the mere repetition of meaningless detail. Its strength—as aspiration, for the accomplishment is almost nil—is polemical, not creative; negative rather than positive. It is related to
the grinning infantilism of the Dada-ists by its laughing nihilism, and represents, as does the Dada-ist impulse, the breaking-point in the reaction against an
over-ordered, over-logical, formal, all-too-formal universe. When all is said and done, the past is an inevitable component of present and future, and the
Futuristic movement, through its very excesses,
hastened its own descent into the very past that it
abjured.

THE "TEATRO GROTESCO": LUIGI PIRANDELLO ET AL

It will be recalled that the Futurist movement in the theatre, though it employed the stage in an effort to further the war, was born before the outbreak of the great conflict.   So, too, was the so-called "grotesque" theatre, which, in its similar reaction against conventionality, resorted to methods less extreme, less offensive to the static bourgeoisie, if at times almost as disconcerting.   If to-day the grotesque theatre is not a vital factor in Italian drama, and more a symptom of artistic restlessness than a promise of achievement, it is more important potentially than the Futuristic drama.   Pirandello, only incidentally a "grotesquer," has alone done things that seem more than ephemeral, and despite all that may be urged against his plays, has brought to the Italian drama that breath of novelty which the Futurists, for all their manifestoes, could not infuse.

One of its possible sources has been traced to Bernard Shaw—chiefly on the strength, one imagines, of the designations that he has adopted for various of his plays, such as "a conversion in three acts," "a debate in one sitting," "a sermon in crude melodrama."   So do the grotesquers avoid the simple designation, in productions which, from the standpoint of content rather than nomenclature, have suggested comparison with the Grand Guignol. Chiarelli's *La Maschera e il Volto* (*The Mask and the Face*), which set the movement a-going, is called a "grotesque," whence the descriptive adjective of the school.   Pirandello's *Cosi è, se vi pare* (It's So,

If You Think It Is) is subtitled "a parable." *L'Ucello del Paradiso* (*The Bird of Paradise*), by the young and daring Enrico Cavacchioli, is denominated "a confession"—just what sort we shall presently see. And thus the style flourishes.

Silvio d'Amico[1] flouts the Shavian source. "He who knows what truly constitutes the secret of the Shavian theatre," writes the discerning Italian, "the essentially moralistic reasons behind his overturn of technique . . . will hardly succeed in discovering any substantial identity between the Christian spirit of the Irish writer and the . . . apparent frigidity of the Pirandellian forms, the prevailingly funereal, lugubrious, macabrous tones of the young authors, who think of everything except social preachment." This is, on the whole, quite so. Yet in Pirandello especially, and from the very beginning, there are social implications. What is more, a rather close comparison of the Irishman and the Italian would bring to light a certain underlying Christianity in both. D'Amico is nearer to the true state of affairs when he declares that the new dramatists can no longer believe in their own creatures— a phenomenon surely not limited to the stage nor to latter-day Italy. "Finding themselves compelled to write in a time in which, according to the assurances of the well-informed, all possible stage situations have been used . . . they try a new game. They take the old situations and try to lend them new flavor by forcing some of the elements (Chiarelli) by decentralizing them (Cavacchioli, Antonelli), by grouping them into a violent synthesis (Rosso di San Secondo). . . . In substance this is a mechan-

[1] See his very interesting *Il Teatro dei fantocci*, Vallechi Editore, Firenze. (No date.)

ical game, which in the end confers upon the plays
the single trait truly common to this entire theatre
—a marionette-like concentration." The more to
impress this point the critic indicates that the very
name "Guignol" comes from the corruption of Chig-
nol—a Bolognese puppet transplanted to France.
Your "grotesque" play, moreover, though "humoristic," is not necessarily an hilarious affair; it may
hold as many thrills as any Grand Guignol "nerve-
wrecker," but the thrills—and possibly we have here
a true distinction between the two types—may be
cerebral as well as physical. That is, the interest
may be centered not alone upon events but upon
the confusion of thought, the bewilderment of attitude induced by them.

As an example of the more obvious type of "grotesque" play, I would give the original form of Fausto
Maria Martini's *Ridi, Pagliaccio,* a one-act play
suggested by the clown of Leoncavallo's opera.

We are introduced to the waiting-room of a very
modern nerve specialist. Several patients are awaiting their turn, and with that companionship which
the discussion and exchange of symptoms so often
develops in sufferers of more or less imaginary ailments, they converse about their pet maladies,
much to the perturbation of Federico, Professor
Gambella's assistant. That worthy, who has picked
up a scrap here and there of neuropathological
knowledge, is certain that this verbal contagion of
nervous symptoms is bad for the patients; they
must tell their troubles to the doctor alone. Among
the patients is one who is sunk into a chair, as if
on the verge of complete collapse. Another, il
Cavaliere Strappa, begins a windy relation of his

particular mania to a woman patient at his side.
He cannot resist the temptation to laugh at everything; no matter what he beholds he is at once
seized with an uncontrollable impulse to shriek
with mirth; he beholds everything through grotesque
spectacles. He has come to Professor Gambella in
the hope that this torturing malady may be al-
leviated.

The patient who hitherto has listened in silence
approaches the couple; he begs their pardon; he has
been attracted by the nature of their discussion,
which, under the circumstances, he could not help
overhearing. Signor Strappa's malady interests him
exceedingly; all the more so, indeed, because it is
the very reverse of his own. He, poor fellow, has
lost his power of laughter; whatever he gazes upon
at once is transformed into a source of tears.

At last comes the turn for this gentleman's interview with the psychiatrist. His name is Giovanni
Scheffi. The doctor, quite cocksure in his powers
of divination, puts him down for a man of leisure,
since hard-working folk cannot afford the luxury of
mental ailments. Scheffi offers no contradiction.
He submits to the tests necessary to discover his
nervous reactions and patiently awaits the doctor's
verdict. It is a serious case; fortunately he has
come in time; his chief remedy lies within himself,
in his own will-power. He must above all things,
avoid the suggestions of the disagreeable, the sad.
He must not permit lugubrious friends to cross his
threshold; he must seek amusement, and center all
his efforts upon extracting the humorous from his
daily surroundings. Oh, yes, let him be sure to see
the pair of clowns that go under the name of Flick

and Flock at the Eden—the third number of the program. At this juncture Scheffi turns suddenly pale, and the doctor fears he has had another nervous attack, but the patient assures him that it is nothing. Whereupon the doctor resumes his eulogies of Flick and Flock as purveyors of curative laughter—especially Flick. Yes, yes; take that "number" in and the cure is effected. "To-morrow you'll come back to me and say, 'Dear doctor, I laughed all evening. . . .' And if you succeed in laughing for an entire evening, the victory over your nerves is won. You no longer need me; you are cured. Why, last night the contagion of laughter was so great that . . . the walls of the auditorium simply shook. Flick's comical powers are so deep and so persuasive that they extend beyond the limits of the performance. When you leave the theatre . . . you catch yourself laughing for no reason at all. Just imagine, last night a certain recollection of the performance came to my mind and the first thing I knew I found myself sitting up in the bed laughing away like a child. What had happened? There was the shadow on the wall in the very form of Flick's snout, grinning right at me! . . ."

The patient has become increasingly nervous; the doctor again questions him:

GAMBELLA: But you are ill. What's the matter? Another nervous attack?

SCHEFFI (*utterly dejected*): Ah! This is too much! Too much!

GAMBELLA: But what's the trouble?

SCHEFFI: The trouble is that I shall never again be able to look upon that fellow, Flick, who gave you such

12

pleasure last night. Because that clown, dear professor—
I am that clown, I myself. . . .

(*Gambella is stunned at the news. The two men look at
each other. The professor regains his composure.*)

GAMBELLA: You? You? I am thunderstruck. I must
admit that, as a man of science, this time I committed a
silly blunder.

SCHEFFI (*weeping*): Now you understand that I
couldn't have told you, because if I had, I would have
run the risk of not being taken seriously.

(*There is a knock at the door. Federico enters.*)

FEDERICO: Professor! Professor! Madame Giabutti
has had one of her regular epileptic attacks. Will you
see her now?

GAMBELLA: Prepare some Valerian.

(*Gambella follows Federico; Scheffi is left alone upon the
stage, still weeping.*)

SCHEFFI (*raising his face, which is bathed with tears*):
This, then. . . .

(*He strides with his accustomed bounding step toward the
large hall mirror at the rear, and greedily begins to evoke
his image there. It seems that he finds it difficult to recognize himself. He sits down, then suddenly jumps up,
kicks the chair, which is overturned, and begins to execute
before the looking-glass the twists and turns that he has
regularly performed at his café. In the meantime il Cavaliere Strappa enters through the door at the left, and seeing
that the doctor is occupied with Madame Giabutti, he exclaims:*)

STRAPPA: I can't get to see him to-day. I'll return
to-morrow. (*He crosses the room and surprises Scheffi in
his clown-like performance, and while Scheffi, with his
nose thrust against the surface of the mirror cries: "Flick,
Flick, I alone will be unable to look you in the face," Strappa
nods as if he understands, walks to the door at the right and
says to himself:*)

STRAPPA: He's not a hypochondriac. That man's crazy!

Such is the end of the playlet, which I translate from the printed version now before me; judging from the reports of the critics, the stage version ends with the clown's suicide. It is easily seen that for the stage such a definite conclusion is more effective, more "grotesque." Here indeed we have the Grand Guignol formula adapted to the purpose of intellectual as well as physical shudders.

La Maschera e il Volto, by Luigi Chiarelli, was presented by him in 1915 as a "grotesque," whence, as we saw, the name of the entire school. The plot is that of a husband who has been outraged in his marital rights. His view upon such matters is rigid; indeed, quite comparable with the "point of honor" that so long clamped its virtues upon the Spanish stage. His duty, clearly, is to slay his faithless wife. What is he to do, however, if his courage is not equal to his sense of duty? He conspires with his own wife to have it appear that he has slain her! She leaves for foreign parts and Paolo delivers himself up to the authorities, averring that he has strangled his wife and thrown her into the lake. He puts his case into the hands of his lawyer-friend Luciano Spina, ignorant, of course, of the fact that Spina is the seducer of his wife. Paolo is acquitted and returns to his home. Lo, the body of a woman is found in the lake; he must pretend to identify it as his wife and go through the funeral rites. And now appears a veiled woman, returning from her concealment in London, to congratulate her husband upon his acquittal. They arrange a clandestine meeting within a few paces of the corpse. The next morning a series of contretemps brings Savina face to face with Luciano instead of her husband, but it appears that her passion for him has cooled, so that Paolo may really feel forgiveness in his heart. But unforeseen complications arise. If he confesses the deceit practiced upon the law, he renders himself liable to thirty months' imprisonment. "What? When they believed that I had slain my wife, they let me free. Now that they discover I didn't kill her, they imprison me?" Flight is the sole resource, and off they fly, to the strains of the funeral march being played for the other woman. The corpse is a symbol of the erring wife's dead self; the new Savina "is present smiling at her own funeral, leaning on her husband's arm."

Even d'Amico, who sees in this play the one valid product of the whole movement, finds it rather conventional in dialogue and not really "grotesque" in substance. "It is only a happy ironic invention; and . . . a colorful satire upon the contemporary powerlessness to live, treated in large, certain lines, which really revive the fine comic effects, the savory scenic strokes and the caricaturesque deformations . . . of the good old times, the possibility of which has been forgotten for years." The play was a great success and went into the Italian repertory.

Taking the grotesque movement in its widest application, we find the figure of Luigi Pirandello easily the most interesting, the most pregnant in suggestion, the most successful in practice. Foreign critics will insist upon his lack of modernity, native critics will point out his essentially Sicilian make-up, but the student who approaches him undefiled by preconceptions finds in him a peculiarly sympathetic personage, easily understandable upon the basis of our common humanity. If Pirandello is a "grotesquer," then the school is as old as his literary career; if he is not—and these labels matter little— he has added to the Italian repertory a unique series of plays, of uneven worth, but of undoubted originality and not without their own suggestiveness to the sensitive contemporary in quest of deeper and wider spiritual realms.

Pirandello was born on June 28, 1867, at Girgenti, Sicily. After a thorough education in Italy he went to the University of Bonn, where he was graduated in philosophy and philology. His subsequent career has been devoted to professorship, but has permitted him enough leisure in which to produce a veritable library of books, covering a wide range and revealing a fine quality. From poetry he progressed to the novel, to criticism, to the theatre. His novel, *Il Fu Mattia Pascal* (1904), which has been translated into French and German, is one of the most original Italian books of the twentieth century, and was responsible for his stepping across the national frontier. It is written in a witty, fluent, Boccaccesque style, in which the author displays his characteristic capability of treating humorously situations of underlying seriousness. If Chiarelli's *La Maschera e il Volto* demonstrates, in d'Amico's words, the modern "powerlessness to live," what shall we say of *The Late Mattia Pascal*, who dies more than once in the course of the strange narrative? In his fiction, Pirandello has been called a "gay pessimist"—a sobriquet that seems to match his paradoxical style with a corresponding paradox; his pessimism, however, is found not to be the Anglo-Saxon type, for underneath it seems to flow a current of faith. The man's writings are really topsy-turvy, compounded of cynicism jostling against sentimentality, Christian self-abnegation rubbing elbows with anarchic denial. He is an "intellectual." One suspects in him the man whose emotions and intellect have never reached a state of stable equilibrium; now one, now the other is uppermost, with a resultant kaleidoscope of many-colored notions, ideas, feelings, reactions. He has been credited with having brought to the stage his own peculiar humor, upon which, by the way, he has written a tightly packed volume. Like most of the leading Italian men of letters, he writes too much. His best, however, is so plainly expressive of a decidedly arresting personality that it will remain as one of the traits of contemporary Italian belles-lettres. And though it is foolish to hazard prophecies, I am quite sure that his countrymen will remember him as much for his plays as for his fiction, though it is held by a number that his plays are the lesser aspect of his fecund talents.

Such an early play as *Lumie di Sicilia* (*Sicilian Limes*) is the farthest remove from the later Pirandello. It is a sweet little one-act trifle in which a rustic youth whose sacrifice has enabled his sweetheart to develop into a world-famous prima donna, comes to meet her years after their childhood days. The gulf between them yawns despairingly great; he is the simple countryman still, she the spoiled beauty of a hundred capitals. The great singer, educated at the expense of her provincial lover, has achieved her fame at the cost of her better self, while the lover, outwardly a boor, is inwardly the artist he had hoped she would become. At the end Sina distributes to her assembled guests the Sicilian limes that her lover had brought for her; even so prodigal has she been with her own transplanted gifts. Tender sentimentality, then, but simple and affecting; more's the pity that in a recent revision of the play Pirandello saw fit to spoil it all by having Sina burst into a momentary fit of remorse while the rustic leaves her implacably.

It would be bootless to take up the entire Pirandellian output. Certain of the larger plays stand out for novelty of presentation or ingenuity of construction, and it is these one should know for a proper appreciation of their author's relation to the Italian drama.

We may, then, pass over with scant attention, such productions as *Pensaci, Giacomino, Il Giuoco delle Parti, Ma non è una cosa seria,* and even the recent *Come prima meglio di prima* and *Tutto per Bene.* The first, *Just Think, Giacomino,* is a queer mingling of farce, comedy, and melodrama, illustrative of Pirandello's pitying attitude toward the creatures of life who are plunged by circumstances into ridiculous ventures. There is plenty of indignation against conventional morality, but it comes from a figure who is not so much a character as a stilted principle in action. The fillip of the play derives its force from the situation of an elderly professor who, having married a very young girl in order to wreak vengeance upon the government, which will have to pay her his pension for many a

year, acts as intermediary between her and her
lover. So, too, *The Chess Game* is a drama of situation in which the supposedly meek husband sends
his wife's lover to the duel brought about by the
wife's machinations, thus turning the tables. *It's
Nothing Serious* depicts the fortunes of an amorous
blade who weds a homely boarding-house girl in
self-protection, finally falling in love with her as she
shows her true mettle and improves in looks as a
result of the care and air she never knew before.
(A sort of inversion of the theme treated by Sabatino Lopez in *Il Brutto e le Belle*.) Like *The Chess
Game*, this is a comedy of intellectual rather than
external situation, yet quite devoid of more than
passing humor or characterization. One may not
question the human significance of the puppets,
but they lack dramatic existence. Pirandello, intellectual that he is, finds greater interest in themes
than in persons; if his theatre is largely a play of
marionettes—as is, for that matter, the theatre of
the "grotesquers"—it is because philosophical preoccupation in all artistic forms tends to reduce
human beings to symbols of thought. It is the rare
artist who vivifies the symbol that is every human
being.

The better Pirandello is discoverable in such striking, ingenious tours de force as *Così è, se vi pare*
(*It's So, If You Think It Is*), his very recent *Sei
personaggi in cerca d'autore* (*Six Characters In Quest
of a Playwright*), and the social drama *Se non così*
(*If Not Thus*), lately re-entitled *La ragione degli
altri*.

Se non così seems to show the influence of Bracco's
feministic plays and is interesting as tract, if nothing

else.   But Pirandello is always seeking the novel
point of view.   His treatment of the eternal triangle, whatever else it may lack, does manage in
the numerous plays he has dedicated to it, to get
out of the beaten path.   The play turns upon the
desire of Leonardo's wife to have a child, even if it
be the daughter of her husband by his mistress,
Elena.   And in the end her plea for this species of
vicarious motherhood is granted by both the willing husband and the reluctant Elena.   Admitting
the plausibility of the wife's views, the play is really
strong and moving.   There is little drama in the
text-book sense of the word, despite some striking
scenes in the second and third acts, for the "action"
consists chiefly in the working out of Livia's views
and the dialogue that arises from the exposition of
them.   In an interesting, somewhat Shavian Letter
to the Female Protagonist of the Play, Pirandello
explains his purpose in the guise of a note, telling
the leading character what an unattractive part
she has, and how difficult it will be for her to find
a leading lady to essay the rôle.

It's So, If You Think It Is is one of the pivotal
plays of the Pirandellian canon.   At the center of
the author's method lies a philosophical conception
of man as a complex of many selves and of reality
as a tissue of countless illusions.   Unity in thought
or action thus becomes but another illusion, and the
true reality is whatever we happen to think at the
moment.   "It's so, if you think it is," and, as the
author might have added, "You are, if you think
you are."   The plot, called a "parable," moves with
a swiftness necessary to such a conception; it becomes bewildering, and, indeed, if it is to delight an

audience, must not permit them to linger too long over the palpable absurdities of the intellectual farce—for such it is. This is not, like the greatest art, an unfolding of beautiful experience. It is an anarchistic philosophical essay written in people instead of words. But the inescapable truth is that it has delighted cultured audiences who do not hesitate to choose between conformity to formula and actuality of impression.

The new secretary to the prefect of an Italian town comes with his wife and his mother-in-law. Queerly enough, his wife is kept isolated by him, and his mother-in-law can go to see her daughter only in the courtyard, never entering the home. This arouses the curiosity of the Agazzi family, whose head is the commissioner of the town and whose wife and daughter are among the leading society gossips of the place. All the more so since the mother-in-law, Signora Frola, lives in the same building as they. Ponza explains that the mother-in-law is demented; that his wife is not really her daughter (who died four years ago), but another, whom she has taken it into her head is her daughter Lina, his first wife. She, on the other hand, tells a different story, saying that her son-in-law so ruined the health of her daughter by excessive love at their marriage that she had to be placed in a sanitarium, and that he became obsessed with the idea that she had died, and that seeing her again, he imagined it a new love affair, and a second ceremony was gone through to humor him. At the same time Signora Frola humored him in his ideas as to her (Frola's) demented condition. Gossip asks which of the two is the crazy one. Sides are taken. Lamberto Laudisi, brother-in-law of Councillor Agazzi, is the raisonneur of the play,—a sort of philosophical gracioso type, who ridicules both sides and so confuses them with added hypotheses that he makes them fear that he'll get them all crazy before the matter is cleared up. Finally it is suggested that if Frola and her son-in-law are brought together in Agazzi's, the truth must come out. In an excellent scène-à-faire this is done (act two), but leaves more doubt than ever! At last Laudisi, maliciously, no doubt, hits upon the idea of asking the wife the true state of affairs. (They have been in an earthquake and all documents of the town they came from have been destroyed, while affidavits from residents of that place are hazy and merely add confusion and perplexity.) The wife comes and says that she is both the daughter of Signora Frola and the second wife of Ponza. Whereupon Laudisi triumphantly bursts out laughing.

SIGNORA PONZA: What? The truth; it's simply this: that I am the daughter of Signora Frola, and also the second wife of Signor Ponza; yes, and to myself, neither, neither!

THE PREFECT: Ah, no, to yourself, madam, you must be one or the other!

SIGNORA PONZA: No, sir. To myself I am that which I am believed to be!

LAUDISI: Behold, gentlemen, how speaks Truth! Are you satisfied? Ha, ha, ha!

In the second act there is an interesting, original, and illuminative soliloquy of Laudisi's with his image in the mirror:

"Well, my dear chap? Which is the madman of us two? Oh, I know. I say You. And you say I.

You, you! And again, I. . . . There, there;
face to face with each other we know each other
well! The trouble is that others don't see you as I
do! And in that case, my dear boy, what becomes
of you? I say to myself that here, in front of you,
I see myself and touch myself—you, as soon as
you're seen by others, what do you become? A
fantasm, dear chap, a fantasm! Well, do you see
these mad folk? Without paying any attention to
the fantasms they carry with themselves, in themselves, they run about, filled with curiosity, in chase
of others' fantasms! And they imagine it's a different matter. . . ."

A philosophical piece, then, in which the author
displays toward the reader the same malicious,
taunting attitude that Laudisi shows toward the
other spectators. As the author says, it is a parable;
plainly, then, he meant to inculcate the lesson that
truth is much a matter of seeming, and that there
may be more than one truth—as many, in fact, as
there are persons and even circumstances. And
when at last we think we discover the truth (Signora Ponza) she gives us a Delphic reply. Is there
truth? Is truth a Delphic oracle? And what a
strange, silly sight we present chasing after it with
more of the inquisitive gossip in us than of the
serious searcher after any real good! And how for-
getful of our own similar position in our inquiries
after the strange aspect of others! Laudisi sums it
up in his talk to himself before the mirror. For
isn't the whole world a mirror, and aren't we con-
tinuously puzzled with our own reflections—whether
they occur in mirrors or in the hearts, souls, and
actions of others?

The end, as in so many of Pirandello's plays, is somewhat weak. Need it be pointed out that the piece is in Pirandello's characteristic, dualistic mood of sober humor?

Later dramas like *Tutto per Bene* and *Come prima meglio di prima* represent industry rather than creative impulse; Pirandello must keep the theatres supplied with fuel, and marks time with just such superficial, conscienceless trash as this. The first has all the earmarks of its pattern: "papers," dubious paternity, and that hoary band. The second is not so much a play of deep passion as of hectic speech, in which a woman, recovering from an attempt at suicide, is taken back by her husband to the household she deserted when her child was three years old—that is, thirteen years previous. Her true status is kept secret for the sake of that daughter, who, coming upon the discovery that no marriage certificate exists (again the "papers!") thinks her father unlawfully in union with this woman. A new baby comes to the mother, leading to the revelation of the truth. Note Pirandello's need of dealing with personages compelled to appear in a double social rôle; his fondness for multiple personality. In his worst and his best alike, the man is primarily a spectator of human complications and follies, atracted more by the intellectual problems inherent in them than by the passions engendered.

Six Characters in Quest of a Playwright redeems him from such pot-boilers as these. Produced this year at Rome with signal success, and shortly afterward acted in London with flattering outcome, it is in the vein of *Così è, se vi pare*. By a natural process of his restless, introspective, curious mind, he turns upon himself with quasi-Shavian satire against the playwright and with comic situations arising from the strange rehearsal into which the players of the piece are forced. Here is a dramatist's holiday, and a critic's as well. He pokes fun at himself, converses with himself about the problems of the drama in general, and finally solves the difficulty with a bullet shot that solves nothing at all. The old plight of Pirandello—and how many countless others!—the hastened, arbitrary ending, so as to have done with it all and ring down the curtain.

Perhaps it is one's hope that seems to detect in this play a sign of Pirandello's coming abandonment of the old-fashioned eternal triangle, to which he has tried to give a new twist, yet which burdens his production unduly. I would not be understood as opposing the "triangle" here on moral grounds, nor would I agree with Dr. Lander MacClintock in his valuable *The Contemporary Drama of Italy* (page 258) that the triangle "is a fashion, a literary convention, and not a record of a social condition in Italy or any other country." Our institution of marriage is breaking up; the triangle, among other things, is a symbol of human chafing in social bonds; it always existed, and whatever the form that eventually supplants marriage as we know it, will always exist as a token of man's (and woman's) rebellion against enforced monogamy. (The important word here is, not monogamy, but enforced.) To return to Pirandello, I merely mean that he is too much preoccupied with it—a question of proportion, not a concession to Mrs. Grundy. Certainly enough it looks as if he had started out this time to write something quite as bad as the two dramas that went before and was seized, in the middle of the task, with misgivings and with a spirit of harsh self-criticism. Having entangled himself in a snarl of marital and extra-marital difficulties, and finding himself hard put to it to extricate not only characters but himself, he seems to have turned about face and aimed the question at the audience. In other words, though the teasing title is *Six Characters in Quest of a Playwright*, the reality is a playwright in quest of what to do with his six characters. And what has he done but bring them upon the "boards" and let them argue out their own case before the public? It is as if the stage has become the teeming brain of Professor Pirandello, and the audience, by some strange psychic license, has been permitted to look right into the throbbing mechanism of a dramatist's mind at work. This sounds something like the monodrama as written and produced by the queer Russian Evreinov, and, to be sure, there is not a little similarity between the manner in which the Italian treats his problem and that in which Evreinov has presented it in his one-act *Theatre of the Soul*. But where Evreinov makes no break between the representation of the soul's unconscious and outer reality, Pirandello is compelled to differentiate between his inchoate characters of the play that is yet to be written and the flesh-and-blood actors and stage director to whom they come in their eagerness to be made into a drama.

The play, nominally, is continuous, but the dramatist manages to introduce two logical waits, during one of which the curtain actually is lowered by a

supposed error of the stage hands. Thus there is
preserved a strict unity of time, place, and action—
more rigid, indeed, than that called for by a much
misinterpreted Greek gentleman named Aristotle.
It must have amused Pirandello that he was able
literally to have unity in variety by lowering partial
"sets" upon the stage, thus achieving the effect of
a change of place without moving from the spot, as
it were. And this, perhaps, was the least of his
pleasures, for the structure of his play affords him
opportunity to play with the new lighting, to indulge in the philosophical chatter that he so dearly
loves, and to disport himself with the paradoxes to
which his very conception perforce gives rise.

As the audience enters it discovers a stage with
curtain raised and no scene set. It is for all the
world as if one had come in just before a private
rehearsal and discovered the theatre in its work-day
clothes. And, indeed, a rehearsal is about to take
place—that of a "play by Pirandello entitled *Il
Giuoco delle Parti*. (*The Chess Game*, one of the
earlier dramas, essentially of situation, in which the
emphasis is shifted to psychological rather than external clashes, and in which the clever husband manages to turn the tables upon his wife and her lover.
Though there is an evident desire to impart new
thrills to the old, old, eternal triangle, there is little
characterization, the humor is acrid, and at times
even grim, while the action is hardly compelling.)
The rehearsal begins and the director is soon argu-
ing with his actors about the merits of the play.
Of course it's ridiculous, he answers, "but what
can I do about it if no more good plays come to us
from France and we are reduced to staging plays by

Pirandello—plays in which you can't understand a
thing, written purposely by the author so as to
make fun of me, of you, and of the public?"

No sooner have they resumed work than the
doorman comes upon the stage announcing to the
director the intrusion of a strange sextet who insist
upon seeing him. (It is to be noted that the stage
directions call for a certain halo of light to surround
the strangers, as a suggestion of their "fantastic
reality." As they advance to converse with the
actors the light disappears, yet they are to preserve
during the entire action a suggestion of their dream-
quality.) These six persons are the cast of the
drama that Pirandello did not write. They have
come to the stage director with their tale of woe,
that he may write them up in a play and thus en-
dow them with that dramatic existence which they
crave. Of course they are received with quizzical
anger, which soon subsides into amused curiosity.

Their tale, as it is slowly extracted from them, is
strange enough. The father, upon the birth of his
first son, sent him off to be nursed in the country,
where he might grow up morally and physically
sound. A rival, at first unwitting, has appeared
upon the scene in the shape of his secretary; at last
things come to a pass where the husband, in all good
humor, sends his wife off to the other man, together
with whom she raises a family. The father, as men
will do, lives a rather careless life until one day he
comes upon his own stepdaughter in a brothel and
learns the horrible truth. The poor mother imagines
that she is earning her living at Madame Pace's as
a seamstress; in reality Madame Pace employs
the mother only as a blind to the real purposes for

13

which she uses the stepdaughter. Here, then, are two separate families held loosely together by the sorrowful figure of the mother. There are other complications that need not detain us; it is important only to indicate the surly reticence of the grown-up son, who has steadily objected to dragging this domestic imbroglio on to the stage, and the quiet youth whose suicide ends both their tale and the play as presented by Pirandello.

The stage director is interested; so much so that he would at once set about arranging the play, distributing the parts and rehearsing the salient scenes. The actors are astonished at their director's resolution. "Is he really in earnest?" asks the leading man. "This is sheer madness!" exclaims the jeune première. And a third: "Are they going to have us improvise a drama here, just as we stand?" . . . "Like the actors of the Commedia dell' Arte!" snarls the jeune premier.

LEADING LADY: Does he imagine I'm going to lend myself to jokes of this sort!

JEUNE PREMIÈRE: Me, neither!

A FOURTH ACTOR: I'd like to know who those people are (*referring to the six persons*).

THE THIRD ACTOR: Who do you think? Lunatics and meddlers!

JEUNE PREMIÈRE: And does he listen to what they say?

JEUNE PREMIER: Vanity, that's what it is. The vanity of figuring as an author.

FIRST ACTOR: Who ever heard the like! If the stage, my dear people, is to sink as low as this . . .

A FIFTH ACTOR: I find this extremely funny!

THIRD ACTOR: Bah! What's the odds? Let's see what comes of it!

As the actors leave the stage the curtain remains
up. The play is interrupted for about twenty minutes. There is something more than mere novelty
in thus leaving the curtain up. The director has
retired with the six persons, so that they may arrange some sort of scenario to follow in building up
the play. By allowing the stage to remain visible
during the interval, the audience is in a sense made
a participant in the wait of the actors. The time
during which the stage is left empty is precisely the
time that passes between what we may call the first
act and the second.

The attempt to enact in rehearsal the scenario
that has been tentatively agreed upon affords the
opportunity for such effects as have now grown
quite old in the service of rehearsal scenes. The
whole story has not yet come out, and as the trial
scenes are gone over, new details keep cropping up,
sounding like one thing as spoken by the persons
who have lived them, and like quite another as
enacted by the artists to whom the parts have been
entrusted. Whence arises cause for speculation upon
the true nature of reality, upon the function of fact
upon the stage as opposed to the higher reality of
art, and sundry other considerations that fail but
rarely to occupy the Pirandellian mind. Enthusiastic
over a culminating scene, the director cries "Curtain!" to signify that the scene may stand exactly
as acted, with the climax at that particular point.
The machinist, mistaking the director's outcry, actually lowers the curtain, leaving the director and
the father before the footlights. They make their
way behind the scenes with the director loud in his
praises of the first act that they have just impro-

vised and rehearsed. Now comes the rehearsal of
the second, in which the trials and outcome are
much like what has preceded, except that the youth
of the tale takes it into his head to end his life, thus
terminating the drama.

What Pirandello has done, then, is to present his
drama without presenting it. He has shown us the
characters, told their tale through their own mouths,
and allowed them to argue the matter out before
his audience. He has, moreover, had them argue
the matter out with the very actors to whom their
parts would be entrusted. And all the time, of
course, he has been discussing the matter with himself. In all conscience, then, this is, as the sub-
title has it, a "play yet to be written." Not a play,
thus, in the conventional sense, yet surely a spectacle upon the stage, and one that affords intellectual delight. It is in no way, however, a practical demonstration of dramaturgy; the foundations
are psychological. "The drama dwells in us," says
the father when he first comes upon the stage.
"And we are impatient to perform it just as our
inner passion urges us." The end suggests the half-
mocking close of the author's best piece, *Così è, se
vi pare*. "He's truly dead!" cry several of the
actors after the climactic shot has been fired. "No!"
cry several others. "It's all a make-believe! Just
make-believe!" Whereupon the father utters a
piercing shriek: "Who said make-believe? Reality,
gentlemen. Reality!" And at last the director:
"Make-believe! Reality! To the devil with the
whole bunch of you! The like of this never happened to me before! And here's a whole day gone
to waste!"

The self-critical implications of the play are quite true to the Pirandellian method, as is the dialogue and the speculation of the characters. So that when the author brings himself and his players upon the scene he is but faithful to his personal methods as already shown in the best of his previous work. It would then be short-sighted to attribute all of the novelty in the newest play to such possible instigators as Shaw's *Fanny's First Play*. That Shaw has influenced Pirandello more or less superficially there can be little doubt; yet as Marco Praga has remarked, Pirandello may be an Italian Shaw, but he is a very Italian one. So Italian, in fact, that few of his plays, in all likelihood, will ever be received outside of the peninsular boundaries, unless by that small audience in every land which realizes the really superficial traits separating one people from another, and is willing to abandon the narrowly national mood for that larger one connoted by valid cosmopolitanism.

"Do you know what I think?" asks the director during one of the many trying moments of the rehearsal added to a rehearsal. "That you people" (this to the unrealized personages) "are trying to adopt the manner of a certain author for whom I feel a particular detestation. . . . In fact, I was just rehearsing one of his pieces when you came in. . . . And here's a fine exchange we've made. From the frying-pan into the fire!" The change from *Il Giuoco delle Parti* to *Sei personaggi in cerca d'autore*, however, is surely no falling from the frying-pan into the flames. The first is Pirandello almost at his worst; the second, Pirandello pretty near his best.

Plays continue to flow from his pen with astonishing ease, perhaps because they are chiefly the product of thought rather than experience, and aim at elucidation rather than illumination of vital passion. The newest, *Enrico IV*, follows the mood and manner of *Così è, se vi pare* and *Sei personaggi in cerca d'autore*. A Roman gentleman on his way to a masked ball in the guise of Henry IV of olden Germany, meets with an accident that makes him really believe he is the ancient potentate; later recovering from his madness, he finds it to his advantage to continue simulating it; when, finally, he confesses his deceit, the confusion is greater than ever. The stock Pirandellian theme of multiple personality, of illusion's predominance over reality, with the same sudden, arbitrary way out of it by means of a bullet.

Pirandello, easily one of the most interesting and entertaining of latter-day dramatists, is not so easily admitted into the ranks of the indispensable few. If, following the rigid canons of Storm Jameson, we must have plays with which to amuse the warrior in his leisure, there they are. Like a lesser Shaw, Pirandello ventilates issues, shifts personages over the chess-board of his fancy, forms new combinations with the colored glass of his dramaturgic kaleidoscope. Far less of a dialectician than Shaw, inferior to him in a grasp of the modern world, in wit and contemporaneity, he yet suggests the Irishman by his very dilution of these qualities. What has he written? Are they plays at all? I leave such questions to the pedagogues. Pirandello's best productions are a welcome addition to the modern

stage; if no category exists for them, why, someone
will have to invent one for them, that is all.

The activities of the rest of the "grotesquers" are
more fervid than important. A few representative
examples will suffice.

Rosso di San Secondo first came to Italian notice
with his *Marionette, Che Passione!* (literally, "Puppets,
What Passion!"), in three acts and a prelude, not
including the advice given by the author to the
actors in a page of the printed version. "The actors
must bear in mind," he writes, "that this is a play
of desperate pauses. The words pronounced in it
always conceal an exasperation which cannot be
communicated except in sapient silences. The ar-
bitrariness, moreover, that may appear in the play,
resulting from the torment in which the personages
are plunged, should not give way to comic effect,
but rather to a feeling of tragic 'humorism.' For,
suffering indeed profoundly human pangs, the three
protagonists of the drama are like marionettes, and
the wire that pulls them is passion.

"They are all human beings: human beings reduced to puppets.

"And therefore, deeply pitiful!"

The prelude is a quasi prose-poem, apostrophiz-
ing the "long Sunday afternoons, with the deserted
streets, the closed shops, and a desolate grey sky
over the grime of the city!" It is not part of the
action, but seeks to do for it, interpretatively, what
the advice to the actors would do histrionically.
The action itself takes place in Milan, on a Sunday
afternoon and evening. The "grotesquers," then,

have not altogether abolished the unity of time; since in this respect, through this play, Rosso di San Secondo is more Greek than the Greeks. Such reversion to antiquity is one of the queer signs of ultra-modernity. The characters have no names; they are such creatures as "The Woman in the Blue Fox," "The Man in Grey," "The Gentleman in Mourning," "The Singer," "He Who Should Not Have Come," and others less distinguished but hardly less vague. We are introduced to a telegraph office, into which, even on a Sunday, come rushing all the phases of life from birth to death, with the mid-point of marriage. The "Man in Mourning" strikes up an acquaintance with "The Woman in the Blue Fox;" each has an unhappy connubial past and is drawn to the other by nascent hopes, perhaps of a better future in common. The "Man in Grey" overhears and impulsively urges them against such a course. Yet the next act finds him following close upon "The Man in Mourning," into the house where the blue-fox lady stays. The men quarrel over the woman, swayed this way and that by passion, and at last, reconciled, plan a party with the woman and her friend, "The Singer." They adjourn to a hotel for their supper of reconciliation, when who should appear at the crucial moment but Mme. Blue Fox's husband, who wins his spouse away from the disconcerted diners. "The Man in Grey" takes poison; "The Singer" mourns him, while "The Man in Mourning" turns now to "The Singer" for consolation. The curtain descends upon the general dissatisfaction of the actors —and of the audience, too, if the printed page counts for anything.

There is evident attempt to bring to the stage new backgrounds, new personages. The total effect, however, is one of hysteria. The directions for the first act are that it be recited throughout in a low voice punctuated by long pauses. Not linked sweetness, but disjointed gruffness, long drawn out. Even from this play it is discernible that the grotesque theatre seeks to be largely a theatre of ideas, even of abstraction, reflected in a distorting mirror. Lawyers, business men, and the regular types are yielding to psychiatrists and that ilk, in both fiction and the drama—and discoverably in the United States as well as in Italy. The ghost—nay, too often the corporeal substance of Freud—stalks through the pages of our native products. Glaspell, O'Neill, and, in a humbler way, Miss Gerstenberg, bear testimony for the stage of America; in Germany, Wedekind; in Russia, Evreinov; in Italy, Cavacchioli—the names are juxtaposed without any implications of artistic equality. We are in the psychoanalytic age of letters and the stage yields its share of the evidence.

Rosso di San Secondo's latest play, a recent one, is called *L'Ospite Desiderato* (*The Desired Guest*)—a "tragic event in three acts." Here, too, is advice for the actors, which reads as follows: "The action of the drama, though essentially human, is born of a nightmare-state of the mind. Reality is, therefore, there transfigured into alarmed and varied syntheses such as characterize horrible dreams. The actors, therefore, both in voice and in gesture, will convey throughout a suggestion of the somnambulistic and the anxious that shall transmit to the spectator not only the essential trait of the per-

sonage represented, but the atmosphere of painful
lyrism in which that personage moves." In contrast with the previous play, the persons are only
five in number.   Melina uses her servant Adelgisa
as a sort of cat's-paw, attributing to the servant all
her own feelings and desires.   The same methods
she employs with her husband, Paride Malviti, almost convincing him that it was he, and not she,
who desired as guest Stefano Brosia.   The guest
himself is somewhat in the dark, but he comes.
Why has he been invited?   The question rises
stronger than ever in the second act.   Was it that
Melina wished variety?   Because her husband
needed him?

In any case, Melina is a bare-faced, cunning siren,
who works her will upon poor Adelgisa until the
servant rebels, going so far as to offer herself to
Stefano rather than see him a slave to the volup-
tuous mistress.   At a banquet (Act Three) prepared
by Melina for Stefano, the latter pretends, at the
climax of the festivities, to hear his friend Malviti's
groans.   He goes off to fetch the husband and suddenly turns about face in attitude, declaring that he
will accept Adelgisa's offer, and that Melina still
loves her husband.   The angry Melina dashes for
Adelgisa, but the guest gives to the servant the
knife with which she may slay the mistress.   And
now Stefano cries to the husband that they are both
free of the servant and the mistress alike; he summons help to catch the murderess in *flagrante delictu*,
as it were, and together with the maltreated husband
makes his escape.

Thus recounted, in staccato form, the play sounds
worse than it is, for the reader cannot deny it several
dramaturgic qualities of a fairly high order.   Grant-

ing the special technique, the dialogue is at times fine, as is the peculiar psychology and the suspense. One does get a real feeling of Melina's wiles; her words, their visible influence over the characters, her cunning art of so shifting her wishes that they appear the wishes of others—these are tokens of a gift that seems, on the whole, somewhat misemployed, or rather, tentatively groping. Grant the sincerity of these new writers and it is easy to feel a certain relief that they choose such queer channels for their art rather than the deep ruts of older paths. But sincerity is the one thing that some of their critics refuse to attribute to them. Melina, in the second act, recites her own defense—and, for that matter, the defense of the woman whom she typifies: "No, my friend. Don't wonder that I should be able to play a part so well. Leave, I pray you, to woman her rights to falsify . . .   She has recourse to it perforce; to make men understand certain details that, in any other manner, they would not grasp; to lead them toward necessary resolutions, which otherwise they would not reach, restrained as they are by a thousand scruples that we women don't possess. . . ."

Worse, if possible, though not less interesting from the student's standpoint, is Cavacchioli's *She Who Resembles You* (*Quella che t'Assomiglia*), which, from beginning to end is, as a play, utterly bad. A technique of spectres, puppets, and abstraction furnishes amusement of a sort not intended by the young writer. Here, as in *The Bird of Paradise*, is an inept mingling of this world and the other, of genre and device, constituting a distinctly retrogressive step. Because a man is of the scientific persuasion, he must go around, to reveal his engineering proclivities, with small wheels where his eyes are supposed to be. The professor of the play —a chiromancer, by the way—uses different lights in his office, according to the supposed nature of the visitor. One of those visitors must, of course, be a woman with whom he develops a liaison. Her husband, a new Enoch Arden, returns from the war, blind. The struggle is now between the two men for the woman, who, when at last the choice is definitely presented to her, repeats the tale of Ibsen's *Lady from the Sea* and Shaw's *Candida*, by choosing the husband.

Most outlines violate a play so sketched; this one does the play more than justice, for it does not mention the child's play of the engineer's puppets, used much as Marinetti has used similar marionettes in his *Elettricità Sessuale*; it does not tell of the ghost of Gabriella's husband, who alternates with his own reality, nor of the mystical effects of organ tones and like theatricalities. It conveys no notion of the actual nightmare-effects achieved. The strange part of it all is that these plays have been produced, and by such actors as Virgilio Talli. For a combination of distraction, imagination gone astray, emptiness of content, and futility of means, they are difficult to match in any civilized nation. It is not a question of a new technique that must companion a new idea. These writers have no new ideas. Pirandello, eminent before them, retains his pre-eminency now. He is bigger than the "grotesque" movement, which, thus far, has but groped in the dark to a greater darkness. As an æsthetic, as well as a national institution, the Italian theatre is in a bad way.

SOUTH AMERICA

SOUTH AMERICA

The drama in South America, whether in the cluster of republics that speak Spanish or in vast Portuguese-speaking Brazil, has undergone but sporadic development. Though in a number of the countries it may be studied with interest in the work of salient individuals, it yet fails to present that ordered progress which produces the impression of a national product. If, then, I choose the stage of Buenos Aires and Montevideo for chief consideration, it is because here, at least, may be followed something like an evolution from mere imitation to autonomous production, and because, moreover, that stage presents a number of historic novelties. The history of most drama reveals a religious origin; the Yiddish stage, however, was born of the restaurants of Rumania, with their song-loving exiles; the Argentino-Uruguayan stage possesses the unique distinction of having been cradled in a circus-ring. Here, too, we come upon the romantic figure of the *gaucho*, who has not yet disappeared from the national literature, though he is as extinct in national life as is our own cowboy counterpart. And, to prove that one touch of civilization makes the whole theatrical world kin, the Argentine stage to-day boasts as trivial comedies and revues as may be matched in any capital of Europe or the United States, with an organization of managers that is as

impervious to beauty as any Broadway potentate
of the proscenium.

The immediate outlook for the genuine development of the theatre in Argentina is not regarded as
highly encouraging, despite a number of authors
capable of good work. The comment of those
critics whose lines are worth reading is anything
but cheerful, and it is to be suspected—from such
as we are able to read in print—that the dramas to
which their profession takes them provide only too
valid a basis for their plaints.

Two chief causes have been brought forward to
explain the undoubted decline through which the
better play is passing in Buenos Aires: first, the exaggerated commercial character of the managers—
a cry that has become synonymous, it would seem,
with management the world over—and second, the
Society of Authors, where the chief topic of discussion is not drama, but money.

A sign of the times appears in the announcements
issued by stage managements and by the authors'
society itself: the amounts of money made on the
various plays are blazoned forth, and the authors
are listed, by their own society, in the order of their
financial success for the preceding season. All this,
and more, from the pen of Antonio Viergol, who is
not an Argentine, but who is so well known in the
country and knows its stage so well, that his opinion
was requested and given—be it said in his honor—
with the utmost candor.

Viergol finds the Argentine stage suffering from
what he calls "metalization"—the greed for coin.
The artistic aspect has so far disappeared that the
business is really a form of industrial exploitation,

and the aims of the founders have been forgotten. A veritable "manufacturers' trust" is the result, through which the supply of plays is controlled by a would-be monopoly, as in any industrial circle. Such a state of affairs works in two directions. By its positive action it vitiates the public taste and the authors who are willing to cater to it; negatively, it keeps the genuine artists from producing the plays which are foredoomed to inadequate presentation and reception. Among these better dramatists are men like Iglesias Paz, González Castillo, Martínez Cuitiño, Otto M. Cione, García Velloso (author of a history of his nation's letters), Pérez Petit (a good novelist), Roberto Payró (another). It is the opinion of more than one competent judge that the times are ready for change. The query is, how long will it take for the change to become effective?

One question—and a fundamental one—that Viergol did not touch upon in his reply, which was in reality a personal letter to a friend rather than a treatise, was years ago pointed out by the best known Argentine theatrical critic, and, incidentally, one of the most readable of the modern men of the theatre. Juan Pablo Echagüe, critic for the *Nación*, is in his writings a well-balanced nationalist, alert to the sincerity of real artistry.

As far back as 1907 he indicated the root of the evil that blighted so vast a percentage of native dramaturgical effort. That effort was not genuinely native. It did not observe directly from life, but wrote with an eye upon other nations and other men's books. It had no feeling for the sterner art of the theatre—that art which eschews extended exposition and the relation of events instead of

14

presenting them synthetically. He had harsh words for the contemporary productions, but his harshness was born of his love for the theatre, for his nation and fellow men. If he spoke of "desolating mediocrity" and the "disquieting superabundance" of the plays, he was none the less eager to praise the good, and his labors are indubitably one of the factors that will aid in the restoration of the Argentine theatre.

To Jean Paul the Argentine stage, from the very circumstances of its surroundings and its soil, should be essentially a place of optimism and confidence in the present and the future, "with a comforting moral leaven." Just what is to emerge from the contemporary era of money and trade cannot be predicted, but so perspicacious a thinker as Francisco Garciá Calderón, in commenting upon a collection of Jean Paul's critical reviews, sees the rise of a new comic impulse, which will be fed by the types produced in a country where new fortunes make a sort of new-world "bourgeois gentilhomme"; he sees, too, the possibility of a varied scene revealing the contact of the different races that are building up that new world, the drama of advancing democratic ideals, and so on.[1]

But there is little to feed such hopes, in the present product, at least. To have great poets, Whitman told us, there must be great audiences, too. Argentine has the poets, the playwrights; but has it,

---

[1] See Echagüe's *Un Teatro en Formación*, Buenos Aires. Señor Echagüe's views exhibit a somewhat excessive eagerness to turn the stage to didactic, and even "moral," purposes. He does not seem to possess a deep sense of dynamic æsthetics, and his otherwise admirable critiques suffer from an undercurrent of moralistic suggestion. He is, in short, a transition-critic of a transition-drama. A useful book to be read as a corrective to Echagüe is Alfredo A. Bianchi's *Teatro Nacional*, Buenos Aires.

yet, the audiences, the managers, the national auditorium?

THE "GAUCHO"

For a proper appreciation of the strange plays that developed out of the circus-ring interludes, one should have an outline knowledge, at least, of the poetry of Argentina and Uruguay as represented by those authors who helped to establish and carry on the literary tradition of the *gaucho* type. The *gaucho* himself, if not entirely a mystery, is much of a puzzle from his very origin. Indeed, the word itself is a philological problem. We have it on high authority that it was neither known nor written in Spain before it was brought over from the western hemisphere. According to the noted Argentine scholar, Paul Groussac, it is an Incaic term, signifying orphan, abandoned, wandering, with a somewhat derogatory connotation, and was originally *guacho*, the change occurring by the well-known linguistic phenomenon of metathesis. It was this form of the word, by the way, that Walter Scott employed, being the first to give the term wide currency in our tongue. And it was Carlyle, in his essay upon the Paraguayan tyrant, Dr. Francia, who presented an interpretation of the *gaucho* which has won high praise from South Americans for its perspicacity. According to another etymology, *gaucho* comes from an Araucanian word for "comrade." The origin of the type itself, however, is less troublesome; the *gaucho* is not an indigenous product; he is, like his songs and his troubadours, (called *payadores* or *cantores*) of partly Andalusian parentage. From birth habituated to the vast extent of the pampas he acquires a bravery that is, like his other attributes, the product of his environment acting upon mixed hereditary influences—often the union of Spanish and Indian blood. That same vast solitude is perhaps the cause of his pensive moods; his poetry is the reflection of his heart. He is a born singer. In the lines of Hernández' famous *gaucho* poem *Martín Fierro:*

> Yo no soy cantor letrao
> mas si me pongo a cantar
> no tengo cuando acabar
> y me envezco cantando.
> Las coplas me van brotando
> como agua de manantial.

(I am not a lettered singer, but once I begin to sing I never can stop, and I grow old singing. The verses gush from me like water from a spring.) His poetry is half his interpretation of nature as he knows it; superstition is the other half. Witches and medicine men play an important part in his life, as do music and love. He is generous to a fault, and indolent as well. His independence, upon provocation, becomes a romantic sort of outlawry; his love, likewise, may blossom into bloody flowers; even into his poetry and minstrelsy he injects the element of rivalry, and enjoys the spectacle of two contesting bards determined to outwit each other at the game of jesting and caustic improvisation.

In the opinion of a recent writer upon the attractive theme, the *gaucho* was (for the type is fast disappearing) above all a transplanted Andalusian. In the early days of emigration to the New World, Andalusia, because of its situation, furnished a ready point of embarkation.

These transplanted Andalusians felt quite at home on the sunny stretches of the Rio de la Plata. Themselves a fusion of Aryan and Semitic strains, they reproduced their ancient life in their new surroundings, even carrying over peculiarities of the Andalusian dialect. From Andalusia, too, they imported their beloved guitar, as well as the sensual sadness of their songs, and the *payador,* their minstrel. And just as the *gaucho* was largely a product of the new surroundings, so is his disappearance due in great measure to a change in the economic environment. With the development of civilization came a regularity that the free spirit of the pampas could not brook; the *gaucho* withdrew into his own realm, proud, defiant, even arrogant in his defeat.

From the fourth decade of the previous century, down to the threshold of the twentieth, poetry in the Argentine has occupied itself with the *gaucho.* Notable exponents of the theme were J. M. Gutiérrez, Bartolomé Mitre, Hilario Ascásubi, Ricardo Gutiérrez, Estanislao del Campo (author of the famous, humoristic *Fausto*), and José Hernández, poet of the still more famous *Martín Fierro.* Rafael Obligado, whose death occurred on March 14, 1920, also belongs in this list. In prose the *gaucho* is best known through Sarmiento's *Facundo* and Eduardo Gutiérrez' novel *Juan Moreira,* which, by some, he is supposed to have elaborated into one of those circus pantomimes that led to the *gaucho* drama.[1]

---

[1] See, however, the Introduction to *Three Plays of the Argentine,* translated by Jacob S. Fassett, Jr., with editorial material by Edward Hale Bierstadt, New York, 1920. Bierstadt asserts that the dramatization was made by Podestá, and cites as support Rodolfo Fausto Rodríguez' *Contribución al estudio del teatro nacional.* The whole matter is somewhat uncertain. ". . . Many of the plays are dramatized versions of actual poems, which served almost as substitutes for the novel in tne earlier days of Argentine literature. The result is that the original poems and the later plays are sometimes hopelessly confused." Page xxxiv.)

Traveling circuses became an institution in the early days of the republic, and were gradually varied by short, quasi-impromptu plays that could appeal to the scant intellectual equipment of their rustic patrons. "These plays," says Mr. Bierstadt, "were for the most part frank melodramas which were all written about the national figure, the *gaucho*. In time the plays took form until there came to be a definite repertory, and, after a certain point, no additions were made to this, so that we have a small group of plays repeated for years all over the country, adored by the people, and, in due course, scoffed at by those wise ones whose taste had been benefitted by European excursions. And the plays grew in body and interest until, from being merely an act of the circus proper, they divorced themselves from their progenitor entirely and demanded a place of their own. The two great theatrical managers of Buenos Aires to-day—they are actor-managers and producers—are the brothers Podestá, who many years ago began their career as members of a family of acrobats in a traveling circus which included the *gaucho* plays."

The native product, then, springs from the circus ring, and is less than forty years old. Of course, dramas had been written in Argentina long before the eventful July 2 of 1884, when the tale of the *gaucho* Juan Moreira was enacted in pantomime as the novelty of a circus performance; yet it is this humble occurrence, together with the production, in April, 1886, of a spoken version of the same renowned tale, that founds the native drama of the Argentine. What had gone before was imitation and perpetuation of Spanish models. Here, how-

ever, we come face to face with the scenes, the types,
the temperaments of the land; rough, devoid of art,
defective in a hundred ways, if you will, but unmis-
takably of the soil and destined to bear ripe fruit
within two decades.

For a time the native stage is trod by an army of
gaucho heroes, all cut from the same pattern. There
are Martín Fierro, Juan Cuello, Julián Jiménez,
Juan Soldao—a sturdy band of outlaws in conflict
with a nascent civilization. Bold men these, but
not wholly bad, incarnating the rough honesty of a
pioneer epoch. But the type begins to undergo a
change, and the change is at last definitely impressed
upon the spectators by Martimano Leguizamon,
with his *Calandria*. This play, first given on May
21, 1896, marked the reaction against the exaggeration of the *gaucho* drama, though it is a brother to
the long line of predecessors. Leguizamon's significant contribution was, in the words of Roberto
F. Giusti,[1] his conversion of the "rebellious, quarrel-
some *gaucho* into a good, industrious native; he
abandoned the routine of bloodshed and interpreted
the natural evolution that had taken place in the
fields. The national theatre, born of the truculent
melodrama, was shown to be improving within its
own mould."

During all this time the taste for music and dance
with the plays had not gone unsatisfied. As the
gaucho themes began to show signs of having yielded
all the variety of which they were capable, popular
taste veered to the national equivalent of Spanish
reviews, zarzuelas, and one-act musical farces.
Here, as in the previous orientations of the Argen-

---

[1] See his important book, *Florencio Sánchez*, Buenos Aires.

tine stage, the Podestá brothers were the path-
blazers, and when, on April 6, 1898, they established
themselves in the Teatro Apolo, they gave to a
drama that they had originated in the sawdust ring
its first permanent home.

This hybrid entertainment was of most varied
nature, presenting a host of types whose background
was usually the slums of the suburb. Not the plot
itself, but its ingredients, was the important thing.
We learn that this stage was even used for moral
purposes, being converted by some authors into a
strange pulpit whence issued "between a tango and
a scene of seduction" the bitter philosophy that is
born of life in the slums. Giusti relates this doc-
trinaire tendency to the influence acquired by
Gorki, who grew popular as one of the results of the
Russian revolution of 1905.

The point is worth passing notice, nor is it by any
means the sole instance of Slavic influence in Spanish-
American letters.

The Teatro Apolo encouraged native authorship
greatly; it was not yet a question of anything like
art, however. Subjects multiply, views and aims
whirl about in unconscionable confusion in the labors
of a new birth. And surely enough, upon June 16,
1902, there is given the initial performance of Martin
Coronado's *La piedra de escándalo*, which achieved
the startling record of more than a thousand performances. With this play yet another phase of
the *gaucho* is signalized—that of the former nomad
now domesticated in the rural scene.

A split between the Podestá brothers soon resulted in José retaining the Apolo and Jerónimo
assuming charge of the Teatro de la Comedia. At

the Comedia it was that the next important step in the evolution of the Argentine theatre took place, on the 13th of August, 1903. The play was *M'hijo el dotor* (*My Son the Doctor*), by Florencio Sánchez. The date marks the definite entrance of modern realism. It is only right to indicate, as Giusti and others have done, that Sánchez was by no means the sole innovator; a number of men whose names are important in the history of Argentine and Uruguayan letters served as collaborators in the transformation, among them Victor Pérez Petit, Enrique García Velloso, David Peña, Roberto J. Payró, Alberto Ghiraldo, Julio Sánchez Gardell, Vicente Martínez Cuitiño. The public was all this time being prepared, and, to employ a useful figure, Sánchez was the crest of the wave rather than the wave itself. From the date of this historical production through the following five years a strenuous activity is felt in the field of the drama. Sánchez himself, who was destined to live but seven years longer, wrote twenty pieces, a large proportion of them worthy of preservation. If, since his death, the stage has declined, there are several valid reasons. Natural reaction may be one; a too indulgent attitude from the critics, another; a third, the Society of Authors, which seeks long and profitable "runs" rather than lofty, artistic goals. Indeed, Señor Giusti, whose work as a critic is characterized by a certain aloofness of manner, and whose style is straightforward, lacking the usual embellishments of the Spanish-American temperament, openly declares in his recent little book on Florencio Sánchez that ' the Argentine theatre is commercialized, and its war machinery is the Society of Authors; the

Uruguayan, for obvious reasons, is not yet commercialized. Though these theatres were born together, already they are beginning to show each other their teeth."

FLORENCIO SÁNCHEZ

By interesting coincidence in the literary history of Uruguay, two of its noted men, toward the unsuspected and premature end of their lives, sought the inspiration of Europe. José Enrique Rodó, himself one of the great apostles of travel as a stimulus toward unceasing self-renewal, left for the Old World during the war that was ushering in a new, but what he considered the journey's beginning proved the journey's end. Death overtook him in Italy—a wretched figure many leagues from home, fairly abandoned, stranded. To be sure the oversight was later atoned for, and when Rodó's remains were returned to his native land they were received with the honors shown to a president.

With Florencio Sánchez, perhaps the most vital of latter-day Spanish-American dramatists, the case was somewhat different. His goal had always been not so much Europe as the boot-shaped peninsula in particular. He knew Italian and the Italians, whom he had portrayed in his plays; he had profited by suggestions from the modern Italian dramatists; he had felt that Italy would spell another step toward fame. In Italy it was that he found, outside of his native scene, the most sympathetic appreciation. Yet death, not glory, greeted him there, and though all this happened some years before Rodó followed him thither, only the other day were the remains of Sánchez returned to the land of his birth,

where representatives from four nations received
them with the highest honors. It was in 1910 that
Sánchez died of tuberculosis; perhaps the recent
return of Rodó stirred up a cry for similar honors
to one who had brought similar distinction to
Uruguay. At any rate, the man who, living, found
it so difficult to procure governmental assistance for
his voyage across, found a host of prominent Uru-
guayans, Brazilians, Argentines, and Chileans awaiting him on his delayed return.

It should not be inferred from this, however,
that Sánchez was a neglected genius, for his labors,
once they were definitely launched, met with generous and continued response. The roots of the
romantic career led by this gifted dramatist lie elsewhere than in the indifference of a public and the
critics' lack of discernment; they sink deep into the
personality of the man himself. Sánchez was essentially a wandering, bohemian spirit, a slave to his
instincts, writing chiefly under the compulsion of
need; he was generous, yet like so many generous
persons, withdrawn; he became, after his early experiences in internecine warfare, radical and unre-
strained; he was successful, appreciated, and, despite what more than one apologetic spokesman
has written, was prevented only by his personal in-
adaptability from enjoying a long life of increasing
success and fame. This is not said by way of re-
proach, nor written from a lofty moral eminence;
Sánchez was the most tolerant of mortals, harsh
though some of the theses of his later plays may be,
and we may well display his own human spirit in
considering him. Out of his personal frailty he
built some plays of enduring note—dramas that will

live in the history of the Continent as part of its intellectual development. They will not for a while provide texts for professors of literature to annotate and to comment upon; they spurted like huge sparks from the furnace of life and not infrequently display the defects, as well as the virtues, of spontaneity and improvisation. But they are so human in implication, so intimately bound up with the history of Sánchez, of his day and his milieu, that to study any one of these elements is, by connotation, to study the others.

The outstanding figure of Spanish-American drama was born on January 17, 1875, in Montevideo. He was the first in a brood of children that was to number eleven. He received a common school education, which was later added to by a course in a *liceo*, and it was not long before he was scribbling away during moments stolen from his position as clerk in the Junta Administrativa. As early as his fifteenth year he felt the thrill of beholding his work in print, and it is significant that his first efforts were in the direction of miniature social satire, under the English pseudonym, Jack the Ripper. He was of the wandering fraternity, and it was always far more easy to find him among the newspaper offices or amidst the popular tumult than at home. Withal, he was a good-natured sort, and if his schooling was limited, he made up for this in part by a quick mind and a ready observation. From the start, in his literary beginnings he exhibited a preference for the dialogue method of composition, as if feeling in him the eventual call to the stage. His short experience as assistant in the office of police statistics and measurements was valuable.

A letter written to a friend when Sánchez was in his eighteenth year shows the future dramatist, however, to be an outspoken liberal of anti-clerical beliefs, and anything but a model law-abiding citizen. But this marked element in the man's nature did not burst forth until the Revolution of 1896. His part in the actual fighting has not yet been made clear, but it is believed that he was in the thick of some of the fighting; there is even a story that during the battle of Cerros Blancos, which lasted through May 15 and 16, he was so overwhelmed by the horrible sight of national fratricide that he began to shout protest at the top of his lungs. This marks the definite turning-point in the formation of the man's mentality, and is at the same time a symbol of his attitude toward that greater battle which he called life.

Sánchez' reaction to these experiences revealed itself in a period of bohemian anarchism. Often he took the trip between the sister cities of Monte-video and Buenos Aires, now in quest of work, now intent upon eluding the pursuing police. Since these ardent spirits cannot separate politics from literature, the International Centre of Sociological Studies, which he joined, gave theatrical performances in Spanish and Italian; Sánchez acted in some of these, and recited for the assembly his social crit-icisms in the form of dialogues. Here he probably received his definite impulse toward dramatic author-ship, presenting a small piece called *Ladrones* (*Robbers*).

The year 1898 found him back in Buenos Aires, on a new periodical, but not for long; he simply could not submit himself to routine or regularity.

That he was cognizant of his own shortcomings is
shown by his letter of resignation, in which he declares his inability to change his reprehensible ways.
As so often happens, the man who had such a trenchant pen for the evils of society could not check
his personal extravagances; perhaps, indeed, his
lifelong criticism of society, mankind, and life itself
was a projection of his conscience into the field of
art. He who had once been so fervent a nationalist
was now writing articles turning a cold shoulder
upon the *gaucho* tradition and looking resolutely
toward the future. This, again, is one of the elements that is to make of his drama a distinct contribution to the progress of the stage. In 1901 we
discover him established in Montevideo and trying
to infuse life into a daily devoted to the interests
of the working-class and called *Trabajo* (Labor).
The founder, however, could not be got to live up
to the noble name of his organ, and as a result his
friends quarreled with Sánchez, who flew off again
to Argentina. He engages in one venture after
another, now at the head of a newspaper, now won-
dering where his next meal is to come from. He
summons energy enough to think of a maid and
marriage, and the new ideal instills new life into him.
He keeps his journalistic employers uneasy, lest he
print something that shall bring the law down upon
their offices; he writes a play that is but the continuation of his social criticism, and does not trouble
to disguise the persons against whom his attack is
launched, but the piece is prohibited in time, through
the efforts of the chief figure satirized. Not without
a battle, however, in which Sánchez is seized by
the police, only to be freed through the muscular

intervention of spectators who resented the over-officious brutality of the gendarmerie.

The ambition for success on the stage now throbbed powerfully in Sánchez' veins. His fourth composition, *Canillita*, actually provided a new word for the Argentines, who, since the first production of the little piece in Buenos Aires, have given that name to the news-vendors. But before this piece had reached the Argentine capital, the central event in Sánchez' life had taken place: *My Son the Doctor* was produced, as we have seen, in 1903, and established its author at once. Inspiration there may have been; accumulated experience and observation were present in appreciable quantity. But the driving force in the writing of the play was the author's need of money with which to get married. Four years previous he had met Catalina Rabentos and, romantically enough, had vowed that they should wed when he became famous. If the girl's family did not look with kindly eye upon the match none could blame them, nor was the news that reached her of the sort to inspire continued confidence. Toward the end of 1902 Florencio was given to understand that he must get famous in a hurry, or else the match was off. His widow—still living—has told of how he was thus brought to the verge of suicide. Instead, he wrote the play that brought him renown and a wife. Its first name was *The Two Consciences*, which states more plainly than the final title the struggle between the ideas of father and son.

Various tales of this period have gained currency, differing in details of greater or less importance, but alike emphasizing the poverty-stricken condition of the author. The very doorkeeper of the theatre where the play was being rehearsed refused him admission because he looked so much like a tramp; an advance was given him so that he might purchase a suit of presentable clothes; he might, at the time, have been under the influence of drink, too, for he was no stranger to the cup that inebriates and by no means always cheers.

From this point the career of Sánchez merges with the history of the Argentine theatre. Giusti, who made his acquaintance at the time when the author of *M'hijo el dotor* was emerging into fame, describes him as being tall, thin, with stooping shoulders, and with a certain gentle face that revealed traces of an Indian element; his lower lip fell toward a large jaw, imparting an air of a goodnatured rustic. There was nothing about the man to proclaim his gifts. When interested in the topic of his conversation he would swing his ungainly arms about and laugh with a laughter that ended upon a note of melancholy. He was one for those who knew him to love, and he showed the need of their affection. Though he found much to poke fun at and deride in human nature, he was fond of the individual. Indeed, in him, as in many a proclaimer against the evils of society, there was a strange need of individual kindness and a deep love for his fellow man. His anarchism has been called lyrical, and rightly. He was the friend of all the poor folk with whom his plays are peopled; he was very fond of children, though he never had any of his own; he liked animals, particularly birds; there was always much of the child and the bird of passage in him, and in his own home he was known as the

"Santito"—the little saint. Legends to the contrary notwithstanding, his friends were numerous.
He met with the envy and jealousy that all success
inspires, as well as with the academic opposition of
critics who, not able to institute facile comparisons
with Æschylus and his compeers down to the latest
innovation of the French dramatists, dismissed his
work as lacking literary qualities. The morality of
his plays was attacked. He was accused of plagiarism. But he was, on the other hand, wined and
dined, flattered by the critics, followed by the
public.

He began to yearn for wider horizons, and after
long knocking at the governmental door succeeded
in being named an official commissioner for the
republic. His nominal duty was to make a report
upon the advisability of his nation's taking part in
the Artistic Exposition at Rome (1909). He was
given a royal send-off and his parting words were
full of a new aspiration. A winter's trip through
France and Italy, and a final settlement in Milan,
soon led to straits in the latter city. His money was
fast disappearing; his health was following it. This
he must have foreseen, for his plays reveal preoccupations with illness. Even upon his deathbed he
held to his anti-clerical views, though he was ready
to welcome the priest as a human friend. On November 7, 1910, he died and was buried in the
Musocco Cemetery of the city, whence only lately
his remains were transported to his native land.

Those of Sánchez' critics who declaim against
the unliterary character of his plays are partly right.

15

Sánchez was no closet spirit; he wrote, moreover, in haste, almost improvising. His early poverty had forced him to steal even the paper upon which he composed his pieces: he would go to the telegraph offices, pretend absorption in the writing of a telegram, and manage to make off with a block of sheets. So accustomed did he become to writing plays upon the back of these telegraph blanks that in later life, when comparative affluence was his, he would purchase blocks of them at the office, as he found it impossible to compose upon the expensive paper presented to him by admirers.

And to most of his plays there is a certain stenographic rapidity of progress that actually suggests the concise phraseology of telegraphic despatches. Even the longest of them are short, always containing a first act notable for the swiftness of the exposition. He dashed the plays off at fairly lightning speed, rarely revised or even re-read his work, did not always even spell correctly, paid little attention (as might be supposed) to the niceties of composition, and was a failure when he attempted stylistic flights. Into some of his best plays creeps an occasional speech that smacks of Echegarayan rhetoric whose death decree was signed by the "generation of 1898" across the ocean. But in recompense for these defects his dramas present us life in action; if he did not create character, he was a natural master in the depiction of types and the presentation of backgrounds.

His plays have been generally grouped as (1) portraying life in the country, (2) life in the city, especially among the lower middle class, and (3) presenting problems. He is a realist first of all, and

draws chiefly upon persons and scenes that he knows
intimately.   Always he is preoccupied with problems that life has suggested.   Now (*My Son the
Doctor*) it is the conflict between new ideals and
old; now (*La Gringa*) the conflict between the native
who must yield up his holdings to the more industrious business-like foreigner; again, as in *Barranca
Abajo*, or *En Familia*, the portrayal of a family
falling away to moral ruin because of the reverses
that overtake them.   Himself a sick man, he has the
courage to write a harsh play like *The Rights of
Health*, in which the thesis is a Nietzschean disregard of the weak.

Much of this was the application of foreign suggestion to the native drama, but such a statement
should not be interpreted as implying anything like
direct imitation.   Sánchez had lived and seen too
much to need such aid.   On the other hand, intensely
fond of the stage, he could not help being influenced
by the 1904 season in Buenos Aires of the Italian
actor, Ermete Zacconi, and the plays thus revealed.
There are external resemblances in some of his
plays to those of Bracco, but in theme only.   Of
course the critics had to talk of Ibsen, as if Ibsen
were not part of the prevailing atmosphere.   At this
time, it will be recalled, Gorki had been brought
forward by the Russian revolution of 1905.

That there is a Grand Guignol element in Sánchez is shown by Antoine's comment after witnessing a performance of *M'hijo el dotor*: "It's a piece
that seems to have been written for my theatre,
with an admirable sincerity of intention and simplicity of means.   I almost feel like giving it in a
translation at Paris."

Yet, even allowing for these varied influences, Sánchez is Sánchez. His own life had brought him face to face with the drink evil that he studies in *Los Muertos;* his own experience with and against the police had brought him into contact with the low types he portrays so well in pieces like *Moneda Falsa;* his personal health could have suggested the entire pessimistic facture of his plays, though it has been noted that whenever he looks toward the coming day he is optimistic. Such, for example, is the end of *La Gringa*, where the son of a foreigner marries the daughter of the conquered native and prepares to build the new civilization of the future. This is the optimism of the lyrical anarchist at battle with the present; it is the optimism of a consumptive Sánchez, too—a "spes pthisica"—finding vent in his work. It is the optimism of the man who, facing a lonely death in Italy, could speak of his future labors with the accents of youthful hope.

Sánchez, in brief, was in a good sense of the term a man of the theatre. Faults his plays reveal a-plenty: in *My Son the Doctor*, for example, the son, who supposedly incarnates the new ideas, is far below the father who exemplifies the old, and the woman in the case is an impossible creature. The play, because of its historical importance, has been much overpraised by Spanish-American critics as a work of art.

It has been estimated that the actual time consumed in the writing of the author's entire output was thirty-five to forty days. Sánchez died at the beginning of his career. His plays, though they are not "literature," read well, even compellingly. Time, said the admirable Brazilian critic, Verissimo, does not respect works in which it has not been made a collaborator. Yet it might be answered, on the other hand, that the life put into a work lives in it. And though Sánchez did not make Time a collaborator, he had a faithful ally in Life. His plays mirror a certain progress not only in the Argentine drama, but in life itself in the neighboring nations. Belonging thus to history and to national development, they may safely hope to find a permanent place in the history of literature.

It is inevitable that, in the criticism of such works as these, the moralistic note should creep in. Of this, the best example with reference to Sánchez, is, I believe, the one hundred and thirty odd pages of homiletic futility perpetrated by Carlos Roxlo in his *Historia Crítica de la Literatura Uruguaya*.[1] It is not worth dwelling upon. The drama has a more beautiful purpose than serving as a text for ethical exhortation. What is worth dwelling upon, however, is the other danger of mistaking the dramatist's views for dramatic accomplishment—of taking the drama as a text for a more liberal-minded exhortation, but exhortation none the less, which betrays the commentator into paths of philosophical polemics. "Sánchez' theatrical works," writes Roxlo, "whether in the ideas they treat or in their depiction of manners, seem to me a mob theatre, hardly lofty in character and often coarse without need; but it is not the coarseness of a Shakespeare,

---

[1] Uruguay, one of the smallest of nations, has in this huge seven-volume opus one of the longest of literary chronicles, running into the thousands of pages. Señor Roxlo is nothing if not erudite, and is capable of introducing a summary of all Greek tragedy as a prelude to the discussion of the innocent Sánchez! This is a morbid example of the pompousness of the lesser Spanish and Spanish-American critics; it reveals the self-proclamative bombast of an eminently righteous soul. The chapters on Sánchez (Vol. VI, pages 297 to 433) are valuable solely for the liberal extracts from Sánchez' plays, which the author uses as texts for his windy sermons.

which is betimes great, rather the coarseness that
takes me back to the circus in which, with their
bilingual gringos, the Podestá brothers got their
start." Well it is for such as Roxlo that centuries
of commentators intervened between him and Shakespeare. Otherwise, should we not have him declaim-
ing upon the low life of the English bard and telling
him that life's philosophies are not formulated in
ale-houses, even as he says of the author of *M'hijo
el dotor?*

Because of the importance of this play, let us
pause for a moment upon it, as upon a few of its
fellows. Sánchez' dramatic personality will be the
clearer for it.

My Son the Doctor, as we have seen, is representative of the eternal struggle between the old
and the new; it furnishes the turning point of the
Argentine theatre even as Hasenclever's *Der Sohn*,
with its similar ideology, provides a rallying-point
for the young German Expressionists. Julio is
here the rebellious youth; Mariquita his fond, for-
giving mother; Olegario, the stern, tyrannical father.
Jesusa, loved by Eloy, upon whom Julio has drawn
a forged check covered by Olegario, is attracted to
Julio and loves him, when she discovers his attentions to Sarah. The situation is all the harder since,
as might be expected, she is on the way to motherhood with Julio's child beneath her heart. The
youthful doctor tries to justify his position with a
somewhat preachy speech on his doctrine of moral
non-responsibility. Olegario threatens to kill his
son if he does not marry the seduced woman. Julio
is even induced, by his mother, to wed the girl, and
begins to behold in her a nobility not before ap-

parent; Jesusa, however, fears that he will go back to Sarah after all. The end is somewhat indecisive, though Julio and Jesusa lead Olegario to believe that they will marry.

There can be no doubting the notable purpose of the drama; but the ideas suffer through insufficient and not wholly convincing characterization. Just as the old ideas are more firmly established than the new, so here the older personages seem more real than the young, erratic doctor. Julio himself does not show a real understanding of the free notions he professes. At best he is a transitory figure who has glimpsed a new truth, but has sullied it with mistaking freedom for irresponsibility. This, however, may be just what the author desired to impress. The first act has been called one of the great moments of Argentine drama; the other two, however, are far inferior. The play as a whole is important rather historically than as an example of successful artistic creation. It has been elevated to the position of a dramaturgic idol; Spanish-American critics will, as a group, recede from this untenable position to something more closely approximating an æsthetic view.

La Gringa, of the following year (1904) is a mirror of the transition from indigenous to cosmopolitan outlook. Its action is characteristically swift— dramaturgic stenography, in fact—and up to the very close presents a fine theme, well-handled. The most convincing character is the old Cantalicio, as if in Sánchez there were a secret sympathy with, and a better understanding of, the older régime, just as, despite his Nietzschean *Los Derechos de la Salud*, he was himself a sick man and kind to the weak and oppressed. In *La Gringa* no sides are taken; the foreign "intruder" and the native are seen, eventually, to merge quite as naturally as the past with the present. A similar sense of situation, a similar human insight and pathos inform *Barranca Abajo* (1905), in which the hardness of character in Zoilo and his rebellious daughter and his sister, mirrors the rigidity of the theme, which recalls Giacosa's *Come le foglie*. What this play does for family degeneration in the country, *En Familia* (1905) does for a like disintegration in the city. Again we have father versus son, with the son at the same time winner (morally) and loser. As usual, Sánchez is more concerned with dramatic situation than with psychology, yet he can make skillful use of situation to throw light upon character. He studies not so much the ruin of a family as the results of that ruin; not the process but the consequences.

Los Muertos (1905), Sánchez' fourth play for that year, is more than simply another picture of a family's dissolution through the father's vice of drink. Here is a milieu where man's beastliness is enthroned by the tenets of social law and religious custom. The background against which Lisandro stumbles on his way to ruin is drawn with the effective, broad strokes that we come to expect of Sánchez. But what seems to have escaped his critics is that in Amelia we have one of the rare women rebels in Spanish-American drama. True, when she exchanges Lisandro for Julian, she but exchanges masters, but the quest for happiness, so long thwarted in her, at least finds vent in one mad dash for such freedom as she comprehends. She has a worthy, if more understanding, companion in the play *Liberta*, by the Cuban dramatist José Antonio Ramos.

Nuestros Hijos (1908) is important for its plainly autobiographical content; it is yet another of the plays in which youth and age wage their unending battle. As so often with Sánchez, and most other playwrights engaged upon problems, the ideas are more important than the personages supposed to represent them, though here the motivation is conscientious, even if but sketchy. The economy of words is telegraphic. In contrast to *M'hijo el dotor*, here it is age and experience which see farther and more resolutely than youth and its facile conventions. The author achieves his satire of the shallow, charitable soul at the cost of exaggeration, yet a hot sincerity born of the writer's actual experience manages to fuse these touches of Ibsen, Bracco, Giacosa, and lesser social dramatists into something like a personal entity. In general outlook the piece companions Benavente's *Los Malhechores del Bien*, while in the figure of Mecha it presents another of the rare rebellious women.

Mecha, seduced and deserted by Enrique, scorns him, though she would marry him to save her family anguish. Her father is a queer, liberal-social spirit, seemingly daft upon the subject of illegitimate children. Her mother and sisters "do charity" with the automatism of most superficial dabblers engaged in that work. On the very day inaugurating the campaign in behalf of abandoned children she reveals her condition to her father. Alfredo, her brother, fights a duel with Enrique, but neither is hurt. Mecha, now the target of her aunt's moral arrows, is almost convinced to go to a convent. Her father, however, stiffens her fibre. She no longer loves Enrique, and when his mother comes with his offer to marry her after all, her father refuses in her name, afterward receiving her approbation. Mecha has now her brother's insistence to conquer, and this she does, refusing of her own free will to wed Enrique. The son threatens to have the marriage consummated by force and (as the father has foreseen) to have their obdurate parent shut up as insane. At the height of the argument the father lets slip a word about his wife's infidelity; he has letters as proof. Alfredo is too overwhelmed to reconstruct his life, but father, daughter, and unborn child go forward to a new day, a new life built upon their own truths.

It is the last of Sánchez' important plays, *Los Derechos de la Salud* (*The Rights of Health*), 1908, that has long been the topic of excited comment. It provides excellent fare for such critics as Roxlo, treating, as it does, so revolutionary a theme as the right of health to love, even if the weak must suffer. It helps to reveal the difference between such critics as Echagüe and Bianchi. Where the former finds only gloom, unreality, and false psychology, the latter (erring, in my opinion, toward the opposite extreme) discovers a play which, if it had been produced originally in French, would have established its author's reputation instead of proving, as it did, a failure in Buenos Aires. The truth, as so often, lies in the middle. *Los Derechos de la Salud* is a compelling, cruel play in which the hardness of the thesis appears in a certain hardness of the characters who exemplify it. It contains more than a touch of melodrama and more than one artificial situation. Nor is it so convincing as some of the other dramas in which Sánchez treats of principles and problems. But its cruelty is part of the inherent cruelty of nature, and, as in so much of what Sánchez has written, there is a singular appeal born of passionate intensity that vivifies the crudeness.

It was natural that the very title of the play, as well as the projected piece *Derecho a la tristeza* (*The Right to Sadness*) should bring to the mind of critics the play by Roberto Bracco called *Il diritto di vivere* (*The Right to Live*). It is recalled, too, in this connection, that Sánchez, like Bracco, received his initiation into adult life by way of the police court. But Giusti is right in checking the comparison right there. "He lacks Bracco's grace, his sparkling, ingenious dialogue; he lacked (nor is this to be deplored) the subtlety that so often converts the great Italian dramatist into an extravagant casuist. . . . By that same token Sánchez is more genuine. Wherefore every one of his works is a valuable document of a psychology and a sociology that are eminently true to our life. Because of them, if we consider their human content and their rich originality, Sánchez is superior to many celebrated foreigners, mediocrities who conceal beneath a gracious, refined art their feeble conception and their superficial observation."[1]

The play itself is characteristically brief: some less than sixty pages of ordinary print. Luisa is a consumptive, the wife of Roberto; he is slowly falling in love with his sister-in-law, Renata. Luisa, with the perspicaciousness of illness, suspects her

[1] *Florencio Sánchez*, page 96.

sister; Renata, learning of this, decides to leave the home—in which she serves as Roberto's amanuensis,—but Roberto is beside himself at the news. The wife, piqued at this practical demonstration of affection for the woman who loved him before she herself did, tries to reach a revolver locked in Roberto's drawer. Her death, in any event inevitable, is hastened by the domestic imbroglio. Roberto, who is a writer, and who pities his wife deeply, defends the right of health to the happiness that illness cannot provide for it. The end is foreseen; Luisa will die; Renata and Roberto will marry.

There is something in Sánchez that, to an American of the North, suggests a fleeting comparison with Eugene O'Neill. Like Sánchez, O'Neill has brought to a stage infested with unrealities a breath of the everlasting that informs all reality. To speak in text-book terminology, part of O'Neill's work represents, upon our stage, the belated arrival of European realism. But Sánchez stopped writing four years before the war began; O'Neill began writing in the year of the war and lived through those horrible years. He has learned, and quickly, what Sánchez would have learned with equal rapidity: that narrow realism is not enough. Wherefore he abandons his early melodrama for a more plastic medium, thus bridging, within the space of a few years, several distinct epochs in the evolution of dramatic form. In O'Neill, as in Sánchez, there is a certain stenographic quality born of a multifarious, restless life; in the North American, as in the American of the South, there is the same succinctness, the same sketchy psychology, the same raciness of dialogue and nearness to the soil, the same lack of "literary" graces—as if "literature" and "style," rather than extraneous ingredients that may be mixed into a work, were not organic components of the creative entity! In each, action is more important than lengthy speech; O'Neill, the equal of Sánchez in reproduction of ambient, is his superior in dramatic projection of character. Our own writer is one of the hopes of the native drama; Sánchez is, thus far, the chief dramatic glory of his continent. That glory, as we have seen, rests upon his personality, his importance to his epoch, as much as upon the plays produced by this errant, human, striving child of the early twentieth century. Yet one would gladly surrender many a work by such "famous" playwrights as Bernstein, the later Brieux, the later Echegaray, and a number of the European mediocrities, for the crude life that pulses in the dramatic output of Florencio Sánchez. Passionate sincerity is not enough to create a work of art; it is always to be preferred, however, to that passionless excellence of the artificer who has nothing to give because he garnered nothing. Others to come will go farther than Sánchez, but they will be the stronger for his having labored.

JOSÉ ANTONIO RAMOS

If I now take up the work of a semi-obscure Cuban who has spent much of his life in the diplomatic service of his country, who has contributed too much of his strength to political turmoil, and has had to rob the very time in which his dramas have been written, it is as much to pay tribute to the man as to his work, and to give some notion of the difficulties under which dramatic authorship especially labors in the various countries of Spanish America. It is doubtful whether the drama exists today in Colombia, Cuba, or, for that matter, Brazil. There are theatres, of course; there is a social audience; but there is not that highly organized, concentrated body of playgoers that is at once inspiration and goal. The younger playwrights are too ready to let second or third best fill the place of their highest efforts; log-rolling and facile interchange of meaningless praise is the rule rather than the exception; ideas are not digested, they are seized upon as so much grist for the theatrical mill. The result is that thesis-pieces abound; they are an easy substitute for the oratory, the rhetoric, the exhibitionism that come too easy to the Latin youth. On the other hand, the social problems presented by the shifting scene are many, and the dramatist—a human being after all, eager to lift his nation to a place of eminence—attacks these through the play as through the speech or the press. It is next to impossible to produce great literature under such circumstances; merely to follow the literary career represents a physical, a moral triumph. Yet the artist must write, and if players are not found for his work, he is not discouraged; he prints it, usually at his own expense. So doing, and in the absence of the actors, he runs the risk of producing "literary" drama, "not for the stage"; but there are other dangers that he may steer clear of, notably that same stage and those same actors. The theatre is a social institution; the drama, an individual.

"You resign yourself to publishing this work,"

wrote Benavente to Señor Ramos, with reference to the Cuban's play *Liberta*, "certain that you will find neither managers nor actors who dare to present it. You know that not all that is of the theatre is art, and vice-versa. You know that the public assembled in a theatre flaunts a morality that may be taken off like a garment and again put on. . . . If I were a manager, I would produce your work; and if I were a theatre-goer I'd be more interested to witness it than some play like *Maître des Forges*, *Fedora*, or *Madame Sans-Gêne*. But you may take my word for it that, for my part, I lose nothing by reading it and perhaps gain by avoiding a production given by a bad company.[1]

"Your play is a work of art and it is something more. Something more, what though the partisans of art for art's sake may think different. . . . I must confess that as regards free love I have my own opinions; there is no need of expounding them here. We all are free to love when and wherever love summons us. But what I don't believe is that we should be free not to accept the consequences, the duties, that such liberty imposes.

"The most interesting part of your work seems to me the situation of the heroine after her first lapse, when everybody denies her the right to a new love and would prefer to have her consume her life in dolorous expiatory penance.

"But, you know it as well as I; if you wish to be a popular author, don't look for plays in life; thumb over the theatrical archives and be one of the regular gang.

---

[1] This view is interesting, as coming from a highly successful playwright. It is almost a restatement of the quotation from Charles Lamb in the opening chapter of this book, and provides an argument for the opponents of the Castelvetro doctrine that a play is not a play until it has seen actual performance.

"If you wish to be . . . yourself. Ah! Then compromise a bit, for in Art one must be an opportunist, as in politics, as in all things. . . . Deceiving is not the same as treason."

The letter, especially toward the end, throws light upon one source of Benavente's own shortcomings in the drama. But it reveals him here as a ready friend of promising youth. With similar sympathy he has studied the stage in Argentina.

Ramos' *Liberta* is denominated by the author a scenic novel in four acts. It is not the swirling stage kaleidoscope that Benavente's similarly named pieces are, resembling rather the Galdosian application of the novel technique to the stage. Mercedes is to become the mother of a child by Luis, who is leaving for a career, with the promise to return and claim her. Elvira, her elder sister, has a talk with Luis, threatens to tell Don Justo, her father, but is prevented. Mercedes' perturbation is taken by the parents for girlish hysteria, and she is not permitted to accompany her sweetheart to the wharf. Three years go by. Mercedes' lover has not returned and she has been in disgrace and in seclusion with her child. But she has learned rebellion, and far from giving herself up to repentant resignation, she forgets her unworthy lover and exercises her right to find happiness in another, Arturo. Her father discovers this; there is a scene in which his old ideas and her new ones are contrasted; he demands that she change her place for a more secluded one on the floor below; she refuses, and prefers to be cast into the streets. Arturo, overhearing her declaration of love for him, climbs back to the balcony to her. Six years after his disappearance, Luis, semi-con-

trite, returns to see his child. Mercedes' mother is
eager for "rehabilitation"; so are the others, but
Mercedes has found a fiercely loved freedom through
all her suffering. She really cares for Arturo, though
she sees that he, too, is an egotist. Four more years
go by in the scenic novel. Mercedes has had a
varied experience among different men of her choosing. Again she is visited by Luis, who is married
and has a child. She plays cruelly with him, forcing
from him a confession of man's sexual egotism, refusing to flee with him, inciting him to ardor, and
finally consenting to remain with him for the night
in "sexual friendship." This, it seems, is the lesson
of sexual freedom that she has learned and taught
him.

The writing is clear, swift, natural; the characters
really live, if at times they do too plainly voice the
author's pros and contras; the drama has grown out
of an inner attitude. And something of the hazi-
ness of the attitude contrives to wrap the personages
in a similar haze. The evolution of Mercedes from
the "clinging vine" type to a master of men shows
a gap at the one place in which we are most interested; the period between Luis' desertion and the
advent of her rebellious spirit. Luis' conversion at
the end is suspiciously sudden. Some might ask
whether Mercedes could or would justify herself in
taking Luis away from his family. Persons who
think their way to freedom are not wont to exercise
it in such a fashion, especially after years have
matured their beliefs. Yet there is a basis of depth
in Mercedes' character. The spirit of Ibsen and of
the Italian Bracco strive somewhat murkily in this

16

lone Cuban woman. And Ramos, her creator, is just as lonely in Cuba as is she.

Peculiarly enough, he is not quite so successful in his patriotic plays, perhaps because of a political eagerness to impose rather than elucidate and vivify an attitude. Only the evident sincerity of *El Hombre Fuerte* (*The Strong Man*, 1915,) saves it from the fate of melodrama. As it is, the same patriotic symbolism that pervades *Tembladera*, likewise a drama in three acts, obscures the effect, though never descending to the ineptitude of the one-act piece, *The Traitor*, which is as bad as our own Mackaye's *Sam Average* and for precisely the same reasons. *El Hombre Fuerte* seeks to represent the triumph of spirit over brute force, with Elena (standing, perhaps for Cuba) as the pawn. Ramos understands readily enough the craft of the stage, yet the play as a whole is of gradually declining interest and presents a thesis worked out in arbitrary fashion. *Tembladera* is better; it may be enjoyed without reference to the patriotic symbolism, and merges his favorite themes,—woman, Cuba, progress, justice, humanity—into a highly readable, actable work.

None better than Ramos appreciates his shortcomings and the external as well as inner reasons for them. In his interesting foreword to *Tembladera*, he argues for a Cuban literature and a Cuban criticism—for a national personality. He advances the arresting idea that, far from having gone through its period of Romanticism, Cuba, like the rest of Latin America, has yet to experience it; this time, not as the mere echo of a European outburst, but as a manifestation of national and continental selfhood.

BRAZIL: CLAUDIO DE SOUZA

The history of the Brazilian theatre, despite Sylvio Romero's effort to divide it into no less than eight distinct "periods," is hardly of great consequence.[1] Many plays can no doubt be assembled; I question whether some of them even belong to Brazilian literature, as, for example, those of the famous Jew (*O Judeu*, his contemporaries called him) Antonio José da Silva, who was Brazilian only by birth, and died in early manhood at the hands of the Portuguese Inquisitors. Our only interest in the Brazilian theatre is to discover what its practitioners are doing to-day; this we may glimpse in the work of the most popular of the dramatists, Claudio de Souza, author not only of some highly successful stage pieces, but of works upon pathology and social hygiene.

The most popular of his pieces is the three-act *Flores de Sombra*, which reached the rare number of three hundred performances—a figure that is quite as commercially respectable in New York as in Rio de Janeiro or São Paulo. It dates back to 1916.

It is easy to see the reason for the popularity, though such critical wisdom after the fact should not deceive us into excessive confidence. In the first place, it upholds the good old times, as represented in the mother of the *jeune premier*. It pre-

---

[1] In Senhor H. Marino's *O Theatro Brasileiro* (Rio de Janeiro, 1904), to which Romero contributes a short introduction, the student will find precious little about the drama of Brazil. He can well dispense with it until something more substantial appears. Romero, as students of Brazilian literature are aware from his thick tomes upon the national letters, dearly loved to catalogue by periods, and changed around from one set of periods to another.

sents, as companion of this prodigal son, a French-
ified dandy with a vagabond's philosophy of the
world, a winning way with the ladies, and, in the
end, a heart far softer than the rapier edge of his
tongue.   There is much playing with frilled suggestiveness.   The sweetheart of country days is,
for the nonce, vanquished by an adventuress from
the city.   The son, forgetting his better self, is about
to talk marriage to her when his sharp-tongued,
modernist chum wins her away from him.   Treachery? Betrayal of friendship? So we imagine, until
in the end he confesses that he had no intention of
marrying the lady.   He merely wished to save his
friend, who is true to his mother, to the country
sweetheart, and to the past after all.   For he marries
the modest flower of his childhood days and all is
well.   Even the servants, as per prescribed formula,
make up their parallel differences, and Bless You,
My Children, is the word for all.

Among the latest of his plays is *A Jangada*, bearing the symbolic title of the raft, or the mutual
support of two stray logs dashed together by the
rush of the torrent.   Coelho Netto, himself one of
the more prominent of latter-day Brazilian dramatists, has praised it with all the weight that derives
from membership in the national academy of letters.
Claudio de Souza, he has written, is to-day, "incon-
testibly, our chief playwright. . . . His pieces
run along smoothly, naturally, without the slightest
effort, which proves his technical knowledge; in
them, moreover, all the personages are of our own
ambient, the milieu is ours, the speech. . . .
Claudio de Souza creates a worthy theatre because

he makes it Brazilian, not alone in the plots but in the rôles; in the scene as well as the sentiment."

Which, with all due deference to Coelho Netto's remarkable powers as an opulent writer of tales, is but a quarter true. The dramatist's Brazilianism we will not question; his plots, however, are no more of Brazil than of New York. Sánchez, for example, wishing to contrast the notions of the old generation and the new, writes a genuine play in *M'hijo el dotor*, propelled, despite its faults, by the inner sincerity that engendered it. It is far different with Claudio de Souza's *Flores de Sombra.* His people are mere stage figures; they come on and off at the wire-pulling of the author; they say what he wishes them to, and when; they are the arbitrary puppets of his purpose. They do things that hundreds of similar puppets perform on the stage of a score of nations; they are the lines of the author's text.

Similarly, when another critic praises the psychology of the leading pair in *A Jangada*, he indulges in the amenities of social compliments—a weakness long inherent in the Portuguese on both sides of the Atlantic. The truth is that Claudio de Souza has themes, but not dramatic imagination. In *A Jangada*, certainly, he gets nearer to the core of his theme, but he is unable or unwilling to abandon the easy aid of "comic relief," cheap punning, very obvious *scènes à faire*, and such ancient devices.

In *La Petite et le Grand* (I know only the translation into French) he is capable of a war dialogue on the theme of Belgium and Germany that is every bit as bad as Harold Brighouse's *Maid of France*.

In the conventional sense, Claudio de Souza is a good enough manufacturer of plays; he has intuitions of life's beauties; undoubtedly he feels the stir of social purpose. But he does not lift the Brazilian stage to the level of dramatic artistry, and only in isolated instances, thus far, does he seem to grasp that higher conception. His critics have, wittingly or unwittingly, praised his purpose rather than his accomplishment.

FRANCE

FRANCE

A NOTE ON ROMAIN ROLLAND, PLAY-WRIGHT

The danger common to all movements for bringing art to the masses is that the artist, in his attempt to "elevate" his audience, will descend to the level of the common denominator of that audience. He will, in a word, become less the artist as he succeeds in a conscious generalization of his power. It is one thing to bring art to the masses and another to write for the masses an art designed particularly for their tastes. Economic sympathies aside, the masses, as such, are inimical to art—more inimical, perhaps, than the static bourgeoisie. Leisure confers opportunity to cultivate taste; excessive labor at minimum wages robs the worker of that opportunity. The proletariat, as proletariat, is artistically inarticulate, and even its leaders, its Marxes, Engels, Kautskys, come from the despised bourgeoisie. This is not to say that its ranks do not contain gifted spirits, intellectual aristocrats, if you will, just as the ranks of the economic aristocrats teem with companies of intellectual laggards and maligners. But it is an error, and a serious one, to mistake sympathy with the plight of the downtrodden for the justification of lowering one's artistic standards by an inch in an effort to "bring art" to those downtrodden. It is significant that the more enlightened of the workers' leaders are as

vociferous in their objection to literary propaganda
as is any upholder of the strictest artistic individuality.

This, then, is not to say that the proletariat, as a
subject of art, possesses no tragic beauty; it is not
to say that their condition of economic servitude
adds to their numerous burdens an arbitrary exclusion from the realms of the beautiful. But it is,
however, meant as a protest against some of the
implications contained in such theories as Rolland's
theatre of the people.

"The summons was two-fold," writes Zweig, in
his panegyric of Rolland, discussing the vicissitudes
of Rolland's popular theatre, "to the writers and
to the people, that they should constitute a new
unity, should form a people's theatre. Since the
forces of the people are eternal and unalterable, art
must accommodate itself to the people, not the
people to art."[1]

Here, in so many words, is precisely the notion
that vitiates so much of Rolland's theatre and that
I have been trying in the opening paragraphs to
oppose. It is not a question of Rolland's idealism
or the undoubted nobility of the man. As an intellectual force, however one may regard his views,
he is one of the outstanding personalities of our
time. "Valueless also, in Rolland's view," continues Zweig's interpretation,[2] "are the attempts
made from time to time by the Comédie Française

---

[1] *Romain Rolland, the Man and His Work.* By Stefan Zweig. Translated
from the original manuscript by Eden and Cedar Paul, New York, 1921. This
book contains an excellent bibliography, including translations into various tongues.
As a work of biography it is high-flown, poetic, eminently readable; it converts
Rolland, however, into a hero of predestined glory, an epic intellectual, a moral
king who can do no wrong. It is the work of a disciple, a eulogist, rather than
of a critic. Page 90 et seq.

[2] Mr. Barrett H. Clark has translated, in addition to Rolland's plays, *The
Fourteenth of July* and *Danton*, the same author's *Theatre of the People*, New York.

to present to the workers the plays of such court
poets as Corneille and Racine. The people do not
want caviare, but wholesome fare. For the nourish-
ment of their indestructible idealism they need an
art of their own, a theatre of their own, and above
all, works adapted to their sensibilities. When they
come to the theatre, they must not be made to feel
that they are tolerated guests in a world of unfamiliar ideas. In the art that is presented to them
they must be able to recognize the mainspring of
their own energies."

Again, a dangerous and debasing view, over-
idealizing the "people" and what is more, cramping
the artist at the outset. The very member of the
masses whom, unconsciously, Rolland was striving
for, had already reached a sterner and purer conception of the dramatic art. Rightly was Rolland fired
by Goethe's literary internationalism, but in using
the German's words as a clarion-call to the formation of a popular art, he but exchanged the restrictions of nation for those of semi-articulate ignorance.
The way to art does not lie in that direction. If the
masses are to be "saved," truckling to their æsthetic
insufficiency will not do it; and the first to inform
Mr. Rolland of this vital fact would be the artistically emancipated worker himself. He does not
want to be "saved." He comes, sooner or later, to
the realization that art is fundamentally human,
with its roots in the common life that is our heritage
as creatures of the earth, but with its flowers in
personality. He who writes plays "for the masses"
but repeats, on a larger scale, the error of the mere
technicians with their wise gabble about the "psychology of the crowd." Of course there is a psy-

chology of large assemblages—the mere contagion of numbers; so, too, is there a psychology of the masses. But do artists write for numbers? Do not the individuals of those very numbers, once they have come to an appreciation of art, refute the whole "mass-art" idea in their very search for the world's salient minds and works? To-day, yesterday, to-morrow—art is in essence of the intellectual aristocracy; it may be colored, inspired by mass problems, mass aspirations; in such a sense, art of the masses may exist and does. But art *for* the masses, art consciously *directed* by mass problems, is a simple self-negation. Art may pass through many mediums, but it begins and ends, as we have already said, in the individual.

And this is true, even of Rolland's theatrical art. That same longing for vast canvases, that led him to project his works not in books but in series, reaches out to the vastness of the people and the vastness of the stage that he has projected for them. His internationality is the philosophic aspect of this craving. Nor are his plays always the evil fulfillment of his theories. A large simplicity they attain; Rolland, too, in his own way, felt the need of getting the audience to join the actors, of bridging the gap that yawns between stage and auditorium. Thus, in his note to the final scene of *Le 14 Juillet* he writes that the public is to join in the singing and the dancing of the celebration. He calls for the public to "mingle not only its thought but its voice with the action; the People itself becoming an actor in the People's fête." He would have as music the famous Ninth Symphony chorus of Beethoven, or something similarly inspired by revolutionary spirit; he underlines his desire to have choruses distributed in every part of the theatre, or even miniature orchestras, framing the public and "compelling it by sheer moral force to sing with them. If this public is composed, even in part, of members of the common people and of young folk who feel personally the passions of the Revolution, I can answer for their taking up the strains."

Thus, Rolland's plays may have failed in their primary purpose, which was in theory antagonistic to the life of art, but they are not without their suggestiveness to the creative dramatist, nor can it be said that they are totally without effect in actual production, as recent performances of *Danton* in Germany have shown. The latest of his plays, the acrid war satire *Liluli*, contains, among other things, the novel possibility of enacting a play not against a curtained background, but against the selfsame humanity that is the spiritual background as well.

Curiously enough, his two great dramatic inspirers were Shakespeare and Renan; yet his own theatrical work displays neither the universality of the one nor the beautiful doubt of the other. In the world of the modern drama Rolland is important historically, as an experimenter. He has created little dramatic beauty, not merely because his theory precluded it, but because of that deeper something in him which made of him a notable power for world peace and could in the first suggest to him that theory. Rolland the man is far greater than Rolland the dramatist.

A young contemporary of his, much less heard of, has been more successful with similar aims; more genuinely the dramatic artist than Rolland, he is perhaps even farther distant from the masses for whom avowedly he wrote.

GEORGES DUHAMEL

The name of Georges Duhamel became known in the United States during the recent conflict, after our entrance into it, for several books of vital experiences and human vision. Yet long before this, the noted physician had initiated his literary career with many verses and three dramas which, if not of the highest worth, yet possess uncommon merit. Strangely enough, all three of the plays were in English years previous to the translation of Duhamel's war books, but attracted no more attention then than they have since.[1] They are, like the dramas of Rolland, the result of a theory of art for the masses, yet, like more than one such attempt, go over the heads of their theoretical audience.

"The old art values," wrote Sasha Best, introducing Duhamel and his aims to this country, "have made way for new ideals in which intuition and sensibility are the most important factors. Detail and analysis are no longer sought after, and the harmony to be found in masses is now the poet's inspiration. Only what is general, universal, is of value. The cult of the individual has ceded its place to one that embraces humanity in its entirety. The individual counts only inasmuch as through him the largely human is to be reached."

This generalization, then, was one of the chief traits of that group of young writers to whom the Duhamel of ante-war days belonged. And, ah, the

[1] See *Poet Lore*, summer number, 1914 (which contains *The Light*); autumn number, 1914 (containing *In the Shadow of the Statues*), and vacation number, 1915 (for *The Combat*). The translations, with introductory material, are by Sasha Best.

vagaries of theory! With a similar universality of
program, a similar refutation of analysis, behold
the divergent destiny of the German Expressionists!
The abstractness presupposed in such generalization
has its reflection in Duhamel's dramaturgy. He has
created strong environments rather than strong
characters; at times the background seems to dominate his personages. The men and women do not
speak the language of everyday life; their dialogue
tends to lose verbal character and dissolve into
mood. As Best says, "Duhamel aspires to reform
the modern theatre by adding a lyric idealistic
element to the realistic. Over realistic scenes of
his plays hovers an atmosphere of strange unreality,
in which his characters move and act. A large and
beautiful symbolism prevails."

Perhaps the best expression of Duhamel's purpose
may be gleaned from his own writings. In his
Propos Critiques (quoted by his translator) he gives
to the world his own *ars poetica*, which applies as
well to his plays as to his poems:

The moment has come when man directly must be
addressed. Honor and love to the poet who strives to
be man first and then the poet; honor and love to the
poet who, filled with his mission, zealously seeks the one
word, the one song that will reach all men of all races.
The greatest worth in the poet's art lies in his greatest
generality. And let it, above all, be a living art! . . .
It permits of no rules and regulations, and will come
under the head of no system. We are in the center of a
movement which is at one and the same time a reaction
and a continuation. . . . It behooves a new art, however, to choose among the realities of life those that
preserve the individual in all his native grandeur. The
eyes of the poet of to-day stray less toward the clouds,

but he seeks with his eyes those of his fellow-men. He no longer dwells in towers, but desires to step out and give affectionate greeting to his fellow-creatures.

All of which is written in a style that is not infrequently employed by the persons of Duhamel's dramas. The context, however, is misleading, and, as we have hinted, the noted Parisian's plays are no more for the masses necessarily than the verses of Whitman. The very lyricism of the dialogue, the broadness of the symbolism, the originality of plot, the refinement of passion,—the cult of generality—render the plays inaccessible to the more or less theoretical masses for which Duhamel and his group wrote their works.

The first play to be considered here was produced at the Théâtre de L'Odéon in 1912, under the direction of the famous Antoine, founder of the Théâtre Libre. Blanche Albane (in private life Mrs. Duhamel), the protégée of Sarah Bernhardt, played the leading rôle, as she has done for her husband's two other plays.

In *The Light* Duhamel's main characteristics are strongly evident. It is here a case not of those who have eyes yet see not, but rather of those who, not having sight, yet see. Bernard, who has always been blind, is endowed with a perspicacity that penetrates much further into his environment than the faithful attendants who minister to his needs. Far from being anxious to recover his sight, he discourages his father in any attempts which will lead to such an end. It is true he yields to the latter's insistence, but only out of love to a parent who has gone from doctor to doctor in a vain search to bring back the light to his son's eyes.

Among the persons who make up Bernard's world is a young girl named Blanche, who loves him with a simple, yet deep passion that seeks its happiness in self-effacement and service to the afflicted one. Blanche is not like the other girls; she does not care to go out among the fields and the flowers. She sits embroidering for her Bernard, and through her very love seems to attain the power of looking upon the world even as does the blind man. Her own eyesight, in fact, is failing her, yet she does not heed it.

Bernard, once all hope for his own sight is gone, looks to Blanche for that light which he had desired too late. She shall be his eyes. Through her he shall learn to see the world as do all the others, and thus they shall find happiness. But a strange change comes over Blanche—perhaps a forecast of her own coming blindness. "My words are childish," she says to her sweetheart. "Take them, however, as coming from reflection. Nature has imposed herself on us by every means in her power and has put into our heads something terrible, something overwhelming: and that is the light of our eyes. Ah, well, it is but a perpetual mirage, a perpetual play, that hinders our soul from a communing with itself. I am sure of that; it has come to me since I have known you."

Bernard is frightened at the queer talk of the girl. From the warmth upon his cheek he knows that the sun is shining. He draws aside the curtains and points to the scene outside. He urges her to tell him all that she sees. Upon every word of hers he hangs as if it were an inestimable treasure. He enlarges upon her slightest expression; he drinks in

17

every description avidly and thirsts for more, still more. The bewildered girl, seeking in vain for more vivid terms in which to convey to the sightless one the glories of the sunset, is suddenly stricken blind. She falls against Bernard in a swoon, while he, realizing that something terrible must have happened, cries for aid.

Blanche's case, however, is not hopeless. With diligent care her sight may be restored in a very short while. Together, Blanche and Bernard go walking, she with her eyes bandaged, utterly dependent upon Bernard for guidance. The latter, accustomed to almost every nook of the country because of his frequent walks and his fine sense of locality, leads his charge with full confidence. He brings her to a statue which, when she still had her sight, she had passed often without really appreciating its beauty. He takes her hand and passes it over the form of the sculpture and teaches her to see the various limbs with her hands, so to speak, to grasp the proportion of the whole, the position, the general effect. It is he, the blind, who must see for her, the erstwhile seeing.

A thunderstorm is brewing. The lovers, engrossed in their sightless pleasure, at first do not hear it. But Blanche becomes timid, and in trying to discover the way back both are confused. Bernard tries to distract Blanche's mind from the terrors of the storm, but in vain. Slowly, unnoticed by her companion, she lifts her hand to her bandage, drawing it off from her eyes. For one moment she beholds the landscape, sees how they have erred in their attempt to regain the right road, and then—

an intense flash of lightning which destroys Blanche's
sight forever.

Together, the blind leading the blind, they fare
forth into the storm. A searching party is sent out
for them. Meanwhile they are approaching the
edge of a cliff in the vicinity. Bernard knows the
danger, and only at the last moment, when he feels
that together they are to fall over the height in
their confusion, does he make an avowal of love
that is more like a prayer than a confession. He
draws the entranced girl to him and kisses her. As
he does so the lovers, not without a symbolistic
significance, turn away from the direction of the
cliff's edge.

BLANCHE: All roads now are good for us.
BERNARD: No, no. I don't want to make any more
mistakes. (*They go to the left.*)
BLANCHE: Yes, that is the way we must go.
BERNARD: I think it is there. . . .
BLANCHE: Slowly, let us go slowly. I am very happy.
I am sure now that we shall arrive.

One of the commendable things about the play is
the illusion of blindness which the author conveys
through the very words which Bernard utters.
His speech, its similes and expressions, are those of
one whose sight is all within. To Bernard himself
words become what scenes are to the seeing. "There
are words," he says, in one of the most beautiful
passages, "that have been of such good service, they
have passed so many lips that they possess a personal warmth, and properties that are not merely
borrowed. When you put a shell to your ear you
hear a noise like that of a cascade or a tempest, and

people say that because the shell has lived so long in the sea it has retained its roar. It is like that with words. They grow polished and hard with time and they take on the quality of the things they express. I know nothing about the light, yet when you pronounce with your beautiful, flexible voice such words as light, transparence, or sun, there suddenly are born in me all manner of violent images that cause me to tremble as though shaken by thunder."

The second of Duhamel's plays to be considered was presented in the winter of 1913 on the same stage as the previous drama. The title is slightly symbolistic, as is the play. But *In the Shadow of the Statues* contains less of the symbolistic than *The Light*, and much less than *The Combat*. If the dialogue is less suffused with the idealistic incense in which Duhamel seeks to envelop the speech of his creatures, it is because the play does not demand such a technique as his two others. The psychology of the leading figure, Robert, has clearly been affected by Ibsen's self-asserting men and women.

Robert Bailly has grown up in an environment which has robbed him of every atom of individuality. He is the son of the great writer Bailly, and to the memory of the latter, to its perpetual glorification, he has been unwillingly dedicated. It is almost as if he himself is nobody—merely the son of the great Bailly. Upon the eve of a great event, —the dedication of a monument to his famous father, Robert rebels against the systematized adulation of his father that is robbing him of himself. He views with impatience the intellectual lackeys that flock in the neighborhood, anxious to shine in the reflected glory of a great man.

Worst of all, he must deliever a speech at the un-
veiling of the monument, a eulogy to Bailly.   This
his finer senses simply cannot permit.   He has read
the works of his father, he does not agree with the
opinions there expressed, he opposes them, in fact.
And the writer of these opinions he must glorify on
the morrow!   In a scene with his sweetheart, Alice,
he tells her that his heart is not in the words he
must deliver.   They look out on the garden.   Here
at last Robert seems to find repose from the swarm
of busybodies that fill every room of the home,
rehearsing the activities of the great day.   After a
time Alice points to a table in the garden.   "Is it
true that it was on that table that your father
wrote his beautiful book, you know, *The Power of
Love?*"   At this sudden recalling of the paternal
fame the garden loses all charms for Robert.   He
wishes to be off, anywhere at all, so it be removed
from the Bailly environment!

Throughout that morning a certain Hilaire has
been trying to get into personal touch with Robert.
Only in the afternoon does this patient emissary
break through the barbed-wire of ceremony and
penetrate into an interview with the son of the
famous Bailly.   He whispers a few words to Robert,
then a few more.   A packet of letters is passed into
Robert's hands, and then comes a terrible discovery.
Robert is not the son of the great Emanuel Bailly!
This is so clearly proved that not a shadow of doubt
remains.

Robert locks himself in his room until the storm
within him subsides.   His mother, who has guessed
the cause of his perturbation, takes the matter
quite philosophically and awaits developments.

Later, when Robert sees Alice, his indignation bursts out anew:

I have been thrust into a cold and clinging darkness. . . . I am still too oppressed by the news that a poor devil has brought me without knowing the price of what he was bringing. All those people were there around me to watch my profile and the movements of my face. When I smiled they all said, "There is the smile of Emanuel Bailly!" And when I was calm they all thought, "It is the same gravity!" And when I showed anger, they looked at each other and murmured, "It is astonishing. He resembles him also in his violence and his force." . . . A marionette, the prey of all the photographers and the newspapers! (*Approaches the statue of E. Bailly.*) You can see for yourself that I do not resemble this man: the bone formation is entirely different, and the rest they have transformed by means of discourses and examples. I had to cut my beard like his, and my moustache, and I had to draw back my hair as he used to draw back his. . . .

Alice, true to Robert, is ready to fly with him whither he will go. He will take a poor, unknown name, he will write his own thoughts, not those of another. He shall be something more than a literary shadow. "Oh, Alice! since you love me, tell me that I am not merely a shadow, and that I have perhaps my genius—a genius of my own. . . ."

But it is not to be. The fetters of a lifetime, even though woven of a lie, have been bound round the victim too long thus to be shaken off in a day. There is a strong scene between Robert and his mother, in which she by her masterly tongue, overcomes her son just as he is on the threshold of his soul's liberty. He goes back into the shadow of

his father's statues, a subdued man—the son of a
father who is not his father, the eulogist of a writer
with whom he disagrees. The environment has en-
gulfed its prey.

The Light contained no humor. It was a sombre
drama of the inner person, even as is this. The
real action was an invisible struggle. *In the Shadow
of the Statues* contains several passages that reveal
Duhamel as a clever hand in the humors of both
low comedy and satire. The love element, as in the
two other plays, is distinctly secondary.

It is in *The Combat*, produced in the winter of
1913 at the Théâtre des Arts, that we have perhaps
the best of these three plays. The dialogue is the
author's most lyric-idealistic effort; the background
is portrayed with a vividness that shines through
the speech and the actions of every person; there
is a unity of mood which is atmosphere itself.

There is a land that is ravaged by the regular
overflow of the sea. It is owned by one family, of
which three generations are living. There is the old
grandfather, ninety years of age. Then comes
Vincent, an invalid of sixty, to whom the most
interesting things in the world are his rheumatic
pains. Gérard, the son of Vincent, is a young man
of twenty-three. The family is wealthy; it is charitable, too, yet the misery of the land knows no
bounds. Everywhere land that might be rich with
the bounties of earth lies under a devastating flood.
The very atmosphere of the country is permeated
with a dampness that penetrates the marrow of all.

Hubert, the family physician, is one who sees
beneath symptoms and complaints. He knows the
real curse of the land; he has been in the wretched

huts of the laborers, he has seen the baneful effects
of the inundation. He suggests to Vincent that a
fight should be made against the ravages of the
deluge. Vincent is rich, why not do it?

Hubert has a sister, Anne Marie, who loves young
Gérard. The same cause that the doctor pleads
with the father Anne Marie pleads with the son.
She seeks to inspire Gérard with a determination
to conquer the mighty forces of the water. But he,
with the foreboding of illness, is loath to undertake
a task the end of which he may never live to see.

> I have attempted nothing, and I'm already beaten.
> I was beaten before I was born.
> You want me to be more than a man,—
> A hero, perhaps, a hero!
> But I have reflected—if I were to rise
> And but raise my hand to give an order,
> I know that a sudden sharp pain in my breast
> Would remind me that I had done too much,
> And that those marked for the sacrifice
> Had better never try at all.

Gérard's premonition is only too true. A little
while later he is seized with an attack of coughing
and he must be carried to his room. "You see," he
gasps to Anne Marie, "you see it only too well."

Gérard has a cousin of some thirty years, named
Michel. The latter is an architect, and is at present
at work upon a mausoleum desired of him by
Gérard's father. As Gérard slowly recovers from
his attack, the words of Anne Marie begin to bear
fruit within him. He would take Michel away
from the mediocre occupation of mausoleum building and set him to work upon a dike—a powerful
wall that shall thrust back the waters of the sea

and reconquer the land for the people. Michel is
the incarnation of health and self-confidence; through
him Gérard hopes to accomplish the great task of
redemption.

The architect calculates that it will take three
years to do the work. But more than money will
be needed—the enthusiasm and courage of the
whole people. The fortune is there, the people
must be aroused from their passive acceptance of
the sea's mastery.

When Anne Marie comes to inquire about Gérard's
health he greets her with a new passion:

> My health is not of the least importance;
> It would seem that I am cured—
> What I am now going to tell you
> Is larger than my person. (*Takes her to the table.*)
> Look there! See the picture of the country.
> Look well: my hands hold down the paper;
> Thus will I with these my hands,
> Mastering the earth and all the men
> That are immersed in their labors,
> Force all to obey me hereafter
> Like one who creates—his thumbs in the clay!
> Look again! All the designs of this map,—
> Are they not in truth rocks and sand
> And green fields with their waving trees
> From which I will drive the water
> Because I have so willed it?

The country is aroused. The dike is started and,
after weary labors, nears the point of completion.
There is not a moment to be lost, for the floods are
rising and may soon render the entire work a useless heap of stones. Efforts are redoubled; every
person is enlisted in the final attack. Every person

—except Gérard, who, in the excitement of the finishing touches, is left alone. A woman passing by labors under the heavy burden assigned to her. Gérard, wishing to play some part in the glorious task, if only an insignificant one, attempts to assist the woman, when he is stricken with a hemorrhage and dies. The woman has gone on, and he falls behind a pile of stones, unseen to the triumphant procession that soon comes marching toward the corpse. The crowd acclaims Michel, who holds Anne Marie's hands. Gérard, the real force behind the project, is forgotten in the tumult. He has died in the moment of victory, a victim to the power which he had conquered.

If Duhamel has created any real characters,[1] such was not perhaps his intention. But despite the playwright's theory of generalization, Gérard, Robert (of the previous play), and Bernard of *The Light* are individuals possessing marked vitality; they are more than abstractions. None of Duhamel's women, however, stands out. In *The Combat* Duhamel has given a vivid portrayal of the working folk. If, in some details, he is not above such conventional devices as stage storms and letters that cast a shadow of melodrama over the scene, he has created a little dramatic beauty that even to-day, after so many changes in the fashions of the theatre, deserves the attention of the few that do not wear their ideas in conformity to the whims of our dramaturgic modistes.

---

[1] Of his latest play, *L'Œuvre des Athlètes*, Henry Bordeaux, in *La Vie au Théâtre*, dernière série, 1919-1921, speaks very highly, commending its satirical verve, its humor, and noting a too deliberate presentation of character.

GERMANY

GERMANY
EXPRESSIONIST THEORY

German "Expressionism," in its simplest phase, is a reaction in poetry, prose, painting, and drama against the Naturalism of the Nineties. While it came into prominence during the war, which incited some of its most characteristic efforts, it thus dates back to the earliest dissatisfaction with the exaggerated attention to reality that was the hall mark of the naturalistic school. It has been qualified as a new Storm and Stress period[1]—or, to be more exact, as part of such a turmoil in the arts—and the well-known literary Jew-baiter, Bartels, adduces it as fresh proof of his theory that a new *Sturm und Drang* appears every thirty years, which is to say during every generation. Naturalism would thus reach its apex in 1890, with the present artistic unrest coming to maturity circa 1920. The same theorist would see in Symbolism the first stage of Expressionism, but the truth is that the new "ism" does not represent a clear-cut, unified reaction or progression; it is not, in the pure sense of the word, a movement, composed as it is of protestants who have in common only the ardor of their protest.[2] Close attention to the theory and the practice of the Expressionists renders even a definite distinction between them and their supposed enemies, the

---

[1] *Die deutsche Dichtung der Gegenwart,* von Adolf Bartels. Die Jüngsten, Leipzig, 1921, page 208.

[2] The first clearly recognizable "Expressionist" play appeared four years before the outbreak of the great conflict. It was the pious, ecstatic Reinhard Sorge's *Der Bettler,* prototype of Unruh's *Geschlecht* and Kornfeld's *Die Verführung.*

Impressionists, rather difficult, and when Bartels points to the Symbolists as representing the initial stage of the Expressionist reaction, he but emphasizes that difficulty.[1] The name itself means very little; it tells as little of the aims of its adherents as do such flapping pennons of progress as Futurism, Creationism, and the rest. What, for that matter, do Classicism and Romanticism really say of themselves, unaided by page after page of exegesis? It is high time for a radical reform of all literary terminology.

One undoubted effect of the war in Germany has been to stimulate theatrical production to an unwonted degree. "Seldom," says Manfred Schneider,[2] "have so many pieces been written as in our day." And just as the Italian Futurists, under the lead of Marinetti, attempted to capture the theatre and turn it into the chief vehicle of their peculiar propaganda, so have the Expressionists in Germany, in their desire to reach the heart of the people, invaded the province of the drama with avowed apostolic aims. Art, as one of their slogans proclaims, must become the common possession of the people.

Yet it was through the other arts that Expressionism made its way to the stage. Much of its theoretical background had already been elaborated in painting, which, reacting against that same photographic realism which prevailed in naturalistic drama, sought a certain neo-primitivism by a return to ancient Egyptian art, to the Grecian vases, to the simple, mystic Gothic forms. Unessential detail was abandoned in favor of stylization; in the

---

[1] Bartels indicates, as one of the Expressionist precursors in poetry, the founder of German Impressionism, Arno Holz.

[2] *Der Expressionismus im Drama.* Stuttgart, 1920.

words of one of their chief theoreticians, Konrad Lange, "The illusion of reality is not a condition of the artistic." "One must so transform an object," says another, ". . . as if it never had any relation to any other object." The tendency was toward the passional immediacy of music, which, in Schneider's words, alone of the arts can be "purely expressionistic." But was it not Verlaine, heralding the Symbolists, who wrote "de la musique avant toute chose?" Expressionism is a child of many ancestors; one may not say for a certainty whether it will grow to adulthood; but, like the infant fondly watched over by its doting parents, it reveals in its restless features now the traces of this relative, now of that. It belongs to them all.

Its evolution in Germany has been traced from Kleist, Grillparzer, and Hebbel (somebody, only the other day, was calling "Genoveva" an elder sister of the Expressionists) through to Wilbrandt and Wildenbruch. And why not the youthful Goethe with his "Expressionistic" drama around Götz von Berlichingen? And *Faust*, with its world-wide ideology, its panoramic scenery, its symbolism? And Schiller, with his universal idealism?

The Naturalistic movement, founded upon scientific materialism, had its world-program in a sort of generalized socialism. Bound up as it was with surrounding reality, it sought detail in both matter and mind, leading thus to excess of scenic minutiæ and of psychological probing. Man was the creature of his milieu. The inevitable idealistic reaction was twofold; on the one hand the Neo-Romantics, headed by Hugo von Hofmannsthal, on the other, the Neo-Classicists, as represented by Paul Ernst. A need began to be felt for a more ample sweep, more solid matter, a more plastic medium for the idea. Expressionism thus appeared as the opponent of both Naturalism and Neo-Romanticism.

Art, in the words of Edschmid, chief of the Expressionist manifesto writers, must become positive, active—must rise from the inspection of detail to the all-informing Spirit. (Spirit must dictate, shaping matter and not remaining dependent upon it. Art shall ascend to vision upon the wings of universal feeling. The work of art must germinate from the idea. Detail gives way to the universal, the typical. Both the dramatist and his creatures must bear the impress of a *Weltanschauung*, a philosophy of the world. The accidental gives way to the essential— an essential that acquires firmer outlines, ampler sweep, tenser form. Things and persons are to be released from their manifold interrelationships and speak out of themselves alone. Arch enemy of such a program is psychology, with its attention to things and persons in their interwoven affinity to one another. With man liberated from all limitations he becomes once again capable of deep, immediate feelings. (A neo-primitive, as it were.)

The Expressionist dramatist frees man from his milieu; he writes no mere plays of marriage, no tragedies that arise from the clash of convention against the urge of freedom; he presents no "puppets that hang from the wires of psychological views and play, laugh, and suffer amid the laws, the attitudes, the errors and vices of this man-made society,"[1] (It is amusing to recall that Marinetti,

<hr />

[1] Manfred Schneider. *Der Expressionismus im Drama*, pages 16, 17. (The author summarizes Edschmid's manifesto.)
   Kasimir Edschmid. *Ueber den Expressionismus in der Literatur und die neue Dichtung*. Berlin, 1919.

proceeding from a similar antagonism to psychology
and the man-made world, has given us, in his play,
Elettricittà Sessuale, a play in which two of the personages are puppets who serve the author's exhi-
bitionistic needs and provide an admirable illustration of that very psychology which supposedly is
being flouted.) Such a drama calls for a new technique of acting and production, and Paul Kornfeld
has thus presented his actors' intuition as a substitute for the histrionic realism that was part of the
naturalistic method upon the stage. "Let the
actor take no particular pains in producing the impression that the thought and the word that he is
to express came to him only at the moment when
he speaks them; if he is supposed to die upon the
stage, he has no need of visiting a hospital to learn
how; nor to go to a tavern to study how people act
when they're drunk. . . ." In short, he is to be
no mere imitator; he is not to deny the theatricality
of his calling. . . . "The melody of a great gesture says more than what used to be called Natural-
ness ever could."

So much for theory. If, in certain details it is
difficult to distinguish sharply between Impressionism and Expressionism, what shall we say when
Schneider, in his succinct but sound pamphlet, finds
it hard to draw the line between Expressionism and
that very Naturalism against which it revolted?
The truth is that hate and love connote each other,
and as in life, so in letters, we retain something (now
a little, now much) of what we reject. Schneider,
too, traces the earliest origins of the new attitude
back to the Storm and Stress of the late eighteenth
century. In the young Goethe and the young

Schiller he discovers a similar "fanatical underscoring of the idea, a heightening of the expression, although almost everywhere in the limits of a brilliantly observant Naturalism. The later Büchner and Grabbe withdrew further from Nature and they are looked upon by many as the fathers of the Expressionistic drama." Wedekind, in certain aspects, particularly his free technique and his nightmarish atmosphere, joins the long list of precursors, as does Maeterlinck with his dream fantasies and Strindberg with his mystic visions. Indeed, back of the Storm and Stress of the eighteenth century lie the Greeks, the perennial precursors in whom each age, each movement finds something to support the most contradictory assumptions. To the Expressionists, the Greeks appealed with their symbolic, typical personages, their unnaturalistic technique, their vast simplicity of style. And, as Schneider puts it, the young revoltés of Germany "looked immediately back to them, over the heads of the German classics who had also been influenced by the Greeks." He discerns no effect of Æschylus, most primitive of them all, upon the new generation. The road to Sophocles is clearer. "Is it not significant that already Hugo von Hofmannsthal, in his efforts to defeat bare Naturalism, came to deal with Sophoclean matter, Œdipus and Electra? In most recent times Hasenclever, one of the better-known expressionist dramatists, has harked back to Sophocles with his *Antigone*." In Franz Werfel's *Tröerinnen* the same critic sees the influence of Euripides. But it should be remembered that when the new German dramatists go back to Greece, to history or to the Bible, it is to produce drama of to-day, in which the ancient plot acquires a peculiarly contemporary application.

With reference to Expressionistic production, Schneider points out that Hofmannsthal sought, for his Sophoclean plays, a régisseur who should emphasize the vast, simple line and blend detail into a grand unity. "The movement demanding a strict simplicity in the scenic investiture of dramatic works dates back, in Germany, to Ludwig Tieck and Immermann." The work must speak for itself; color, light, and form are the means for presenting its vast simplicity, replacing the cluttered stage that so often weighs down the piece itself.

"It is not very long since this movement has come to the fore. But one may well maintain that the Expressionistic stage direction preceded the Expressionistic drama. . . . One may even say that the stage was waiting for the Expressionistic drama."[1]

We may, then, before approaching some of the dramatists themselves, attempt a summary of the none too lucid principles that guide the Expressionists in the drama.

Expressionism is as yet more an aim than an achievement. It is a reaction against Naturalism, international in character and spiritual in implication. For all its avowed opposition to Impressionism, it seems fundamentally but a deeper aspect of the same intense subjectivity predicated by the Impressionists. It is complementary rather than antagonistic to Impressionism, and has been termed

---

[1] Manfred Schneider. *Der Expressionismus im Drama*, page 20. This does not seem to agree with Mr. Lewisohn's statement (see his review of Macgowan's *The Theatre of Tomorrow*, Nation, February 8, 1922) that "Hence in Germany the new art of the theater has always followed the development of dramatic literature and has rarely attempted to influence or lead it." Our own new drama, however, has long been preceded by the scenic artists, and now O'Neill, with his quasi-expressionistic *The Emperor Jones* and *The Hairy Ape* seems to have answered the call.

the male element in art, in distinction to Impressionism, the female element.   One might emphasize the difference between them by saying that Impressionism presents the world in terms of personality, while Expressionism presents personality in terms of the world.   The Expressionists are not only Neo-Romantic, they are Neo-Primitive, Neo-Classic, as well.   Were one not afraid of too many terms, one might call them esoteric eclectics; eclectic they certainly are, and if anyone can discover the meaning of half their labors (those of Oskar Kokoschka, for example) he is indeed blessed with second sight. They seek to create a fourth-dimensional technique, in which time and space dissolve into the velocity of thought.   Artifice is replaced by intuition, even in the acting; ideas, not theses, prevail; feeling, not psychology, is dominant.   The materials are to be employed as a composer employs his notes: merging them into the unity of an immediate appeal.   The whole, with its preference for symbolic types rather than characterized individuals, is to be infused with, or suffused in, an atmosphere of exaltation.   And characteristically enough, that same Schopenhauer in whom Remy de Gourmont and the Symbolists found some of their "subjective idealism," has been referred to as one of the philosophic sources of the Expressionists.

The Expressionist critics, who do not differ among themselves quite so radically as do the dramatists, yet reveal interesting divergences.   Bernhard Diebold, in perhaps the best single book dedicated to these lyric dramatists,[1] notes with so many others the yielding of Ibsen and Hebbel to Strindberg and

---

[1] *Anarchie im Drama*.   Bernhard Diebold.   Frankfurt am Main, 1921.

Wedekind as models; he distinguishes between the
various men, agreeing that they cannot be grouped
under any all-inclusive label.   More important still
for the Expressionist drama, he distinguishes between *Seele* (soul) and *Geist* (intellect), indicating
the intensive, instinctive character of the first and
the extensive, formative character of the second.
The danger of the new drama is, that in its ardent
battle against materialism, its almost mystic yearning to merge into universality, it may sacrifice *Geist*
to *Seele* until artistic communication becomes too
difficult.   "The soul as soul alone, without intellectual form or corporeal frame, is impossible in
drama."

As a result of the intenser preoccupation with
self, the new type of play develops particular forms,
which, while they may often be referred to models
in the past (especially *Faust*, which has left such a
numerous progeny), possess a decidedly contemporary significance.   This has aptly been termed Ego-
drama, and has, almost through necessity, developed
into what might be called Alter-ego-drama.   No
longer does man struggle against a Greek Fate,
against other men, but he is at war with his other
selves.   In himself he is a microcosm, the very scene
of all his conflicts.   Hence the frequency of dream-
representations, the many shiftings of scene, the
rapid revue-technique, the telegraphic text.   Much
of this passion for a new spirituality, indeed, suggests a modernization of the mystery, the *auto
sacramental*, the morality; at times it sinks to a sort
of psychoanalytic allegory.   Self often is companioned by counter-self (as in Hasenclever's *Der
Sohn*), or by a multitude of changing selves (as in

Werfel's *Spiegelmensch*). Ancient theological queries
acquire new poignancy, and one feels that a New
Evangel is being preached—one no less strict upon
the individual conscience for all its frequent freedom from orthodox obligations to a personal God.

The drama, in short, becomes autobiographical,
as did the novel before it. Hence these kaleidoscopic
soul-adventures; hence, if Diebold's pertinent suggestion be accepted, the prevalence of historical
plays, which provide the frame for personal views
after the author has used up his own happenings.
And hence, too, the temptation to use the stage for
its own sake, until Diebold, who is fond of punning
(was it not he who spoke of the *Nirvanitas nirvanitatum*, with reference to the deliquescent universality of the lyric dramatists?) may say that the
modern *miracle* becomes a *spectacle*.

Approaching the plays, we need hardly be surprised
to find that the various devotees of the new drama
differ in their application of the theories and in the
results they obtain. As an introduction to the out-
and-out Expressionists I should like to consider
somewhat more than cursorily, one of Hauptmann's
recent dramas, *Der Weisse Heiland*, not only because it has been called a "fairly Expressionistic
work," and the conception and presentation of the
character of Montezuma termed "thoroughly Expressionistic," but because, in trying to reveal the
errors of such a view, we may arrive at a clearer
understanding of the Expressionists in action.
Hauptmann, of course, is no static figure; his outer
growth has paralleled an inner; he is of too wide a
girth to be contained in our convenient "isms"; the

hasty dragooning of him into the Expressionistic
camp attests something eternally young in his own
being no less than the impatience of critics to see
things whole if not steadily. He is no Expressionist,
though he has undergone some of the influences that
have shaped the confused reaction.

HAUPTMANN'S *DER WEISSE HEILAND*

The White Redeemer takes us back to the Mexico
of Montezuma and Cortez, at the time when the
two civilizations met in inevitable clash and the
worshipers of the sun god went down before the
cross of the conquistadores. Hauptmann calls it a
"dramatic fantasy"; he has, in the Horatian phrase,
changed sky but not spirit; it may well be that the
fate of Montezuma, which one German critic strik-
ingly termed Montezuma's Passion, is not devoid of
a certain application to the man of the twentieth
century. We have here an epic tragedy of faith.
Its eleven scenes—there are no acts—are as many
stages of the protagonist's ascending path to martyrdom. From first to last it is his lot in which we
are interested and over which the poet seems most
to have brooded. The play, which possesses no
"love interest," is written in trochaic tetrameter, so
that, naturally enough, as one reads on, the throb
of "Hiawatha" begins to hum outside one's ear;
but the emphasis is not upon the poetry, nor are the
lines often laden with compelling image, deep insight, magic of music. Rather has the author
seemed to concentrate upon the color and contrast
of background, the scenes of culminating antagonism, the effects of grouping and a certain pageant-
like flow of cumulative episodes. He paints in his

background with broad sweeps of the brush; his
personages stand out clearly enough, but more as
huge shadows than as creatures that grow before
our eyes. Montezuma alone is bodied forth in the
round, breathes, lives, and dies within our sight.
Were it not that the unyielding belief in the advent
of the white redeemer is the groundwork of his
tragic faith, the dramatic fantasy might well have
been named *Montezuma*. Hauptmann, however, has
not built up one of the pseudo-historical personage-
plays that have of late come into a new vogue. *The
White Redeemer* is only incidentally and unavoidably
historical in facture. It is, fundamentally, human
and universal.

The play opens upon a scene in a small apartment
of the Temple of Quetzalcoatl at Tenochtitlan.
Montezuma listens to his Priest recount the prophecy
according to which a white saviour shall come to
redeem the son of the Sun and his loyal subjects.
Three thousand summers have followed upon as
many winters' snows; the time for the fulfillment of
the prophecy is near. Montezuma is filled with the
fervor of belief. All signs point to the great and holy
moment. News has come of strange arrivals, who
seem to answer the details of the forecast. These
creatures who have risen from out of the deep,
upon fiery animals—dragons, surely—who bear them
upon their backs,—these white men that carry
thunder and lightning in their hands—are these
not the emissaries of the white saviour? Montezuma's belief is not shared by his advisers; young
Cacamazin warns him from the first not to trust
the demons that the ocean has spewed forth, and
the Emperor's own son, Guatemotzin, adds his pro-

test. Montezuma is deaf to all entreaty; these
newcomers are not enemies. They are the promised
redeemers.

The second scene reveals the full character of
Montezuma's unshakeable faith. He has an answer ready for every adverse interpretation. Besides, are not his loyal subjects rejoicing in the
advent of the white comers? Is there not the
universal cry, "On to Cholula! On to Cholula!"
Let there be no more argumentation, then. "I am
Master!"

If there is discord among the Aztecs, neither is
all harmony in the Spanish camp, into which we
are first afforded a glimpse in the third scene. The
hot-headed Pedro de Alvarado finds his fellow-
fighters not half impetuous enough; tender-hearted
Las Casas rebels against the slaughter of children,
women, and the aged; Gomara thinks chiefly of the
salvation being brought to the heathen by the word
of Him who died on the cross. With unconscious
irony, he asks his companions what the shedding of
human blood matters beside the prospect of plant-
ing the holy symbol in this land of dark horrors.
Alvarado, in the heat of argument, has drawn his
sword against one of his own (the situation parallels one in the previous episodes among the Aztecs)
when Cortez appears from his tent, calling to his
men to distinguish between friend and foe. Cortez
is no Montezuma; he has a clear conception of his
purpose and the method of fulfillment. He has
promised Carlos V to reduce the Aztec emperor to
vassalage and vows to attack his aim with the directness and the fearlessness of the soldier. Even as
Montezuma has imposed his will upon the differences

rife amongst his counsellors, so does Cortez impose his. There is arrant hypocrisy in his reception of Montezuma's ambassadors of friendship; no sooner are their backs turned than he gives orders to advance upon Tenochtitlan.

The reports of the Aztec heralds, however, convince Montezuma more than ever that he has beheld the true vision of fulfillment, and when Cortez arrives to pay his military visit, he is received by the Emperor as the white saviour himself. From the first, Montezuma is religiously humble; from the first, Cortez is arrogantly wily. The land has bewildered the Spaniards' sense; it is a dream of paradise; its wealth of gold stuns them. To such a soul as Las Casas, the picture appears in different colors; to him, the greatest wonder of all is the ruler of the empire. "Never, not even in Europe, have I beheld such a man as this. He seems truly a stranger to this earth, and most lonely." But Montezuma is not really lonely; for him, the end of this world and the beginning of a greater has come; Cortez is the white redeemer; when, he asks the conquistador, will the sun-chariot appear that is to sweep us into the heavens? The astute Spaniard, with his mind upon gold and conquest, honies his lips with a pious reply.

The perplexity of the doubting Aztecs is added to by the similarity between their own cult's symbols and those of the Spaniards; there are analogues to the cross, to the Madonna and the Child. Qualpopoca and his kind, however, refuse to be convinced by such argument. "If the great Huitlipochtli sends us such redeemers," he cries, "then I prefer his Hell to his kingdom of Heaven." The Spaniards are no less surprised to find the semblance of Christian symbols in the temple of a heathen war-god. Cortez' arrogance grows with Montezuma's faith, but there comes a climactic moment when the dawn of the Emperor's disillusionment breaks. The conqueror, less and less disposed to conceal his true colors, finally shatters the image of godhead that he had reared in Montezuma's heart.

> .Nie hat so wie du ein Mann
> seine Gottheit selbst zertreten!

exclaims the undeceived ruler, too late, as he is ignominiously fettered by command of the mortal in whom he had beheld the white saviour.

From this point on the attitude of the populace changes; a holy dance of theirs is by the rashness of Alvarado (temporarily in charge, because Cortez has been forced to leave in order to quell disturbances on the coast) converted into a massacre. The one hope of bringing the wild Aztecs to their senses is to get Montezuma to appear before them in his imperial robes and quell the outburst by his august presence. Montezuma, however, has sunk into a brooding, apparently indifferent silence. The guards suspect him of harboring suicidal thoughts; in fact, Montezuma goes upon what we now call a "hunger strike," refusing to eat and drink. He tries the patience of his captors sorely, and Cortez harbors a final means. If he must, he will have Montezuma forcibly attired in his regal splendor and shoved out in sight of his subjects. This the conquistador is compelled to do. The Emperor is thrust into his jewels and his cloak, and dragged forth. To little avail, however, for Montezuma, instead of main-

taining silence, addresses the multitude, who aim
their missiles not at the treacherous Spaniards, but
at their own ruler. Perhaps he has asked them, in
their own tongue, to do him the mercy of slaying
him. He is brought dying before Cortez, and during
a flicker of consciousness before his last breath
rejects Gomara's anxious plea for conversion to the
faith of his betrayers, rending his fetters in a final
access of frenzied strength.

Such, in an outline that robs the piece of all its
vitalizing elements, is the story of *The White Redeemer*. Montezuma is not only an Aztec king—he
is any man of any epoch who follows blindly a compelling vision and wakes too late to the harsh reality
behind it. He is the trusting soul; were he born a
Spaniard he would have been such a one as the tender
Las Casas, who had sensed the concealed truth that
duty may walk hand in hand with mercy. He is
the symbol of yielding good that is so readily vanquished by gold-dazzled self-seeking. May not
Hauptmann even have had the artistic aim of presenting Montezuma as the one genuine Christ-like
figure in the drama? That this may be something more
than mere speculation is suggested by the author's
evident sympathy for his protagonist. Montezuma
is a lesser Christ crucified by men calling themselves,
and sincerely believing themselves, Christians. He
is the strangely soft product of a cannabalistic cult,
as opposed to the leader Cortez, harsh son of a religion of meekness. Lift the symbol into higher
regions still, above nations and cults and ages, and
you have the unending pageant of human disillusionment. Montezuma the martyr becomes Man

the seeker-martyr. By such signs as these, even
allowing for the personal bias and coloring that is
inherent in all suggestive interpretation, Hauptmann was looking not only backward when he wrote
The White Redeemer, but was regarding the present
and perhaps doubting the future. He has thus not
strayed so far from his characteristic plays as one
might at first blush be tempted to think; his human
interests are strong with the suggestion of contem-
porancity. It is not at all impossible, though the
idea may sound far-fetched, that Hauptmann wrote
with a haunting thought of the late war; those who
are fond of extracting such symbolization will find,
if they seek diligently enough, material for their
pursuit. However, such investigation may best be
left to those who are so minded.

The irony of the piece plays almost constantly
over the action; it appears at once in Montezuma's
inextinguishable faith and follows the Emperor to
the bitter moment when he is forcibly clothed in his
regal robes, into which one of the mocking soldiers
blows his nose. There are moments of intense
pathos, as for example the final interview between
the ruler and his brave son, in which both vow
themselves to a defiant death. Effective scenes of
debate, of dissension in council, alternate with the
tumult of color, tempests of sound, and anguished
silences in which Montezuma comes to realize his
unwitting betrayal of his people.

Yet the movement is not, on the whole, essentially "dramatic." Montezuma is a psychological,
rather than a dramaturgic, creation. His thoughts,
not his deeds, are presented. It is through his spoken
emotions that he wins the reader's and the spec-

tator's sympathy, rather than through acts that translate those emotions. (All this, not so much to imply inferiority as to note a distinction in style.) Certain figures Hauptmann has touched off with a happy stroke, while others, and notably Marina— Cortez' paramour—are merely suggested and not made clear.

Now, how is this an Expressionistic work? Because of its numerous scenes? Scenic discontinuity alone cannot make Expressionism in the restricted sense of the new German experimenters, else Shakespeare would be the central Expressionist of them all. Besides, Hauptmann does not here play with time and space. Montezuma? But he is a compelling psychological creation in just the sense that the Expressionists repudiate! The background? But Hauptmann uses it for its colorful suggestion, independent of the purely symbolic practice of the Expressionists, who aim at the generalized emotionalization of the inanimate object. The poetry? But it is all-too-monotonous in its regularity, and too crystal clear for "Expressionism." Too mature, shall we say? Too human? Too coherent? Too intermediate? All these things, and more, from the point of view of the new revoltés. Hauptmann, one fears, must be left in the seclusion of his own preeminence.

WALTER HASENCLEVER

Perhaps the most widely known of the pure Expressionists in the drama is the young half-Jew,[1] Walter Hasenclever, born on July 8, 1890, at

---

[1] See, on this score, Adolf Bartels, *Die deutsche Dichtung der Gegenwart*, page 229. In all that Bartels has written the Jew is one of the arch-villains of German literature, together with the Protestant and other pet animosities.

Aachen. He has studied at Oxford University, England, where he wrote his first book. "The cost of printing it," he has written, "I won at poker." In 1909 he proceeded to Lausanne, thence to Leipzig. He has traveled in Italy. He served during the war as an interpreter, purchaser, and kitchen-boy. He has won success as a poet, and his works for the stage include *Der Sohn*, which was completed in 1914, *Antigone*, *Die Menschen*, *Die Entscheidung*, *Der Retter* (a dramatic poem), and *Jenseits*.

As the writers of the new drama differ within the sphere of their common revolt, so do the plays of Hasenclever differ among themselves. At times they baffle ready comprehension—particularly *Die Menschen*, which, suggestively enough, begins and ends in a graveyard, and, among other things, makes an excursion into a madhouse where the inmates crawl about in lycanthropic abandon. At others, as, for example, *Der Sohn*, the play is quite coherent, and for all its strangeness would produce undoubted effect upon a contemporary audience of a certain sensitivity to experimental novelty. Whatever the worth that may ultimately be assigned to the movement, it has already earned, then, the right to be examined, and the investigation is productive enough of pleasure, surprise, bepuzzlement, and occasional frowns.

Take, for beginning, the five-act piece, *Der Sohn*. *The Son* was begun in 1913, and published in the opening year of the great conflict. It has, incidentally, sold like a popular novel into the thousands, and the reason for its popularity is implicit in the very title. The play, like the movement that it represents, is a revolt of the sons against the fathers,

of the new against the old. The son stands for
everything that is everlasting change, the father for
all that is philosophically and self-protectively conservative. Between these, despite all that links
them to each other, is a species of eternal warfare,
now underground and muffled, now overt and implacable. The victory is always to the new, which
in its turn becomes the old of a newer generation,
and thus onward ad infinitum. An old, old theme,
this struggle of the emerging new, nor has Hasenclever brought anything thematically novel to its
unfolding; the novelty, then, lies in the treatment;
from our point of view, plot is distinctly secondary,
as perhaps it was with the author. Expressionism is,
from its very title, new more in manner than in
content, though a thorough change in the one implies a change in the other.

The Son fails in his examinations and, after a
talk with his Instructor, is brought by his thoughts
to the brink of suicide; a sudden reaction is wrought
by a vision, and he decides to live. Now that life
possesses a new sweetness, he looks with different
eyes upon the Governess who serves as guardian
over him during his father's absence. He demands
that his father be sent for; he wishes to have it out
with his parent once and for all.

Act Two: a love episode between him and the
Governess is interrupted by the arrival of the Father,
whereupon ensues a bitter—and highly effective—debate between the two men, ending with the Father's
decision to lock the boy in his room. The Father, a
physician, considers his son temporarily deranged
by a fever, so strange does this rebellious talk come
from a child hitherto amenable to every paternal

wish. But revolt, as well as love, laughs at lock-
smiths, and the same friend who has visited the Son
in the previous act appears now to the strains of the
chorus in Beethoven's Ninth Symphony and wafts
the Son forth through an open window to lead the
revolt of the world's suppressed sons.

Act Three: A society of youth has assembled in
annual meeting and is to be addressed by Cherubim, a sublimated stump-orator eager for effect
rather than for sense. Just as his triumphant speech
is about to be delivered, enter the Friend, who
challenges Cherubim and all he stands for. Rebellious youth, it seems, has differences in its own
ranks; it has been whispered somewhere, I believe,
that there are fathers "younger" than their own
sons. The upshot of the Friend's arrival is that
instead of Cherubim winning a rhetorical triumph
with his merely epicurean oration, the Son, under
the hypnotic influence of the Friend, delivers a revolutionary appeal; the society for the propagation of
joy is won in a campaign against the fathers. "Death
to the dead!" becomes the slogan a phrase deeper
than the mere paradox that at first appears. The
Son's triumph has saved his own life, for behind the
scenes the Friend has stood ready to shoot him if
he should fail to capture the sentiments of the
society.

Act Four: The Son surrenders to a sentimental
interlude with Adrienne, a daughter of joy. He is
naïve; she would be his teacher; for the nonce his
violent speech has escaped from his memory. "What
is eight hours old has already become historical to
me." But the Friend, who plays, from the beginning, Mephistopheles to the Son's Faust, arrives

with the news that he himself has informed the
Son's father of the escaped child's whereabouts.
The Father has sent the police to apprehend the
young rebel. And now, according to the mysterious
Friend, comes the supreme test. Will the Son,
leader of the world's revolting sons, slay his own
father if that tyrant really has sent the police upon
his trail? The promise is exacted and made; and
surely enough in come the police, to whom, without
a struggle, the Son surrenders. The Friend, his
mission now fulfilled, yearns for death, the vision
of which blends with that of the returning Adrienne.
"She will bring me annihilation in a drop of cham-
pagne."

Act Five: The Father and the Police-chief, who
is also a father, discuss the case of the Son. The
first is the obdurate Roman parent, kindly in his
own way, but firm in his interpretation of filial
duty and paternal authority; not so the other, who
counsels leniency. Led back to his father, the Son
determined if necessary to slay a tyrant who refuses
him liberty, assumes the attitude of judge rather
than defendant; again the old debate is resumed,
with increasing fury and at the very moment, it
seems, when the Son is ready to shoot, the Father is
stricken with apoplexy. A short epilogue is spoken
(in rhymed verse) by the Son, who proclaims a
mission in which sacrifice fructifies deeds:

> Denn dem Lebendigen mich zu verbünden,
> Hab' ich die Macht des Todes nicht gescheut.
> Jetzt höchste Kraft in Menschen zu verkünden,
> Zur höchsten Freiheit, ist mein Herz erneut!

On this note of the defiance of death in the spreading
of a libertarian gospel, the play comes to an end.

Governess and Son walk hand in hand off the stage, leaving the corpse alone in the middle of the room.

As to the technical aspects of the play, there is much to be said. Note at the very start the return to the five-act form. Note, too, that there is the occasional use of rhymed verse. As we have already learned, the soliloquy is self-conscious; indeed, there is a repeated use of stage figures of speech that seems to attest an added wish of the author to impress the theatrical atmosphere. Thus, at the opening of the play, when the Son wishes to be left alone, his instructor asks him: "What are you going to do now?" Whereupon the Son replies:

Probably indulge in a soliloquy. I must have a talk with myself. You know formerly this method was despised. But I've never found it blameworthy to kneel down before my own pathos, for I know how poignantly real are my joy and my sorrow. Ever since my earliest childhood I have learned to love the solitude around me, until it spoke to me in tones. Even to-day I can go into the garden and stand before a few trees, directing a symphony and playing the tenor of my own opera. . . . Don't you know that feeling?

The Instructor, a workaday soul like ourselves, is embarrassed for reply; here is something not in his books, so all he can say is, "We live on an upper floor." We have, in this paragraph of the Son, a hint of what is, as we have said, coming to be called the presentational method. The Son not only emphasizes the fact that he is an actor, but fairly states the dramatist's apology or justification for the use of soliloquy; he turns commentator, critic, theorist, and, what is more, is practically addressing the audience, though well within his rôle. The mood is the "exalted" one so sought by the Expressionists.

Examine the third scene of the second act; the Son has been locked up and despairs in a brief soliloquy. Suddenly his friend appears outside the window, announcing that he has circumvented all precautions. The Son is overwhelmed with joy.

SON: It's you! You love me! Good God! God!

FRIEND (*half of him showing through the window*): Have I come at the right hour?

SON: Can anyone yet befriend me, as forsaken as I am?

FRIEND: Have you forgotten that Beethoven lives? You no longer recall that we sang in the Chorus of the Ninth Symphony? Would you not embrace all mankind? Up, my youth, it is daybreak! . . . Let us wander amidst the echoes of joy as once, after the concert hall was closed, we wandered together into the night.

As they escape through the window, the spectator beholds the lights of the distant city. Over the wind come faintly wafting the strains of the finale of the Ninth Symphony, tenor solo and male chorus:

> Froh wie seine Sonnen fliegen
> Durch des Himmels prächt'gen Plan,
> Laufet, Brüder, eure Bahn,
> Freudig wie ein Held zum Siegen.

And "joyous as a hero to victory" the Son leaves on his high purpose.

At the end of the third act the programme of the Ninth Symphony chorus yields to the war-cry of the Marseillaise. The Prince himself, won over by the

Son's eloquence, leaps upon a table and starts to sing:

> Aux armes, citoyens!
> Formez vos bataillons!
> Marchons! Marchons!

We have found, thus far, a medley of the realistic drama (the hot debate between father and son), the verse play, the opera. Once more, at the end of the fourth act, when death seems to beckon this time to the Friend, since his mission in directing the Son's actions is at an end, there is a self-conscious soliloquy, with a critical remark seeking to explain and justify. "Soliloquies before death are frequent," he tells himself. It is the somewhat hazy figure of this Friend that imparts to the play the character of a quasi-mystical drama. The "raisonneur" is not dead; he lives again in contemporary drama, now frankly enough, as in Molnar's *The Devil*, now in such another avatar of Mephistopheles as this selfsame Friend. The reminiscence of *Faust* is not due solely to critical perspicacity; it is suggested by the dramatist himself, in yet another passage of the play that indicates the author's desire to impress upon us the essential artificiality of his medium. The Son has just recited a rhymed soliloquy of some seventy verses, when the Friend mysteriously appears.

FRIEND: I heard that you had failed in your examinations. Were you about to commit suicide?

SON: To be brief—yes.

FRIEND: Well, why didn't you?

SON: I decided to live.

FRIEND: You owe your life to a plagiarism of Faust.

Aren't you allowed to read Goethe yet? Does your father at least let you go to theatre?

The latter-day Mephistopheles, however, tempts his Faust, not with women, but with ideas. Before the end of the play has been reached, it is not only the fathers against whom the sons of the world are to revolt, but the entire family system. The characters of the play are, as may easily be seen from what has been written, types rather than individuals; the Friend, in addition, is a vague type, tenuous, suggesting even an intellectual attribute of the Son himself, and from such a point of view to be considered as a complementary self, somewhat in the manner of Leandro and Crispin in Benavente's sparkling apologue, *Los Intereses Creados*.

The Expressionists, having disavowed psychology, would logically have little use for character in the realistic sense of the word. If Hasenclever's people are schematic, symbolic personages, embodying the various postulates of the author's inner debates, this is not through dramaturgic deficiency; it is part of his avowed manner. The same must be said of his scenes, which may be coherent enough when his purpose seems to demand it; usually, and more notably in his later work, they are capricious, shifting like the imagery of thought rather than progressing in conformity with the unity of place enforced by the exigencies of the modern stage.

The Expressionist may repudiate the thesis play and speak of the substitution of ideas for theses (nor is the distinction new, for there is a genuine difference between the problem play and the thesis play, though the terms are often employed inter-

changeably).[1] Yet such a play as *Der Sohn* is a
thesis play, or very near it. Its intent is unmis-
takable; to be sure, we have a certain feeling that
the dramatist has tried to be fair; he has presented
good fathers (the police chief) as well as frivolous
sons; the name of the play, however, and its course,
plainly reveal the author's sympathies. To attempt
an appraisal of its values would be premature, as
it would be in the case of the other plays to which
we shall presently come, because the medium is
new and one must allow for mental habits. Several
readings seem to indicate that the play would
easily interest a trained audience; it has high moments, high purpose, and its author is plainly an
intellectual force.

Antigone, which followed *Der Sohn*, owes only its
material and its personages to Sophocles. In the
hands of Hasenclever the plot acquires a pacifistic
passion; Antigone blames herself for having dwelt
in passive pleasure while the war just ended raged
in its path.

> Ich klage mich an, die niedrichste Magd von allen,
> dass ich lebte und wusste: Wir töten uns,
> dass keine Stimme von Gottes Himmel
> mich erweckte als Retterin.
> Ich klage mich an, dass in meine Kissen
> nicht die Wunden eiterten hinein,
> dass ich schwebte auf blühenden Girlanden,
> solange ein Mensch noch hungrig war.
> Ich klage mich an—ich habe Gutes genossen,
>   doch nichts Gutes getan, sonst wären Meschen
>   nicht feind.

---

[1] The thesis play, for example, elucidates a foregone conclusion; the problem
play presents, rather than solves, an issue.

The chorus of the poor (and Greek-like choruses, much transformed, are common in Expressionist drama) proclaims the new day:

> ˮFriede allen Nöten.
> Friede allem Leid.
> Schon auf Morgenröten
> grüsst die neue Zeit. ˈ

Antigone is the leader of her people, even in her chains. Schneider complains that it is too theatrical, that its language, especially that of King Kreon, is too rhetorical, and that the inartistic parallel between the king and Wilhelm II injures the artistry. Yet he finds in the play, which he considers superior to *Der Sohn*, a wealth of deep passion, a great longing for justice and human solidarity.

From now on Hasenclever's plays grow misty, like an ill-focussed slide upon a murky screen. Take, as instance, *Die Menschen* (1918), another five-act play, but almost distinct enough from *Der Sohn* to have come from another hand. Dialogue has been reduced to a semi-comprehensible minimum; what is more, there is no logic to the act-divisions, and such coherency as binds them must be deduced, although a scene here and there adheres to some cogent principle. The technique is fairly Marinettian in its Futurism; time and space are the playwright's toys and even severed heads may speak. The whole flickers past the vision like a badly edited film, and the words click like the telegrapher's key. *Der Sohn* is as a set of kindergarten blocks compared to the Expressionistic filming of *Die Menschen*. As to the plot, I offer, in all humility,

such a narrative as two puzzled readings have
yielded up from the mad succession of scenes.
Alexander, rising from his grave, meets a murderer
who cries aloud his crime, at the same time passing
to him a sack with the head of the murdered person.
The murderer descends into the grave and Alexander throws earth upon him, leaving then upon a
series of adventures; he comes upon a couple of
lovers, the lass crying that she has betrayed her
swain; he enters a café in which a murder is being
discussed; through deception and robbery he stalks,
in high places and low, perhaps in quest of himself,
for at the end of the first act he asks, "Who am I?"
There are episodes with prostitutes, gloomy prog-
nostications by a fortune-teller, made to the youth
and lass of the first act, and surely enough we next
find them in the doctor's office, he suffering from the
unmentionable disease and she big with child, yet
winsome enough to attract the physician. Now
comes Alexander to save the maid from suicide and
the youth as well, for the next scene shows them all
in an opera box. "Where are we?" asks the maid.
"Resurrection," answers Alexander.

The following acts bring like adventure of like
significance. "Who are you?" asks the father of a
little girl whose mother Alexander has befriended.
"I am looking for myself," is the reply. "Mensch!"
(i. e., human being) is the father's monosyllabic
exclamation. Then comes a hospital, with an almost unmentionably cynical episode of a child's
birth; in a later scene the cynical doctor is himself
done away with for his money; there is a court trial
in which Alexander is found guilty of the murder
committed, persumably, by the man who replaced

him in the grave. In vain he offers evidence, repentance; "All are murderers!" he cries out, and is
thereupon sent to the madhouse. He returns at
length to the grave, the man he left there comes out,
Alexander gives him back the sack, empty, and
descends into the tomb as the murderer, stretching
out his arms, cries, "I love!" Gruesome, path-
ological, grotesque. But art? One recalls a useful
distinction, insisted upon somewhere by Wilson
Follet: art is not merely self-expression, but self-
communication. Hasenclever doubtless expresses
something or other in *Die Menschen;* he is imbued,
as are his fellows, with a sense of our common guilt,
our need of merging that guilt in an all-embracing
love; as to what he communicates needs further
thought. Plays such as these, it seems, demand
discussion in terms of Freud; indeed, an American
analyst, Dr. Brill, in his latest book, suggests a
comparison between the auto-eroticism of the infant
life and the contemporary artists whose compositions are understood only by themselves. The normal child as it grows older learns the proper transference of its affections to an outside object; corresponding art likewise communicates the author's
emotions in degree. Mere expression stops upon
the threshold of the shut-in, the self-preoccupied personality. Of course such comparisons properly concern only the genesis of a work of art; they cannot
replace the final æsthetic criteria. And it is just this
æsthetic sense that Hasenclever so amuses and
puzzles in *Die Menschen.*[1]

Der Retter was written previous to *Die Menschen,*

---

[1] The psychoanalysts no doubt could tell us pretty things about the constant
use of severed heads by these writers. We might call it the John-the-Baptist
"complex!"

in 1915, and not unnaturally deals with the problem of those days. The King, his Minister, the Field Marshal, and the Poet are the chief figures, with a vision of Saint Paul lending a mystic touch and a grand apotheosis in which the Queen appears. The Poet is a man of peace and would work his way with the King, who feels for him, but national necessity forces the monarch to place all power into the hands of the Marshal, who demands and receives the life of the Poet. Essentially the play, which Hasenclever calls a dramatic poem, is social, pacifist, poetically Christian. It is written with a high intensity that at times attains to eloquence; music, light, and scenic effect play parts analogous to those in *Der Sohn* and in the new play, *Jenseits*, as in a moment we shall see. The author is very evidently fond of the debate as a dramatic tool, and no doubt this answers a need felt by him as a critic of society. Again it is worth while calling attention to thesis implications of both theme and treatment.

Jenseits (1920) is less easy to understand than *Der Sohn*, but not quite so baffling as *Die Menschen*. In any event it is a play in simple language that almost eludes understanding. Hasenclever is not an abstruse writer; his style is usually clear in expression; it is the combination of events and the sequence of images that alternately attract and repel the critic. The technique here is largely that of the presentational method; for recent psychology in the drama it substitutes a new psychic suggestiveness; at times the dialogue (or the monologue) is naïveté of a medieval order. There are but two persons in the play, Raul and Jeane. In the other plays we have considered there are stage directions; here they are reduced, as are the personages, to a minimum. The place of action is "the house," and the various scenes take place in different parts of the house, now at the window, now in a room, again near a telephone or on a bed. Perhaps Jeane is the eternal woman, true to her first husband and to her child rather than to Raul, the eternal man, slaying love through very excess, that he may be free of its fetters.

The "plot" of *Beyond* is perhaps implied by such an interpretation. The dramatist's means are characteristic. The very opening, for example, shows Jeane at the window, talking to herself:

This is my house. This is my window. This is the sky. The sun is shining. I know that I am alive. I am happy. I am beloved. (*She takes a couple of roses.*) Summer is coming. Yesterday was Sunday. When Sirius rises, it is night. Night, when I kiss. Night, when I love. I am born. I am with thee. No garment hides me, no veil. I stand naked before thee. Only a few hours. Time is eternal. Come soon. Come again. I love thee. (*She opens the window.*) This is my house. This is my window. These are flowers in my hand. If they could feel as I feel! My friend! My beloved! My husband.

Her husband, however, is killed in an accident, and instead, there comes his friend, Raul. Thus begins the course of their love, which Jeane is soon to repudiate as an act of madness and grief on her part. The coils, however, tighten around them both, and this way and that they are torn in the conflict of their emotions. The presence of the husband returns to hover over them and add to their confusion. A child forecasts its coming, and serves to divide rather than unite them. Raul goes mad. "Let the world crash to ruin! I preach annihilation in my name. . . . Free! I am my own judge. The world belongs to me. Love is death!" Yet again he appeals to Jeane, who literally tells him to take everything but "spare my child!" Her greater allegiance, however, is to the child, and when Raul sees this, he stabs her even as he is kissing her. Whereupon, according to the stage directions, "invisible hands bear off the house. The walls noiselessly collapse, the various objects sink into the depths, the chandelier sways on high. The window in the background disappears." Raul's head is bathed in a light that seems to issue from his own forehead. "I see the light. I see into Life. I see into the kingdom of all things transitory. For the last time I have been a human being. I am illumined. I am ready." Curtain.

It is interesting to note a strange blending of the ancient with the futuristic technique in the course of these short five acts. We have heard Jeane soliloquize, we have heard her ask in melodramatic accents that her child be spared; so, too, there is (as in other plays of Hasenclever) the old device of transmitting information across the footlights. On the other hand, to companion such effects as speaking heads[1] (and did not a certain Will Shakespeare employ them in *Macbeth?*) there is the material representation of psychic effects that Marinetti has tried to build into independent plays made up of inanimate objects. So here, in the first scene of the

---

[1] Compare the scene in Wedekind's *Frühlings Erwachen*, in which the boy comes out of his grave, with his own head under his arm, for a talk with his old schoolmate. Bartels has called *Der Sohn* an example of immature Wedekindism.

fourth act, "the moon fills the room with spots. The various pieces of furniture assume faces. Behind the wall appear the silhouettes of beckoning arms and legs."

Hasenclever is not an isolated phenomenon; he is a popular member of a groping group that is more positive in its reaction against previous methods than in its advance toward anything like definite accomplishment. He is not, in these plays, national; the milieu is everywhere in general, the core of his feelings is broadly human and universal. Neither is he, it may be added, erotic, though persons with a penchant for psychoanalyzing literature may detect the symptoms of certain "complexes". Indeed, *Der Sohn* would by these students be referred to the Œdipus cycle of literary manifestations.[1] In company of most dramatists who write with a purpose, he lacks humor. Yet even as the Italian Futurists, for all their overemphasis upon subordinate details, are not to be dismissed without a fair examination, so the wildest of Hasenclever's creations may yield —together with the other new German dramatists —a tithe of permanent gain, a new flexibility, a new suggestive power, to the dramatist and the theatre that live on, above the welter of "isms" and "ologies" in the upper regions of art.

GEORG KAISER

That the Expressionists form a loosely allied group rather than a concerted reaction or a centralized movement, is further emphasized by consideration of some of the more striking members

---

[1] I am sure that some German student will soon write an essay upon *The Œdipus Situation in the New Drama*. There is abundant material!

of the nucleus. And there are groups within the group, as witness the *Aktion* and the *Sturm*.

Kaiser has been called a number of names at home and abroad. Financial difficulties (so readily solved in his plays, thick with millionaires, banks and floating notes) brought him a couple of years ago into notoriety, and it was even suggested by part of the German press that he needed seclusion in a sanitarium rather than punishment behind the bars. Later, when his *Von Morgens bis Mitternachts* was put into English, The Morning Post of London made the discovery that Kaiser was a "Bolshevik dramatist,"—a judgment and a phrase that means nothing, either to art in general or with special reference to Kaiser's plays. The man may be, as Kerr of the *Berliner Tageblatt* has said, half-Expressionist and half-bluffer, but he has written some things that, if as a whole they reveal the influence of Ibsen, Wedekind (his *Rektor Kleist* is another edition of *Frühlings Erwachen*), and Sternheim, in turn will influence the younger generation.

Even Kaiser's "bluffs," if such they really are— for example *Europa*, a "play and dance" in five acts, or *Der Gerettete Alkibiades* (*Alcibiades Delivered*)—contain undoubted moments of beauty; and if no single play can be pointed to as an immaculate accomplishment, there is in the sum of his work a suggestion of a novel nuance in the contemporary drama. There may be a question as to whether that nuance is rather pictorial than essentially dramatic; as to whether Kaiser has any definite knowledge of what he is striving after, or, as I am inclined to think, he is roving about half lost, like so many of his fellows. In any event, he is not the mystifier that Kokoschka plainly seems to be; if he is not always clear, one feels that he actually is expressing something and in his own way. Call him what you will, discover the origins of his work—and a varied, wavering line his labors trace —in whatever impulse you please, the man has intuitions of beauty in the drama. He is intense in spots, rather than complete; he is a playwright of fascinating fragments; in continuing and elaborating the "speed-technique" of Wedekind he has sacrificed the continuity to which we have long been accustomed. But not merely for the sake of covering more ground or in an impatient desire for an art of outbursts. Kaiser, in his more thorough-going pieces, seeks something of the expressional power of music. If not every word be grasped, not every idea linked to the remaining phrases in a chain of logic, little harm is done. These scenes, these people upon the stage before us are visions, emotions made visible. It is the succession of emotions, the surge of feeling, that counts.

Among the new dramatists Kaiser is relatively old. He was born on November 25, 1878, at Madgeburg, and followed early in the footsteps of his father as a merchant. Business took him for three years to Buenos Aires, and on his return he married. His plays already number at least a score. The Expressionists, even those that belong to the out-and-out ranks, are none too consistent in their production; clarity and obscurity sit side by side in the same play, let alone the list of their writings. So that in the case of the half-Expressionist Kaiser we are not surprised to find pieces ranging from the transparent action of *Das Frauenopfer* (which may, with close approximation to its actual contents, be translated into the banal title *A Woman's Sacrifice*) to the murkiness of *From Morn to Midnight* and yet again to the alternate light and shade of *Europa*. Nor do these varying manners follow any chronological order. *Das Frauenopfer*, for example, belongs to 1918, being preceded (1917) by *Die Koralle*, an interesting bit of pure Expressionism (if there be any such thing) and followed by *Gas* of the same year and *Hölle Weg Erde* of the next. A zig-zag spirit, then, both in the line traced by his entire output and in the rhythm of the separate pieces.

Die Judische Witwe (1911, *The Jewish Widow*) is a Biblical play on the Judith theme; *Die Bürger von Calais* (1914) is likewise historical, going back to the tale of the six victims demanded by Edward III., for England; *Das Frauenopfer* is part history and part fiction, recounting the story of Madame La Valette, who, saving her husband after he has been condemned to death following the downfall of Napoleon, saves him once again—and by the same subterfuge of putting on masculine apparel—when the soldiery comes in pursuit of him. The play has more than the significance of an altered historical tale; it seeks, not too successfully, to contrast the sacrificing spirit of womankind with the narrow, jealous heart of man. La Valette, for example, learning that his wife, having taken his place in the cell when he walked out in feminine garb, dallied under compulsion with the guards so as to give him more time in which to make good his escape, bursts into possessive fury. But the plot is too strained for reality; it is too obvious for symbolism; it falls between two stools into a species of grotesquerie.

20

Two years before, in *Konstantin Strobel*, known also as *Der Zentaur*, Kaiser had written a play which blended reality and fantasy in even less separable fashion. The first half of the play is in what for him we may call the realistic fashion. We divine that Strobel, engaged to Judith, has been straying with a common house-servant. And we divine also, though less clearly, that in this seemingly ignoble act was the germ of something that was meant to be noble. But the relation between end and beginning is not clear.

Between these plays and the others, however much one may discern in the first type signs of Kaiser's more Expressionistic moods, there is a fairly distinct line of cleavage. Yet little is gained by such distinction. Either Kaiser is comprehensible or he is not; either he affects the spectator or not. It is easy enough to show just where and wherein he is of this dramaturgic persuasion or other, and all that is required for such a purpose is a decent library of dramatic criticism, a pair of good eyes and the infinite—if none too fruitful—patience of the pedant. More to the present purpose is Kaiser's quest for beauty. For once and again he seems to gain it through a plastic use of the human figure (in the individual and in the mass) to express fundamental spiritual reactions. Let us examine first the piece that introduced him to the English-speaking public, *Von Morgens bis Mitternachts*, both in London and in New York.

From Morn to Midnight has little plot; plot is so secondary to the Expressionists that they are quite as willing to remake ancient plays as to borrow more modern tales, much less devise fables of their

own. Not the plot but the immediately communicated thrill of emotion is the thing. Here we
have a married bank clerk, who is fascinated by a
woman whom he believes accessible, and for whom
he steals sixty thousand from his institution, only
to find that she is not for sale. He has made the
leap and now he must plunge on to the bitter end.
Before he does so he visits his home—a bourgeois
domestic interior—and upsets it by his sudden leaving, before eating his noonday meal. The break
with routine kills his mother, but he receives her
death with a cold, Kaiserian remark: "Daran stirbt
sie, weil einer einmal vor dem Mittagessen weggeht"
("For once in his life a man goes out before his meal
—and that kills her").

The excitement that the woman from Italy has
denied him the fugitive will seek elsewhere—at the
howling enthusiasm of a six-day cycle race, which
he showers with prodigal prizes; at a high-class res-
taurant, at a Salvation Army hall, where confession
and repentance may ease his soul of the day's many
burdens. But the crowning irony comes when he
casts his money to the winds before the audience of
penitents. Instead of spurning it, they make a dash
for the precious paper. And the girl who has led
him to the sinner's bench betrays him to the police
for the sake of the reward offered for his apprehen-
sion. Suicide is his one recourse, and shortly after
the shot, all the electric globes explode in a vast
crash; the fugitive from justice, the seeker after
emotional intoxication, staggers with outspread arms
to the cross upon the curtain. "His groan rasps
like an Ecce; his gasp moans like a Homo," runs the
rather futile symbolism of the stage direction. The

prosaic officer closes the play with the curt remark that "Es ist ein Kurtzschluss in der Leitung,"—in briefer words still, "a short circuit."

And so the play, too, with its flash of light and the surrounding darkness, is artistically a short circuit. The closing scene in the Salvation Army Hall is a play in little—excepting, as we easily may, the childish Ecce Homo episode of the very end, which, for that matter, need not be heard in performance. The separate confessions of the penitents, leading up to the clerk's own public repentance; his scattering of the money and the consequent scramble, are conceived in a search for a rhythmic plasticity that serves the author's revelation of human nature. It is the culminating scene of the play and the most expertly managed. It is compact; it does not, like the opening scenes, wander; it produces an emotional effect independent, not of the words, but of their individual meanings. This is the "exaltation" after which the Expressionists strive and to which occasionally they attain. A play that could do this in its entirety would deserve the word "great," regardless of the "ism" that hatched it.

Largely on the strength of an acquaintance with this play, some of our native reviewers have somewhat carelessly spoken of O'Neill's "Expressionism" in *The Emperor Jones* and *The Hairy Ape*. But affinity is not identity, and if O'Neill were in search of "models" for his free structure he need hardly have gone abroad while Broadway or its vicinity harbored the "formless" plays of Gorki, Molnar and their kin. There is never a moment, for that matter, when O'Neill's artistic aim is in doubt; he makes no cult of personal mysteriousness; more than Kaiser he seems to know the reason for his various changes of form. He is, like the German, a fallible playwright, but one feels that he will elude the snares that his critics have set for him, with their overpraise and their eagerness to show that we, too, on this side of the ocean have new "isms" and "ists."

Did these critics of O'Neill know *Die Koralle*, surely they would have suspected some connection between the theme of *The Hairy Ape* and one of the episodes in the German piece. The coincidence of facial resemblance seems to have occupied Kaiser's thoughts at the time he wrote the play, for in *Das Frauenopfer*, which preceded it by a year, the resemblance between husband and wife played no little part in her deception of his captors. Similarly in *Die Koralle* the resemblance between a philanthropic millionaire and his secretary provides the pivot upon which turns the impossible plot—in which we are asked, for example, to believe that not even the man's children can distinguish him from his physical alter ego. The son in whom he centres his hopes runs off—as a stoker. The daughter likewise rebels. His secretary has lived a peaceful youth that the millionaire would enjoy if only in retrospect. Thereupon the moneyed potentate slays his counterpart and pretends, for the sake of that vicarious, retrospective enjoyment, to be the man whom he has slain. From this decision not even his children—at last ready to reveal his true identity —can move him.

Of course, if you are one of the initiate, you will know that the secretary is, in the first place, *another aspect* of the millionaire. In slaying the secretary, then assuming his identity, the millionaire merely returns to that other aspect of himself. But this, as a drama, is a metaphysical rebus.

The play exists for its detail; it is not an artistic entity. Kaiser is fond betimes of preaching through the mouths of his characters. So, in the second act, there are interesting arguments on board the millionaire's yacht, which has set out in chase after the *Albatross*, upon which the son has sailed as stoker. They overtake the son, who has learned humanity at the mouths of the furnaces. He has the nostalgia of the boilers; a man turned hairy ape, as it were, out of understanding and sympathy with the men below decks, rather than a hairy ape frustrated in a blind, boastful groping after place in the scheme of society. "On the deck," he cries, "the passengers stroll in their gay clothes, chat and are merry. A few metres below is hell. There human beings burn with quivering flesh in hot shafts before holes that belch fire. So that we can have a swift, jolly voyage. . . . Fever seethes under the soft soles of your white shoes. Everything in half-darkness!—Rip up this wall of lumber —such a thin wall, but what a gruesome partition it spells!—And look down—all of you—live through it, so that the words will stick in your throat when you try to be uppish to any of the fellows from down there!" As in Hasenclever's *Der Sohn*, so here there is a scene in which the son threatens the father with a revolver. There are interesting, but hardly beautiful, moments.

More successful, from the standpoint of the playwright's aim, is *Hölle Weg Erde*, which, it may be mentioned in passing, seems in its printed form to prefigure what may be called the Expressionist typography. Time and space are telescoped as far as possible. Lead is not rubber, as the compositor will tell you, and there are limits to such compression. The piece is printed ":solid;" every scene forms an unbroken paragraph; stage-directions are done in italics, while the only device that separates the speaker from what is spoken is the printing of the character's name in capitals. The spiritual theme is that of human solidarity is good and evil —an ancient one, in all conscience, since there, but for the grace of God, goes any one of us. "Not the Murderer, But the Murdered Is Guilty," runs the title of a novel by the brilliant young Expressionist, Franz Werfel; so here, not the robber but the robbed seems to be guilty. The résumé of a plot, always an unsatisfactory substitute for the original, is triply so with reference to these pieces. As they aim at evoking an emotional flux, so must they be discussed in terms of those emotions.

"Wer is nicht schuldig?" asks the protagonist, Spazierer, in the second part of the play. "Who is not guilty?" And it is this theme that receives quasi-symphonic treatment toward the end of the piece. Spazierer, in need of funds with which to save an anguishing soul, is enraged to find how easily that same money is spent upon such luxuries as jewels for women; he visits his fury upon the jeweler, serves his term, discovers that prison is really a punishment of society by the ill-understood criminals, and comes forth to convert the very society that was responsible for his incarceration. There is a fine effect of antiphony in the prison yard when, with Spazierer as a sort of spiritual chorus director, the two large divisions of the prisoners on one side and the distant crowd on the other cry out their confession, which is at the same time purification. "We are guilty," chant the prisoners, while, from afar comes the answer of the crowd, "We are innocent!" "We are innocent!" echo the prisoners, while the crowd responds, "We are guilty!" And soon guilt and innocence blend into one vast human chorus wherein they are almost indistinguishable. It is at such moments as this that Kaiser suggests the potentialities of the new method. The themes are not so new as is the attitude, which determines the new form. What is thematically new about *Gas*, with its millionaire's son who renounces his fortune (the son in *Die Koralle*) and ventures forth to combat the machinery of capitalism? And what is new about the skeptical attitude of the very masses whom he seeks to benefit and who prove themselves as yet unready for redemption? And just how "Bolshevik" is a play with such a theme and such an outcome?

Kaiser's relative importance, then, lies in his development of the "speed-technique," in his "exaltation," his blending of pictorial plasticity and choral emotion—as if sculpture were made to live and communicate feeling. In *Europa* he does this through an effective scene in which Europa's suitors seek to win her in competitive dance against the disguised Zeus. The play, as a whole, is a satire against the æstheticism of Stefan George and his followers, much as—mutatis mutandis—Gilbert's *Patience* satirizes Wilde. And Kaiser's "fleshly" moral is that Europa is weary of her perfect, terpsichorean suitors and would enjoy some healthy

animality. More body, less soul, is her desire.
And that is a large part of Kaiser's own doctrine.
In *Der Gerettete Alkibiades* he achieves the same
effect more than once—in the scene with the crowd
of fisherwomen, and again when Phryne tries without
success to enamour Socrates; later, too, in the
trial scene, where Socrates appears to answer the
charges against Alcibiades, who has fled. Once
again Socrates saves the hero whose gratitude is
strangely mingled with resentment.

In all these plays there inheres a decided reassort-
ing of dramatic values. If Kaiser is a "bluff," then
one wishes for a "bluffer" like him with more talent
for maintaining the dramatic level—a difficult feat,
it may be added, since a continued maintenance of
"exaltation" wears out the very emotions which are
meant to be stirred. With all his faults, mystifica-
tions, grotesquerie, and restlessness Kaiser may be
one of the precursors of a new orientation in the
drama. This need not, except to the fanatic in art,
mean abandonment of the past; rather it is an en-
richment of the future. Why is it impossible, side
by side with the drama of character, plot, and continuity, to harbor the drama of type fragment and
immediate emotion? It is not. All that is required
is the dramatist of genius and the audience of re-
sponsive talent. A large order, that, but it can be
filled.

OSKAR KOKOSCHKA

The theory of the German Expressionists elucidates, ostensibly, a desire on the part of the new
dramatists to get closer to the hearts of their audiences—to present emotion as directly as may be,

without the baffling intervention of craft, homily, or convention. Yet their practise, with scant exception, has been quite the opposite. They have enfolded themselves in thick esoteric veils and, so clad, lead themselves and the spectators a merry dance that leaves one at the end about where one was at the beginning. To be just, some of this difficulty is due to an excess of earnestness; to continue to be just, some of it is seemingly nothing more than an attempt to amaze the uninitiated, to confound the bourgeoisie. It is precisely as such an example of shell-shock "artistry" that one should approach the so-called "Expressionist" dramas of Oskar Kokoschka. If his paintings are at all comparable to his stage-pieces, they must be, to say the least, interesting psychological documents though hardly chefs-d'oeuvre.

Kokoschka was born in 1886, in Austria. The four dramas for which he has become notorious are *Mörder, Hoffnung der Frauen* (1907), *Der Brennende Dornbusch* (1911), *Hiob* (1917), and *Orpheus und Euridyke* (1918). If any definite idea is to be picked out of these swirling sands, I must confess ignorance of the process. When the Italian youngsters wish to become "grotesque" they often get silly, but rarely turn incomprehensible. Things are done, persons come and go; they may be followed, if only with amused disapproval. Kokoschka is comprehensible only in tiny oases, and then the æsthetic reward is almost nil. One may easily imagine, in not so many years to come, a laborious critic coming upon the finely printed volume of Kokoschka's *Vier Dramen*, shaking his head sadly and exclaiming: "How cheap must paper and labor have been in those gladsome days! The plays mean next to nothing, but what excellent typography, what ample margins, what pride of craftsmanship! The plays may not be easy to understand, but heaven be praised that they are at least easy to read, and physical comfort compensates for the intellectual dismay."

Criticism implies an open mind, and it is unfair to oneself, let alone the creative artist, to be swift with condemnation or ridicule. The Expressionist Movement, like others that went before, has committed its follies, but it has at least brought the suggestion of a modified technique based upon a modified attitude toward the world and life. So doing, it has exaggerated with the ardor of the new convert, but it would be folly to condemn it out of impatience or a desire not to be bothered. "Expressionism" is, in short, a symptom of a changing world and is as likely as not to produce the genius who will transcend its circumscribed tenets. That is what geniuses are for. But such a spirit of tolerance, and such an eagerness to understand the multiform strivings of the artist to express himself, need not deter us from sweeping aside altogether, on occasion, the merely wilful mystifier of a school or sect. Such a playwright is Kokoschka, and his plays are to be read accordingly. For here is an Expressionist who expresses nothing.

Take, for beginning, *Murderers, the Hope of Womankind*—a name to conjure with. The action occurs in antiquity before a tower bathed in the glare of torches. The characters are nameless, as in most of the "Expressionist" plays—The Man, The Woman, Warriors, and Maidens. The playwright seems to have attempted a depiction of the savagery that flows beneath our civilized love-making. His verse is free; his scenic grouping suggestive of canvas effects, with a certain oscillation of feeling between the warriors led by The Man and the maidens led by The Woman. One might venture to describe the short piece—it is in a single act—as a species of esoteric sadism. But even then, it needs the exegesis of a psychoanalyst. As creative art, it "says" next to nothing.

The Burning Bush, likewise in one act, is a little less obscure. In the manner of the new playwrights it makes prominent use of shadows, "spotlight" effects, symbolic lights (white while The Man speaks and red for The Woman's answers), transformation scenes and choruses. Its theme, similar to that of the preceding play, is voiced in the chorus of the second scene:

> Wer himmlischer Liebe Schlüssel hat,
> Dem nie erstirbt die Stund.
> Wie süss wird's ihm erst sein.
> Ird'sche Liebe ist nur ein' Pein,
> Ein Rosendorn am Pfad
> Zum Gartentor von Golgotha.
> Seele, bleib noch nicht da. . . .

A mystic theme, then, of love reconciliation in the beyond, presented in mystifying fashion.

Hiob is a step in advance, if only because its anti-feminism becomes fairly clear in a clumsy rehash of Job's woeful tale. Its motto is "Pein für Bein" and is elaborated in six lines of sterile satire:

> Als Adam schlief auf grünem Rasen,
> Erbarmte Gott, die Sonn' im Mittag stand
> Und dem vor Langerweil schon um Schlafen sei.

Weint Adam, in der Nacht von einem Rippenstoss
  erwacht: "Ei"
Und da mit Eva sich begattet fand:
"Mein Gott, hätt'er mir nur mein Bein mit Ruh gelassen."

Kokoschka's Adam would rather surrender his Eva
and have his rib back, and it is likewise with Job
and his wife, Anima, who brings him to an unhappy
end. "And Anima," as the closing lines of the play
inform us, "who placed upon Job's shoulder the
burdensome cross—is Eva." The play does not
limit itself to human beings; there are parrots, dogs,
heads poking up through apertures in a canvas that
is painted with the bodies of men clad in mourning.
"How love has turned my head," groans Job, "since
in this empty house the gentle voice of a woman
called me unto her." If Kokoschka intended to
suggest, in his action, the turning of Job's head, he
has at least met with outward success—and communicated that turning to the reader as well.
"Essig gab und Wein dafür wollte," says Anima in
one place. And that is what the author has done
with us: given us vinegar and asked wine for it.
This is a mere toying with theatrical mechanism, a
rather faded novelty that irritates, because it serves
no significant purpose. So, too, the Italians have
played with marionettes upon the stage, with alter-
nating lights (though not yet with severed heads)
and have run into the same alleys of fatuity. It is
not at present easy to explain the Expressionist
predilection for severed heads—a fondness derived,
perhaps, from Wedekind's *Frühlings Erwachen*.

As for Kokoschka's *Orpheus and Eurydice*, no
purpose would be served by expatiating upon it.
If stage directions made a play, perhaps this impo-

sition in three acts and an epilogue would achieve
comprehensibility. As it is, some things pass understanding; others do not reach its threshold. This
play barely steps across. Kokoschka's "advanced"
strivings, if they are sincere, have moved in a circle
that brings him back somewhere behind the point
from which he set out. He is not to be thought of
in the same connection as Hasenclever, who is a
serious, if sometimes indistinct, artist; or Fritz von
Unruh, in whose work an ethical aim inheres; or
Georg Kaiser. Kaiser is no genius, nor, for that
matter, has the "Expressionist" group thus far produced any personage approaching Hauptmann's
stature. But Kaiser does "express" something in a
personal, recognizable medium. Kokoschka reduces
the theory to absurdity. Somewhere, I believe,
there was report that one of his plays had caused a
riot. Perhaps this is not quite the sort of participation aimed at by the "Expressionists" in their
fusion of audience with stage, but in the case of
Kokoschka it is the one kind that may be understood at this distance. The most appropriate simile
one may suggest for his plays is that flickering
phantasmagoria which parades under one's lashes
just before the sufferer sinks into a fevered slumber.

OTHER DRAMATISTS
STERNHEIM, KORNFELD, VON UNRUH, WERFEL, GOERING, TOLLER

The fairly detailed consideration of Hasenclever,
Kaiser, and Kokoschka has given, I hope, a notion
of the newer dramatists' practice, both near the
heights and toward the depths. The first two, how-

ever, are no more necessarily the best of the dramatists than Kokoschka is necessarily the worst. Carl Sternheim, for example, would make quite as interesting a subject as Georg Kaiser; both stand out from their confrères for a certain aloofness from their material, for a certain restlessness that is reflected in their numerous and varied plays. Sternheim, in Diebold's phraseology, is the ironic "grand-seigneur" whose skepticism destroys the will to the ideal; he is *précieux;* he employs, chiefly, anti-lyrical puppets whose significance is made clear not so much from what they say as from what occurs in the tale itself. He is chiefly *Geist,* with little *Seele*—the cynical anti-Philistine. Paul Kornfeld, on the other hand, derives from the Storm and Stress, and is as soulful (in Diebold's sense) as Sternheim is intellectual. His *Die Verführung* has been called, indeed, "an inexhaustible, ever-repeated eruption of a volcano of suffering." His personage, Bitterlich, has become one of the salient types of the new drama: he is the love-seeker who, unable to recognize love when it comes to him, is damned. For love must bring sacrifice, not pride. *Himmel und Hölle* shows the reverse of the coin; instead of a proud, blasphemous Bitterlich, a humble, dutiful Jacob, spokesman of mankind.

Fritz von Unruh, who, in *Offiziere* and *Louis Ferdinand, Prinz von Preussen,* wrote two plays of high merit, though they are not definitely in the Expressionist category, rose to new renown through the unfinished trilogy that comprises, thus far, *Ein Geschlecht* and *Platz.* The motto of his *Louis Ferdinand* affords an insight into his ideology: "Wie ueber Sterne das Gesetz, erhebt sich ueber

Menschen das Pflicht, gross und ernst." "As law above the stars, so reigns Duty above mankind, vast and solemn." It is the direction of that duty and its ancient conflict with desire which engross the impassioned mind of von Unruh.

Such is the conflict in *Offiziere*, Naturalistic in facture, though with forecasts of the writer's later Expressionism. Such is the conflict of *Louis Ferdinand*. Such, with a change of direction, is the conflict of the trilogy. That Duty exists is, to von Unruh, a cosmic axiom; it must shift from the service of Might to that of Right. *Ein Geschlecht* raises the figure of the suffering mother (the *Mater Dolorosa* theme of the Expressionists) to that of a powerful, eternal symbol—Mother Earth herself, forever bearing that her offspring may forever return to her bosom. This is not only protest against the madness of warfare but an image of life's own cruelty.

The most considerable production of Franz Werfel in the drama—for he is an able poet and novelist as well—is, thus far, the panoramic, phantasmagoric *Spiegelmensch*, denominated by its author a *Magic Trilogy*. Spiegelmensch himself (i. e., mirror-man) is one of the numerous alter-egos of Expressionist drama, one of the many children of Goethe's Mephistopheles. He is the counter-protagonist of what may well be called a twentieth-century morality, only that this morality is replete with high moments, though more effective in episodes than as a whole. An alter-ego-drama, then, redeemed from unoriginality by its poetry, its strange conceptions, its instinctive artistry, its effective portrayal of our many conflicting, deceptive selves forever in a new disguise assumed by Spiegelmensch. Its renunciatory moral would seem to be a sort of *Nirvanitas nirvanitatum;* one feels uneasy amidst the hectic self-dissolution of these young spirits.

One must nevertheless recognize that far from shirking the discipline of an ordered life, not a few of the Expressionists are Puritanically severe in their very Un-Puritanism. Our own Mr. Arthur Davison Ficke, in his *Mr. Faust,*[1] has written some lines that might serve to characterize the new strivings of such of the Expressionists as Werfel; they are all the more significant in that the Devil, in Ficke's play, tempts Faust, not with woman or wealth, but with that selfsame paradise of spiritual peace which Werfel's Thamal has sought through all the trickeries of his alter-ego Spiegelmensch:

> . . . I will create,—
> I and the souls that after me shall come
> By passion of desire a pillar of flame
> Above the wastes of life. If no God be,
> I will from my deep soul create a God
> Into the universe to fight for me.

How the false gods arrive with the hocus-pocus of their "religions" receives dramatic commentary not only in Spiegelmensch, but in Werfel's newest piece, *Bocksgesang.* Only one wonders, contrasting the mirror-like clearness of the first with the hazy action of the second, whether Werfel has not been indulging in a little bit of dramaturgic hocus-pocus himself.

Questioning of God, Fate and man is not confined to the modern morality type; it occurs even in the

---

[1] Cincinnati. 1922.

so-called revolutionary Expressionist plays, of which Reinhard Goering's *Seeschlacht* is a noteworthy prototype. I do not think that the charge of being a mere propaganda play may justly be brought against *Seeschlacht* any more than against Toller's *Masse-Mensch*. There is no conspicuous distortion of events or character to a foreordained end. Goering's tragedy is in a single long act, more lyrical than dramatic, yet undoubtedly effective, depicting the nascent revolt that brews in the armored turret of a battleship. But does it take much discernment to see that this is no mere battleship, for all the inspiration of the piece in a war-time mutiny? "I know," says the Fifth Sailor, the guiding inspiration of the piece. "What we are doing is madness and crime . . . for there are things between one human being and another which it is a more sacred duty to fulfil than any other battle."

Again a conflict of duties between man as State and man as Mankind. It is a similar conflict, with the distinctions more finely marked and more clearly presented, that is dramatized in Ernst Toller's notable piece *Masse-Mensch*. The very title emphasizes the important theme of the play, for *Masse* stands for man in the mass, while *Mensch* is man the individual, the human being, the freely developed personality. A revolutionary play, indeed, but directed against the very revolutionists themselves. And written in that same prison wherein Toller composed his latest drama, *Die Maschinenstürmer*. Toller was Minister of Justice in the Communistic government that lived for a short while in Bavaria, and is now—at the age of twenty-six—serving a twenty-year sentence. His first play,

Die Wandlung, is an ego-drama, turning upon the
experiences of the sculptor-hero, Friedrich, who en-
lists as an escape from ennui; at the end of the hair-
raising spectacle, with its pandemonium of the living and the dead, the sculptor smashes the statue
upon which he has been working,—a statue dedicated to the glory of his nation. Symbolism could
be no plainer. *Masse-Mensch,* however, is of far
better stuff. It is no mere propaganda of the
proletariat against the patrician. Indeed, in his
foreword to the second edition[1] he states expressly
that he does not believe in a proletarian art except
in so far as that art merges into the universally
human. And what is the purport of the play itself
but to free the mass from the raw, brutal force of
its own numbers and point the way to individual
creativeness? Moloch is Moloch, whether it be the
conservative State that slays or the revolutionary
Mass. Murder is murder; war is war. The Christ-
like woman protagonist, Sonja Irene L. (the only
person in the play who is named) goes to her death
at the hands of those for whom she has lived, because her message is sounded too soon. She is not
understood by the very men and women who have
called upon her leadership and rejected its far
vision.

There is art in this proclamation, as there is humanity. Toller makes highly effective use of the
dream-technique (three of the seven scenes are
presented as visions); he employs with skill choric
effects and plastic, sculptural groupings of crowds.
There is color, rhythm of motion, antiphony. There

---

[1] Potsdam, 1922. "Es gibt eine proletarische Kunst nur insofern, als für den
Gestaltenden die Mannigfaltigkeiten proletarischen Seelenlebens Wege zur For-
mung des Ewig-Menschlichen sind."

is an emotional surge that companions the progress of feeling in his character symbols. This is not allegory that evades expression; it is expression highly concentrated into symbolic figures who do not lose their human significance. In coherency, plasticity, management of the speed-technique, the play betters Kaiser's *Von Morgens bis Mitternachts*. It is one of the outstanding products of the new dramaturgy.

Die Maschinenstürmer relates, ostensibly, a tale of wretchedness among the English weavers in 1815, when machinery began to displace hand labor at the looms. Here, too, is a leader slain; here, too, machinery wrecked. And here, too, the new order brings misery, as did the old. By these tokens Toller means not only England and not only 1815. Yet, though he dedicate his plays (*Masse-Mensch*, for example) to the Proletariat, and write with conscious contemporaneity, he has done some work that will in all likelihood outlast the ferment of to-day.

To these names, to these plays, a goodly number might be added, for the dramatic fervor runs high in contemporary Germany. Out of the welter rises the one great contribution of the new dramatists: a new soul, a new intellect for a new world.

It is not necessary to "judge" the Expressionists at this date; they may disappear with the course of time, leaving only whatever vital elements of their theory prove available to the purposes of the ones that follow. That they have brought a *nouveau frisson* to the drama is undeniable; thus far they seem to have affected the paraphernalia of the stage rather than the inner life of the drama. They are, then, experimenters. In so far as they are frankly propagandistic, they must share the obloquy of all such special pleaders in the arts, however much one may sympathize with their noble outlook. Claiming recognition as social forces, they often defeat even this purpose with a highly individualized practice; their avowed universality becomes the property of a small, initiated clique; ostensibly directing their efforts toward international mankind, they frequently display a disconcerting esoterism, far more difficult of access than any ivory tower. These artists, like all others, whatever their professions, do not exist for the mass; the masses exist for them. Yet, despite these tendencies toward a dehumanization of the stage, toward geometric stylization of life, they have achieved moments of beauty that may, in the hands of the not impossible genius, be lengthened into hours. They have brought a colorful sweep, a massive plasticity, a musicality of method that address a need of the soul; they have assembled the elements of a new art, if not the finished product.

THE YIDDISH DRAMA

THE YIDDISH DRAMA

A HISTORICAL AND CRITICAL SURVEY

One of the chief effects of the war upon the lesser peoples has been the rekindling of the Jewish national spirit. This phenomenon is always closely related to the Yiddish language, which, in the course of its precarious existence has on numerous occasions been given premature burial by the learned and the pessimistic, only to rise, like the Phœnix, new-born from its own ashes. The war has helped, moreover, to shift modern Israel's literary center of gravity from Warsaw of the old world to New York, the metropolis of the new.

Pessimism with regard to the Yiddish tongue naturally extends itself to the institutions using that tongue, so that prophecies of imminent dissolution of the Yiddish theatre have been rife during the past twenty-five years. Yet, though such pessimism is well-founded, the Jewish theatre persists in flouting the prophets, and where some see the embers of a dying fire, others, even to-day, behold the first rays of a new dawn.

However that may be, there are distinct signs that the Yiddish spirit, craving self-expression and foreseeing to-morrow's possibilities, will in this country adopt the national language when necessary, even as have the Irish dramatists, whose first efforts were written in Gaelic. Long ago the Jewish publications found it necessary and profitable to

329

issue English supplements; more recently poets like
Rosenfeld and Yehoash have written in their adopted
tongue as well as in their vernacular. To-day translations of Yiddish plays are being presented in
English, not only to Gentiles, but also to Amer-
icanized Jews. The step from translation to original
productions in English is a short one. There is
thus a conservation of energy in art as well as in
science; though the great languages, like the great
nations, absorb the smaller, yet the spirit of the
latter persists through the transformation.

Yiddish, variously termed Jewish, Jargon, and
Judeo-German, is closely related to High German,
and in its dialectic variations, which are not few,
follows the High German dialects of the Middle
Rhine, with Frankfort for its centre.[1] The infusion
of Hebrew words, outside the purely ritualistic
terms, probably occurred during the sixteenth century; at this time also, Slavic elements were added,
due to the intercourse between the Jews in Bohemia,
Poland, and Lithuania with those they had left
behind in Germany. Thus, despite the mixed
character of the Yiddish vocabulary, which is further
altered by the language of the immediate environment, its speech remains fundamentally a German
dialect.

Curiously enough, as shall soon be noted in connection with the earliest Yiddish plays, the Yiddish
tongue received strongest opposition from the Jews

---

[1] During the hysterical period of accusations that added grim humor to the
late war, an Englishman made the startling discovery that though the letters of
Yiddish are Hebrew characters, the language is fundamentally German in structure. This he proceeded to publish as if the Hebrew characters were a species of
camouflage! One wonders whether he ever discovered the vast Teutonic element
in English.

themselves,[1] even as among the French Canadians
to-day the use of French is by some considered to be
a prejudicial influence, while among the "West
Britons" Irish is considered too primitive.

It is but one of the many ironies in the history of
the Hebrews that a race whose tragedy has occupied
the world-stage for more than a half century of
centuries should have established its national theatre
only within the past fifty years; yet since the year
1876, which witnessed the founding of the Yiddish
stage, Jewish drama has passed through several
distinct phases. That one of the oldest of peoples
should possess the youngest of stages is not so paradoxical as at first appears. Religious opposition to
the theatre is not an attitude confined to the pious
Jew, nor are conditions which favor the stage apt
to arise among a people whose fate it has been to
wander over the length and breadth of the earth.
In the arena of the ages this nomad nation has been
too intensely occupied in living its drama to have
had the opportunity to simulate it in the theatre.

The early Hebrews founded no stage. Some in-
vestigators have discovered in certain well-known
parts of the Bible examples of incipient dramatic
form, such as the Song of Songs and the Book of
Job, but later critics have dismissed the evidence.
It is the festival of *Purim* (Feast of Esther) that is
of practically sole importance in connection with
the origin of Jewish drama.

The Talmud makes mention[2] of representations,

---

[1] The Yiddish poet Yehoash tells of an amusing episode in Palestine, where
a band of Jewish students, in their fervent advocacy of Hebrew as a national
tongue, refused to listen to a lecture and a play in Yiddish. And this only yesterday.

[2] Megillah, 7, II; Sanhedrin, 7, II. See M. Pinès, *Histoire de la Littérature
Judéo-Allemande*, page 494.

not of a very high order, it is true, held at Purim. These were more or less imbued with the dramatic spirit and contained the germs that were to develop into pieces comparable to the mysteries whence the modern European theatre evolved. It became customary for Haman, who stood as symbol of the foes of Israel, to be burned in effigy "on a small pyre, over which the participants jumped a number of times in gleeful rejoicing over the downfall of their worst enemies." Spontaneous merrymaking would naturally arise under such circumstances and the better jests would be transmitted from year to year until the ceremony took on a more ordered form. This phase, approaching the dramatic in its formal dialogue, was reached in fifth-century Italy. But such approaches to dramatic representations were sporadic.

✓   The first real Jewish contribution to the drama is a dramatization of the story of Esther, which dates from the ninth or the tenth century; four hundred years later we find records of Jews participating in similar productions having for their subject the story of Haman's punishment. Here the chief element of fun was the dressing of men in women's garb (an act forbidden by the Bible) and general hilarity. Were it not for the greater freedom permitted from the earliest times on this holiday, religious prejudice would have perhaps forever stifled the chance for the development of a Jewish stage.

These same Purim plays (*Purim-spiele*) furnish the subject for the earliest Yiddish pieces, the high mark in the popularity of which was reached in the eighteenth century. The first printed text, entitled

Ahasuerus play and anonymous, was published at
Frankfort in 1708; before 1711 another Purim-spiel
appeared, in the form of the German farcical clown-
dialogues, based upon the story of the sale of Joseph, and written by Bermann of Limburg. This
was perhaps the first Yiddish "hit," for when it
was produced two years later, at Frankfort, with its
scenic accessories, costumes, and stage effects, so
great was the excitement among the denizens of the
ghetto that two soldiers were detailed to manage
the crowd. The play was acted by Jewish students
from Prague and Hamburg, and practically the
same company later produced the play at Metz.
The low comedy part devolved upon a character
named *Pickelherring,*—not a creation of the author,
but rather a stock merry-andrew in earlier and contemporary pieces.[1]

To the foregoing plays may be added *The Sacrifice of Isaac* and *David and Goliath.* These pieces,
of small literary value, indicate German influence.
Many of the details are coarse, resembling the
comedies and burlesques then in vogue among the
Gentiles. Like those of the earlier continental
mysteries, their subjects are taken from the Bible,
and the comic element introduces a secular note.
The acting of them, too, was in mediæval fashion,
as may be gathered from texts, where the characters,
upon entering, first address the audience. The
actors of the first Jewish pieces were student amateurs. As may be expected, the success of the
Biblical plays bred a host of imitations, some of the
latter rivaling the originals in popularity. Most

---

[1] The popular mind names its merry-andrews often after dishes. Pickelherring
is the Dutch analogue for Jean Potage in France, Hans Wurst in Germany, Jack
Pudding in England, and Signor Maccaroni in Italy.

liked of all, perhaps, is the tale of Joseph, which, in
Eliakum Zunser's modern dramatic version represents the best Yiddish work on the subject.[1]

While these early pieces possess a certain interest
as Jewish dramatic products, they did little or nothing toward founding a national theatre.[2]

I

In the early nineteenth century, long before the
definite establishment of the Yiddish stage, there
had arisen a Jewish literature in dramatic form
which, aside from purely dramatic considerations,
presents a worthy and authentic picture of the
time from the standpoint of Jewish social and political life. The plays thus written were not intended
for presentation, but were the offspring of that
movement for reform and enlightenment known in
Jewish history as the *Haskala*. Originating with the
German philosopher, Mendelssohn, prototype of Lessing's *Nathan der Weise*, the Haskala propaganda,
among other things, directed its forces against
Judeo-German, upon which it foisted the appellation
jargon. It sought also to promote the study of the
Bible in a rational spirit and to combat the fanaticism of the Khassid sect.

For the jargon the Haskalites would substitute
German, although under the rule of Alexander II
in Russia the Russian tongue loomed large as a
possible linguistic substitute. The onslaught against

---

[1] See Leo Wiener: *A History of Yiddish Literature in the Nineteenth Century*,
page 231 seq.

[2] Those who read Yiddish will find a wealth of valuable material in B. Gorin's
Die Geschichte von Yiddishen Theater, 2 vols., New York, 1918. He refers to a
number of Jewish playwrights in Spain, Portugal, Italy, but since they used the
language of these respective countries and dealt with contemporary themes they
do not properly belong in a history of the Jewish drama. Another work worth
consulting is M. Seiffert: *Die Geschichte von Yiddishen Theater, in Drei Zeit-Perioden*,
New York, 1897.

the humble language of the people, however, was of no avail, and Yiddish came out victorious through an epoch of intense hatred and factional strife. As late as 1862 a petition was presented by Jews to the Russian government, asking for the prohibition of publications in Yiddish, with the exception of religious works. And, as another irony in the history of the race, a Russian refusal taught the Jews toleration toward themselves.

The Khassid sect—that other target of the Haskalites' aim—lived in enthusiastic, whole-souled worship. They obeyed not only the spirit which giveth life, but also the letter that killeth. The Khassidim were fanatics who expressed their extreme ideas even in their manner of dress and personal grooming. Their queer caps and long coats with the inevitable girdle, their locks of hair coming down over the temples, their sacred beards, have long formed a stock topic for satire in Yiddish literature. The Khassidim believed their favorite rabbis to be quite as omnipotent as the Lord himself; such a rabbi, for instance, could send children to barren wives, forecast the future, save hopeless invalids, and what not else. Much of this fraudulent practice was forced upon the rabbi by the sheer ignorance and superstition of an uncultured, barely civilized community, which demanded miracles, and the demand was met with the facility and ambiguity of the oracle at Delphi.

It is this Khassid element that furnishes the humorous content of the dramatic literature inspired by the Haskala and the social-political conditions of the Jews at the time which we are considering. Thus in Gottlober's *The Marriage Veil*

(1838), Yossele is a hero impregnated with the new
thought of his day, and loves Freudele. But the
course of their love is too true to the proverb, and
far from marrying each other they are to meet, on
the same day, a most dreadful fate. Yossele is to
wed a one-eyed Yiddish *Katisha*, while Freudele is
to be united for life to a fool. Yossele, however,
knows the people with whom he is dealing, and
realizes that he can play upon their superstitions;
which he does so well that when the marriages take
place it is he who is united to Freudele under the
marriage veil, while with justice more poetic than
probable the one-eyed Gorgon is married to the
dolt.

Fools, it may be noticed in passing, have acquired
a popularity upon the Yiddish stage quite parallel
to their vogue in Elizabethan drama.

One of the best Yiddish comedies, Ludwig Levinsohn's *The Women's Knots* (i. e., kerchief knots,
where money is hoarded), directs its humor similarly against the Khassidim. Through an inventive
lie told by one of the sect to his wife, the news is
spread all over town that monogamic restrictions
among the Jews are to be abolished. This is to be
done so as to enable the Jews to raise enough money,
by the multiple dowries coming with several wives,
to pay off the town's taxes. Rather than face such
a calamity the moral wives get together every coin
that they have stored away in old stockings and
knotted kerchiefs and bring the tax-paying fund of
virtue to the assembly of Khassidim, which promptly
proceeds to spend it on a junket.

The type of the termagant has acquired a constant, if not creditable popularity upon the Yiddish

stage. In the comedy, *Serkele*, by Solomon Ettinger
(not published until 1861, some six years after the
author's death), we find the prototype of a long line
of Jewish Xantippes whose collected oaths and imprecations represent a most formidable arsenal of
depreciatory volubility. Here again we find a similarity in the Elizabethan audience and the Jewish.
Go no further than King Lear's curses upon his
daughters and you will find a wealth of condemnation comparable in vehemence to the Yiddish, with
a rich resonance that falls (independent of its content) with pleasing familiarity upon Jewish ears.
Domestic quarrels particularly, and the choice oaths
they engender, have from the beginning been one
of the mainstays of the Yiddish stage, and it is as
well to remember that these oaths, if literally translated, convey to the Gentile reader a distinctly
wrong impression as regards both the morality and
the wholesomeness of common Jewish life.

Ettinger was thoroughly conversant with German
literature, a knowledge of which reveals itself in all
he has written; *Serkele* is constructed upon the
model of Lessing's dramas. The sordid machinations of the virago, Serkele, to deprive her niece of
costly jewels and to marry off her silly daughter to
advantage, lead us through a melodramatic plot,
with Serkele exposed as thief, liar, and diabolical
plotter in general. The play, however, ends happily, through a train of events which contributes to
our pleasure by taxing our credulity. "As in all
the early productions of Judeo-German literature,"
says Wiener, in his account of the play, "there are
in that drama two distinct classes of characters: the
ideal persons . . . and the real men and women

who are taken out of actual life. On the side of the first is all virtue, while among the others are to be found the worst forms of vice." For the rest the characters are well depicted, and the scenes have value as contemporary documents.

In Aksenfeld's *The First Jewish Recruit in Russia* (a drama in eight scenes, and, like his other works, a study in manners) we find one of the most important of this period's plays. We know from contemporary evidence that Aksenfeld wrote his pieces in the second decade of the nineteenth century, but not until forty years later were they published, and then in part only. The author had been a personal witness to the terror among the Jews when the *ukase* of 1827 was promulgated by Nicholas I, requiring each Jewish community to contribute its share of recruits to the imperial army. These terror-stricken figures move through the drama, while their leaders, with the hope that springs eternal, see in the communal calamity an opportunity for the Jews so to distinguish themselves in battle as to win from the monarch concessions for their oppressed race. It is finally decided that since someone must be sent to the army, it may as well be Nakhman, who is the terror of the town because of his propensity for practical jokes. The better to accomplish this, Nakhman is induced to volunteer himself through his love for Frume, the beautiful daughter of the tax-collector, as he has been told that his bravery will be the condition of her acceptance. As luck will have it, Frume really loves Nakhman, and when she hears of the practical joke that has been played upon the practical joker, she suffers all the pangs of torture, but hides her woes, finally dying from her unuttered sorrow. Nakhman's mother, discovering the deception practiced upon her simple-minded son, comes to the home of her son's lover only to stumble upon Frume's corpse. In a touching scene, where Nakhman's mother addresses the dead body, the play closes.

The theme of recruiting is naturally as popular in Yiddish literature as it was unpopular in Jewish life, and early appeared in J. B. Levinsohn's essay *Die Hefker Welt* (The Topsy-Turvy World, 1828, circulated in mss. form), which has been called by Pinès the first original production of this epoch. This work, in some respects a Jewish *Utopia*, contains, among other things, complaints against communal grafters and recruiting abuses whereby the sons of the rich escaped service. These find a most powerful echo some thirty years later in the most important play of the period preceding the founding of the Yiddish stage—Abramovitsch's *The Meat Tax*. Here the reformatory spirit of the times reaches its highest dramatic and most significant social expression, not by drawing only from the religious life of the day, but also from the political.

It was Abramovitsch who brought to the Yiddish language and style a beauty, a capacity for expression which finally effected its triumph as a literary medium. From the beginning he had felt a call to serve God through serving man. "It appears," he says in his reminiscences, "that from very birth I was destined to play the rôle of writer for my people —a poor and wretched people. And in order that I might know this life in its entirety, early in life God said to me, 'Go, my little bird, fly about the world and be the unhappiest of the unhappy—the

most Jewish of Jews.' "   Abramovitsch differs from
the preceding writers in emphasizing the necessity
for proper material conditions before spiritual expansion is possible.   In conformity with such an
economic tenet he turned his attention to communal
improvement, and his *Meat Tax* is a powerful example of Yiddish social drama—powerful not only
intrinsically, but in its immediate effect upon the
conditions and the persons against whom it was
written.

The play is founded upon the meat and candle
tax, then one of the greatest hardships of the Jewish
community, for both articles are much in demand.
The tax was farmed out to the *kahal*, the body which
ostensibly represented the Jewish community, and
was supposed to go to the support of certain communal institutions.   Altogether too much of it, however, found its way into the kahal pockets.

In the figure of Spodek, the ring-leader of the
kahal grafters, Abramovitsch has created a Yiddish
minor *Tartuffe*.   Outwardly Spodek is a man of
holiest thought and deed, but he knows the value
of a cringing manner and a pious lamentation.   He
knows, too, that he profits most from his fellow-men
when he seems most humble,—that beneath his
mask as a social benefactor lurks the grin of the
communal parasite.

There is a striking episode, Act II, scene III,
where the members of the kahal are discussing the
details of a newly planned tax.   Suddenly the news
is brought that the government has sent an auditor
to look over accounts.   Spodek, inwardly overwhelmed at the possibilities suggested by the unpleasant announcement, affects the religious whine

which precedes his greatest perfidies. "Alas," he begins, with blasphemous piety, "how dire is our exile! Here comes an auditor to examine our accounts! It is because of our sins that we are in exile. May God—praised by his name—have pity on us. . . . With God's help," he adds, significantly, "everything can be arranged. Do you understand?" His companions understand. For Mammon is the god whose help Spodek means to invoke, and Russian officials, like Pooh Bah, are ever ready to be "grossly insulted" by the healing bribe.

Wecker, the young hero of the play, is an up-to-date fellow who has been in Spodek's employ and knows that worthy's methods only too well. He tries to arouse the people against their grafter-"benefactors," only to be met on all sides by ignorance, indifference, cowardice, submission. There is nothing left for him to do but abandon the fight, placing his hope for the future in the beneficent actions of the government.

Aksenfeld's *First Jewish Recruit* had expressed a similar faith in the government's protective powers. This trust is one of the characteristics of the Haskalite literature. At the time Abramovitsch wrote *The Meat Tax* the anti-Jewish riots of 1881 were still far off, yet the dramatist himself, in his noted prose work *Die Kliatsche* (*The Dobbin*), foresaw the miseries in store for his people.

We find, then, that the Jewish literature in dramatic form which was written in the era that preceded the founding of the Yiddish stage by Abraham Goldfaden was characterized by a didactic strain, drawing upon actual life and actual problems. It was sporadic and reformatory in nature, and in the case of *The Meat Tax* actually became a power in social conditions. So well did this play perform its mission that the rôle of Spodek was recognized in real life and the sanctimonious grafter's prototype was forced into bankruptcy by an outraged population.

Owing to the peculiar conditions with which Goldfaden had to contend, Jewish drama soon took a direction quite different from that so promisingly indicated in these early plays. The serious element of the drama resolved itself into almost a stereotyped repetition of Haskalite arguments against the Khassidim, while the comic element, plus song and dance, assumed first place. Goldfaden and his followers wrote for a seeing and listening public, not for a reading and thinking individual, under circumstances which are best examined in connection with the life of the man who adapted them to the crowning achievement of his career.

II

Even as the Yiddish stage furnishes one of the most absorbing by-paths in the lore of the drama, so is the figure of its founder, Abraham Goldfaden,[1] one of the most picturesque in modern theatrical history. Had he never written anything other than poetry, he would be gratefully remembered by his fellow-men for his two allegorical poems, which glorify his religion and its Sabbath, and his numerous lesser writings, all replete with a spirit of modern, yet fundamental Judaism. His popular songs have

---

[1] The name was originally Goldenfadim, and was changed by him to Goldenfaden and finally to Goldfaden.

sung themselves into the hearts of his people, where, too, he himself has found a place.

Abraham Goldfaden was born on July 12, 1840, at Old Constantin, in the southern part of Russia, government of Volhynia. His father being a staunch adherent of the Haskala, the son grew up in an atmosphere of enlightenment, and his early education, besides Hebrew—in which he showed his poetic powers at the age of ten—included Russian and German, with Yiddish, of course, as the domestic tongue.

At the government school Goldfaden became friendly with his teacher, Gottlober, the well-known poet and dramatic author. The latter, besides writing Hebrew verse, set the lines to music himself, and encouraged his pupil in similar pursuits. From Gottlober, too, Goldfaden imbibed a love of the drama, which is later evidenced by plays which reveal the direct influence of the instructor.

Another important influence in firing the lad's enthusiasm for dramatic representation was a play performed in 1855 at the Rabbinical college, whither he had been sent upon completing his grades with distinction at the community school. This drama, written by one Kamrasch, was given in honor of Alexander II's coronation, and depicted the life of a Jewish soldier and the environment of the Jewish folk. The entire student body had been enthused with the Thespian spirit as the result of other Jewish teachers' successes at Berdichev, and the event made a deep impression upon the fifteen-year-old Talmudist, who soon became acquainted with Ettinger's *Serkele* and stored it up, perhaps unconsciously, with the host of other impressions that were later to show themselves in his work for the stage.

At college Goldfaden was very popular. Daily the students would gather in the arched halls and sing in sonorous voices the Hebrew and Yiddish songs of their talented colleague. In 1865 appeared Goldfaden's first collection of Hebrew poems, and in the following year, which witnessed also the completion of his studies at Zhitomir, was published his initial group of Yiddish poems, under the title *Dos Yidele* (*The Jew*).

The end of Goldfaden's studies was the beginning of his trials. Soon disgusted with his position as government teacher, which yielded the princely sum of almost ten dollars per month, he abandoned the profession for undertakings in various directions with much more versatility than success. We discover him now as cashier (by this time he is married), now as proprietor of a large millinery establishment, now plunged into bankruptcy, with only his bitter experience as an asset. For a time his eyes turn toward Munich, where the medical profession beckons, but fortunately the world is spared a bad doctor. Only one makeshift presents itself, and Goldfaden enters journalism. His first venture (the humorous journal *Yisrolik*, established in conjunction with Linetzki,[1] author of the widely read Yiddish satiric classic *The Polish Boy*) is throttled by the Russian government after six months, and he moves from Lemburg to Czernowitch, where, in 1876, he issues the *Bukowiner Israelitischer Volksblatt*. Matters go from bad to worse, and Goldfaden seems at the end of his resources, yet this is the very

---

[1] (1839-1915). His satire is all the more effective since it proceeds from a member of the Khassidic sect that is pilloried.

year which is to bring him distinction. He receives a letter from one of his Roumanian subscribers, Mr. Librescu, urging him to come to Yassy, where dwells the largest Jewish population in the country, and where a journalistic venture may bear more fruit. The drowning journalist grasps at the financial straw and goes to Yassy.

Before we follow him thither, let us take a glimpse at the two plays which he had already written under the inspiration of Gottlober and Ettinger.

The Two Neighbors and *Aunt Sosie* were published in 1872, and are both in comic, even farcical, vein. The first is just a dialogue between two friends whose little ones are playing on the floor. In honied phrases the women express their intimate regard for one another, and with maternal fondness look forward to the time when they shall dance at their children's wedding. But the harmonious ecstasies of the parents are by no means mirrored in the children, who, while their parents have been marrying them off, have started a quarrel. One of the tots is hurt, whereupon a sudden change comes over the mothers. Each upholds the blamelessness of her offspring; kisses, weddings, dances—all are forgotten. Compliments yield to curses, and a characteristic scene of abuse ensues. *The Two Neighbors* is thoroughly enjoyable satiric farce, with a genuine insight into human nature.

Aunt Sosie, despite its evident indebtedness to Ettinger's *Serkele*, contains some of Goldfaden's best work, and has been called his masterpiece. It is based upon the Jewish life that its author knew, and is in plot more complicated than Goldfaden's later stage pieces. Sosie's husband is a hen-pecked spouse, who nevertheless succeeds, by enlisting deceit in the service of his timidity, in marrying off his ill-treated niece to Sosie's own brother. Sosie, who turns all her efforts to marrying off her sister, finds out just in time that the Lithuanian Jew upon whom she had looked as an excellent match, has already been married. The timid husband is thus a far better matchmaker than his termagacious mate.

Goldfaden did not come to Roumania unknown; his songs were sung in all the coffee houses and had been popularized by the balladists who constituted, outside of the synagogue precentors, the Jewish population's sole musical diversion. The taste of this public was little refined; from the religious preachers it absorbed, through the synagogue, the serious thoughts which were part of its daily life. Here, too, the Jews indulged their love of music, and a precentor who could sing well was always sure, as he is to-day, of a large audience. For the comic relief in the drama of their daily existence there were the badkhens, or wedding-jesters—parlor entertainers whose powers of improvisation some-times reached artistic significance.[1] The lieder-singers in the restaurants pursued similar methods.

These singers, however, were not merely vocalists. Their work comprised not only songs, but called also for a certain amount of acting ability, since the songs were sung in costume, accompanied by ap-propriate facial expressions and gestures. It was moreover a common practice for a singer, if the song called for more than one part, to have the

---

[1] The last of these picturesque improvising minstrels was the beloved Eliakum Zunser (1836-1913). His collected work, in three volumes, exhibits three distinct strains: (1) the homiletic, (2) the satiric, (3) the nationalistic. He is at his best as a spontaneous, simple wedding-jester.

assistance of a second person. We have here the practical beginnings of genuine drama. Indeed, it was while listening to such a singer performing one of his own songs that the idea came to Goldfaden to write out the action of the song in the form of a prose play.

Goldfaden's journalistic prospects were quite as gloomy in Roumania as they had been elsewhere. He must have money. It so happened that when he arrived at Yassy, Gradner, a singer of great versatility, was giving a concert there. Goldfaden saw here an opportunity to sell a few songs, for he knew that Gradner made a specialty of singing some of his old ones. The playwright has left us a humorous account of how, when he broached the matter to the lieder-singer, he was met with the reply that his only pay for the poems would be in the popularity which Gradner's singing would bring to the author. All of which, though it soothed the soul, could not still the stomach. But this meeting was fraught with far greater consequences.

Gradner was not the common type of lieder-singer; he succeeded in raising the standard of his popular art. He was not content to be a mere badkhen for the pleasure of wedding gatherings, nor did the narrow sphere of the coffee houses appeal to him. He sought out the large centers, and as soon as he arrived, would hire a prominent location, put up a platform, have seats arranged and numbered, and spread notices that he sang the songs of the most popular folk-poets.

Among the latter, of course, Goldfaden figured. In Gradner, Goldfaden was quick to recognize a baritone voice of undeveloped beauty and a mimicking talent capable of high attainments. Through Gradner, Goldfaden learned what the public for which he would have to write really wanted, and that whatever attempts he might make must be based upon the lieder-singers. He knew also that from certain quarters he must expect very little aid or sympathy. The more intelligent class of Jews was of cultured taste, preferring the Gentile theatre with its literary offerings and trained personnel. As it had opposed the spread of the Yiddish tongue, so would it oppose the founding of a Yiddish stage, and later fight that institution in both Russia and America. Goldfaden must build from the bottom. Accordingly, fired by his new idea, he sat down, wrote a few songs, and set to work immediately preparing them for performance with Gradner, and the latter's assistant, Goldstein.

This first piece was built around songs. No set dialogue was written down, but more or less in the fashion of the *commedia dell'arte* the writer got his two chief actors together, gave them hints as to interpretation, and suggested an outline of whatever action the piece contained. While the songs were being learned the dialogue would be worked out, and if the actors forgot the exact words the audience would be none the wiser for their improvisations. The first play was thus a mere hodgepodge of songs, quarrels, amorous complications, curses, and plenty of horse-play. There was the inevitable Khassid, the dressing of men in female garb, and the now traditional imprecations.

By comparison with the two plays which Goldfaden published in 1872, we can easily see that in this first stage play, written in 1876 and produced at Yassy, the author wrote consciously down to his audience. This was an absolute necessity under the circumstances, if any sort of stage at all was to be established. Goldfaden soon went with his men to Batishani. The Russo-Turkish war was now in the air and Roumania was laying hands on every available Jew to press him into service. Terror reigned in the ghetto, which was full of Jews who had escaped from Russia in order to avoid military slavery. With difficulty the founder of the Yiddish stage himself eluded the hands of the *khapers* (catchers). Productions naturally were not to be thought of, but as Goldfaden lay in hiding he had plenty of time to consider his plans, and it is not strange that his second attempt should take the form of a play dealing with Jewish recruits.

Goldfaden's piece, however, is not, like Aksenfeld's on the same theme, a drama. The action of *The Recruits* is very simple, and depends, as do all of the writer's theatrical works, very largely upon the songs interspersed. The Jewish recruits, in this case, prove so manifestly useless for the service that they are released, but not until they have furnished plenty of antics for the crowd. The farewell of Zadik, one of the Jewish students who is seized by the *khapers*, is a parody on Joan of Arc's farewell at the end of the prologue in Schiller's *Jungfrau von Orleans*. Soldier farewells, moreover, are very common in Jewish folk-songs.

Goldfaden's fortunes, or perhaps misfortunes, brought him soon to Bucharest. Here, at the headquarters of the Russian staff Jews had gathered from all points to make a living in wartime activities. Goldfaden, adding to his company, and tak-

ing advantage of the community's humors, hastily
concocted some very light pabulum for the palates
of these wearied men of affairs. The pieces are of
meagre plot and worth, and moreover have little
inner connection with Jewish life. They consist
mainly of couplets set to music by the author, plus
situations suggested for the most part by French
originals which Goldfaden used as models. The
songs are still popular, though few who sing them
know their origin.

It was at Bucharest where Goldfaden remained
until the end of the Russo-Turkish war (1878) that
he formed the acquaintance of the talented actor,
Mogalesco, whom he persuaded to remain upon the
Jewish stage. Here, too, Gradner, because of professional jealousy of Mogalesco, and not entirely
without proper personal reasons, left Goldfaden for
good.

From Bucharest Goldfaden went to Odessa, where,
at the Maryinski theatre, his company met with
immediate success. Other writers were attracted,
among them Katzenellenbogen (perhaps the most
original of the number), Lerner, Lillienblum, and
Shaikewitsch. The dramas of this period, though
not of great intrinsic merit, were better than the
products soon to flourish in America. Lerner's
adaptations of German pieces such as *Uncle Moses
Mendelssohn* and Gutzkow's *Uriel Acosta*, particularly the latter, proved very popular.

The financial success of the theatre at Odessa,
however, prepared the way for the rapid downfall
of the Yiddish theatre in Russia. Actors and ac-
tresses became unduly impressed with the idea of
their own importance and began to demand salaries

commensurate with their conceited notions. Dissensions arose and the original troupe divided in two, Goldfaden taking the directorship of the first, while Lerner took charge of the second.

Goldfaden now undertook a tour of the principal cities of Russia, meeting with varying success. In some places he was welcomed by the Jewish population, while in others the troupe met with the opposition of the more cultured element, who looked upon the project as a retrogressive influence. During this time, in order to provide a wider repertory of somewhat more substantial appeal, Goldfaden wrote *Doctor Almosado*, *Bar Kochba*, and *Shulamith*. With the last two pieces, says Seiffert, Goldfaden "made himself immortal, and secured for the Yiddish stage a long future. Even more than the historical subject, the sweet music, the genuinely Jewish melody, achieved the greatest success. Later they were translated into Polish and produced at the Polish opera with the most gratifying effect. These two pieces are the quintessence of the entire Jewish repertory."

Meanwhile matters connected with the Yiddish stage were going from bad to worse. As if internal intrigues were not enough, it is averred by some that Gentile actors, jealous of the Jewish successes, whispered into the official ears that the Yiddish stage was a hot-bed of revolution. The Russian minister wearied of reading all the evidence submitted to him by the rival companies; on the 14th of September, 1883, a decree was issued in which the further continuance of the Yiddish stage was forbidden. "Like a father in despair," Goldfaden has written, "I rushed to St. Petersburg to beg mercy

for the child of my spirit. It was all in vain." For
a short time the decree was evaded at Warsaw by
giving the Yiddish plays in a so-called "German"
theatre, but a second *ukase* put an end to this subterfuge. The career of the Yiddish theatre in
Russia had thus lasted but five years.

The more mature pieces by Goldfaden forsake
French models for German, and draw their inspiration from the Bible or from history. The songs
from some of these form part of every Jew's heritage.
As composer, Goldfaden is distinguished for a tender,
lyric melancholy which reaches straight to the heart
of singer and hearer alike. Through these songs
he lives in the hearts of his people in a very vital
and enduring sense.

In his later European and American activities
Goldfaden added nothing substantial to his achievements. In him the man and his work were so intimately fused that a full appreciation of the one
is possible only through a knowledge of the other.
When, in 1908, he died in New York, he left behind
an intellectual legacy that will, after all is said and
done, consist of two or three stageworthy productions, numerous folk-songs, a fair variety of poems,
and the historical distinction of having laid the
foundations of a Yiddish drama that for too long
remained without any worthy superstructure.

Goldfaden had come among an ignorant public
whose tastes were of the most uncultured. He had
quickly discerned the elements in their amusements
which could be fused into a stage, and had set about
the work with astonishing energy. Himself without
experience as an actor, he developed his raw material

into an aggregation that scored success wherever it
appeared. Handicapped, until he came to Russia,
by the absence of women, he trained men for female
parts. And although his pieces are by no means
realistic plays, as a producer he sought realistic
effects. Thus the soldiers at the end of the second
act in *The Recruits* were real soldiers, hired for the
occasion, since our producer feared to entrust the
part to civilians. Wherever possible in such minor
rôles, Goldfaden would seek out in private life the
very types for which the play called, and train them
for the production. As an example of this, Gorin
relates an anecdote of Goldfaden and a cobbler,
told to him by the playwright himself. In one of
the early plays a cobbler was needed to portray a
quarrel. The part was more than mere "suping,"
and Goldfaden was short of actors. Setting out
about town, he found a poor fellow at his bench,
told him the plot then and there, rehearsed him,
put him on the stage, and made an actor of him.
To train synagogue singers into theatrical choruses
was of course an easy matter for a man who, in his
early productions, acted himself, built his own stage,
and painted the scenery!

Whatever there is of serious thought in Goldfaden may be found in all the popular poets of his
day, and is usually part of the Haskalite propaganda. Here Goldfaden strikes no new note.
The real contribution of his pieces lies in the genuine folk-humor and the caricatures of Yiddish
types. Some of the latter have furnished new expressions to the Yiddish tongue, and a *Kuni-Lemel*,
as a byword for an awkward, inconsequential sim-
pleton is just as well known to Jews as is, for in-

stance, among the English, Pooh-Bah as a type of grasping politician.

The first to write for the Jewish stage, Goldfaden impressed his form upon all his immediate successors, thus founding a distinct school. The rhyming couplets, the song and dance, the horse-play, the jester-type (containing points of resemblance to the Spanish *gracioso* as well as to the Elizabethan clown)—may all be traced to those separate elements in the diversion of the Roumanian Jews which Goldfaden found ready to hand for combination. This pattern was to cling to the Yiddish stage with a grip that long stifled all genuine progress towards the legitimate drama.

III

Since 1908 the government of the Czar had not been so strict in its attitude towards the Yiddish theatre. The effects of the rescripts of 1883, however, were to disperse the actors and to shift the scene of the Yiddish drama to America, whither a large host of Jews had emigrated to escape from persecution.

The development of the Yiddish theatre in America is practically synonymous with the development of the Yiddish stage in New York. The larger Jewish centres, like Chicago and Boston, now have companies visit them for shorter or longer stays, but the dominant influence is naturally that of the metropolis which contains almost half the Jews in the United States.

Boris Tomasheffsky, to whose enterprise the foundation of the Yiddish theatre in America is due, had been one of the early Russian-Jewish immigrants into this country. It was he who effected the transference of a London Yiddish troupe to New York, and presented it, amidst almost insuperable difficulties, to an audience that filled the Fourth Street Turner Hall. Due to the intrigues of the Jewish opposition, however, the performance fell flat and the company disbanded.

The history of the various theatrical ventures and ensuing rivalries presents too many details to be entered into at length. They may be epitomized, however, in the competition between the companies that finally occupied respectively the Bowery Garden, renamed the Oriental Theatre, and the National Theatre, renamed the Roumanian Opera House. With the Oriental Company came Lateiner as staff playwright. The Roumanian Opera House Company arrived in 1886, their staff writer, Hurwitz, following soon after. In general, the plays given by the first troupe were better than those offered by the second, while in the matter of acting the case was reversed. Gradually, because of this superiority in acting, the Roumanian Opera House forced the Oriental Company into the background.

The rivalry between these two houses was not slow in producing evil effects analogous to those which had helped to disrupt the stage in Russia. Hurwitz, especially, was quite unscrupulous in his methods. The rivalry took on an amusing phase in the fashion of singing couplets at one theatre antagonistic to the fortunes of the other. These couplets were obtruded into the plays without any concern as to their inappropriateness to the action, and found further extension in the campaign of scurrilous handbills which was initiated. Actors were enticed from one side to the other, and cases are recorded where a player would appear in one act at one theatre and in the following act at the other playhouse!

At this time the coming of Goldfaden might have had salutary effects, but, due to the hostilities, he was excluded altogether. He left New York in disgust, and was soon replaced by Shaikewitsch, who could write a play "while you wait." The latter ground out one production after the other for the Roumanian Opera House troupe. The various plays written by the other dramatists of the time are too much alike in their general unworthiness to require any special mention.

With the arrival of Jacob Gordin in the early nineties came a breath of new life into the Yiddish stage. The time was ripe for reaction. The plays hitherto produced were of a type that was fast declining even from the Goldfaden pattern; there was no attempt to be true to life. As frequently happens, the pendulum, in the reaction, swung too far in the opposite direction, and Gordin's welcome introduction of realism often degenerated into a riot of sensationalism and grotesquerie. On the whole, however, he exercised upon the stage an influence decidedly beneficial, and initiated a new epoch. His works repay special treatment, and will therefore be reserved for the fourth section of this introductory outline.

There soon came a rage for the classics, not without its ultimate benefit to the public taste. The actors, advertised as the equals of Booth, Salvini, Irving, found in Goethe, Schiller, Shakespeare, and others an opportunity for indulging their histrionic conceit. The most popular plays of this period, judging from the financial returns, were *Othello*, *Hamlet*, and *Romeo and Juliet*. Of two versions of Hamlet, one is quite close; in the other, Hamlet is transformed into a Rabbinical student, with an uncle conspiring to have him sent to Siberia as a nihilist. Of course the uncle himself meets that dire fate, while Hamlet dies of a broken heart. The classics prepared the way for the denationalization of the stage, and its degeneration through box-office standards.

Since the first days of the stage in New York changes in theatres, in troupes, and in plays have been many. Of the numerous actors, some have become known outside their particular environment and have won the approbation of American critics. Most prominent is the veteran Jacob Adler. To him belongs much of the credit for obtaining a hearing for Gordin. A lover of realism himself, he recognized the merits of its Yiddish dramatic exponent. Tomasheffsky, as actor, has been found wanting in expressional power and miming capacity. He represented formerly the best Yiddish type of matinée idol, and was the actor and the type for whom Lateiner wrote his hero rôles. Bertha Kalish is known favorably to the English stage, although she confesses a marked preference for the Yiddish audience. The Yiddish stage has undoubtedly produced, in its short career, some half-dozen artists that would, if they acted in a tongue more widely known, have achieved far greater distinction.

As for "Moishe"—Moses—that collective name by which the less discriminating part of the Jewish audience is known—he is a fellow at once difficult and easy to please. Give him and his female companion something to laugh at or weep over (for lachrymose tendencies form a noticeable weakness in the Jewish audience, even among the men), and he is content. But if you please him not, he is less reserved in the expression of his dissatisfaction than is his American neighbor. The Jew, Bertha Kalish has said in an interview, "approaches the theatre with a great love, particularly for his favorite player. He listens attentively. More than that, he is figuratively on the stage in the very scene, a tense spectator. If a line or situation doesn't ring true, he shakes his head. If it gets him down where he lives, he is silent or yells as the reaction takes direction."

The dramatic output from the beginning of Tomasheffsky to the coming of Gordin is merely a continuation, or even a dilution, of the Goldfaden model. With the freedom of thought and worship in America the necessity for Haskalite agitation had vanished, but nothing had been found to replace this serious element of previous plays. The epoch, dominated by Hurwitz and Lateiner, was one of great activity but of no permanent accomplishment. With all his talk of technique and his derogatory reception of Gordin's progressive plays, Hurwitz wrote nothing that will live. Lateiner, less pretentious, but scarcely less productive, is in the same class with his rival. The first, specializing on what he called the "culture" play—well termed by a Gentile critic the "sentimental representation of inexact Jewish history"—is, if possible, the worse.

IV

Gordin's original intention in coming to the United States had been to start a communist colony. Born in 1853, at Mirgorod, the same town that had given birth to the great Gogol, Gordin grew up into a lover of literature and the drama, becoming a follower of Tolstoi. Unlike Goldfaden, who, despite his reform beliefs, was opposed to assimilation, Gordin cherished the hope that some way might be found for reconciling the Jewish and the Christian religions. The massacres of 1881, however, shattered his syncretist aims.

Ten years later he turned to America. Here he was quickly disillusioned about the "golden land," and found himself face to face with the disheartening problem of making a living. Gordin had edited a Russian paper and was well acquainted with the literary and dramatic currents of his native land; there he had become known as *Ivan der Beissende* (Ivan the Incisive) for his biting style, so that it was natural for him to take up the pen as a means of support in the new world.

His first visit to a Yiddish theatre in New York disgusted him, and he was impelled to write a play that would not be a disgrace to the race. Whatever the real value of his first effort—entitled *Siberia*—he made an honest attempt, as he said, to fashion each word a pure one and each thought a holy one. The radical element of the ghetto received Gordin's drama with loud acclaim; their preoccupations with the sordid details of everyday life and their knowledge of the best in world-literature rendered them especially sensitive, not only to the need of change, but to the appearance of its champion. Gordin was hailed as the apostle of realism.

The Jew is forced by the pressure of his experience to be more or less an eclectic. Gordin's career as playwright illustrates this fact with strong emphasis. He has adapted or translated Shakespeare, Goethe, Hebbel, Ibsen, Hugo, Lessing, Schiller, Hauptmann, Gogol, Grillparzer, and Ostrovsky. In many cases the adaptation is in the nature of a Yiddish analogue suggested by the Gentile plot. Gordin knew little of the intimate lives of the ghetto's people; he was never really a part of them, so that his realistic endeavors could scarcely look to the creation of a genuinely vital Jewish play. What he did seek, and in a measure attain, was the problem play, although the Jewish element in the problem was too often superficial.

Gordin was not truly a creative spirit; he could, as an educated writer, galvanize plays into the semblance of life, so to speak, and having received his training from the Russian realists, he naturally fell into the handling of the domestic problem, in the style of Ostrovsky. He certainly succeeded in making his atmospheres thoroughly Jewish, even if the problems were not always essentially racial.

Gordin's best play is reckoned by many to be his *Gott, Mensch und Teifel* (*God, Man, and Devil*), inspired by *Faust*. Here, at least, the German classic is transformed into a Yiddish play with a vital Jewish problem—a play that is, despite its source, thoroughly original and deserving of a wide acquaintance outside the ghetto. Instead of Faust, we have the poor Yiddish scribe, *Herschele;* instead of a Mephistopheles who tempts with the pleasures

of youthful passion, we have a Devil, who seeks to
purchase the scribe's soul with sordid dollars and
cents.   Instead of a Gretchen who is seduced, we
have a wife who is abandoned in favor of a younger,
more attractive woman.   These changes from the
German original operate also in an altered environment that raises the play above mere imitation.
Gordin was no Shakespeare, but for once, in this
play, he used another's plot to make his own play.

The Devil, however, is cheated out of Herschele's
soul at the very moment of his apparent triumph.
Despite the riches heaped upon him and the business
career which threatens to ruin the former scribe's
finer self, an accident in Herschele's factory, which
kills the son of a boyhood friend, awakens Herschele
to a sense of his debasement.   With all the power
that gold has brought to him, with all the domina-
tion over his friends and fellow-men, it has taken
away something more precious—his joy in righteous
living.   Believing himself beyond redemption, Herschele hangs himself.   As the Evil One is forced to
confess, "Even the power of money is limited, for
though through it man may be deceived, perverted,
mutilated in soul, he cannot be ruined entirely."
The piece stands out with particular significance
in the repertory of a stage whose people have been
unjustly reputed to love money above all things,
and though it has certain defects, which we shall
touch upon when we come to Gordin's technique,
it is none the less one of the salient achievements in
Jewish drama.

Gordin's adaptation of *King Lear* is far less felic-
itous.   As has been noted by more than one critic,
the piece has extent rather than depth; it is spoiled

by the intrusion of the song-and-dance element. Where the great Bard portrays the agonies of a soul, the Jewish dramatist depicts merely the external sufferings of a body; Gordin is physical where Shakespeare is psychological; the one fashions events, where the other creates character.

In the version of Hauptmann's *Fuhrmann Henschel*, which is known to the Yiddish stage as *Die Schevoah* (*The Oath*), the playwright has taken many liberties with the original. At the point of death, but with the passions of life still active within him, a peasant exacts from his wife an oath that she will not marry again. The oath is soon forgotten, the widow marrying her steward, who proves faithless. Only death can end the woman's misfortunes, and when her child is drowned, the only link that connected her with life is snapped; she burns the house over her head. As an instance of the telling use which Gordin makes of Jewish beliefs and customs, we have the theatrical scene where, at the mother's second marriage, her young boy blows out the candles which are burning in commemoration of his father's death anniversary. It is a Jewish superstition that while the anniversary light burns the soul of the departed is present and can see all that is taking place. To extinguish the lights before the twenty-four hours of the anniversary have been completed is an impious act; but here the simple mind of the little boy, feeling that his dead father is witnessing a wedding which violates a sacred promise, blows out the candles so that the departed soul may not behold the wife's infidelity.

In the Jewish *King Lear* we have the self-sacrificing father. In *Mirele Efros* (looked upon by many as superior to *God, Man, and Devil*) it is the mother who has sacrificed herself to the upbringing of children only to see them depart from the maternal guidance. The father of the Jewish *King Lear* sinks into insignificance beside Mirele the mother. Mirele is perhaps the one instance in Gordin's career as playwright where he built up a complete character. Not that the same may be said of the play as a whole, but here at least the leading character is real, the events typically Jewish, the use of the religious atmosphere intensely effective. Mirele grows with the action; she is not a rôle, but a living personage.

For the rest there is little comment to make upon the stories of Gordin's numerous productions. He covers a wide range of problems, involving filial duty, religious faith, racial weaknesses, mixed marriages, and so on. He wanders from one theme to another, not as an artist expressing, like Ibsen, for example, his mental growth in his dramatic output, but rather exploiting the ideas of others, or his own preconceptions, in theatrical guise.

The great contribution of Gordin, then, to the Yiddish stage is that in place of the falsities of life and character that had flourished in the Lateiner-Hurwitz régime he brought truth, character, art. Starting out not far from the beaten path of Goldfaden, he achieved a personality of his own, despite the intrusion of the vaudeville element which had to be endured for the sake of a public. His plots sought intimate relation with actual events, and if they were more complex, they were more real. Even if Gordin did not succeed in writing perfect technical compositions, his intentions were so evidently sincere, and in such marked contrast to his predecessors that intention alone almost equaled achievement.

Gordin's dialogue is noted for its rugged power, as are certain of his episodes for their individual strength. Indeed, Gordin, in much the same way as the Elizabethan Marlowe (guarding proper distances), has been looked upon primarily as a writer of scenes rather than plays, and too often of rôles rather than characters. His most serious defect lies in just this inability to create character. The beginnings of his plays are usually the best part, for here he poses his problem, arouses our interest, and then—shirks the vital point in the problem. He gives the primary dramatic impulse, but can rarely carry it through to the end.

Thus in *God, Man, and Devil*, as Pinski,[1] with the perspicacity of the serious creative artist, has pointed out, the one great necessity in the play was to show Herschele's *first* step in his debasement through the power of gold. It is just this step in the change which makes of a pious Jew a conscienceless exploiter that the author shirks. In *Mirele Efros* a similar omission mars what would easily have been a masterpiece of character portrayal. For here the author has sustained our interest to the very last, only to leave out the identical scene for which he has been preparing us with a cumulative power that renders the spectator almost breathless with anticipation. Will the mother be reconciled to those from whom she has been estranged? After all who could hope to win her over have been sent, will she be able to resist the pleadings of her grand-

---

[1] In *Dos Yiddishe Drama*, New York, 1909. This pamphlet is one of the best pieces of dramatic criticism in Yiddish.

child? This is the turning point in Mirele's life; it is the great scene of the play—if only it had been written. But no, instead, we have it merely related to us that the grandchild has carried off victory where his elders failed.

That Gordin was alive to his shortcomings is amply shown from his own words. "I want to say publicly," he wrote, as early as 1897, "that the Yiddish theatre will never be in a position to undergo normal development as long as the intellectual Jews continue to disregard a problem so important to the masses as the upbuilding of a literary, serious stage. The Yiddish theatre, despite the hundreds of thousands who form its audiences, cannot hope for the arrival of a powerful, talented writer so long as the majority of its authors will, like me, be men who take to dramatic writing through accident, who write pieces only because they are forced to do so in order to make a living, and who, like me, are isolated and see about them only ignorance, jealousy, enmity, and rancor."

Gordin died in 1909. True to the eclectic spirit in which he had at first sought to reconcile Judaism and Christianity, and later ransacked the world's library for material, true to his intensely theatrical instinct, he made his last exit, not with a Jewish word upon his tongue nor with his own thought, but with the closing line of *I Pagliacci:* "La comeddia è finita"—the comedy is over. To his final words Gordin was a man of the theatre.[1]

---

[1] This same story is told of so many men that, though I record it, I choose to take it with a grain of salt larger than the usual dose.

V

His example attracted a number of followers. Although the plays produced under this imperfect realistic influence are not usually remarkable for art in its deeper significance, the dramatists were learning how to speak, as it were; they needed only something to say.

Few of Gordin's disciples add anything to the leader's accomplishments. Libin, for example, has been spoken of as the compromiser between the literary drama and popular trash, but there is too little of literature in the compromise. His real field is the short story, in which, together with his contemporary, Kobrin, he discovered the new-world tenement to its bepuzzled denizens. In a few plays by Kobrin and Asch, in the dramas of Pinski and Hirschbein, we find what is best in the Yiddish drama of to-day—a drama that is practically divorced from the stage that should have been its home. There is here a triumph over the vulgar and ubiquitous intrusion of the song-and-dance element that helped to vitiate even serious plays ever since Goldfaden started the fortunes of the genre; indeed, the third phase of Jewish drama consists in just this liberation from the trammels of badly mixed moods, in the attempt to treat vital Jewish themes, in attention to art rather than to mere substance as such. At times the reaction, like most early reactions, swings to extremes, as in some of Hirschbein's idyllic, symbolic sketches, which are quite unsuited to the stage. On the whole, however, we find in this period the best works that have been written for the Yiddish theatre.

The new impulse came, not from America, but from Russia. Attracted at first by the naturalism of Gorki and later by the mystic symbolism of Andreyev, the Jewish writers fashioned works distinctly racial, at times with a breath of the universal about them.

We may, in a few words, dismiss both Isaac Loeb Perez and Sholom Aleikhem as dramatists. The debt of Yiddish literature to both is infinite; Perez is regarded as the peer of the literature, a master of many forms, and an aristocratic soul who forsook a career in Russian letters, that he might serve his own humble folk with an artistry which— ironically enough—they will perhaps never fully grasp; Sholom Aleikhem, the greatest of the Yiddish folk humorists, is nearer to his people's hearts and to their comprehension. But neither Perez nor Sholom Aleikhem was a dramatist of power or depth. The human touch was there, the pure intention, but not the accomplishment; they are occasionally produced, particularly Sholom Aleikhem, but they have been without any abiding effect upon the drama of their people. The latter's short pieces are little more than sketches; in such a hodge-podge as *The Divorce* he strikes the muddy bottom of bathos; in *Zeseit und Zerspreit*, a play in three acts, he touches upon the dispersion of a Jewish family: the children of Meyer Shalant come to a pretty bad end, Volodia being arrested as a revolutionary, Khayim going to Palestine as a laborer, Khanna preferring study to marriage, Matvey mingling in evil company, Flora eloping. There is a resemblance to Naidenov's *The Children of Vaniushin*.

For the better drama of more recent days, then,

we must look to Leon Kobrin, Sholom Asch, David
Pinski, Perez Hirschbein, and to a few new pieces
that have been brought to the attention of Jewish
audiences in America through such pioneers as
Maurice Schwartz and such institutions as The
Jewish Art Theatre.

LEON KOBRIN

Kobrin was born some fifty years ago in Vitebsk,
White Russia. As early as his fifteenth year he had
begun to write sketches and tales in Russian. Emi-
grating to the United States in 1892, he commenced
the following year to pen stories in Yiddish, based
upon the New World atmosphere, which he was
one of the earliest to bring into Yiddish letters. For,
during his first six years in this country, he engaged,
with as little patience as success, in shirtmaking,
breadbaking, weaving, and newspaper-selling; all
this time his chief desire was to devote himself to
literature.

It was with his first book, *Yankel Boila and Other
Tales* (1898), that he won recognition from critics
on both sides of the ocean. Professor Wiener, of
Harvard, who has since abandoned his Yiddish
studies, hailed the author as the Yiddish Gorki.
Successive productions in fiction (*Ghetto Dramas*,
1904; a nine-hundred-page collection of tales, 1910;
the novels, *The Immigrants*, *Mother and Daughter*,
The Professional Bridegroom, *The Tenement House*,
The Rise of Orre) picture the multiform phases of
tenement life and ghetto adventure in the new land,
with their exotic milieu and their peculiar psychology.

As a pioneer in Yiddish literature in America,

Kobrin will always be remembered as the discoverer of the tenement. He and Libin have been called by their associates the twins of the tenement, because of their preoccupation with the many themes furnished by the East Side in the early days. Kobrin has a deep sense of the environmental influences of the gloomy structures upon the dwellers, so that his numerous tales possess a historical interest. For a whole generation, indeed, Kobrin and Libin dominated Yiddish letters on this side of the Atlantic. They both began with the sketch and the short story, thence to the drama and finally to the novel. In Kobrin may be studied the evolution of the immigrant psychology, from his homesickness for the "old country" to the direction of that yearning upon himself, and by a natural process, to the formation of a strong nationalistic feeling.

The author's dramas number some two dozen, and he is still active. Of these a surprising number have been successful, although upon the stage he seems too ready to strain the truth for a situation. Without a doubt, however, Kobrin has had a wholesome influence upon the Yiddish drama, having followed the Gordin tradition of personal tenacity and fought unceasingly for "playwright's rights" as against managerial dictatorship. His first play, *Minna*, was produced in 1899, having been written in collaboration with Gordin. His second, *The East Side Ghetto*, played in the same year, brought to the attention of the public the varied gifts of Bertha Kalish, who has since achieved a reputation among English playgoers. It was on the occasion of the production of *Two Sisters*, 1904, that Israel Zangwill

24

wrote a very favorable report of the play in the
New York *Herald*, later meeting the author and
requesting him to translate into Yiddish *The Children of the Ghetto*. When that work was done and
the play presented in Yiddish, Zangwill exclaimed
enthusiastically to the translator, "Now I realize
that I have translated you—not you me!"

"Three years ago," said Kobrin to an interviewer
in 1915, "I organized all the playwrights, about
twenty in number, into a society known as The
Jewish Playwrights' Association. Our common aim
was to make the dramatist independent—to make
it possible for him to express himself freely as he
feels, and not as the manager expects him to."
A further insight into the writer's independence is
afforded by an interesting detail in the history of his
play, *Children of Nature*. (The play, by the way, is
founded upon his early tale, *Yankel Boila*, and was
several years ago produced with great success in a
Russian version at the Moscow Art Theatre.) The
Yiddish original was accepted in 1912 and rehearsals
were begun. The author had received seven hundred dollars in advance royalties. At one of the
early rehearsals, however, the manager showed a
disposition to change the plot—a phenomenon not
unknown to the English "boards." Kobrin could
not see the point, despite the manager's most earnest
protestations. The latter, as a final resort, exclaimed
that unless the author conceded the issue he could
take his play back. Whereupon the playwright
took the play and returned the advance. Other
managers proving just as obdurate, Kobrin decided
to produce the play himself, and surely enough,

when it was given at the Odeon Theatre on the East Side, its immediate success justified the author's confidence.

Children of Nature is the tale of a village boy who falls in love with a Gentile lass. The two have grown up together. Yankel's father dies, and extracts, upon his death-bed, a promise that his son will not marry out of the faith; that instead of wedding Natasha he will take a cousin, who happens to be a silly child and an invalid to boot. Matters are further complicated by the fact that Natasha faces motherhood. Upon hearing of Yankel's promise to his father, she is compelled to leave the village. Her suffering proves too much for Yankel; yet he is bound by a sacred oath and is, withal, of an intensely superstitious mental cast. Marry the idiot cousin he cannot. On the day of the wedding he is found hanging, dead, in the home of the prospective wife.

Such violent contrasts as suicides on wedding days are dear to the hearts of lesser playwrights, yet this should not obscure the intellectual honesty of the drama. So evident was this at the very first performance that the critics found Kobrin too fair, so to speak. The Gentile characters of the play, notes one, are more amiable, and draw more deeply upon the sympathies of the audience, than do the Jewish. A more serious fault has been indicated— one that strikes at the roots of the protagonist's character. Kobrin, in accentuating the superstitious nature of Yankel, makes his hero weaker as a dramatic force. Would so superstititious a fellow have dared to continue to love out of the faith?

Could he have risen, another critic has asked, to the solution of suicide, if his beliefs in after-world punishment were so strong?

In more than one other of his longer plays Kobrin deals with a similar contrast; now it is between two brothers, one of whom has abjured the faith (*Back to His People*), now between the real Jewess that is Hadassah Polakoff, the singer of international repute, and the "distinguished foreigner" that she becomes in the hands of her press-agent and an adoring public (*Israel's Hope*). Such plots are often, in their very essence, artificial, and betray their fundamental falsity in the melodramatic jerkiness of the action. They possess full significance only to that portion of humanity which has lived through the double life forced upon the Jew; they fall short of the highest art because they strain a truth which reality itself has strained in the first place.

Kobrin has translated *Faust* and *Hamlet* for Jewish readers; he has also made Yiddish versions of some of the works of Echegaray, a writer whose frequent excursions into melodrama contain something that should appeal to the less discriminating members of the audience—which everywhere means most of it. His other translations include the works of Turgeniev, de Maupassant, Hugo, Gorki.[1] Kobrin's highest achievement is not of the stage; it is a short idyll—this, of all things, from a writer deeply sensual and as capable of bare literary brutality as

---

[1] It is Kobrin, I believe, who may be said to have "discovered" Gorki outside of Russia. He had noticed in a Russian publication the tale *Makar Chudra*, signed by a then unknown name. He at once translated it for the Yiddish *Zukunft* (Future) a New York publication that even today has few rivals of its kind in the nearby English magazines. It was Kobrin who brought Gorki to Professor Wiener's attention. The latter, on his return from a visit to Russia for the purpose of collecting material for his book upon Yiddish literature in the nineteenth century, brought back with him the first three volumes of Gorki's works, which were later put into English by Isabel Hapgood.

any disciple of Zola!—called *A Lithuanian Village*.
It is one of the finest productions in the Yiddish
tongue.

SHOLOM ASCH

Asch is to-day one of the most widely read of the
Yiddish writers and at the same time one of the
most naturally gifted. His prose, at its best, is a
highly flexible medium, as ready to the purposes of
the sternest realism as to the softest idyllic effects.
He is not, in the rhetorical sense of the word, a
"stylist"; he is an artist by virtue of his spontaneous
response to the manifold beauties of his ever-changing scene. His very lapses emphasize the spontaneity of his expression without impairing its
efficacy. By these tokens he is not to be classified
with the conventional symbols of genre or outlook;
he is realist, romanticist, idealist, playwright, novelist, conteur,—all in one. He has made of the
despised "jargon" of the Haskalite scorn an instrument of beauty whose melodies are rivalled only by
such contemporaries as Pinski and Hirschbein. Much
of what he has written will perish with most of the
other works of man, but at his best he has given to
Yiddish literature some of its most enduring pages.

He is to-day in his forty-second year; his peregrinations have carried him to the four corners of the
earth; he is a restless mind in a restless body. As
early as his twenty-fourth year he achieved a reputation with his first book, *The Town*, a series of
vignettes of provincial Jewish life in Russia, and
followed up this success with a steady number of
short tales in which the multiform phases of his
people's life—sacred and secular—were depicted

with a deep yet unobtrusively poetic insight. Of his novels, *Meri* and *The Road to Self*, which form a continuous whole, depict with a wealth of color and episode the wanderings of Jewish souls in search of self-realization. The background, mainly that of the Russian revolution of 1905, shifts, as the author himself has so often done, to various parts of the globe. Such places as the thirteenth chapter of Part One of *Meri* and the forty-first in Part Two of *The Road to Self* exhibit the same linguistic iridescence that was early forecast in his shorter tales. *Mottke the Vagabond* and *Uncle Moses*, both now available in English, witness the novelist's essential traits: a relative carelessness as to the mere plot in itself, while attention is concentrated upon illuminating detail, upon character in action, poetry of scene and situation.

Since, as Lewes has told us in his biography of Goethe, "the whole man thinks," these qualities of Asch, more or less diluted, are to be found in his dramas. Best known of his full-length plays is *The God of Vengeance*, of which more in a moment. The shorter pieces present a motley crowd that troops in fictitious existence across his stage: drunkards, fallen women, rabbis, pious provincial Jews, sophisticated new-worldlings, defenders of the old, pioneers of the new. In these plays, as in the longer, it may be said that Asch, generally speaking, is either too intent upon symbolism for its own sake or too easily drawn into the methods of melodrama. On the one hand his idealism is apt to be translated into material too tenuous for effective production; on the other, his equally powerful sense of the real finds expression in an insistence upon theatrical externals. Yet such a one-act production as *The Sinner*, which deals with the refusal of a Jewish grave to receive the corpse of a man who has married out of the fold, is developed not only with impartial outlook, but with a certain successful projection of the uncanny situation. The effect of the play is that of a blind power; one is conscious of strength even where one is puzzled as to definite significance. The religious may interpret it as orthodox, the advanced may see in it even a certain sympathy for the mysterious figure of the woman who has been the companion of his ungodly life; none can deny it, however, a suggestion of an ineluctable fate. I have hinted that such pieces as *Night* are too tenuous for production, yet this should not diminish its worth as a bit of highly original and effective impressionistic writing; the newer methods of production, moreover, will do much to destroy former talk about what is stageworthy and what is not, and this daring interlude in which a prostitute's face for a moment lights up with the pallid holiness of the Madonna's image may appeal to lovers of the drama that is imagination as well as physical movement.

The God of Vengeance, upon which Asch's reputation as a dramatist may be said to rest, was first produced outside of its local habitat by the famous Reinhardt, at the Deutsches Theater, Berlin, in 1910. The powerful play quickly made its way to the chief stages of Europe. It has been played all over Germany, Austria, Russia, Poland, Holland, Norway, Sweden, and Italy; in the country last named it produced a marked impression during the entire season of 1916.

Its plot, simply narrated, is that of a father who, having accumulated a modest sum through the brothel that he runs in his cellar, aspires to redeem himself and his wife in the eyes of God with his daughter Rifkele. The money that sinks its roots in impurity shall flourish into a tree of sanctity. Yekel presents a Holy Scroll to the synagogue; he consorts with the holy men; he admonishes his wife to keep a sharp eye upon their only child. Their vigilance proves of no avail; Rifkele, fascinated by the life that her mother has led and that her father fosters in others, is led astray through the offices of one of the inmates. With his hope of redemption thus shattered, Yekel goes mad with rage and thrusts his daughter down into the brothel with the rest of the prostitutes. Not pleasant stuff this, nor very close to the life that most of us know. Yet there is a certain beauty here—a rugged beauty that was born in no literary hot-house and much dimmed, perhaps, by the repellent human beings who are its carriers,—but beauty none the less.

It is interesting to consider Asch's *The God of Vengeance* in connection with a play like *Mrs. Warren's Profession*. To be sure, there is no technical resemblance between the two dramas; nor, despite an external similarity in backgrounds, is there any real identity of purpose. Asch's piece glows with his characteristic poetic realism and re-counts an individual drama not without symbolic power. Yet the essentially moral earnestness of both Shaw and Asch brings the circles of their themes in a sense tangent to each other. And I use the word moral in its broadest, not its narrowest, sense.

Mrs. Warren, for example, cherishes no delusions about her dubious profession,—neither the sentimentality that has long swathed so much talk about the prostitute nor the delusion of the conservative, conventional horror before an institution for the perpetuation of which—in its uglier phases—conservatism and conventionalism are much to blame. If Yekel and his wife, in Asch's play, are not so enlightened as Mrs. Warren upon the traffic off which they live, they are in their own crude way equally sincere in considering it a business quite as legitimate as any other. With the same inconsistency that Hindel displays in imploring heaven for aid in achieving her nefarious aims, after which she promises to be a model wife and mother, Mrs. Warren, at the end of Shaw's play, swears by heaven that henceforth she will lead a life of evil.

In the case of Yekel and his wife, and in Mrs. Warren's, another touch of inconsistency is added by the agreement that theirs is not the best of professions. Crofts, too, in the English play, discusses the business with all the matter-of-factness of Asch's pimp, Shloyme, yet considers himself a gentleman none the less.

Rifkele, the seduced daughter, is no Vivie. Asch's simple-minded Jewish girl is a victim, not a rebel. Yet in either case the daughter is lost to the parents, and the power of money cannot win back the child. And just as Yekel, in his impotence, blasphemously thrusts the Holy Scroll from his household, so does Mrs. Warren, defeated in her attempt to regain her daughter, cry, "From this time forth, so help me heaven in my last hour, I'll do wrong, and nothing but wrong. And I'll prosper on it." Perhaps, too,

the retribution which in each case is visited upon
the parent arises from the fact that both Mrs.
Warren and Yekel have, in Vivie's accusatory,
Ibsen-like words, "lived one life and believed in
another."

The God of Vengeance, despite conclusions too
easily drawn, is not a sex play; I mention this, not
because I believe any odium attaches to sex in
literature, but out of a desire to make a distinction
between values. When Asch wishes to deal with
sex he is not afraid to handle the subject with all
the poetry and power at his command. Such a play
as his *Jephthah's Daughter* treats the elemental urge
of sex with daring, beauty, and Dionysiac abandon,
while a golden symbolism wafts through the piece.
Again, in his novel *Mottke the Vagabond,* he has
given us scenes from the underworld of Warsaw
that are hard to parallel for truth to detail. *The
God of Vengeance* is no mere brothel-drama, but is
instinct with a connotation of genuine artistic
beauty and ethical verity. Nor is it a drama with
a moral purpose (employing the word now in its
narrow sense), as Mr. Mencken interpreted it in
one of the few intelligent criticisms that greeted its
appearance in English.[1]

When he came to the United States some seven
years ago, he expressed, in an interview, a desire
to eliminate from the Jewish theatre the commercial atmosphere that was its bane. "One way to
do this," he suggested, "is to introduce into the
representations of our modern life, and ultimately

[1] Mr. Mencken was the first, among English critics, to recognize Asch's gifts
as a novelist. His critique of this play as a moralistic tract may be traced to the
intensely religious atmosphere upon which much of the force of the issue depends.
Asch is an independent mind, least likely of all his confrères to preach morality
either upon the stage or upon the printed page. He is, as his symbolic pieces show,
eager to reveal beauty, but never to debase his medium.

into the life itself, our beautiful Hebrew traditions. A great many of them are pagan—I confess—but beautiful nevertheless, and contributory to a fine culture." That phrase, "pagan—I confess—but beautiful nevertheless," is an excellent commentary upon this artist when he is at his best. None of his plays, however, has had such an influence upon the Jewish drama, which for the most part plods along the road of mediocrity, quite impervious to the labors of the better spirits. The plain truth is that in the United States most cultured Jews seek the Gentile drama, and the average audience for the Yiddish product is—average.

DAVID PINSKI

Mr. Pinski stands well in the forefront of his people's prose artists and dramatists. Hostile tactics of the East Side press and the cliques that control it long kept his name from achieving the fame that was its due, yet there is in his work a something finer that limits his appeal to a small circle—an aristocracy of attitude that is the full flower rather than the inconsistent antithesis of his democratic, universal aspirations. Something of this there is in the writings of Perez, who was, with his characteristic perspicacity, the first to discern the natural gifts in the young man.

To the literature of the Jews Pinski is known, not only as dramatist, but as the discoverer of the Jewish proletariat in fiction. Yet, paradoxically enough, the very people whom he so discovered has yet really to discover him, and while third- and fourth-rate dramas weigh down the boards of the

Yiddish theatre, it is left for Europe, and latterly, non-Jewish America, to appreciate at their proper value dramas which have, in some cases, been before the Yiddish public for years. This is all the less excusable on the part of Yiddish critics, in that Pinski has been a resident of New York since 1899, and has, with the exception of *Isaac Sheftel*, written his best works in that city. Yet in all the years he has lived in New York he has not secured a regular Yiddish publisher. It would seem, once more, that a dramatic prophet is not without honor save in his own land. This, however, should not give the impression that Pinski is unknown to the Jewish reader. Far from it. His stories are widely read by an ever-increasing number, both for their intimate and artistic pictures of working-class life in Europe and their skillful, melodious use of the Yiddish tongue, which we shall later see has been moulded by the author into a thing of beauty that at its best rivals the harmonious language of a Yeats, a Maeterlinck, or a Lord Dunsany. His plays, too, are known among the more discerning. But it has been left, after all, for America really to discover David Pinski.

Born on April 5, 1872, in the government of Mohilev, Russia, of pious parents, he was early destined for the career of rabbi. At the age of seven he began the study of the Talmud, and in a few years became widely known as a learned Talmudist. At the age of ten he rebelled against the narrow intensity of his training and first felt his inspiration to become a writer. This ambition had its initial glowing success the next year when, in his grandmother's home, before an audience of some twenty persons who had paid admission, there was given a piece which he himself cannot at present recall except that it brought much laughter and tears to the eyes of the spectators—a recipe that still holds good for success on the stages of more than one country. This was his only attempt at drama until 1899, the year of his one-act *Yisurim* (*Agonies*) and the three-act *Isaac Sheftel*.

When he reached the age of thirteen his family moved to Moscow, where his secular education began, but this was soon put a stop to by restrictions against the Jews. The year 1892 finds him in Vienna, this time preparing for the medical profession, but the expulsion of his parents from Moscow brought him back to Russia, where, in Warsaw—the Mecca of Jewish literary talent—he took to writing the stories that soon made him known. At first he wrote in Hebrew and in Russian, but as early as his seventeenth year he saw that if he was to help his people, he must use their tongue, and he gave himself definitely over to Yiddish. In 1893 with the story, *The New Madman* (known now as *In a Madhouse*), he made his successful debut as author. Not long after, together with Isaac Loeb Perez he founded the so-called *Holiday Pages*, a publication which owed its name and its method of publication to a peculiar Russian law against regular periodicals in Yiddish. To get around the censor, the enterprising partners took advantage of the fact that Jewish holidays came with comfortable frequency. Perez was the guiding spirit of the publication, while Pinski was its organizing power; here again his modesty kept him from having his name appear upon the editorial page, so that his association with Perez is little known. The year 1896 found Pinski in Berlin, where he made a study of German literature and philosophy and established friendships with the leading literary and dramatic spirits of the country. Here, too, he conceived his first important drama, *Isaac Sheftel*, under the influence of the Naturalists. By this time his name had begun to be known among the Jews of New York, and he was offered a place upon the editorial staff of a weekly there. He was prompted to accept by the fact that New York had an established Yiddish theatre, and that his play might be produced. Judge of his surprise when he learned upon arriving that the Yiddish managers would not even consent to read his play, because—it was written in three acts, and they demanded four. From that day to this Pinski has gone his own way, and it is significant that more than one of the plays that soon followed was written in three acts, and even one.

Once, in 1903, Pinski was even upon the verge of giving up his literary career. He entered Columbia College, prepared to receive the Ph.D. degree after a year's study and to teach German literature and drama. But his natural gifts proved too strong for him. On May 20, 1904, when he was supposed to go to the doctor's examination, he sat down and instead put the finishing touches to *The Zwie Family*—about which for many months there raged a discussion that has not yet quite subsided. Only two years later he was to write *The Treasure*. From that day to this he has been steadily engaged upon his literary work, singularly unmindful of all influences not directly concerned with the highest that there is in him. "My work has become," he said to me some years ago in his Bronx home, "almost a personal rite. I have forgotten what the voice of the critics sounds like. And as for my life itself, it is, and has been, very uneventful. Its greatest joy has always been my wife. Its greatest sorrow, the loss of my seven-year-old son in the recent epidemic of infantile paralysis."

Pinski's first significant play, written at the age of twenty-seven, is a natural development from his early tales. It is not, however, as might have been feared, both from the age at which he wrote it and the tales from which it evolved, spoiled by any propagandistic aims; indeed, it is a psychological study rather than a plea for a class. More, despite its Jewish background and its poverty-stricken milieu, its leading character, the factory-worker, Isaac Sheftel, is a symbol who rises above class or race into the universal. Sheftel's tragedy is the tragedy of us all—the tragedy not only of the unfulfilled, but of the unfulfillable. This worker, whose vision sees so much farther than his meagre mental equipment can carry him, has invented one or two simple machines, and has sold them for a mere pittance to his employer. Suddenly he is seized with a new idea that promises a masterpiece of invention; he cannot sleep, he cannot eat; he even takes off three days from the shop, despite his dire poverty, so that he may finish the work. His wife nags him for his selfishness; his neighbors ridicule him; his employer sends to inform him that if he does not return to work that very day, his place will be filled by another. In stubborn silence Sheftel works away at his contrivance, baffled and

beaten. His inborn creative intelligence is balked
by his mental and technical limitations, and fairly
crazed by his wife's unceasing nagging and the
wretched surroundings of his cellar home, he smashes
the entire device and returns to work without
having eaten a bite. His shopmates receive him
with taunts, and soon begin to ply him with liquor
to revive his sunken spirits. In this condition he
answers his employer's recriminations by smashing
the machines which had been previously bought
from him. He rushes forth from the factory, evades
pursuit, and for the rest of the day wanders madly
through the woods. That night he returns to his
home, exhausted; the better part of him, his beloved
inventions, is already destroyed; no one understands him; he cannot express his own visions.
Thus dejected, and half unwittingly, he commits
suicide by drinking rat poison. Even his death is
ignominious.

The playwright has been commended for his
handling of crowds upon the stage. Here, in his
first large effort, is afforded an excellent instance of
this particular skill. The second act, which shows
the interior of the factory, is admirable not only for
its group-technique; the whole life of the worker—
his ready humor, his inappreciation of his position,
his incapacity to understand the Sheftel type, is
drawn in rapid, vivid strokes that forecast the
notable fourth act of *The Treasure*.

From the man Sheftel, Pinski, in *The Zwie Family*,[1]
(1904), went to the race. Here are represented,
under one roof, three generations of the Zwie family
—not as in *Milestones*, for instance, by means of

[1] In the English version this is called *The Last Jew*.

acts with the years between them, but all simultaneously gathered in one home, and symbolic of the three generations of present-day Jews. Old Reb Maishe, the city preacher, is the type of religious idealist that is fast disappearing; his son Yankel mouths the words of God, to be sure, but his mind is upon the accumulation of money. Yankel's sons, on the other hand, flame with an idealism no less than that of their grandfather; but it is an idealism that looks away from the old city preacher's goal. The one is a Zionist, the other a Socialist, the third believes in assimilation. And so, under one roof, five worlds. Suddenly occurs a massacre, and each world reacts in its own peculiar way to the stress of the horrible day. The old grandfather, intent upon saving the holy scroll of the synagogue from desecration, wanders through the city in vain to find defenders. His own family deserts him, each going his own way. The leaders of the community, more intent upon business than religion, likewise turn a deaf ear to his entreaties. Baffled, old Zwie makes his way, alone, to the synagogue, where he is soon to die by a stone hurled through the window. Too late comes aid from his grandsons; he is dead, and the old order with him. But a new one shall arise, and the torch-bearer will come from the third generation.

Obviously such a play (erroneously interpreted by a leading Russian-Jewish critic as a mere pogrom-drama) can have its chief interest only for the race whose trials it symbolizes. It represents perhaps the author's most intense outpouring upon the question of his people; the tragic figure of the protagonist is a second Moses, as it were, whose following aban-

25

dons him at the crucial moment. The intense pessimism of the early scenes gives way, at the very end, to a ray of hope.

Following closely upon this play, in the same year, came the one-act *Gluecksvergessene*, known in English as *Forgotten Souls*. Here, as in the majority of Pinski's works, the Jewish background does not tend in the slightest to smother the universal note which must sound beneath all work that is truly great. Rarely has the pathos of self-sacrifice received treatment at once so simple, so ironic, so tenderly human. Fanny's self-effacement so that her sister may be happy is a trait that makes her kin with all who have suffered for another's joy. The jubilant opening of the act and its steady progression to the passionate, pathetic close, is accomplished with a crescendo that is one of the author's distinctive technical traits. It was already evident in the second act of *Isaac Sheftel*; it forms one of the chief charms of Pinski's highly original war piece, *Little Heroes*, one of the miniature masterpieces that grew out of the savage conflict.

The year 1906 marks a distinct step forward in the playwright's career. It is the year of *The Eternal Jew*, of *The Treasure*, and of *Jacob the Blacksmith*. From the crushing sense of life's sterner realities he had by this time distilled a vision, a sense of color and movement which, added to the intense power of his earlier style, soon resulted in a series of plays which for sheer inner beauty, chastity of art, and pregnancy of imagination, will long remain unsurpassed, even as they are now unapproached, in the history of Jewish drama. Together with all this came a new rhythmic prose that

lends itself most naturally to the expression of
Jewish thought. Pinski has made of the long-
despised "jargon" a thing of flexible beauty, of
infinite tenderness or crushing power, a stream of
melody that only rarely is disturbed by an occasional construction that is too German for the
idiom. Without the suggestion of preciosity, he
chooses even his vowels with a poet's ear, and his
later plays demand to be read aloud, if even to one's
self, for their fullest effect.

The Eternal Jew, besides being the first of a series
of plays founded upon the Messianic idea, is also
the first of a tetralogy, each act complete in itself,
based upon the fascinating subject that has inspired
so many writers before him. Here, for the first
time, appears the sense of the color and glamor of
history which is to come to full fruition five years
later in *The Dumb Messiah*. Here, too, makes its
initial appearance another characteristic, later to
receive greater exemplification in such a piece as
Mary Magdalene, or the beautiful series of one-act
plays, five in all, written around the wives of King
David, and thus constituting, as it were a Biblical
Anatol. Pinski, in drawing upon the Bible or upon
Talmudic legend for inspiration, uses his source
merely as a suggestion. He seizes upon his personages, studies them, penetrates their inner life,
and evolves the details of the action in strict consistency with the character of the actors; his plays
not only fill out the mere suggestions of his source,
but interpret them as well. This is well shown in
The Eternal Jew, where the author has quoted his
source in the original Hebrew, translated it into

Yiddish, and embodied it in a dramatic form that glorifies the dull iteration of the original.

Perhaps it is more than mere coincidence that two of the leading plays produced by the Yiddish theatre are on the subject of money. Gordin's *God, Man, and Devil* is a thesis-play, like many others that Gordin wrote, differing from them, however, in the success which attended the author in his remaking of Goethe's *Faust* into an original drama of undeniable potency. But Gordin, a born man of the theatre, lacked the refinements of higher art. He did not possess the keen psychological insight which is one of Pinski's chief gifts as dramatist; so that in many respects the difference between *God, Man, and Devil* and *The Treasure* represents the great stride taken by Jewish drama in the few years that separated the writing of the two plays. The earlier one is the acme of Gordin's theatrical talents; together with his *Mirele Efros* it represents the high-water mark of the third distinct epoch in the evolution of the Yiddish drama. An intense action, determining, rather than determined by, the characters; a ready flow of speech; a certain brutal strength; an obvious thesis worked out with suspense, crisis, and ultimate catastrophe.

In Pinski's *The Treasure* (produced in 1910 at the Deutsches Theater, Berlin, by Max Reinhardt) one notices immediately the touch of a master hand. No longer do the personages make the ready slaves of the dramatist; they are the germ of the action, which rises most naturally from their own natures. Tille, despite the fact that her father is a grave-digger, and that the cemetery is a daily reminder of the vanity of earthly pomp and possession, yearns for the power that beauty and wealth may wield.

Not even the Ninth of Ab, one of the most solemn days in the holy calendar, can take her mind from the contemplation of handsome young men and brilliant matches. And what if the handsome young men don't look her way, and the brilliant matches do not appear? Can she not imagine them? Is she not, at least, queen of that realm? And what shall prevent her from imagining, for instance, that she is Rothschild's bride? In the midst of such a mood in comes her half-witted brother Yudke, who has just buried his dog and has found in the earth thus dug up a handful of shining gold pieces. Seized by one of his numerous whims, he places them all in Tille's hands. Following, as they do, fast upon her golden visions, what more natural than that she should seize upon her father's suggestion that probably there is a treasure buried where Yudke has interred his dog? She refuses to surrender the gold pieces to her parents, jumps merrily out of the house, and, regardless of the sacred character of the day, runs off to the city to deck herself out in the finest that the department stores can provide.

She returns late that evening, in a carriage, if you please, leaving behind her a trail of open-mouthed citizens. For she has not bothered with details; since, doubtless, an enormous treasure was buried near Yudke's dog, and since he would surely recall just where he had interred his pet, as soon as the forgetfulness which always followed his epileptic attacks would pass over, she has spread the report that her folks had upon their hands a great fortune in gold pieces, yielded out of the bowels of the graveyard.

At once the entire community comes fawning at

her heels. The leading matchmaker calls to arrange a splendid union, the humble grave-digger begins to receive more visitors in a single day than had ever before graced his dwelling in his entire life. All manner of complications begin to arise, prompted by the jealousy and covetousness of his neighbors, until it is impossible to manage the pretense any longer. But now that the finding of the treasure is denied, who will believe the denial? And when Tille's poor father tells the tale exactly as it stands: that his son found a few gold pieces where he buried a dog, and that he cannot now recall where the place was, the report spreads like wildfire, and the excited community, believing that there is a fortune where the dog lies buried, begins to ransack the cemetery and dig it up from top to bottom in the search for the gold. The whole town turns out; in the anxious search, graves are desecrated. And when finally Yudke remembers where he buried his dog (in the grave of a holy man!), it turns out that there is no treasure at all, and the crowd disperses. It is the dead of night, and the souls of the departed, literally awakened by the search for the treasure, discuss the eventful day in mystic epilogue to the "bitter comedy." . . . "Money, money, money," sound the mysterious voices of the shades. "And yet it must lead to something. Surely there must be a goal. . . . Only God knows that. . . . And man must learn what it is. That will be his greatest victory. Man's greatest victory."

SEVERAL OF THE DEAD: Man's. . . .

OTHERS: The living one's. . . . And we? (*A ghostly breathing of laughter and sighing.*)

THE FIRST: Man's greatest victory. . . .

And the curtain descends upon the enigma.[1]

It is no small tribute to the author that the play rises most naturally into the mystic close. Money, the dead seem to whisper to us, and the possessions which it represents, have thus far mastered humanity; but some day humanity will master it. The meanness in man that pursuit of wealth has called forth will then vanish in the proper appraisal of that wealth as a means, not as an end; money may be, until that day, at the root of all evil, but the struggle after money is not a search for evil; the evil is incident to the search. And man's greatest victory will be the mastery of his possessions.

The opening act is an admirable example of expository art; the second and third acts, in the humor and satire that spring spontaneously from the germ of the action, reach a level rarely attained in American or continental drama. Professor Baker has already signaled out the closing act as being remarkable for its handling of the crowd in the cemetery. The entire play, so significant in its literal action, rises to universality in the unobtrusive, yet inescapable symbolism of its inner development.

Symbolism is almost as natural as speech to the

---

[1] Since it was Ludwig Lewisohn's English version of *The Treasure* that brought Pinski to the Gentile reader of this country, and thus elicited from Professor G. P. Baker, of Harvard, a fulsome measure of praise that further established the Yiddish dramatist in the favor of a discriminating few, I give here a short article written by Baker for the Boston Evening Transcript of March 31, 1917, to companion the discussion of Pinski written by me for the same issue. The present section on Pinski is a revision of that discussion. Said Professor Baker:

"When *The Treasure* came from the publisher, the name of its author, David Pinski, meant nothing to me. I opened the book, thinking wearily, 'One more play to read,' but I read it with such growing enthusiasm that I have come back to it again and again. *The Treasure* is a comedy—or is it a tragedy? In any case it rests on intimate knowledge of life among the poor Jews in a Slavic city. The observer is sympathetic, yet not limited in his judgments by their prejudices and conventions. It is a play which oddly combines intense realism of details with broad, imaginative sweep. Though there is an admitted general dramatic principle that to mingle the realism of every day with the supernatural is dangerous except in the hands of a master, so perfectly does Mr. Pinski use the two in *The Treasure* that I more than suspect he is a master.

"When I look about in English literature for a parallel to this play, I think of

Jew, yet too often trammeled by an overinsistence upon detail that ends by becoming too monotonously obvious or, on the other hand, involved and even far-fetched. Thus Sholom Asch's *Jephthahs' Daughter* falls into the first category, while more than one piece by Perez Hirschbein inclines to the other extreme. Pinski was saved from this in *The Treasure* and other pieces by his thorough immersion in the theme and his freedom from the trammels of conventionalism. More than one will object that there is a mite too much of talk in the play, as, indeed in the drama built around the Zwie family; the criticism applies more to the latter than to *The Treasure*, however. In the Zwie play the protagonist's exhortations are largely repetitions and delay the action not merely in the conventional, technical sense, but in the deeper and more legitimate sense of emotional unfolding.

Jacob the Blacksmith is hardly worthy of the two pieces that preceded it in the same year. It possesses too many of the qualities that insure rapid success upon the Yiddish stage—a success which it has had and still continues to enjoy. It looks like a "pot-boiler"—revealing, no doubt, the hand that

---

Ben Jonson's *Volpone*. There is in both plays something of the same mocking laughter, the same bitter recognition of the humor there may be in sordidness and horror. Both are largely and finely conceived. If *The Treasure* lacks the poetic expression of *Volpone*, it has finer truth of characterization.

"This grim comedy of the effect upon a community of some money, found in the Jewish Cemetery by the demented Yudke, is certainly one of the most remarkable plays written in the past ten years. Successful on the Yiddish stage of New York, produced by Reinhardt in his Deutsches Theater in Berlin, because he recognized its more than local significance, it has not been seen on our stage even a year after its appearance in an admirable English translation. It is easy to see why amateurs should hesitate to stage it, for it requires a large cast and very careful producing. Its difficulties, however, are of the sort to stimulate a producer of the best type to his utmost endeavor. Sympathetically and thoughtfully staged, it would certainly produce a strong impression. Produced according to formula, as are so many of our plays on the New York stage, it would be so twisted and contorted as to lose most of its chief values. Is it not a great pity that our present conditions do not even permit our public to judge for themselves a play as thoughtful, as free from conventionality, yet as essentially dramatic and as individual as *The Treasure?*" The play was later produced by the Theatre Guild.

wrote it, but none the less reflecting little credit upon the author. Its main theme, that of a wayward husband regenerated by the confidence of his wife, is important to us mainly as indicating the entrance of the dramatist into the field of the drama based upon sex-problems. The characterization is not clear, and despite the strong act in the blacksmith's shop, it is one of the least convincing of the writer's published works.

With the poetic *Gabri and the Women*, however, written two years later, Pinski is more successful. The drama is not particularly Jewish in tone (and after all, even for Jewish dramatists, the essential thing is to write first of all a good play) and may be compared, in theme, with such a play as *Candida* or *The Lady from the Sea*. Only here it is the man that wavers between two women, going back to his wife after having received from her his freedom of choice. The piece is distinguished by the exquisite prose that embellishes so much of Pinski's work; one trembles to think what it would become in the mouths of the ranters that constitute, in altogether too great number, the Yiddish world of actors. Here, again, especially in the second act, the delicate symbolism heightens the significance of the action. The drama is further distinguished from the European plays just mentioned in the fact that The Little One, who has for a time won Gabri's love away from his wife, in turn transfers her love to one of Gabri's sons, even as he has transferred his from his wife to her. *With Banners of Victory*, a one-act play of the same year, dealing with a similar theme, is not among Pinski's happiest creations; it seems forced and not sufficiently characterized.

Two years later, 1910, came *Mary Magdalene*, the name of which calls to mind, among the moderns, Maeterlinck and Paul Heyse. Yet Pinski's conception of the historical figure has little in common with either, and is in some respects perhaps superior to both. Maeterlinck's play has plenty of the poetical, of the spectacular; there is little or no psychology; his Mary, moreover, is another Monna Vanna, with time and circumstance altered; indeed, it is perhaps the very element in Heyse's play which placed Mary in a forced choice between her carnal and her spiritual love that so attracted Maeterlinck to the play from which he borrowed the two situations which afterwards occasioned the quarrel between him and Heyse, who was himself no small borrower from early Italy and Provence. Such choices were dear to Maeterlinck's heart, and had already occurred in more than one of his plays. Heyse's play, more involved than the Belgian's, is more essentially dramatic. Neither attempts to depict the process of Mary's conversion; it is taken for granted and exploited for the chief situation, which is in both plays the same—that of Mary's choice between her lover and the Nazarene. And in each case, of course, Mary prefers to let the Nazarene die rather than save him at the cost of violating his own teachings and the faith he has inspired within her.

It is characteristic of Pinski's dramatic method that in his treatment of the theme he has taken Mary at the moment the conversion begins and has chosen to make a searching analysis of her soul. The play is at once a drama of sex, with all the freedom of treatment that the subject connotes, and a drama, so to speak, of Biblical reconstruction, thus uniting two of the dramatist's manners. But, like all of his historic or legendary plays, this one possesses a most human and contemporary application. He conceives Mary as a woman who has erected within her a Venus-religion, a faith in the all-compelling power of her own beauty. Her meeting with the Nazarene, reported by herself, has caused her faith to waver, but before surrendering she determines to make a desperate resistance, to try her charms upon the holiest men—upon Alexander, one of the leaders of the zealots and hater of women; upon Amram, most pious of the Jews. Having conquered them, she proceeds to a second assault upon the Nazarene (again reported upon the scene as having happened) and this time her Venus-faith is shattered. The dramatist has dissected the woman's soul; here is no spectacle, no melodramatic choice between the two sharp horns of a dilemma; the drama is an inner struggle. Neither Maeterlinck nor Heyse has attempted so minute a characterization. In neither of their plays is there the humor by which Pinski has relieved the tense poetry of his Mary's struggle. Pinski's Mary, moreover, stands out in all the bolder relief for the figure of the courtesan, Isabel, who pokes fun at her companion to the last, and robs her of her jewels in the final act of the three. The closing act, by the way, is another splendid example of the playwright's crescendo effects; opening upon a scene in which several suitors of Mary engage in a drunken brawl, its gradual ascent to Mary's noble renunciation is accomplished with a skill that achieves all the simplicity of the inevitable. For the rest the dramatist has lavished upon the play some of his most poetic passages, which are the despair of the translator. And in one respect, at least, there is no doubt that he has surpassed both Heyse and Maeterlinck; the fascination of his Mary is shown in the very words she utters; in the uncanny cleverness with which she outwits the arguments of the holy Amram and baffles all but the Nazarene, whose silent goodness at last conquers her loquacious sin. In the moral of the play (to risk a word that connotes a pulpit-thumping which is furthest from Pinski's methods) as in the treatment of the subject, he differs from both the German and the Belgian. The plays of the latter emphasize Mary's conversion as a divine effect of Jesus' influence. Pinski's play, while showing this in all the soul-struggle of its consummation, adds to it the note of toleration—"Judge not, that ye be not judged"—which was the very element in Jesus' human message that so stirred Mary back to the life of a good woman. For the very men in the Pinski drama who have most condemned Eleazer, the leader of the zealots, for his slavery to Mary's charms, are themselves ready victims to it. *Mary Magdalene* belongs at the side of *The Treasure* and *The Zwie Family*.

In the following year (1911) came *The Dumb Messiah*, another in the historic series, which, in the list of the playwright's chief works, must be placed together with the three just mentioned. The play, suggested by the expulsion of the Jews from France in 1306 by Philip IV, and their return nine years later under Louis X, is built upon an original plot and placed in the mythical land of Illyria. The leader of the Jews here has had his

tongue cut out for his utterances against the harsh
King Philip, and together with the whole Jewish
population is expelled from the country. The tongue-
less Menahem has beheld a vision in his prison cell,
and has felt that he has been called as the Messiah
of his people, to lead them back to Zion. His daughter, Rachel, shall be his tongue; and with her great
eloquence inspired by her faith in her father, she
so moves the suffering multitude that they com-
mence the long and weary journey to the Holy Land.
While they are on the way messengers overtake
them, telling them that the old king has died, and
that the new monarch, Louis, calls back the Jews.
Menahem and Rachel are overwhelmed; their
dream of Zion threatens to evaporate. Hillel, who
has fallen in love with Rachel, even attempts to
persuade her and her father back to Illyria, but
Menahem holds tenaciously to his fanatic Messianic belief and still controls his daughter, his other
self, his voice. The faith in his belief is strengthened
when Leah, the mad-woman, suddenly hails him as
the Messiah amid the awe-struck wonder of the
crowd. Rachel, who has begun to doubt, is thus
also reënforced in her faith. Suddenly, in the midst
of an impassioned speech in which Rachel is winning
the wavering Jews back to the Zionist dream, Leah
begins to call the beggar the Messiah, too, and even
Blanche, the prostitute. The charm is broken; the
people turn from wonder to derisive laughter;
Rachel loses belief in her father's mission, while he,
choking with rage in his powerlessness to speak,
rushes upon a rock and jumps into the sea. Leah,
in her crazy dance, shrieks "The Messiah! The
Messiah!"

Here again Pinski has triumphed over the technical difficulties of the crowds which he is fond of assembling; here again, athwart a background of mediæval persecution and a case of the religious mania which it so often inspires, he has thrown a drama that abounds in color, spectacle, striking scenes, and penetrating touches. Menahem is a religious Sheftel; he, too, has in his own fanatic way, beheld a vision beyond his powers to communicate to those about him, and seeks his refuge in death.

The Mountain Climbers (1912) is the most purely symbolic of the dramatist's work, much weakened by the somewhat trivial personages and insignificant action which contrast too strongly with the attempted grandeur of the theme. The ascent of his troupe, and their final arrival at the hotel at the top, where the great inn-keeper receives them all after their weary climb, is an obvious symbol of life's progress—as obvious, for instance, as the burning candle in Andreyev's *Life of Man*. With the ascent of his characters, so ascends the dramatist's action, from the placid and promising opening of the first act, through the varied tribulations of the four couples depicted in the next two, and the peaceful close, which, from the standpoint of pure symbolism, is the most successful of the four. At the very end of the play, the great inn-keeper, whose visage is veiled by the eternal clouds of the mountain-top, warms his hands at the fire which has been made by the two poetic lovers from the twigs of a tree on which they had carved their initials in token of their great love. The inn-keeper approaches the fire, after he has closed the door of the hotel upon the last pair of lovers, and, rubbing his hands over the flames, exclaims, "At such a fire, I, too, may warm myself!" It is significant that Pinski looks upon life as an ascent and upon love as its really vivifying principle. To this year belongs also *To Each Man His Own God*, in which Menasseh Rivkin, a poverty-stricken immigrant, overcomes the temptation to deceit forced upon him by his needy dependents. Losing an arm in a street-car accident that was meant to produce but a profitable bruise, he refuses to accept the damages that the company is only too willing to pay. He regards the loss of his limb as a punishment from God and his renunciation redeems him. Though there are good scenes in the play, it does not rank with his best, any more than does the play of the following year (1913), *Better Unborn*. This is conceived in a spirit of intense idealism, but the insistence upon harrowing detail only serves to impress the contrast of the central deed to the circumferential passion of nobility. From the brutal murder of the little girl discovered at the opening to the expiatory suicide of the murderer at the close, the drama envelops the auditor in an atmosphere of gloom. True, the play was not written for the sake of the tense situations; here, as always, Pinski is the psychologist, and what most interests him is the struggle that begins in the protagonist's mind after he has, in a moment of bestial passion, committed so vile a deed and then been convinced by his father that for his own sake, as well as to erase the blot upon his family and his race, he must pay for the girl's life with his own. For persons with oversensitive nerves *Better*

Unborn is better unseen and unread. There is a Brutus-like nobility in the stern father, but the regions are not lofty enough for tragedy; there is something just as barbarous about expiatory suicide as there is about sadistic child-murder.

We come to far better stuff in the series of five one-act plays written around the wives of King David; this, begun in 1913 with *Bathsheba*, includes *Michal*, *Abigail*, and *In the Harem*, all of 1914, and *Abishag*, 1915. In his foreword to the translation of *The Treasure*, Ludwig Lewisohn ventured the opinion that the prose of these exquisite plays is "as subtly beautiful as Maeterlinck's or Yeats's; in passion and reality the Jewish playwright surpasses both."

Although the plays were inspired by the Bible, they are by no means ancient in action or outlook. It is one of Pinski's distinguishing traits that whatever he turns his hand to—be it the proletarian drama, the Messianic legend, or the theme of dominant sex—he is, first of all, the modern psychologist, thoroughly alive to what might be called, only in seeming paradox, the everlasting contemporary. The King David plays receive their suggestion, and in places, their very text, from the Holy Book, yet so deeply has the author penetrated into his subject that his dramatic version often interprets his source. He has not hesitated to introduce illuminating interpolations nor to alter chronological sequence. And above all the figure of David stands out, not as a mere reconstruction of sacred history, but as a living creature, a vital personality that becomes naturally a symbol of Man the Lover.

At first thought one is prompted, in seeking for analogues in the modern drama, to call *King David*

and His Wives a Biblical *Anatol.* I am not at all
insensitive to Schnitzler's magic of mood and his
deep sense of man's passional transiency, and though
I make no pretense to establishing ultimate hierarchies, I find in the succeeding scenes of the New
York Jew a pleasure equal to that afforded by the
Jew of Vienna. The significance of the Biblical
series is no less pregnant and human; it possesses
coherence and cumulative power; the plays (each
complete in itself) are more than links in a chain;
they are the rungs of a ladder, while Schnitzler's
episodes lack this rising continuity. Pinski's dramas
probe into the hidden recesses of a man's soul,
not—as do Schnitzler's episodes—into an interesting corner of it. Where the Austrian dramatist
refines upon a type, the Yiddish writer reveals a sex.

Such a comparison, of course, is hardly fair; it is
merely a personal expression. One is foolish to seek
in Schnitzler something that he did not intend to
put there. As a study in a lover, *King David and
His Wives* excels in poetry and vision; it is inferior
to *Anatol* in wit and incisive dialogue. One thing,
however, I should like to emphasize: Pinski's series
is just as contemporary as Schnitzler's. The Yiddish dramatist's David is, in a sense, modern man
searchingly analyzed and revealed. And modern
woman? How rich is Pinski's series in feminine
portraits when his women are compared with
Schnitzler's cocottes and demi-mondaines. There is
Bathsheba with her withering scorn for Uriah's
obedience to his lustful monarch; there is the beauty
of Abigail's submission, the piquant quarrel of the
mistresses in *In the Harem*, the proud Michal, who
will not share her love even with God. Already in

26

In the Harem we find David awakening to the realization of oncoming age; in *Abishag* the burden is heavy upon him. The voluptuousness of self-abnegation is not often so potently displayed. Old David, afraid to taste young Abishag's beauty because to enjoy it would leave nothing more to be desired,—old David living solely for the goad of that eternally unfulfilled desire—such a figure and such a conception is a successful incursion into Schnitzler's very province. David is Anatol turned poet; the Hebrew king is man, the creature of passion, a ruler even while he is ruled. Without any intention of implying relative values, it may be said that Anatol is a jester in the court of King David.

Diplomacy (1915) is a rather obvious satire upon war-makers, while *Little Heroes* (1916), in its presentation of childhood's innocent suffering during the senseless savageries of its elders, achieves genuine pathos in its grim humor. *The Phonograph* (1918) is chiefly noticeable as a recent refurbishing of a theme that preceded *The Treasure* and indeed suggested it. Of the long plays, the best recent one is *Nina Marden's Loves* (1915-16). The piece belongs with those in which the author is chiefly concerned, with the psychology of woman, and is a natural outgrowth of the Biblical series of one-act plays. It is, shall we say? a sort of feminine *Anatol*. It is written with an economy of means rather unusual in Pinski, and follows the adventures of Nina after her marriage. It is her fate to seek, by her power and beauty, to draw out the best in men, yet never to succeed. She is of the type that can love more than one at a time; perhaps at the end she is herself spoiled by the contagion of evil. On the evening of her marriage she discusses love with former suitors; in the second episode she attempts to infuse a new soul into the actor Henderson, only to discover at the end that her appeal to him has been but a superficial one; in the third, Nina encounters a changed revolutionary agitator, and at the end, the close of her career is foreshadowed by a diplomatist's threat to destroy within her the idea of youth. Nina is thus a spiritual sister of Mary in *Mary Magdalene*, of Tille in *The Treasure*. Like Tille and Mary, so Nina lusts for power.

As Pinski's women lust for power, so his men yearn for spiritual conquest. Isaac Sheftel's intense will to be and to do crumbles upon the ruins of his scant foundations. Reb Mayshe, of the Zwie family, falls upon the threshold of a vision never to be beheld by his eyes. The soul of the obsessed Menahem Penini founders likewise upon the rock of disillusionment.

Throughout most of what Pinski has written for the stage there is a humanness, a passion, a vein of satire and genuine humor, a freedom from propagandistic tendencies (despite his own definite opinions upon the questions that vex the world) and a sincere dedication to the best that lies within him. He is a realist who knows that life is more than tears and mire; a poet who wanders in the clouds without letting his feet long leave the solid earth; a thinker free from the curse of pedantry. A full man, a rare spirit, an artist soul.[1]

---

[1]*The Treasure, Three Plays,* and *Ten Plays* are issued in English at New York.

PEREZ HIRSCHBEIN

Hirschbein has just passed his fortieth year. Born the son of a poor miller in a small Russian town, he became known at twenty-five as a writer of drama in Hebrew, later in Yiddish.

He has been much influenced by the French symbolists and mystics, as is attested by the dialogue of his plays and the beauty of his prose-poems, though often the dialogue is too tenuous for sustained action and the beauty proves largely verbal. In many of his one-act plays particularly he is a dramatist in a secondary sense only.

Take, as an instance of his early labors, the one-act *Solitary Worlds.* During the short course of the play there is little, if any, genuine dialogue. The characters speak to us by speaking only to themselves. One curses his fate in a withering invective; another has gone mad over Talmudical disputation; a young child draws designs upon the floor and talks about the music upstairs as if it were—as indeed it is—in another world, and so on. Here is a cellar full of people, yet each is a world unto himself. Symbolic, of course, as so much of Hirschbein's work is, yet at times too fragile, pictorial rather than sustained by inner passion. There is something of this symbolic pictorialism in most of the man's short pieces, whether we examine his *Grave Blossoms* of 1906, or the cluster of miniatures written during 1915,—*Raisins and Almonds, On the Threshold, Bebele, The Storm, When the Dew Falls.* One exception, surely, must be made: *In the Dark,* which belongs to 1906. Here plot, poetry, and symbolism are fused into a genuinely dramatic whole; the tragedy of poverty and shattered illusions is depicted with a poignancy and power that entitle the piece to a place among the best in its province.

Yet there is a certain beauty in even an idyll like *Bebele*, recounting the superstitious penance which a mother takes upon herself for her daughter's welfare. And charm there surely is in *The Storm*, with its illustrative sub-title: Once Upon a Time the Jews Revelled.

Hirschbein is strongly attracted, both in his longer and his shorter pieces, to the type of the rebellious young girl. In *In the Dark* the moody heroine plunges from the darkness of her daily life to the deeper darkness of eternal sleep, impelled to suicide by hopelessness. *On the Threshold* shows Rosie superior to her environment, refusing to sacrifice her youth to the dictates of unsympathetic tradition. So, too, in *When the Dew Falls*, we meet the everlasting contrast between that "crabbed age and youth" which cannot live together. At the falling of the dew old age seeks refuge while youth begins its revels. Again, in the early *Grave Blossoms*, the spirit of youth rebels against the sterile rites of mourning; while Bella, the depressing, imaginative sister, sees horrors in the grave, Rivke, the buoyant, gathers beautiful blossoms amid the tombs. Man, with his own hands, buries worlds of beauty; such is the burden of the song at the close. Yet again, *Sparks* (1913), is symbolic of the undying sparks of passion in the heart of youth that has early been bereft of companionship through illness or death. Everywhere, it would seem, Hirschbein is preoccupied with youth; his old folks talk of it, his young ones live in its rollicking insouciance.

Yet only rarely is this youth a passionate, understanding, revolting call. The maidens are most often village hoydens; their swains, kind-hearted bumpkins. Unless it be an Itsik of *The Haunted Inn*, little daring enters the breasts of these tradition-bound sons of the soil. It is from the girls, nearer the core of being, that hope of freedom comes. Yet, too often, only hope. They burn with a momentary flame of rebellion, skip a few steps of the treadmill, then resume the weary round.

Of the longer plays, I should like to consider some half-dozen; a complete edition published in 1916, in five volumes, contains twenty-six pieces in all—including the shorter ones—and is for those who love poetic beauty, haunting charm, humanity in strange moods, delightful genre pictures, and a certain fantastic glow.

Carrion was written in 1906. It deals with the rivalry of Mendel and Berrel for the hand of Rosie, a poor lass who suffers maltreatment at the hands of her mother. Rosie allows Berrel to buy her a pair of much-needed shoes, thereby inflaming the jealousy of Mendel. He is goaded to propose to her, and she refuses him, telling him that he smells of the carcasses in which he deals. Overwhelmed, the simple youth goes to his father, and in wild tears asks why he has been made a carcass of; to add to his woes, he gets news of his mother's illness, and is bewildered between the two blows of misfortune. The carrion-odor, the loss that it seems to have brought him, his resentment against his father, all conspire to madden him; at the end he is mad indeed, having slain his father and appearing all bloody from his own scratching, speaking incoherent snatches.

Rosie is but another of the Hirschbein creatures who lust for life all the more because of the terrible privations of their desolate cellar existence. But the play is noteworthy chiefly for the portrayal of Mendel's madness. Hirschbein either cannot, or will not pay much attention to the upbuilding of an inevitable plot, conditioned by the unfolding passion of the characters themselves. He always interests, but often fails to convince. He is very evidently a fine spirit, yet, as we have already hinted, his conception of the drama widens it to include much of the pictorial and the conversational as ends in themselves, rather than as the environment of a dominant action.

Of texture less stout is *The Earth* (1907), which is symbolic in a rather derogatory sense, replete with poetic discussion and Maeterlinckian languors. That the play is not essentially Jewish need bother us little; more to the point, the little plot there is suffers from a set of static symbols that should have been dynamic personalities; there is no character development. The play seeks to emphasize the sanative quality of contact with the common mother earth; it displays, even more, the unhealthy quality of the dramatist's contact with French symbolism at its most deliquescent.

The best of Hirschbein's longer plays are those in which he himself establishes a restorative contact with the earth that his early years have known, with the simple folk among whom he was reared, with the bumpkins and hoydens of peasant life as he saw it and felt it. Here he is simple, yet vigorous; the symbol arises, as always it should, from the bare facts of human intercourse; the poetry is inherent

in the expanding souls rather than in the words
applied. Two or three of these folk comedies repay
more than passing attention.

A Forsaken Nook was written in 1913. It is folk
drama of the most legitimate appeal, simple in atmosphere, technique, plot, and language, and in the
best sense of the word, wholesome. Filled with
deep sentiment, it never degenerates into sentimentality; this little corner of the world, far from
the hurly-burly of agitated modernity, is yet a
replica of the greater bustle without; it has its
own commercial rivalries, its own love difficulties,
its own philosophies, none the less profound for
being couched in the humble tongue of humble
folk. *A Farvorfen Vinkel*, from one standpoint, is
a miniature Jewish village *Romeo and Juliet*, ending,
however, in joy rather than tragedy, with a victory
for ebullient youth over the prejudices and obstinacy
of middle age. And appropriately enough, the reconciliation is effected by old age, which has known
both the turbulence of youth and the bootless
animosities of the middle years.

Notte, the son of Tudrus and the father of Tsirrel,
has fallen out with Khayim Hersh, the father of
Noah, because Khayim owns the only wind-mill in
the remote spot and opposes Notte's wish to branch
out as a mill-owner himself. Notte is a grave-
digger; his daughter Tsirrel, he begins to think,
must be brought up in some other environment
than that of tombstones, and he himself would
welcome a change from a business that is sure enough
to find customers, but which has its unpleasant side.
Noah, recking little of parental disputes, is the young
and ambitious suitor of Tsirrel, who, like more than

one of Hirschbein's maiden characters in his numerous plays, is of the rebellious type. She herself may not fully understand her rebelliousness, she does not reason the matter out, but rather follows the dictates of her instincts, which lead her to return the affection of Noah. Yet if the hostility between their parents is not strong enough to keep them altogether apart, it provides fuel for lovers' quarrels; and since our village pair are both young and self-willed, unmindful of spring days that speed all too soon on the wings of memory, they waste precious moments in recriminations that neither means. There is another young man in the case, it appears, Khatskel by name. Not that Tsirrel smiles upon his suit, but Khatskel, taking for granted the father's authority over the daughter, woos her through his favors to the father rather than directly.

Khayim Hersh, getting wind of his son's courtship, is seized with anger. This is downright treachery, right in the bosom of his family. Notte, it seems, has taken definite steps toward the erection of a rival mill; the site, the lumber, and the stones have been procured; this news is not calculated to sweeten Khayim's temper, and a family row is provoked, in which not only Noah, but little Khayya, show their aggressive mettle. At the height of the domestic squabble who should enter but Krayne, Notte's wife. Noah and Tsirrel have had words, and Tsirrel has been taken ill; perhaps Khayim's wife, Krayzel, can step over and banish the effects of the evil eye that has looked upon the child. It may be noticed here that the wives of the men are by no means so prompt to yield to the animosity of rivalry as are the men; it is only when the business virus enters the blood of such as these that they are infected with the dubious virtues of their husbands' combativeness. Throughout the play the wives of both contending parties cannot see why peace is not possible, though at moments they forget their mission of peacemaking, influenced more by their men's demeanor than by their own desires.

Notte, fully as obstinate a fellow as Khayim—just as much the stern father and the domineering husband—traces his wife to the home of his enemy. There is a glowering encounter between the men, but Krayne saves the day by pulling her bellicose husband out of the hostile household.

Khatskel's influence over Notte begins to appear in all its scheming and cunning. He it is who has advanced the money for the new mill's materials; he enters the home of his Tsirrel with the confidence of victory through paternal support; Tsirrel, however, will have none of him; this she makes clear to Noah, as well as to her sympathetic mother. A visit from Khayim Hersh to discuss matters ends in a break, and since Khatskel (having heard that the bringing of the material will be opposed by machinations of Noah) has hired some Gentile peasants to be ready to earn their brandy by the strength of their arms, surely enough a brawl occurs as soon as the material heaves into sight. Noah, whose eye has been seeking Khatskel everywhere, catches the fellow and chases him into the home of his prospective father-in-law. Stones crash through the window of Notte's home and as the curtain comes down upon the third act, the family feud has reached its climax.

Throughout the preceding action we have noticed

that not only are the women of the contending
households inclined to a peaceful view of matters,
not only are the youthful lovers faithful to one another despite their pretended coldness and their
boastful aloofness, but that Tudrus, Notte's father,
looks with little favor upon the squabble. He is an
old man, with a sense of life's true values; he has
known Khayim's own father—was, indeed, the man
who helped him get a start in life, and buried him
with his own hands. As the father of Notte the
grave-digger, who bequeathed to that worthy his
trade, Tudrus feels that Notte belongs at his old
established business; as one who has seen children
born and who has buried their parents, he knows
the moments that really count in the span between
the cradle and the grave. And if these middle-aged
fathers are intent upon letting their quarrel interfere with the happiness of their children, why, he,
too, is a father, and will impose his will upon Notte.
He wishes, and will have, peace between the families. What has an out-of-the-way spot, a forsaken
nook like their hamlet, to do with two windmills
turned by rival hands? Why this unnecessary warfare? Away with such obstinacy! Let the scheming Khatskel get his investment back and cease
bothering Tsirrel with his unwelcome affections; let
Noah and Tsirrel marry and run the new mill themselves—Noah has enough to pay back Khatskel for
the raw material.

The fathers make a show of resistance, but, like
so much resistance that has begun to crumble inwardly—like that stubborn opposition which is
itself often a sign of unspoken willingness to compromise—the feud comes to a happy, sudden termina-

tion. Tudrus' simple reasoning, added to the unspoken predisposition of the men, the tears of the
women, and the stout determination of the children,
leads to the closing "Mazel Tov!"—the congrat-
ulatory cries of good luck for the young couple.

There are other characters in the play than those
mentioned; particularly Dobbe, the crazed mother,
whose five children lie buried in Notte's grounds;
at first blush it would seem that she is a superfluous
personage; she appears but a few times, producing
upon spectator and personages alike an eerie effect.
Yet is she not a characteristic figure of such vil-
lages, and moreover calculated to impress the audience with the fleeting days of childhood and the
inherent folly and wrong of thwarting the legitimate
aspirations of the younger generation? Not that
Hirschbein uses this rôle or any other to impress a
preconception; nothing could be further from prob-
lem-drama or thesis-drama than *A Farvorfen Vinkel*;
it is the folk-play raised to a very high artistic degree; the action is compact, the dialogue natural,
these are genuine, unvarnished folk, whether in
their hatreds or their affections. Here art conceals
itself, indeed, and a natural effect is achieved with
unaffected directness.

The Blacksmith's Daughters is, like *A Forsaken
Nook*, a genuine idyll. What permanent feuds may
develop in a milieu such as this, where the inhab-
itants take with pious seriousness the injunction
that enemies must make up before the annual Day
of Atonement? What wild romances of the heart
may blaze up amongst youths who ask fathers for
their maidens' hands with all the deference that
they themselves, when they shall in turn become

fathers, will expect to receive from the children of the next generation? The average maiden in these forsaken nooks goes whither her father sends her; father and daughter alike hearken to the advantageous matches which the traveling book-vendor carries around together with the sacred books he sells; and the vendor, who hawks hearts as well as tomes, finding every maiden beautiful and every wight sturdy and able, is himself a sort of symbol as to how marriage is looked upon. Not that there is no love amongst these youths; not that marriages of convenience arranged in haste do not in a surprising number of instances lead to long years of happy married life; not that there is an undue admixture of mercenary motives. But these simple folk have acquired no coat of sophistication; they speak their true mind as often as not; the girl is hardly ashamed of wooing her chosen youth, and she will fight openly for her right to him; the obdurate father will listen to reason, and if he has two daughters, provided the elder is married off first to a person of worth, the important thing is to marry the second off and free himself of a double burden—the duty to marry off his child and the ease that comes with knowing that he need no longer support her.

So, in the play we meet the two daughters of Nakhmen Beer, the blacksmith. Leah Dobbe and Zelda are twins; since, in the orthodox Jewish household the matter of precedence among daughters is of no small importance, these two maidens are often at odds as to which is really the elder. To be sure, Zelda, if strict chronological order is to be observed, was born first; but then, hasn't Leah grown up to be a big, strong lass, and does not her very appearance proclaim her virtual seniority? Zelda, self-willed and high-spirited as she is, resents such a usurpation of her rights; nor is the resentment based upon merely abstract principles; there is a very concrete reason in the person of her father's hired blacksmith, Nisson Alter. Nisson is an active, industrious fellow, who has brought a great deal of trade to his employer, and when the latter praises him with generous words, he plucks up the courage to ask for Zelda's hand. But just at this point a traveling blacksmith comes along asking for work. As Nisson has only a moment before been complaining that the establishment needs more hands, and as the applicant looks like a worthy chap, he is engaged. He will live with the rest of the household and make the place his second home.

The coming of the new workman, Borukh Mayshe, brings new dissension into the sisters' lives. The mischievous self-willed Zelda, who at first "stole" Nisson away from Leah, now has taken a fancy to the new man. Still, she and Leah are sisters; beneath their rivalry is the blood relationship, and Zelda, for some purpose of her own, and to show that she is not trying to steal Borukh away from Leah, will even let her sister have some of the love-powders that she has got from an old woman skilled in such matters. These Leah takes, and determines to put in Borukh's soup that night; carefully she does so, and is about to serve it to the young blacksmith when Zelda manages to strike her sister's arm, and the precious bowl of love-laden soup goes crashing to the floor.

Zelda is induced by her sister to stay over at a

relative's until the holidays, when the family will journey over by wagon and take her back. In the meantime—and perhaps without Leah's wishes— Nisson seems to have turned his affections from one sister to the other. He is happy with the one dear charmer while the other is away, and now approaches the father to ask for Leah's hand. The parent is willing; after all, a marriage is a marriage, be it Zelda or Leah. But once again Nisson's proposal is upset, this time by Zelda's unexpected arrival from her relative on the wagon of an itinerant book-vendor. Homesickness—and a bit of lovesickness, too—has brought her back thus early, bringing upon the scene the picturesque vendor himself.

The hawker of hearts and books for a moment sees good prospects of earning an honest ruble by matching off the youths upon whom he comes. Zelda, however, is of the type that matches off her-self; perhaps her short absence has taught her that Nisson is the man she really wants. At any rate, like the perverse imp she is, no sooner does she get an inkling that Nisson desires Leah than she desires Nisson with all the energy of her willfulness. Borukh has a word to say in this, too. What does Nisson mean by trying to take away Leah from him? If the match is a settled one, very well; he will leave. Fortunately here is the itinerant vendor, who will take him off to some other spot, where he can hire out his services anew. But where are his tools? Who has hidden them? (Zelda could answer if she chose. Once she wished him to stay because she thought she would like to have him for her own; now let him stay so as to remove Leah from between her and Nisson.) Surely enough Borukh has his way with Leah, and Nisson, who was fond of Zelda in the first place, is fond of her in the last, too.

Here, as in *A Forsaken Nook*, there is a wise grandfather, whose favorite Hebrew chant about praising God at dawn for the light of the stars is redolent of that deep appreciation of youth which rises from so many of Hirschbein's dramas. Like the play of the village *Romeo and Juliet*, so this rustic *Comedy of Errors* is simple, idyllic, pictorial, though by no means static, and in more than one point well sustains comparison with the plays from the Irish company that made Lady Gregory's name well known in this country. And, if there must be comparisons, the folk-pieces of Hirschbein are to be found much nearer in spirit to the comedies of Lady Gregory, let us say, than to the sterner realities of Synge. But let us not hasten to compare. It is in such pieces as these, free of the sometimes baffling symbolism of such of his dramas as *The Earth* and *The Haunted Inn* that Hirschbein is refreshingly himself. Here he is not only the playwright, but the poet as well—a writer of a charm that is something more than the echo of words and the melody of phrases; above all these quarrels of lovers, these domestic altercations, these tea-pot tempests that loom so large in the pastoral regions where his muse has her favorite spot, rises an aroma of enchanting powers—a volatile essence, indeed, but as rare upon our stage as any other of the more delicate qualities of art.

The same wholesome simplicity—both of the life pictured and the means by which it is portrayed— informs the comedy *Green Fields* (1916), in which a

wandering pious student innocently disturbs the
hearts of a pair of lasses who at last break down his
adolescent asceticism. Of course he can marry only
one, and before that one wins him definitely away
from the other, the parents of both are drawn into the
inevitable rural feud, which ends quite as suddenly
as it begins. There is a family resemblance to these
folk comedies of Hirschbein, as there is to his one-
act pieces; yet it is an engaging family, and one
that is met too infrequently upon any stage.

Of the more serious pieces, *A Life for a Life* (1915)
contains good dramatic action, though it is, like so
many of the man's other pieces, deficient in characterization and in the delineation of the minor
figures. Israel Neakh offers, for the privilege of
laying a synagogue cornerstone, to donate the
weight of the stone in gold. His wife, Pearl, is
thunderstruck when she hears of it, but her dumb-
foundedness increases when Israel's partner, Tevye,
bursts into her home and declares that it is his
money that will really build the edifice, and that he
will proclaim it to the world. Neakh, in truth, is
reduced to poverty; his daughter's marriage is thus
postponed indefinitely; his wife, having lost all desire to live, regains her passion for existence as she
feels a new life burgeoning under her heart. Neakh
subsequently refuses his former partner's offer to
begin anew in the old union; he has taken his past
to heart; rapidly he fails, at last expiring in the
Rabbi's arms. His own life thus has paid for the
life of the child whom his prayers and charities (at
Tevye's expense) have called into being. Now Pearl
will live for her child, and the marriage of his
daughter is assured.

27

There is a certain power in the treatment of the
Jewish theme; Israel Neakh is a salient figure, strong
and implacable.

It was with *The Haunted Inn* that Hirschbein's
name really cleared the barriers of the Yiddish
milieu and for a while attracted the attention of
Gentile critics. This was the play with which the
Jewish Art Theatre of New York, under the direction of Mr. Emannuel Reicher, inaugurated its career
in the autumn of 1919. By virtue of the striking
production and the acting of Mr. J. Ben-Ami in
the rôle of Itsik, the drama was soon the talk, not
only of the Yiddish reviewers, but also of the critics
of the English press, who forsook Broadway for
Madison Avenue and Twenty-seventh Street and
long made the play the subject of enthusiastic comment. It is this play, indeed, that led to Mr. Ben-
Ami's rapid transfer to the English-speaking stage;
all the more pity, then, that when it was given in an
English version it was badly garbled, the last act
omitted, and the entire emphasis of the play shifted
from that of a symbolic presentation of youth's raw,
shifting instincts and parental harshness amid an
atmosphere of superstitious obsession, to one of
aimlessly romantic maundering.

Although I believe Hirschbein's folk-plays of
better stuff, there is good writing in *The Haunted
Inn*. So much of the drama is done with Mr. Hirschbein's sensitivity to subdued tones that not a little
of its quality is sure to be missed by most spectators untrained to alertness for subtle values; here
color tends to subside into nuance, and action is
refined into the suggestion of impulse and mood.
Thus, at first blush, the opening act seems a calm

procession of rustic types, yet every event and mood of the play is introduced and forecast. The arbitrary choice of Meta's husband by the fathers on both sides; the previous understanding between the girl and Itsik; the motif of the abandoned inn and the unmentionable spirits supposedly inhabiting it; the rebellion of the daughter as foreshadowed by the closing scene, in which she waves her hand to Itsik in the darkness; the entirely natural chatter of the grandfather bent upon the barn and its calves, in which are seen symbolized the home and the girl's eagerness for escape into a life of her own— in these we have the play in little, of which all that follows is the logical unfolding.

One thing in particular deserves emphasis: throughout the play the mysterious and supernatural mood is upon us, even as upon the dwellers in the hamlet of the action. Yet in no instance does the playwright summon the aid of arbitrary forces; nowhere does he introduce any element not inherent in the very existence of his characters. To them their superstitions are part of their every thought and act, not, as with our more sophisticated selves, an amusing and instructive detail of psychological study. The spirits of the inn are real; they may be offended, they may pursue their victims, they must be propitiated. Hirschbein here achieves an effect of other-worldliness, of unreality, without once employing any means other than those of everyday reality. I have mentioned the spirits of the inn. Take now the merchants of the colorful wedding scene in the second act. Nothing more natural than that a party of men should pause on their way to join the festivities, providing not only

music, but handsome gifts for the couple, and then
pass on. Yet to the relatives and guests assembled,
in whose minds the inn is closely linked to the dowry,
and in whom stirs the uneasiness of having disturbed
the evil ones in their nest, the strangers, because of
their very strangeness, may easily become ambassadors of those spirits. Add to this the kidnapping
of the bride by her primitive lover, Itsik, and how
can they doubt any longer that malignant influences
are at work?

What does the abandoned inn symbolize? Parental restraint of young daughters, which often ends
by conquering the daughters themselves? As suggested, for example, by Meta's desire to jump into
the flames whence Itsik saves her? Is Itsik the
symbol of crude unconventionality? Bendet, the
obdurate father, becomes so obsessed with the fear
of the spirits that he flees from them and finally
sets fire to all his possessions. He presents, indeed,
an interesting study in the progress of superstitious
fear, perhaps remorse. The play, however, is not
exclusively symbolistic; it has its moments of
realism and romantic ardor, and is, as a whole, distinguished for a subtly managed mood of mystery.
Of character portrayal there is characteristically
little; mood foreshadows mood, much as in other
plays events foreshadow events. Even to the Jew
the whole is somewhat exotic.

NEW WRITERS

Kobrin, Asch, Pinski, Hirschbein—they are all
very active yet, and anything like definite pro-
nouncements upon them would be premature.
Among the lesser lights, a number of men show

promise, one of them a recent arrival from Poland, Fishel Bimko by name. Maurice Schwartz, to whom the Yiddish stage owes some of its most artistic ventures, introduced him here through the play called *Thieves*. Bimko is on the sunny side of forty and has, besides writing a long list of short stories, been occupied in journalism for the leading newspapers of the foreign Jewish centres. He has to his credit two or three other dramas of a symbolic, mystical cast—and how the Jewish mind is betrayed into these alluring pitfalls!—but *Thieves* is reality almost photographic. It has been given some two hundred times in Warsaw and Vilna.

There is little in the play to suggest the symbolism and mysticism of his other work; it is, in no derogatory sense of the word, sternly realistic material, treating a subject that to many must be of the most repulsive nature, yet so handling the matter as to produce a certain dramatic beauty—the beauty of the sun illuminating an infested marsh.

Here we have, in the first place, a half-dozen underworld men each engaged in the same traffic, yet requiring distinct characterization if they are not to become a six-fold, boresome reflection of a single type. Here we have a slum woman, raised by preference of the gang leader to the relative dignity of wifehood, such as their milieu knows it. Yet even these lawless haunts feel the necessity for some higher striving; though they may find ready excuse for the trade they ply, though they may consider themselves even removed from the necessity of justification, there are those among them who long for something better. It may be the reawakening of religious fears instilled in childhood;

it may be simply the natural desire to excel, to stand out from one's fellow-men, be the claim to distinction ever so small. But the feeling is there, and even among these Gorkian "ex-men" there is the sense of caste.

Shloyme Shuver, who has married Gittel, granddaughter of the barber-woman, Keyle, is the leader of the thieves. Ever since his marriage, however, his hand seems to have lost its cunning, and his heart has gone completely over to his wife. As it turns out later, he beholds in her, not only the woman, but the vessel of redemption. It is the child that she will give him who will come to wipe out his past—to cleanse him of the evil which blackens his soul. The rest of the gang are disgusted with this change in their chief. Not only can they not understand his altered ways, but they poke fun at him for his chicken-hearted courtship of his coquettish wife. He is so "touchy" about her—so watchful, that none may approach her—as if she were indeed a lady. The tragedy of Shloyme's life begins with his realization that he cannot have a child, and that the trouble does not lie with his wife. He broods himself into utter uselessness as a gang leader, and all the while his wife's affections really belong to Mazik, as spry and handsome a thief as ever carried a jimmy. The inevitable happens; Mazik and Gittel have secret meetings, and before long Gittel confides an interesting secret to her grandma. The latter, at first uninformed as to the whole truth, receives the news with all the joy that it would bring to the orthodox Jewish household; indeed, even old Keyle has a little religion in her for all her living in a thieves' den.

Has she not sent Gittel to the rabbi, even to witches, for a remedy against the curse that has brought Shloyme such agony?

Slowly the truth unfolds. Shloyme himself suspects, and after the child is born he spends hours gazing at its face, trying to make out whether it resembles him or another. Because of his preoccupation with the infant,—a preoccupation that is steadily growing into an obsession—the gang's plans go awry; his fellow-thieves tease and taunt him with cutting references to the dubious paternity of the child, and at last, from the lips of his own wife, who has long since lost all love for him, comes the confession that Mazik, not Shloyme, is the father. Obsession now flames to insanity, and in a wild fury, after gathering some clothes and setting fire to them so as to burn down the house, Shloyme strangles his faithless wife.

It is characteristic of the entire play that the strangling scene does not take place in view of the audience; nor is this because the Jewish spectator shares any Greek aversion to the representation of such events. *Thieves* is genuine drama, with little affinity to its step-brother melodrama; its characters are well distinguished from one another, and though it would be presumption for one who does not know the Varsovian underworld to comment upon the author's truthful portrayals, it is enough for the purposes of art to agree that he makes us feel they are true. The play as a whole has been called a Yiddish *Na dnye* (Gorki's *Night Lodging*), and, to be sure, there is a certain resemblance. In both plays there is a motif of violent love, in each there is a breath of aspiration to higher things, though this is conveyed more poetically, more elusively, by Luka of Gorki's striking piece; in each there is a well-differentiated group, though here again the advantage is with Gorki, whose drama is of deeper philosophical import and of broader application. Bimko's thief-psychology is an incidental, however, rather than a salient, trait; it is directed not so much upon the group, as in Gorki's piece, as upon Shloyme and his strange, though by no means unnatural, desire for redemption. *Thieves*, then, has stronger ideological resemblance to Sholom Asch's *The God of Vengeance*. And it is, by the way, this same Sholom Asch's picturesque novel *Mottke the Vagabond* (*Mottke Ganov*), which, in its third part, gives us an intimate insight into the very Varsovian slums that provide the background for Bimko's play. Yekel, in the Asch play, it will be recalled, cherishes the same eagerness for redemption through his daughter, and even gives holy gifts to the synagogue, paid for with money made in the most nefarious of trades; yet despite his attempt to bribe the Lord, his daughter falls a victim to the very brothel her father runs. In each play, then, is a theme of retribution that falls upon the perpetrators of evil and sweeps even the innocent in its path. In both is a strange yet characteristic separation of secular and sacred, and an unsuccessful attempt to reconcile them. Though once more the advantage may lie with the other author, *Thieves* may well be said to provide a worthy addition to the Yiddish repertory of "unpleasant" plays.

And, finally, before leaving a by-path of the drama over which we have lingered only because it is so unlikely to receive adequate attention among its own people, let alone those outside the pale of tongue and temperament, let us consider the bold choice made by Mr. Schwartz for the opening of the season of 1921-1922 in the Jewish Art Theatre.

An-ski's *Der Dibbuk* belongs to the dramatic literature that must be taken largely upon faith; it is a world where Hamlet's father may return as a ghost without being assailed upon scientific and rational grounds; a world in which the dead may converse with the living; indeed, an inter-world. The Vilna edition of 1919, as a matter of fact, bears the sub-title, *Between Two Worlds*, thus revealing this sense of a spiritual limbo.

Schwartz's venture was daring in more ways than one; the piece is in reality a transcription of folklore. It is necessary to recall, even for many Jews, the peculiar background against which it is played, —the intense Khassidic life where the most ardent fancies somehow acquire a reality almost as real as the very ground over which the engrossed Rabbis wend their way from synagogue to home and back again. The piece requires a sympathetic heroine in whom the male voice of her departed lover speaks his soul through her body. The full production involves about a hundred persons, of whom twenty-five take active parts.

The title of the play is a Hebrew word of kabbalistic derivation, signifying an evil spirit that enters a person.

We are here in a world where the dividing line between the now and the beyond is a tenuous one; the "true world," in fact, is the hereafter, and it is so named. Yet the dead form part of the present existence almost as much as when their bodily

forms strode through it; their graves are regularly
visited, and they are spoken to, communed with
upon the most intimate secrets, invited to the weddings of their orphans, taken tender leave of when
their offspring depart for distant lands in quest of
a better fortune. These strangely living dead appear
in dreams and make their wishes known, recite
their grievances against the dwellers in the present,
and even answer summonses to rabbinical trials in
which the merits of the case are heard before a holy
tribunal.   Almost literally, then, the Jews of this
Khassidic sect and milieu live "between two worlds,"
communing too much with the life everlasting to
remain wholly on this side of paradise. It is such a
world in which An-ski's peculiar play comes to pass,
and in a reading of the drama or in any discussion
concerning it, care should be taken not to dismiss
as palpably unreal, or unconvincing, episodes that
would hardly be questioned by the persons among
whom the events supposedly occur.

S. An-ski's correct name was Shloyme Zalmon
Rappoport; his recent death removed from Yiddish
letters a beloved figure who was very close to the
soil of the folk. In a sense he is said to have been
much closer than the greatest writer in the short
but intense history of Jewish literature, Isaac Loeb
Perez.   Perez, intellectual that he was, was also
more the artist than An-ski; he could not be content
with mere transcription of folk-motives, though he
is thoroughly imbued with the folk-spirit. Where
Perez would elaborate without destroying, An-ski
would reproduce faithfully.   Such a method, of
course, entails the risk of certain defects of stagecraft, and we shall note that An-ski has not escaped

them. It responds, however, to a strong need of the Jewish reader and audience, satisfying a pleasure of recognition that forfeits with a certain ease most claims to more refined artistic treatment. This is not to say that An-ski's play lacks art; but surely, either through temperament or set purpose, he has in *Der Dibbuk* eschewed delineation and development of character and concerned himself chiefly with pictorial presentation.

This is not at all an unwise course to follow where legend lies at the root of life. Moreover, so remarkably has the dramatist reproduced the throng of religious devotees that the drama as a whole is steeped in the communal character. So well has this part of An-ski's labor been performed that the play, despite any dramaturgic shortcomings that may be urged against it, has been hailed upon both sides of the ocean as an epoch making event in the Yiddish drama, and even as the "first Jewish national play." Perhaps, and perhaps not. An intimate view of a certain phase of Yiddish life it doubtless affords. But "national"? In what sense? Certainly not that of national aspirations, with which it has nothing whatsoever to do. And is the view of love —that of a foreordained union with which mortals vainly interfere—a typically Jewish one, a national view? In such a sense, is not Hirschbein's *Green Fields* just as "national" as *Der Dibbuk?* In the politico-philosophical acceptation is not Pinski's *The Last Jew* (*Die Familie Zwie*) just as "national"? At any rate, questions of priority are meat for historians' appetites; they have nothing to do with art. It is easier to grant the epoch-making qualities of An-ski's play, which let us summarize before appraising.

The auditorium is plunged into dense darkness, out of which, as from a distance, floats a soft, mystic chorus. In this the dramatist has perhaps sought to concentrate the underlying thought of his play; I translate it rather closely:

> Wherefore, O wherefore
> Is the soul
> Fallen from highest estate
> Into darkest depths?
> Within itself the fall
> Bears the ascension. . . .

Then the curtain rises upon the play.

Hannon, a poor student of religious lore, is by nature given to mysticism and the maddening intricacies of kabbala, according to which every letter, numeral, or word has its occult significance in the unraveling of the divine mysteries. Homeless wanderer that he is, he has been taken in by the wealthy Reb Sender, according to a charitable custom whereby the better-favored Jews freely boarded the humble students of the local House of Study. In this prosperous home Hannon conceives a passionate affection for the daughter, Leah—a typically pious, obedient child of the race. It is common talk that Sender seeks for his child the most advantageous match he can find, and the tale of his quest and his succession of refusals is told by the pious students to one another between devotions. That nothing comes of the attempt to match Leah off is a source of exalted gratification to her lover, for Hannon believes that it is his intense faith and his frequent fastings that have intervened to keep her for his own. Now comes the news that Sender has at last betrothed his daughter to Menassah, son of the wealthy Nahmen of the nearby town, Miropolia. Hannon's pious deeds, then, despite his feeling that a higher power has foreordained him as Leah's mate, have proved of no avail. Suddenly, in the synagogue where the news reaches him, he seems to behold a new light, and falls to the floor in a sleep of death.

A strange fellow, this, who has had the temerity, not only to think queer thoughts, but to utter them to his fellow-students, who gaze upon him almost as if he spoke blasphemy. What else are they to imagine of a kabbalist who tells them that "it is unnecessary to wage war against sin; one need but refine it. Even as a goldsmith purifies gold in an intense fire . . . so should one purify sin of its evil, that only the holy kernel remains." Hannon speaks, indeed, as if he had seen a vision of the essential unity of sin and virtue, for to him, "everything that God has created holds within it a spark of holiness." But three months later, when Leah is to be married to Menassah, Hannon has been quite forgotten; except by her, to whom his grave has appeared in a dream, as well as his spirit. When, just before the ceremony, the bride goes off to the cemetery to the grave of her mother, to invite her departed parent to the wedding, she steals over to Hannon's grave, too, and extends the same invitation. It is here, presumably, that Hannon's spirit merges with her own, for when she returns to her home the great change has taken place in her soul. Scarcely has the ceremony begun when Leah tears off her bridal veil and refuses to go on with the pact. Imploring the intercession of a legendary pair of ever-faithful lovers whose tomb lies nearby, she exclaims, "Holy couple, shield me, rescue me!" and falls to the ground; she is raised, when suddenly she begins to cry, not in her voice, but in the voice of Hannon: "Ah! You buried me! But I have come back to my predestined one, and will never leave her!" The company regard her as a madwoman, but the half-mysterious figure of the messenger, who haunts the action from beginning to end, declares amidst wild confusion that "a spirit has entered the bride."

The possessed daughter is brought to the sage, Rabbi Israel, upon whose powers Leah's father depends to have the spirit exorcised. During an imposing scene, in which the spirit speaks through the mouth of the woman he has entered, the Rabbi concentrates his most intense will upon driving out the intruder, but in vain. The final resort is about to be brought into play,—that of excommunication —a drastic measure that requires the assent of the town rabbi. Consent is given, and Rabbi Israel (who is of Miropolia) sends to Brinitz (the town whence Leah has been brought to him) for the bridal party, as it is essential to marry off Leah the moment the *dibbuk* has been expelled.

It happens that the town rabbi has been visited thrice by a dream in which Nissan, the departed friend of Sender, has appeared demanding justice for a deep injury done him by his friend. The rabbis feel that the dream may have a bearing upon the recalcitrance of the *dibbuk*, and therefore decide to submit the case to a *beth din*—the rabbinical trial— before resorting to final measures in ridding Leah of the spirit. Accordingly, the court-room is arranged, one part being divided from the rest by a white sheet, behind which the spirit of the plaintiff, Nissan, comes to present his case. Surely enough, the complaint of the departed has a direct relation to the peregrinations of the *dibbuk*. Years before, it transpires, Nissan and Sender, upon marrying, had made a pact: should their wives give birth at the same time to infants of different sex, the children should be betrothed. It so turned out in the case of the children born, but the vicissitudes of life had separated the friends, and only coincidence had brought Hannon, son of Nissan, to the home of Sender, father of Leah, as a poor, wandering student. Sender, in tears, protests his ignorance of Hannon's identity, and begs the indulgence of the departed Nissan.

The verdict of the tribunal is as follows: Since Sender is indirectly guilty of Hannon's death, he must distribute half his fortune in charity and for the rest of his life recite the commemorative prayer of the dead (Kaddish) for both Nissan and Hannon. There is no sign, however, that Nissan accepts this expiation or that he forgives his friend. Now comes the awe-inspiring scene in which the *dibbuk* is expelled; only after two vain appeals does the rabbi have recourse to the excommunicatory ban, before which, in the throes of agony, the spirit yields and forthwith abandons Leah's body. With it, life seems to depart, for Leah sinks to the floor in a swoon. Now has come the moment to rush her under the wedding canopy, but the bridal party has been delayed upon the road (more of the spirit's work?), and when it arrives Leah's soul has flown, to merge with that of Hannon. "I have forsaken your body," he whispers to her, "but I come to your soul." Through the wall appears his image, in white, and she goes to meet it. The mystic chorus of the opening is repeated, and the curtain falls.

As may be seen, even from the outline, two separate legends, that of the *dibbuk* and that of the rabbinical trial between a dead man and a living, seem to have been combined by the process of what earlier criticism called "contamination." Anski has fused them into a logical whole, though the dream in which Nissan appears comes somewhat abruptly into the action, with little preparation. Relatively devoid of characterization as is the play, lacking the personal contribution of the author, it yet produces an undoubted effect of simple, yet inescapable power. The opening act is notable for its well-sustained mystical atmosphere—an atmosphere produced not by the extraneous aid of cheap "spiritual" effects, but by the glints of student humor, the strands of Khassidic lore and conversation woven into the fabric of the scene. So, too, the second act—that of the interrupted wedding, in which the haunting suggestion of Hannon's dead grip upon the maiden is impressed with cumulative power. Yet there is overemphasis upon the moody motif. Compare this with the remarkable wedding scene in Hirschbein's *The Haunted Inn*, in which an even stronger mood is produced with an artistry that requires less emphasis for its effect.

The third act acquires its solemn character not so much from the dramatist's skill as from the holy associations of the scenes. The episode in which the Rabbi first tries to expel the spirit of Hannon from the body of Leah, and during which the unruly

dibbuk speaks through her mouth, is one of the most
daring in contemporary drama. It is as if Jekyll
and Hyde were simultaneously present, in opposite
sexes, in the same person. And what shall we say
of the rabbinical trial, in which, through the mouth
of one of the living, the dead man in the shrouded
enclosure makes known his plaints? *Der Dibbuk*
is, first of all, a play of atmosphere; like so much
mysticism, it is founded upon the great, concrete
reality of sex in its most poetic evolution—that of
an eternal love which shatters the laws of both man
and God. Yet before endorsing this phase of it, we
must remember—and the Yiddish commentators
seem to have overlooked the fact—that Leah and
Hannon were not really predestined; they were betrothed before birth, it is true, but by their parents
and not by God, unless in their parents is beheld
the hand of the Lord.

Just how mystical is the play? Is there anything in the action that may not possess its realistic
explanation? I believe *Der Dibbuk* should be sharply
distinguished from those plays in which the mystical element is chiefly poetic suggestion, usually of
a watery sort. For cases similar to that of the
dibbuk under discussion are familiar to students of
abnormal psychology; moreover, the sight of the
legendary lovers' grave doubtless played its part
in Leah's obsession; yet again, Khassidim steeped
in their occult lore are apt to work themselves into
a state of self-deception that would lend the guise
of reality even to a rabbinical trial such as is here
depicted. Khassidic lore surely would seem to support this assertion. So that when Dr. H. Shid-
lovski terms An-ski in this play essentially a realist,

28

he is not so far astray as hasty consideration might make him appear. It is a subjective realism, indeed, in which reality is not what lies without, but all of that which the persons of the drama in their daily life accept as real, regardless of its scientific demonstrability.

Wiener, in 1899, questioned whether the Yiddish stage would last another ten years. That was twenty-three years ago. Since that date have been written the best dramas of the Jewish theatre. The prophecy, however, was founded upon certain facts of which Jewish writers themselves have not been slow to take cognizance. Even though the melting-pot should finally claim the Yiddish stage in this country, the Yiddish spirit will continue to express itself in the adopted tongue, as it has everywhere done; and it will add a distinct note to the literature of the United States, as have the labors of such diverse spirits as Abraham Kahn in fiction, Louis Untermeyer and a group of others in poetry, Ludwig Lewisohn in criticism. To-day, it would seem, Yiddish literature is in the midst of a quasi-renaissance. Its future depends upon those influences that will force together or disintegrate the Jewish people. After all, History has a habit of poking fun at prophecies. What the future holds had best be left to her.

RUSSIA

RUSSIA
EVREINOV AND THE MONODRAMA

The name of Nikolai Evreinov[1] is associated in English with the semi-scandal that attended the introduction of his work to London. By some he was received as a genius, by others as a mountebank. His *The Theatre of the Soul*, produced there at the Little Theatre on March 8, 1915, was later forbidden performance at the Alhambra, what though William Archer found the play extremely original and striking and Mr. E. Spence called it "a weird, clever piece." To make things merrier, another damned it alliteratively as "poor, puerile, and pretentious," yet one seeks in vain, in the piece itself, reason for the antagonism it aroused.

Thus, Evreinov's theory and practise of the "monodrama" enters our dramatic annals as a sort of intellectual undesirable, an unwelcome immigrant. It is by no means the least interesting of the contemporary revolts against realism, and shares with all the other reactions a strange suggestion of the primitive amid its belligerent modernity. And the career of its originator parallels his theory in exotic piquancy.

Nikolai Nikolaievitch Evreinov was born on Feb-

---

[1] In preparing this note upon the provoking Russian theorist and playwright, I have used the following books and translations of Evreinov's pieces: (The name of the author is variously transliterated into English as Evréinov, Evreïnov, and Yevreynoff.)
The Path of the Russian Stage, by Alexander Bakshy, Boston, 1918.
The Russian Theatre Under the Revolution, by Oliver M. Sayler, Boston, 1920.
The Theatre of the Soul, translated by C. St. John and Marie Potapenko.
A Merry Death and *The Beautiful Despot,* translated by C. E. Bechofer.

437

ruary 13 (26), 1879. As a child he was fascinated not only by the theatre, composing his first play at the age of seven, but by music, becoming expert on the flute. Like Benavente, he has followed the circus, whence, perhaps, like the Spaniard, he derived his later fondness for presenting mankind upon the stage in the guise of puppets. It is something more than chance, indeed, that leads the advanced theatrical spirits, whether in Italy, Spain, or Russia, to a new age of the marionette. He has acted, he has traveled far and near, fed early upon the adventure tales of Mayne Reid, whom he emulated by writing his first novel at the age of thirteen. Educated for the law at the Imperial Law School, Petrograd, he pursued his musical studies under the master colorist, Rimsky-Korsakoff; an atheist at fifteen, a Nietzschean at eighteen, at twenty he is led to the gospels through the death of a friend.

From now on his dramatic activity becomes dominant, and in 1908 he is chosen as successor to Meyerhold at the Kommissharzhevskaya theatre in Moscow. The following year, together with this actress' brother, he organizes the Gay Theatre for Grown-up Children in Petrograd, producing there *The Merry Death.* Thence to The Crooked Looking Glass, which he directed from 1914 to 1917, when he left for the Caucasus.

He has been teacher, composer, musician, and even futurist painter; he has written opera bouffe, operetta, and what Mr. Sayler calls a "lyric naturalistic opera," and as if these interests were too narrow, he has added to Russian literature a *History of Corporal Punishment in Russia.*

At the time of his introduction to London he was connected with the Parody Theatre, Petrograd, and had already written a number of the theoretical works propounding his invention of the monodrama; in 1909 had appeared his *Introduction to Monodrama*, followed a year later by *The Representation of Love*, first of the plays to embody his new theory. In 1912 came, on the stage of The Crooked Looking Glass, the much-discussed *Theatre of the Soul* (Sayler translates it *The Greenroom of the Soul*).

"The full and complete development of Evreinov's theory of monodrama as well as his critical opinion of all other forms of the theatre and their apologists is contained in the three volumes of his greatest work in dialectic, *Teatr dlya Syebya* (*The Theatre for One's Self*), the first of which was published . . . in 1915, the second in 1916, and the third after the Revolution in 1917. The first volume is characterized by the author as theoretical, the second as pragmatical, and the third as practical. For its daring and confident advocacy of a new way of thinking in the theatre, for the breadth of its knowledge of the drama and the theatre in all countries and all times, for its eager enthusiasm in the theatre and for its whimsical imagination, it is the most important contribution to the discussion of the drama since Craig published *On the Art of the Theatre*. No summary, no characterization can do it justice."[1] And Sayler adds that among the man's books awaiting type are volumes upon Russian scenic setting, on portrait painters, a novel, an æsthetic treatise, and a third volume of his collected plays.

[1] Sayler, *The Russian Theatre Under the Revolution*, page 228.

Among Evreinov's exploits at the Parody Theatre was his production of Shaw's *Candida*, accompanied by the reading of the stage directions by a black boy, as the Russian producer considers the directions the most brilliant part of the play.

At the same theatre he has presented the first act of Gogol's well-known comedy, *Revizor* (*The Inspector-General*) in several different styles, all in the same evening. The act was thus staged successively in the manner of the Moscow Art Theatre, after the methods of Craig, and so forth. "In this satirical venture," writes Christopher St. John in the introduction to the translation of *The Theatre of the Soul* made by Marie Potapenko and himself, "Evréinof was hitting at the cranks who want to reform the theatre or make a new thing which shall be more artistic than the theatre. He is in the position of being a rebel against rebels, and is no more in sympathy with the Art Theatre, Moscow, and all similar enterprises, than with the ordinary commercial theatre."

The essence of Evreinov's theory of the monodrama, in which Bakshy[1] beholds a development of Meyerhold's playing upon the imagination of the audience, is the psychological fusion of the spectator with the actor, and of the stage with the representation of the acting character. The play then becomes, literally, a "drama of one"; the actor is the spectator, and the scene is reality, not as it appears to another, but as it seems in ever-changing aspect to the actor-spectator himself. All the characters other than the protagonist are not independent individuals, as upon the conventional stage,

---

[1] *The Path of the Russian Stage*, pages 77-83.

but subjective entities, mental conceptions of such personages entertained by the chief figure. In this way Evreinov hopes to concentrate the attention upon the central actor-spectator. The other type of drama, which he does not, by the way, wholly dismiss, he calls "the drama alien to me" (i. e., objective, capable of being viewed from the outside by a spectator who feels a spirit of observation rather than of participation), in contradistinction to his "my own drama" (i. e., subjective, impressionistic, capable of being felt from the inside by a spectator who is the center of the action.)

In connection with this theory Evreinov seeks to reduce the importance of the spoken word; the ears give way to the eyes, or, as he has written, "we hear more with the eyes than with the ears; and this, in my opinion, is in the nature of the theatre."[1] In his monodrama, "only one acting character is possible; in the strict meaning of the word only one subject of action is thinkable. Only with him do I identify myself, only from his point of view do I perceive the world surrounding him, the people surrounding him. In this manner the latter must present themselves through the prism of the soul of the acting character himself; in other words, the spectator of the monodrama perceives the other participants in the dramas as they are reflected in the subject of acting, and, consequently, their living experience having no independent meaning on the stage, they seem important only as much as in them is projected the perceiving 'I' of the subject of the action. On this ground, we cannot in monodrama

---

[1] "I wonder whether I'm not hearing with my eyes?" (Ich zweifle, ob ich nicht mit den Augen höre), says King Agenor in Georg Kaiser's *Europa*, Act III, as he considers Zeus's passionate dancing.

recognize any importance in the other acting characters in the strict sense of the word, and we must in justice set them up as objects of action, understanding the word action in the sense of the perception of them and the relations of the acting character to them."

There is, in all this, not a little resemblance to the dream mechanism as elucidated by the psychological school presided over by Freud, who is no stranger to Evreinov. In our dreams, stripping them for the moment of their condensations, their ravelled symbolisms, their origins in recent impressions and obscure references to a resurgent past, we witness just such a monodrama as Evreinov has developed. For it is our "I" that is at once the sole spectator and the sole actor; the other personages of the dream are surely not themselves, but our perceptions of them; their words are our own, as are their actions; the scenery, which shifts far more rapidly than ever it will upon the most highly developed stage, changes in place and mood with the altered tonality of thought. And, as if to complete the analogy, the ear gives way to the eye.

We may now consider *The Theatre of the Soul* in the light of the playwright's theories; of course all the personages of the cast, with the exception of the porter (and perhaps he, too!), represent a different psychological aspect of the professor and of the other persons as they appear to him. So that, in the cast that follows we have some eight or nine persons in one:

> The Professor.
> M 1, The Rational Entity of the Soul.
> M 2, The Emotional Entity.

M 3, The Subliminal Entity.
M 1's Concept Of the Wife.
M 2's Concept Of the Wife.
M 3's Concept Of the Wife.
M 2's Concept Of the Dancer.
The Porter.

The action passes in the soul, in the period of half a second. (!) There is, of course, a prologue. And what a prologue!

Picture the Professor appearing before a blackboard, in front of the curtain, chalk in hand. "Ladies and Gentlemen," he begins, "when the unknown author of *The Theatre of the Soul*, the play that is going to be presented to you this evening, came to me some weeks ago with the manuscript, I confess that the title of his work did not inspire me with much confidence. 'Here,' I thought, 'is another of the many little sensational plays with which the theatre is deluged.' I was all the more agreeably surprised to gather from this first reading that *The Theatre of the Soul* is a genuinely scientific work, in every respect abreast with the latest developments in psychophysiology."

The Professor then invokes the names of Wundt, Freud, Théophile Ribot, and goes into an obscure discussion of Fichte's "entity of the soul." As he speaks, he proceeds to draw a diagram upon the blackboard, in which he represents the three entities of himself, by the symbols M 1, M 2, M 3. The first stands for the rational entity, his reasoning self; the second, for his emotional self; the third, for his psychical self. And "these three M's, or 'selves,'" constitute the great integral self. Whereupon he writes down: "M 1 plus M 2 plus M 3, equals M, the entire personality."

The ancients, he explains, believed that the seat of personality was placed in the liver. "But the author of the work which is to be presented to you holds, and with far better reason, I think, that the human soul manifests itself in that part of the physical breast which a man instinctively strikes when he wishes to emphasize his good faith. Consequently the scene of the human soul appears to us like this."

Whereupon he draws a plan of a large human heart, with physiological comments as his plan is worked out. The system of nerves he compares to a telephone, and surely enough on the stage that is soon to be revealed to the audience, the professor's plan is faithfully followed out, even to the telephone. "Such is the scene in which the 'entity self' plays its part," he concludes. "But, ladies and gentlemen, science does not confine itself to explaining things. It also offers us consolation. For instance, it is not enough to say: 'I've done a foolish thing.' One ought to know which of the three entities is responsible. If it is M 2, or the emotional self, no great harm is done. If it is the psychical entity, the matter need not be taken very seriously, either. But if it be the rational self, it is time to be alarmed. . . ."

What shall those who object to Shaw's economics-dissertation prefaces (which, after all, may be read or not as the reader desires)—say to this inescapable scientific prologue? The staging of the heart-scene, too, is a matter involving new problems for the modern theatre.

At the production of this play by Miss Edith Craig's Pioneer Players there was used a "queer and fascinating machinery of the simplest kind, by which little was seen of the three entities beyond their faces appearing at different levels out of intense darkness. The heart was represented by a glowing red space, which appeared to pulsate, owing to an effect of light. The concepts of the women were seen in the foreground, and were brilliantly lighted. . . ."

The play itself, outside of the bizarre conception of a cast of characters that represents the multiple aspects of a single personality, and outside of its daring prologue, calls for few words. It depicts, in characteristic fashion, the struggle going on within the heart of the professor between his love for his wife and the fascination exercised over him by the dancer. There is a debate in which his three entities take part, and in which the various conceptions of the different entities appear.

The end of it all is that the professor, in his intense dilemma (a dilemma which is all the more easily conveyed to the audience because of the confusion of symbols amidst which it occurs), shoots himself. A loud, cannon-like report is heard, and a great hole opens in the stage-diaphragm, from which pour ribbons of blood. Darkness comes over all. "M 3 trembles and stretches himself out wearily." A porter carrying a lighted lantern enters, cries out "Everyone's Town," and "M 3" puts on his hat, takes his bag, and follows the porter, yawning."[1]

---

[1] The reasons for the prohibition of the play at the Alhambra are a sort of mystery. There is certainly nothing in the play that a normal person could call immoral. Indeed there was no talk about the play's morality at the time of its performance at the Little Theatre. One of the translators writes that "it was received with indisputable enthusiasm by an audience fairly representative of the best elements in that mysterious entity, 'the Public.' . . ." He adds that there

"Within the narrow limits of subjective illusion-ism," Bakshy has written, "it (Evreinov's theory of the monodrama) doubtless presented an original development. There is, however, this fatal contra-diction concealed in it, that whilst invoking the spectator's power of imagination, in which it is subjective, it is compelled to base itself mainly on the realistic scenic effects, such as are produced by various lighting and musical devices, which illus-trate the changing moods and standpoints of the protagonist. This carries illusionism even further back than the chirping crickets, croaking frogs, cur-tains blown by the wind, and other mechanical tricks of the Moscow Art Theatre." There is an even more fatal contradiction. For the monodrama, as exhibited in *The Theatre of the Soul*, far from creating the spiritual, subjective synthesis of stage, actor, and auditor, produces from the start the very opposite effect. The spectator is transformed into a pupil before a blackboard, so that the gap between stage and auditorium grows wider than ever; he is asked to become an analyst, whereupon the syn-thetic subjectivism, even before the play has begun, is rendered impossible.

Of far better stuff are *The Merry Death* (a har-lequinade) and *The Beautiful Despot*, which are said to be the twin favorites of their author.

The personages of the philosophical harlequinade are the conventional types of the Commedia dell

---

was no suggestion whatever in the Press that the play was one which ought never have been brought "on the loftily moral English stage."

The license for the Alhambra performance was granted, much to the disap-pointment of the theatre's manager, Mr. Charlot, who, for reasons still unknown, had conceived a sudden and unwarranted aversion to the play. And yet, despite the fact that untiring rehearsals had been gone through under the direction of Miss Edith Craig, Mr. Charlot, on the very morning of the day on which the per-formance was to take place (the day was designated "Russia's Day"), summarily and without explanation refused to have the play given on his stage.

'Arte: Harlequin, Columbine, Pierrot; there are, too, a Doctor and Death. To be sure, there is nothing new in the philosophy, any more than in the figures, yet to both the writer imparts a certain new flavor, a modern savor.

The curtain discovers Harlequin asleep. Pierrot, chasing the flies from the sleeper's face, turns to the audience and commences a prologue that is a personal address to every individual in the audience:

S-h-h-h! Quiet! Take your seats quietly and try to talk and turn in your seats less. Even if an ingenuous friend has dragged you in and yourselves are too serious to be interested in a harlequinade, it's quite superfluous to hint of it to the public, which in the main has no affair with your personal tastes. Besides, Harlequin's asleep—you see him! S-h-h! I'll explain it all to you afterwards. But don't wake him up, please! And when Columbine comes on, don't applaud her like mad, just in order to show that you know her, had a little intrigue with her, and can appreciate certain talents.

Pierrot then explains that he doesn't fear any intrigue between his wife Columbine and Harlequin; yet his manner denotes the opposite. Harlequin, moreover, is to die at midnight, and here it is already eight o'clock! Suddenly Pierrot thinks of a great plan: he will push back the hands of the clock two hours! "I always liked taking people in; but when it's a matter of taking in Death and Harlequin at the same time, and as well, for the harm of the first and the good of the second, I don't think you can call this plan anything but a stroke of genius. Well, to work! The performance begins!"

It quickly appears that Harlequin, with the footsteps of Death echoing in every beat of the clock, is determined to meet that lady in most merry mood. "I am Harlequin," he cries, "and shall die Harlequin!" True to his word he proceeds to make merry with Pierrot's Columbine, even to argue with her about the hereafter, and when Death enters, pointing with menace to the clock, he pokes fun at the grim figure. "Look round," he challenges Death, "you are in the house of Harlequin, where one can laugh at all that's tragic, not even excluding your gestures." He invites her to perform the traditional Dance of Death, which she does. A last kiss to Columbine, a parting gibe at Pierrot's cowardice, and Harlequin is dead.

Pierrot's epilogue is even more impudent than his prologue:

I really don't know what I ought to bewail first: the loss of Harlequin, the loss of Columbine, my own bitter lot, or yours, dear audience, who have witnessed the performance of such an unserious author. And what did he want to say in his piece?—I don't understand. By the way, I'm silly, cowardly Pierrot, and it's not for me to criticize the piece in which I played an unenviable rôle. But your astonishment will increase still more when you know what I've been told to say in conclusion by the culprit of this—well, between ourselves—this strange mockery of the public. S-h-h! Listen! "When the genius Rabelais was dying, the monks collected round his couch and tried in every way to induce him to do penance for his sins. Rabelais, in reply, only smiled, and when the moment of the end came he said mockingly, 'Let down the curtain; the farce is over.' He said this and died." Why the graceless author thought it necessary to put other people's words into the mouth of one of the actors, I don't know—I've not a free hand in the matter; but being a respectable actor, I stand by him to the last and so, obeying without dispute the will of the author, I shout mockingly: "Let down the curtain; the farce is over." (*The curtains fall behind him.*)

But the author reserves still another slap. For the epilogue continues to speak, despite the fall of the curtain:

Ladies and gentlemen, I forgot to tell you that neither your applause nor your hissing of the piece is likely to be taken seriously by the author, who preaches that nothing in life is to be taken seriously. And I suggest that if the truth is on his side, then you should hardly take his play seriously, all the more as Harlequin has probably risen from his deathbed already, and perhaps is already tidying himself in anticipation of a call, because, say what you like, the actors can't be responsible for the free-thinking of the author. (*Exit.*)

Now, this is no mere *tour de force* in physiopsychological analysis, as is *The Theatre of the Soul;* this is philosophic drama where the philosophy does not obscure the drama. These puppets, like the puppets of Benavente in *The Bonds of Interest*, are no primitive marionettes strutting across the stage of the Commedia dell 'Arte; they are living modernists, making for once out of the banal eternal triangle a conception of life as a brave adventure not to be taken too seriously, yet to be lived up to the hilt.

Jameson would have it even more. To her it is "a technical masterpiece and a fine drama," and "takes rank with the great Russian comedies. Evreinov has written no other play which approaches its standard of excellence, and his latest work shows a gradual failing of dramatic power."[1]

---

[1] *Modern Drama in Europe*, pages 263, 264.

29

The sub-title of *The Beautiful Despot* is *The last act of a drama*. If the author's rap at the critics in the epilogue of the previous play reminds one of Shaw's episode of the critics in *Fanny's First Play*, the leading figure in *The Beautiful Despot* is of a piece with the lover of the good old days in that satire. It is not so much a love of the past as a scorn for the present, with its withering commercialism (which Evreinov in one place calls "Americanism") that drives the master to become an exile from civilization. He has retired into the year 1808, surrounding himself with the books, the papers, and the atmosphere of that age; thus he lives, as he says, in an attempt "to lose my despair in beautiful folly."

So, when a friend from the contemporary world comes to visit the Master, the servants of the household and the others are told that they are to preserve the illusion of 1808 before the Master's visiting friend. The friend arrives, only to be bewildered by an entire household that denies any knowledge of such new matters as railroads, electric lights, and so on.

There follows soon a most interesting, witty, and well-sustained argument between the Master and his friend, in which the past and the present have their various claims for preference advanced. The friend is almost seduced by the arguments for the antique; he even asks to be allowed to sleep at the Master's that night, even if, the next morning, he intends to take the quickest horses of the Master to ride back into the world and the present.

It is, of course, impossible to give plays like these

their just deserts in a mere outline. In distinction
from the thesis-drama, they might be termed thesis-
farce. And much of the underlying thought in the
harlequinade and in this arraignment of the present
bears strong resemblance. "What's health?" asks
The Master in the midst of a maze of phrases.
"Isn't it money to be spent neither too stingily nor
too prodigally?" . . . Again, "What! Hasn't
the senselessness of existence stared you in the face
yet?" . . . The dialogue, one should really say
the monologue, for all is subordinate to the epigrammatic chatter of The Master, is the typical mockery
of the dramatist. "The hour will come," warns
that loquacious fellow, "when the demon of vengeance will awake in you, the terrible demon of
vengeance, and when you will want to seize the
globe like a stone from the street of the world and
throw it with all your force at the great Policeman."
A strain of aristocratic cynicism runs through the
play. It is hardly putting it too strong to say that
what with glib references to "the new Sakya-Muni"
and "the new Zarathustra" and all this ball-tossing
of Olympianism, skepticism and the rest, this piece
will be more read than acted. It possesses far less
stageworthy elements than *The Merry Death*, and
would seem to have been meant for a little theatre
and particularly sympathetic actors.

Evreinov's better work, it would seem, is done
outside of the monodrama, to which type neither
the philosophic harlequinade nor the satire of the
beautiful despot belongs. The monodrama, at best,
may prove successful pyrotechnics. Its essential
unsuitability to drama of the higher category is

that, though it aims at synthesis, it proceeds by analysis. It originates from no center of passion in the author; it is a product, and a cold one, of the intellect. It does not, in its own creative life, accomplish that fusion which it demands of the spectator. It reveals thought rather than emotion; it is scenic dissection.

From the purely technical standpoint it proposes little that is new. Marinetti, in his futuristic, synthetic plays, has dispensed with dialogue even more than Evreinov, and has, in like manner, so subordinated the ear to the eye that some of his pieces are meant only for the eye, producing their effect either by the sudden revelation of a scene that tells its own story, or by manipulation of the light to create, by shadows, the illusions of moving objects. Pirandello, as we have seen in the chapter on Italy, has lately used the monodramatic idea in conjunction with the regular type of play. And Bakshy points out that some of the monodrama's effects have for a long time been stock in trade of the moving picture.[1]

Its chief interest to the student of the eternal ebb and flux of art is that of the frank invasion of the stage by the new psychology. Like all of the theories that buzz in the wings of the contemporary theatre it brings, at best, a healthy stir of unrest, the contribution of a detail to the complex craft of

---

[1] *The Path of the Russian Stage*, page 80. ". . . the audiences of which, for example, are treated to the illusion of a moving motor car at a standstill, while stationary houses appear to be flying swiftly into the distance. However," he adds, "as far as my own experience goes, I have never, in such circumstances, been under the impression that it was I who was seated in the car and the hero of all the extraordinary adventures which kinema cars are in the habit of undergoing."

An even better example of monodramatic suggestion in the "movies" is Buster Keaton's "The Playhouse", in which by a photographic trick Keaton is made literally "the whole show", portraying every character on the stage.

the drama. And here is its least attractive feature: this suggestion of a preoccupation with craft rather than the passion that creates its own form, becoming synonymous with it. The monodrama is too commentatiously self-conscious; it is, after all, the theatre of the soul, not the soul of the theatre.

THE UNITED STATES

THE UNITED STATES
EUGENE O'NEILL

Properly to appreciate the promise and the performance of Eugene O'Neill as one of the youthful experimenters in the theatre, one has but to have gone through the thousands of pages that his contemporaries have written at home and abroad— the monodramatic extravagances of Evreinov, the lucubrations of the Italian "grotesquers," the mad confusion of half of the German Expressionists. To talk of "placing" O'Neill at this early date would be the worst of academic fatuousness; his work is plentiful, widely varying in quality, and his attitude, perhaps, as his production, is, of choice, experimental rather than settled. Seemingly he marks a new era in the drama of the United States; what one may do now is to examine, at the beginning of that career, the qualities and the works of which it is compounded, following it from the worst of melodrama to the best of realism, and thence to a freedom of structure that approaches Expressionism only in its disruption of conventional form. For, thus far at least, O'Neill has yielded to neither the formlessness nor the incoherence of the more extreme Expressionists; even when his contact with external reality seems least firm, he yet maintains his grip upon the roots of things. There are, in *The Emperor Jones*, for instance, elements of the monodrama, yet O'Neill never becomes metaphysically abstruse as

457

Evreinov; his *The Hairy Ape* may suggest the later Kaiser and the youthful Hasenclever, but it is not of the self-willed, esoteric brood that is signalized by the misty productions of Oskar Kokoschka and his fellow-Germans. In this, the foreign critic, who has his labels as have our own, may be inclined to find a Yankee tendency to stick to facts and not fly too easily off on the wings of fancy or the back of a Pegasus who has broken the reins of the imagination and ranges wildly through stellar space. I rather find it in the man's own personality, in an elemental vigor that sees even phantoms clearly. For it is one of O'Neill's distinguishing traits that he lends a peculiar vitality even to his worst scenes —and there are bad ones even in his later productions.[1]

To Mr. Kenneth Macgowan (see *Vanity Fair* for April, 1922) I am indebted for a full list of O'Neill's plays, written during the past nine years. Arranged chronologically, they are as follows:

1913: *A Wife for a Life*—one act, destroyed. *The Web* —one act, published 1914 with four succeeding plays. *Thirst*—one act. 1914: *Recklessness*—one act. *Warnings*—one act. *Fog*—one act. *Bread and Butter*—four acts, destroyed. *Servitude*—three acts, destroyed. *Bound East for Cardiff*—one act. *Abortion*—one act, destroyed. 1915: *A Knock at the Door*—one-act comedy, destroyed. *The Sniper*—one act, produced by Provincetown Players (1917), destroyed. *The Personal Equation*—four acts, destroyed. *Belshazzar*—Bibiical play in six scenes, destroyed. 1916: *Before Breakfast*—one act. *The Movie Man*—one-act comedy, destroyed. *Now I Ask You*—

---

[1] In the case of O'Neill I assume, of course, a knowledge of his latest pieces, which are readily accessible in print, if not on the stage. All but the first of the volumes (*Thirst and Other One-Act Plays*, Boston, 1914) are published in New York. A special edition of *The Emperor Jones* is issued in Cincinnati.

three-act farce-comedy, destroyed. *Atrocity*—one-act pantomime, destroyed. 1917: *Ile*—one act. *In the Zone*—one act. *The Long Voyage Home*—one act. *The Moon of the Caribbees*—one act. *The G. A. N.*—one-act farce-comedy, destroyed. 1918: *Till We Meet*—one act, destroyed. *The Rope*—one act. *Beyond the Horizon*—three acts, 6 scenes, produced 1920. *The Dreamy Kid*—one act. *Shell-Shock*—one act, destroyed. *Where the Cross Is Made*—one act. *The Straw*—three acts, five scenes, produced 1921. 1919: *Honor Among the Bradleys*—one act, destroyed. *Chris*—three acts, six scenes, produced out of town 1920, destroyed. *The Trumpet*—one-act comedy, destroyed. *Exorcism*—one act, produced 1920, destroyed. 1920: *Gold*—four acts, produced 1921. *Anna Christie*—four acts, produced 1921. *The Emperor Jones*—eight scenes, produced 1920. *Diff'rent*—two acts, produced 1920. 1921: *The First Man*—four acts. *The Fountain*—prologue and nine scenes. *The Hairy Ape*—eight scenes.

In his very first published work appear, in the rough, both the good qualities and the bad that are to haunt his later plays. For the light they throw upon the maturer artist, they repay something more than cursory examination. *Thirst and Other One-Act Plays* comprises *Thirst*, *The Web*, *Warnings*, *Fog*, and *Recklessness*.

The Web is melodrama at its worst, with all the outworn technique connoted by the name, but already there appears, in the sound of Rose's coughing as she is led away by the officers, O'Neill's predilection for the potency of pure sound upon the stage. Time and again this fondness for aural effects is evident; in the remaining plays of the volume, for example, there is the whining of the wireless in *Warnings*, the steamer whistles and the dripping water of the icebergs in *Fog*; there are, in *The Web* itself, the falling raindrops. So, in the later *Bound East for Cardiff*, there is the whistle blowing through the fog at intervals of a minute and, in *The Emperor Jones*, the haunting crescendo of the tom-tom, beating faster and faster with the wild palpitation of terror.

Recklessness, like *The Web*, has all the earmarks of melodrama: the spying maid, the lying mistress, the treacherous chauffeur, the purloined letter proving the wife's guilt, the husband's cruel and sardonic revenge. *Warnings*, the tale of a deaf wireless operator who fails to receive the message warning of a derelict, and who commits suicide on learning that the fault is his, requires two scenes for its setting; the first would not have been necessary in the hands of a dramatist more skilled than was O'Neill at the time; the second scene is better done and is in the nature of a foretaste of the later work. *Fog* is the tale of yet another wreck, brought about by a collision with an iceberg. Best of the collection, easily, is *Thirst*, for the depiction of the raving, wrecked trio afloat on a boundless ocean with a raft for their world is accomplished with true psychological power, vivid scenic sense, and a flair for the abnormal passages in the lives of men and women. One thinks of this playlet as he reads the opening act of *Gold*.

What the earth was to Antæus, the sea is to O'Neill in these early plays. He gathers strength from each new contact. On land, in these same products of his 'prentice days, he fairly wobbles like a sailor on shore leave after months and months on the deep. To be sure, the dialogue as often as not is a string of *clichés;* the characterization is uncertain; but even thus early we have a welcome infusion of the exotic element, a groping after the inscrutable powers that rule over land and sea, a vigorousness, a masculinity, whose muscles were strong with a strength that lacked direction and discipline.

"But the blind sky will not answer your appeals or mine," says the Gentleman in *Thirst*. "Nor will the cruel sea grow merciful for any prayer of ours." Already, in the cannibalism of the negro, resurgent through the ravages of thirst, there is prefigured the regression, through fear, of the burly Emperor Jones—a psychological retracing that, by the way, was accomplished for the group in *In the Zone*, as *The Emperor Jones* accomplishes it for the individual. Already, in *Fog*, O'Neill, like the Dark Man of his play, finds the people in the steerage more interesting to talk to than the second-class passengers; the suggestion of a mysterious grinding power does not harmonize with the realism of the scene, any more than does the philosophical argument between the poet and the business man, but one may glimpse here the original suggestion of *The Hairy Ape*. In *The Web*, O'Neill had spoken, in a stage direction, of an "ironic life-force"; in *Fog* there is talk of "poverty—the most prevalent of all diseases." By which tokens he had levied tiny tribute upon Shaw.

Intrinsically, these early pieces are of meager worth; they are, however, necessary to a fuller understanding of the man, containing, as they do, the suggestions of a number of his later plays.

The Moon of the Caribbees and Six Other Plays of the Sea, though published five years later than the little volume we have just considered, contains plays written between 1917 and 1919. The melodramatic element, though refined, is still there; by now, however, O'Neill seems to have acquired a genuinely philosophic grasp upon his material. Before, he was outside his imaginary world, now he has broken in. Before, he revealed no firm grasp upon character; now he is able to create a little human comedy of the sea, in which the same personages, clearly differentiated, appear in the various plays and are readily recognized for the distinct men they are. *The Moon of the Caribbees* has color, mood, suggestion, action; *Bound East for Cardiff* has all these, and a simple pathos that is the voice of a whole philosophy. "This sailor life ain't much to cry about leavin'," says a dying comrade to his mate. " . . . Just one ship after another, hard work, small pay and bum grub; and when we git into port, just a drink endin' up in a fight, and all your money gone, and then, ship away again. Never meetin' no nice people; never gittin' outa sailor town, hardly in any port; travellin' all over the world and never seein' none of it; without no one to care whether you're alive or dead. . . . There ain't much in all that that'd make yuh sorry to lose it, Drisc." No pretty language there; no romanticizing of the heaving billows and a life on the ocean wave; no stage rhetoric. This is the tongue of reality, with the clear-sightedness of actual contact. It is the language that *The Hairy Ape* is to speak, in harsher tones, down in his hole at the bottom of the ship which is the bottom of civilization as well. Not so good is *The Long Voyage Home*, with its tale of Olson of the Glencairn shanghaied in a London dive just as he is on his way home to a farm, after giving up sailoring for good. This melodrama of types, with its seduction, poisoned drink, robbery, and other familiar devices, is saved only by a tinge of irony, and only for a while. Of better stuff is *In the Zone*, with its war-scarred crew in the mine zone suspecting the lovelorn Smitty of harboring a treacherous bomb in the box that treasures his harmless love letters. *Ile* inclines to melodrama, but is strengthened by its revelation of man's search for power in the face of woman's weakening love, while both *Where the Cross Is Made* and *The Rope* are spoiled by the author's unwillingness to forego the assistance of convention and coincidence. Else, why these foreclosed mortages, these wills, this plentiful passing of information across the footlights, these maundering soliloquies? Yet there is vision in *Where the Cross Is Made*, as the fulfilment of the theme in *Gold* has revealed. And, for that matter, is not the theme of *Ile* deeply akin to the struggle between man and wife in the selfsame *Gold*?

Beyond the Horizon, written in 1918, is the first of the author's longer plays to survive his destructive wrath. Even here, where the domestic tragedy is enacted upon the land, the roar of the sea is heard in the distance. Though the ever-present sea is oftener than not the "ol' davil" that Chris Christopherson is always calling it in *Anna Christie*, it yet may heal, as it does Anna herself, so long shielded from it by her obsessed parent. To Robert in *Beyond the Horizon*, as to Anna of the later play, the land proves a curse; but the sea that heals Anna is kept by the irony of fate from Robert, whom it would have cured doubly, by taking him from Ruth, who was not made for him, and by bringing him the romance that his poetic nature craved. At the end Robert speaks to his returned brother, Andrew, with the clear vision of the dying. He asks him to take care of Ruth, whom Andrew and not Robert should have married in the first place, and of the land, which Andrew and not Robert should have remained to till. "You've spent eight years running away from yourself. Do you see what I mean? You used to be a creator when you loved the farm. You and life were in harmonious partnership. And now—(*He stops as if seeking vainly for words.*) My brain is muddled. But part of what I mean is that your gambling with the thing you used to love to create proves how far astray you've gotten from the truth. So you'll be punished. You'll have to suffer to win back—".

The play was hailed, upon its initial performance, as one of the master products of realism in the United States; O'Neill, who must since have disconcerted the ready prophecies of our pigeon-hole critics with his experiments in the new forms, was looked upon as the founder of a truly realistic drama. Yet from the standpoint of such a realism he has carried over, into the play, some of the less worthy devices of his early pieces. His dialogue is natural enough, the writing is well-modulated, there are high moments, and one feels something like an implacable fate hovering over these toys of the land and the sea. This is a domestic tragedy of might-have-been, permeated with that "ironic life-force" of which the 'prentice O'Neill had written. But to overpraise the play and the author in one's enthu-

siasm at our drama's final attainment of adulthood,
is to be false to both. "O'Neill's future," Mr.
Macgowan has written, "lies along the new way
and he must follow it."[1] Nor is this mere partizan-
ship of the new for novelty's sake. Realism, in the
catalogue sense of the word, holds for O'Neill the
traps of melodrama, of the artistically purposeless
goings and comings of the dramatist's puppets.
This appears in so good a play as *Beyond the Horizon*,
in which Andrew, each time that he comes on a
visit to the old farm, wishes to return at once to
his distant business, the reason for this impatience
being more the playwright's than the character's.
It appears in *Anna Christie*, where her future lover,
though he has been five days adrift with his ship-
wrecked companions, rowing them to safety, must
begin to make love to her no sooner than he has
been picked out of the water. It appears later in
the play, in the inexcusable fourth act, wherein the
author kicks his dramatic and artistic structure to
bits by a sudden reversal of the situation. It appears, in a peculiar manner, in *Diff'rent*, by not
appearing at all, so to speak. For *Diff'rent* is by
implication a psychological contrast, yet the author
presents only the outer ends of that contrast, with
thirty years between the acts. The missing act,
the one he did not write, was precisely that in which
some hint of the process which changed the woman
from a prim Sunday-school mistress to a silly
flapper of fifty should have been presented.

[1] *Vanity Fair*, April, 1922, page 16d. If I concur in Macgowan's opinion,
it is not through definite allegiance to the new way as against the old. The worthy
playwright transcends the limitations of any particular form, and the special form
of a play is determined by the material as it shapes itself in the author's imagination, and by nothing else. That form is part of the matter,—an aspect of it.
O'Neill's outlook upon the world is a peculiar blend of vivid insight and spiritual
groping; it violates itself in the moulds of ordinary realism, as I try to show.

Had O'Neill, for example, treated *The Emperor Jones* (produced in 1920) in the fashion of conventional realism—and there was, one may imagine, that possibility—he would have fallen short of a veritable triumph, not through the accidental use of an inappropriate technique so much as through failure to grasp the essence of his theme, which demanded the form—which *was* the form itself—that he employed. The Emperor, not to be slayed except by a silver bullet, is killed by just such a bullet moulded by his credulous vassals. So, too, are we slain by the very belief of others in our own deceptions. Here we have a masterly presentation of the degenerative process of fear. The Emperor, once he has fled the palace—the first step in his fear, despite all his bluster, which was a sign of fear in the first place—wanders through the forest in rapid regression to primitivity. The tom-tom effect is remarkable, and is the culmination of O'Neill's natural response to such sensory stimuli. This is no mere sound accessory, as it is in the early plays, with their fog whistles, their rain drops, their whining children, and the whirr of the wireless. The tom-tom is part and parcel of the psychological action; at first it is the call to war; then it merges into the Emperor Jones's vision of the slaves rolling to its beat; finally it becomes his own throbbing, feverish temples, and all the while it is our heart beating more and more rapidly as we follow his fate.

Is the play one long soliloquy, practically? But fear talks much to itself. The visions that rise before his eyes? They are such as fear beholds, and truer to genuine reality than would be a blank

stage. It is the surge of the Emperor's speech that
makes these spectres live for us as they do for him.
This part of the play is really of a piece with the
monodrama, in that it achieves complete identifica-
tion of the auditor with the actor, and presents
surrounding reality not as it appears to those outside the action, but in subjective terms of the actor's
self. There are hints of the cinema in the gradual
unfolding of the past as the play progresses—a
series of "flash-backs," as it were; but this is no
mere imitation of a medium; it is inherent in the
character of the play; it *is* the play, and could not
have been presented otherwise. Here symbol and
psychology merge; analysts have found it a remarkable study, fundamentally as true of the white man
as of the black; the Emperor Jones is, in addition,
or simultaneously, an unobtrusive symbol of man's
vain boast of power.

Anna Christie, written in 1920, just before *The
Emperor Jones*, was produced a year later. For
three acts it presents another realistic study in the
"ironic life-force"; the fourth, as we have said already, is inexcusable, except upon the frankly commercial desire to provide a happy ending at whatever cost to the artistic conscience. If Mr. O'Neill
really believes in that final act, the three preceding
ones, with their closely-woven narrative, their
pungent dialogue, their reality to the life they portray, must be a lucky accident. And one refuses to
believe in such fortunate fortuities. Not from the
man who has written the relentless scenes of *The First
Man*, in which the creative soul that is the artist
may tread even upon the creative body that is
woman.

And so, from melodrama and external realism, through the novelty of *The Emperor Jones*, we come to the newest of O'Neill's productions, *The Hairy Ape*, a "comedy of ancient and modern life." The ancient life of the author's sub-title is that same ancient life which sprang into being in the successive downward steps of the Emperor Jones's terror, for in theme and scene *The Hairy Ape* is contemporaneous with the transatlantic steamship on which it takes place, at once realistic background and symbolic, timeless token of caste and character. "The beginnings of it," wrote Mr. Woollcott in *The New York Times* on the day (April 16, 1922) preceding its initial production at the Plymouth Theatre, whither it had moved from the Macdougal Street home of the Provincetown Players, "can be traced back to the days ten or eleven years ago when O'Neill was an able seaman aboard one of the ships of the American Line and came to know a certain stoker on the same ship—a huge Liverpool Irishman, who drank enormously, relished nothing in all the world so much as a good knock-down-and-drag-out fight, and who had a mighty pride in his own strength, a pride that gloried in the heat and exhaustion of the stokehold which would drop the weaklings and leave him roaring with mirth at the sight of them carried out. He was just such a specimen, therefore, as the Yank Smith on whose immense shoulders the ominous, nightmare events of *The Hairy Ape* press down like the crowding phantoms in some fantastic picture of Despair.

"In the mutual snobbery of the liner, O'Neill as a seaman could hardly exchange confidences with the stoker, but they got to know each other ashore

in the greater democracy of Johnny the Priest's
saloon down in Fulton Street just around the corner
from West—the same saloon, probably, through
whose grimy windows the light filtered on the gaudy
hair and cheerless face of Anna Christie.   There,
over his beer, O'Neill was free to contemplate the
immense complacency of the Irishman and his glowing satisfaction with what most folks would have
regarded as an unenviable rôle in the world.   The
memory of that satisfaction furnished a curious
background for the news which drifted up from the
waterfront some years later—the tidings that one
night, when the ship was plowing along in mid-
Atlantic, the big stoker had stolen up on deck and
jumped overboard.   Why?   What had happened to
shake that Gargantuan contentment?   What had
broken in and so disturbed a vast satisfaction with
the world that the big fellow had been moved to
leave it?   O'Neill never heard if any one knew, but
out of his own speculation there took shape at last
the play called *The Hairy Ape*."

The Emperor Jones emphasized the individual's
regression through fear; *The Hairy Ape* shows that
same individual thwarted in his gropings after social
significance, returning in his inarticulate rage to his
savage ancestor of the forest.   The "ironic life-
force" again, tinged with a distinctly social meaning
and attitude.   As the Emperor, blustering in his
consciousness of power before the fear connoted in
his blustering begins to get the better of him, so
Yank the coal-heaver, bellowing his pride of position in the infernal heat of the stokehole—a pride,
already from the first, instinct with the uncertainty
of all exaggerated pride, already betraying the in-

evitable result when stokehole clashes with upper
deck in the vision of a curious daughter of the rich,
who would go a-slumming on the transatlantic and
get a glimpse of life below decks.

Listen to the bluster of the hairy ape, Yank:

Hell, sure! Dat's my favorite climate. I eat it up!
It's me makes it roar. It's me makes it move. Sure,
on'y for me everything stops. It all goes dead, get me!
De noise and smoke and all de engines movin' de woild,
dey stop. Dere ain't nothin' no more! Dat's what I'm
sayin'. Everything else dat makes de woild move, somep'n
makes it move. It can't move without somp'n else, see?
Den yuh get down to me. I'm at the bottom, get me?
Dere ain't nothin' foither. I'm de end. I'm de start!
I start somp'n and de woild moves. It—dat's me! De
new dat's moidern de old. I'm de ting in coal dat makes
it boin; I'm steam and oil for de engines; I'm de ting in
noise dat makes you hear it; I'm smoke and express trains
and steamers and factory whistles; I'm de ting in gold
dat makes it money! And I'm what makes iron into
steel! Steel, dat stands for de whole ting! And I'm steel
—steel—steel! I'm de muscle in steel, de punch behind
it! (*As he says this he pounds with his fist against the steel
bunk. All the men, roused to a pitch of frenzied self-glorifi-
cation by his speech, do likewise. There is a deafening
metallic roar through which Yank's voice can be heard
bellowing.*) Slaves, hell! We run de whole woiks. We're
it, get me! All de rich guys dat tink dey're somep'n, dey
ain't nothin'! Dey don't belong. But us guys, we're
in de move, we're at de bottom, de whole ting is us, see?
We belong!

But "belong" is precisely what Yank does not,
and the eight scenes that comprise the play spell
his disillusionment, until he meets a grisly end in
the arms of a gorilla at the zoo. Ape has come back
to ape.

It is *The Hairy Ape* and *The Emperor Jones* that are the cause of the linking of O'Neill with the German Expressionists. But, as we have seen, the resemblance is by no means identity. He shares their speed technique, but not the telescoping of time and space that is practised by the extremists of Germany, together with their Futurist brethren in Italy. He shares with them, too, an inability to create a perfect fusion of his elements, though he has not so clearly broken away from the old technique, which has a habit of making diconcerting appearances even in his best work. Nor should we forget, in all such comparisons as these, that the term "Expressionism", applied to modern German dramatists, is quite meaningless unless modified by a knowledge of the playwright to whom it is applied.[1]

This, then, is the sketch of a man who is but at the beginning. And with him and Susan Glaspell, it may be, begins the entrance of the United States drama into the deeper currents of continental waters. O'Neill flaunts no narrow, mistaken nationalism; he apotheosizes no "ism"; he digs down into the subsoil of common humanity. Already he has produced, in the new forms, a pair of pieces challenging comparison with the best that foreign youth has brought forth in the same time, and that emerges victorious out of the test. Every favor of circumstance is with him—the press, the critics, the playhouses. The rest is in him, and in his artistic duty not to be content, as heretofore he has been, with second- or third-best.

---

[1] See section on Germany.

SUSAN GLASPELL

Between Susan Glaspell and Eugene O'Neill there
lies a fundamental artistic difference that may be
rooted in the difference of sex as well as of temperament. Allowing for the fact that clear-cut contrasts
are more or less illusory, we may yet assert that
where O'Neill is at bottom the man of feeling,
Glaspell is the woman of thought. From this distinction may be derived a list of antitheses. With
O'Neill's overflow of feeling comes a straining toward
violence and melodrama; he reveals little humor; he
is fond of primitive persons, usually men bent upon
achieving their purpose at whatever cost; he is
voluble, as if his persons' thoughts were struggling
to clarity through the mist of inchoate feelings.
Glaspell's intensity of thought, on the other hand,
induces a straining toward wit, an eminently intellectual process; her humor—leaving aside the
question of its body or successfulness—presupposes
persons of sophistication. As O'Neill inclines toward
the masterful man, so she leans toward the rebellious
woman. Where the author of *The Hairy Ape* spurts
out words like the gushing of a geyser, Glaspell is
reticent, laconic; O'Neill is expression, where Glaspell is repression. "Do you know, dearest", says
Ian in her *Tickless Time*, "you are very sensitive in
the way you feel feeling? Sometimes I think that to
feel feeling is greater than to feel."

Now, Miss Glaspell is indeed very sensitive in the
way she feels feeling, and by that very token is she the
woman of thought, for the process implies an acute
consciousness of one's emotions, a standing outside
of them even as they are being experienced. And

this is precisely what her most significant characters are forever doing, until their very language acquires a difference from ordinary expression that renders it exotic and mirrors the exotic difference of the characters. They speak of their "otherness", of the "outness", or "apartness", as no character in O'Neill has ever spoken. For language, too, is a matter of sophistication, and though O'Neill's people feel their "otherness", they do not feel the feeling, to use Ian's words; they have not achieved self-consciousness. It is thus something more than mere playing with words to affirm that where O'Neill feels his thoughts, Glaspell thinks her feelings. Contrast the descent of *The Emperor Jones* and his white brother *The Hairy Ape* with the ascent of Madeline in Glaspell's *Inheritors* or of the overwrought Claire in *The Verge* and the seeming trickery of words acquires validity. "Do you know why you're so sure of yourself?" cries Claire to her daughter, Elizabeth. "Because you can't *feel*. Can't feel—the limitless—out there—a sea just over the hill." Miss Glaspell's underscoring of the word feel reveals the difference in *thought* which she packs into that word.

But thought, too, has its misty zones, and more than once Glaspell flutters into them. "We're held by our relations to others—"says Fejevary in *Inheritors*. So far, so good. Few plays fill one with a realization of these necessary, yet numbing, ties, as deeply as does *Inheritors*. Then the speaker adds, "—by our obligations (*vaguely*) to the ultimate thing." Now that "ultimate thing" is what troubles one even in Miss Glaspell's best work, such as

Bernice. The *vaguely* of her stage direction is something that bothers, not only Mr. Fejevary, but herself and her women protagonists as well. Now and again her women—whether in her lesser things or in her chief labors—feel "big things", but with that same vagueness which necessitates such words as "otherness", "apartness", and similar crepuscular formations. Not that the dramatist is wholly unjustified either in word or procedure; she is dealing with twilight persons, transitional souls, in the nobler meaning of transition; Claire herself is perhaps as puzzled as we; she is a Madeline of *Inheritors* grown up into motherhood and complex selfhood—a Madeline whose problems are no longer exclusively social, but whose individual problem is badly crushed beneath the weight of social pressure. Such a grip has this twilight "apartness" upon Miss Glaspell that she even hints abstractions in her stage-directions. *The Verge*, for that matter, is one long abstraction in three acts, not entirely untrammelled by a pervading symbolism. Glaspell, then, as a serious dramatist—one of the few Americans whose progress is worth watching with the same eyes that follow notable European effort—is largely the playwright of woman's selfhood. That acute consciousness of self which begins with a mere sense of sexual differentiation (exemplified in varied fashion in *Trifles, Woman's Honor, The Outside*) ranges through a heightening social sense (*The People, Close the Book, Inheritors*) to the highest aspirations of the complete personality, the individual (*Bernice, The Verge*). I would not be understood as implying that these plays exhibit solely the phases to which they are here related;

all of Miss Glaspell's labors are an admixture of these phases, as is the life of the thinking and feeling woman of to-day.   And there is more than rebellious womanhood in these dramas; there is consciousness of valid self, or of a passion for freedom, of dynamic personality; there is craving for life in its innermost meaning.

Miss Glaspell's one-act plays run the gamut from farce to drama. At times her more comic self is the caricature of her more serious.   Even allowing for the influence of collaboration in *Suppressed Desires* and *Tickless Time*, are not these laughable creatures but replicas of her more sober protagonists reflected in a distorting mirror? She can poke fun at amateur Freudianism gone mad (*Suppressed Desires*) and then create serious characters that are almost clinical types for the psychoanalytical laboratory (*Bernice*, *The Verge*). Even her farce reveals her predominantly intellectual interests, as witness *Tickless Time*. Everywhere her ideas, as opposed to her feelings, will out. Thus *The People* is, in part, ostensibly a satire upon the cranks that infest the offices of radical publications, but the dramatist does not seem sure of her footing. Shall it be straight satire, burlesque, or what? As a result the humor becomes too heavily freighted with the suggestion of serious-ness, the characters merge into caricature, and the spectator listens to the preachment of some beautiful thoughts that live as words, as ideas, but surely not as drama. So, too, *Woman's Honor*, containing some acute criticism of the masculine mind, wavers be-tween the farce and the serious play.

Out of the conversation in the sheriff's house,

among the women who have assembled to save the life of a young man by offering as sacrifice their coveted honor, arises a protest against the lily-white ideal of virtue in which men have so long stifled woman's passional existence. They are sick of man's "noble" feeling toward womanhood and recognize, with feminine uncanniness, the source of that feeling in the emotional satisfaction which it breeds in man. "Did it ever strike you as funny," asks the Scornful One, "that woman's honor is only about one thing, and that man's honor is about everything but that thing?" And later in the same piece, from the same personage: "Why, woman's honor would have died out long ago if it hadn't been for men's talk about it." And the Shielded One:

Oh, I hope you women can work out some way to free us from men's noble feelings about it! I speak for all the women of my—(*Hesitates*) under-world, all those others smothered under men's lofty sentiments toward them! I wish I could paint for you the horrors of the shielded life. (*Says "shielded" as if it were "shameful".*) . . . Our honor has been saved so many times. We are tired.

There are ideas enough in this little piece to float more than one long social satire, yet as Miss Glaspell has presented *Woman's Honor* it is, like *The People*, valuable for the detached ideas and for little else. For realism it is patently impossible; for satire it is too bald; for fantasy, too corporeal. The piece asks for different treatment and should receive it; the idea is too good to be wasted upon an indeterminate parlor entertainment.

The same predominance of idea over character and plausibility pervades *Close the Book*, in which the social status of Jhansi, the gypsy, provides the pivot upon which turns a very pithy critique of genealogical snobbery that proves a boomerang. O'Neill's weakness, particularly in his one-act plays, is the degeneration of feeling into a melodrama redeemed by gleams of originality in conception; Glaspell's weakness in her short pieces is the lapsing of intellectuality into brittle, discerning statement with little relation to organic artistry. And as O'Neill triumphs over these shortcomings in his later and longer work, so too, does Miss Glaspell in her longer subsequent pieces. "Life grows over buried life", says Allie Mayo in *The Outside*. And art grows over buried art. The real Glaspell is not in these one-act plays, however often they may be produced and read. It is in the oft-cited *Trifles*, with its tribute to woman's supposedly finer intuitions as opposed to the supposedly coarser fibre of man,—with its wise if overdone reticence—its foreshadowing of the longer dramas.

O'Neill's women do not understand their menfolk; recall the situation between Curtis and his wife in *The First Man*, between the wives and their men in *Ile*, in *Gold*. Glaspell's men do not understand their women. The Prisoner, in *Woman's Honor*, rather than be saved by the chorus of self-sacrificing females, cries out, *"Oh, hell. I'll plead guilty!"* Craig, in *Bernice*, has neither the profound intuitions that flow at the bottom of creative artistry (he is a writer who utterly misses the tragic plot that is his own married life), nor the appreciation of his wife which would have prevented her virtual suicide. Fejevary, in *Inheritors*, only half understands his

niece, Madeline, while Professor Holden, who understands her attitude, cannot after all comprehend her
radical action. As for *The Verge*, most of the men
are entirely at sea as to Claire, and none more so
than her eminently normal husband.

In *Bernice*, first of the full-length dramas, Miss
Glaspell seems to carry her reticence to a fault, yet I
believe her method is fully justified because it is a
spiritual mirror of Bernice's own life tragedy. To
add reticence to reticence, Bernice does not even
appear, she is dead at the beginning, yet alive in
every gesture, every utterance, made by her mourners.
(Compare Glaspell's method in *Trifles*.) Her
presence fills the intensity of a play that is as chary
of deeds as of words; here, too, the idea gives life to
the whole, but a genuine, dramatic life. The talk
is all of her, and out of the stray phrases a vivid
woman arises as if in the round before us. Miss
Glaspell's irony is all the more difficult to appreciate
in that she is as half-communicative as was Bernice
herself; but it is an irony that cuts sharply and deeply
into the quick of existence. A double irony, even as
it is a double reticence; for her women, not understood of their men, but half understand themselves.
That is the price they pay for their ever-groping
superiority.

Inheritors, dealing with a social rather than an
individualistic theme, is clearer in facture, even as
Madeline is more direct in deed. Three generations
pass before our eyes: the visionary pioneer who has
been inspired by his Hungarian friend with an
educational ideal, the son of that Hungarian friend
who marries the pioneer's daughter and becomes the
president of the college founded by his father-in-law,

the motherless niece of that president. Again irony, for the vision of the pioneer degenerates into the corrupted and corrupting opportunism of the college president. But hope, too. For the brave niece refuses to profit by her uncle's social influence; she champions the cause of a handful of liberty-loving foreigners at a time when free speech has been forgotten in her own country, preferring the jail of the body to the jail of ideas. A heroine of the Glaspell tradition, then, who conquers her feelings in the glorious battle of the Idea.

Out of this play rises not only the irony of the succeeding generations, but that of life's inextricable tangle itself. These are no conventional heroes, heroines, and villains of a cause. The danger that besets the dramatist now and again in her one-act pieces is here conquered through a thorough immersion in her theme. "If you sell your own soul," explains Holden, the independently-minded professor who, for the sake of his sick wife, must recede from his noble stand, "it's to love you sell it". Whereupon Madeline: "That's strange. It's love that—brings life along, and then it's love—holds life back." This, to me, is fully as important in the play as are Madeline's social heroics or the shifting of values from one generation to the other. And I may be pardoned if I call attention to the punctuation of the sentence just quoted from Madeline—to the dashes. That is the way Miss Glaspell's women talk—with words occasionally underscored and parted by dashes. This is no idiosyncrasy of orthography, I imagine. It is the intellectual groping of one who feels her feelings.

It is in the final act of *Inheritors* that Madeline's

mentally unbalanced father, Ira, at last breaks his
brooding silence and pours forth a flood of words that
for all their apparent rambling are pregnant with far-
seeing sanity. Another irony, this. And it is in *The
Verge* that insanity becomes almost the only sanity
open to the shut-in personality of Claire. Her
speech in the opening act may stand as epigraph to
the play:

(*With difficulty, drawing herself back from the fascination
of the precipice.*) You think I can't smash anything?
You think life can't break up and go outside what it was?
Because you've gone dead in the form in which you found
yourself, you think that's all there is to the whole adventure? And that is called sanity. And made a virtue—
to lock one in. You never worked with things that grow!
Things that take a sporting chance—go mad—that
sanity mayn't lock them in—from life untouched—from
life—that waits.

Now this, as Dick soon tries to explain, is merely
"the excess of a particularly rich temperament",
and certainly the playwright has succeeded in projecting a sense of the bewilderment that Claire
works upon her husband, her daughter, and her
friends. Among these is included the one whom she
loves, who breaks through to her (to use her own
style of expression) too late. "No, I'm not mad,"
cries Claire as the obsession grows upon her. "I'm
too—sane!"

It would be easy to select strange-sounding passages from the progress of Claire to the murder of
him she most loves, and to make easy mock of them.
Her "outness", "otherness", "aliveness", provide jut-
ting pegs upon which uncomprehending reviewers

may hang the pearls of their journalistic wit. They are, as we have seen, merely verbal images of the woman's difference from her spiritual milieu. A more valid criticism would be directed against the unrelieved tension of its straining toward something which never becomes quite clear. That same criticism may be leveled against *Bernice*, as may the opposite against the too symetrically patterned *Inheritors*. Yet *The Verge* is the brave protest of an artist-soul against the cramping patterns of existence. It is filled with the cry that ends one of Amy Lowell's best poems: "Christ! What are patterns for?" "Alles Ewige die Erfüllung fürchtet," declares someone in Franz Werfel's most recent drama, *Bocksgesang*. "All things eternal fear their fulfillment." True, a paradox lurks in the phrase, but few words could better describe the fear in which Claire lives amidst the plants which she is trying to nurture into new, inedited existences—the plants which are the symbol of her own little world. And something of of this same fear keeps Miss Glaspell at times half mute—chokes her personages with the fulness of unplumbed possibilities.

It is this refusal to be shut up into a shell, this everlasting aspiration toward newer and different life, that Miss Glaspell has significantly breathed into her long plays. All in all, here is a dramatist who oversteps mere national cataloguing. What she has already done pledges her to even higher things.

31

INDEX

1018 College St.

Flem & Bur.